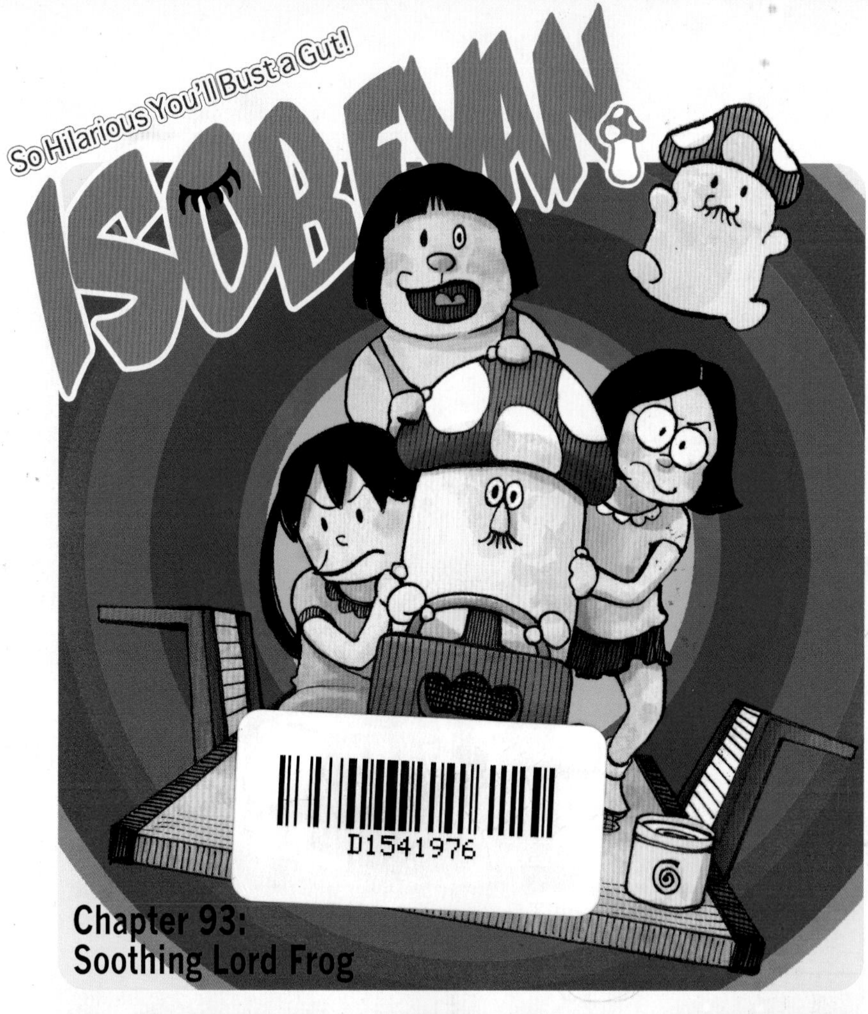
So Hilarious You'll Bust a Gut!
ISOBEYAN

Chapter 93: Soothing Lord Frog

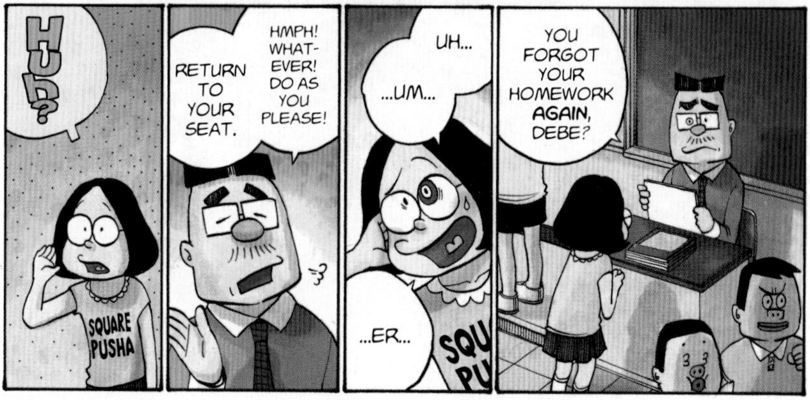
YOU FORGOT YOUR HOMEWORK AGAIN, DEBE?
UH...
...UM...
...ER...
SQU PU
HMPH! WHAT-EVER! DO AS YOU PLEASE!
RETURN TO YOUR SEAT.
HUH?
SQUARE PUSHA

By Bonjiro Isofura

☆ At my elementary school, everyone in class does the Isobeyan Dance on our sports field day. (Taishi Arii, Hyogo Prefecture)

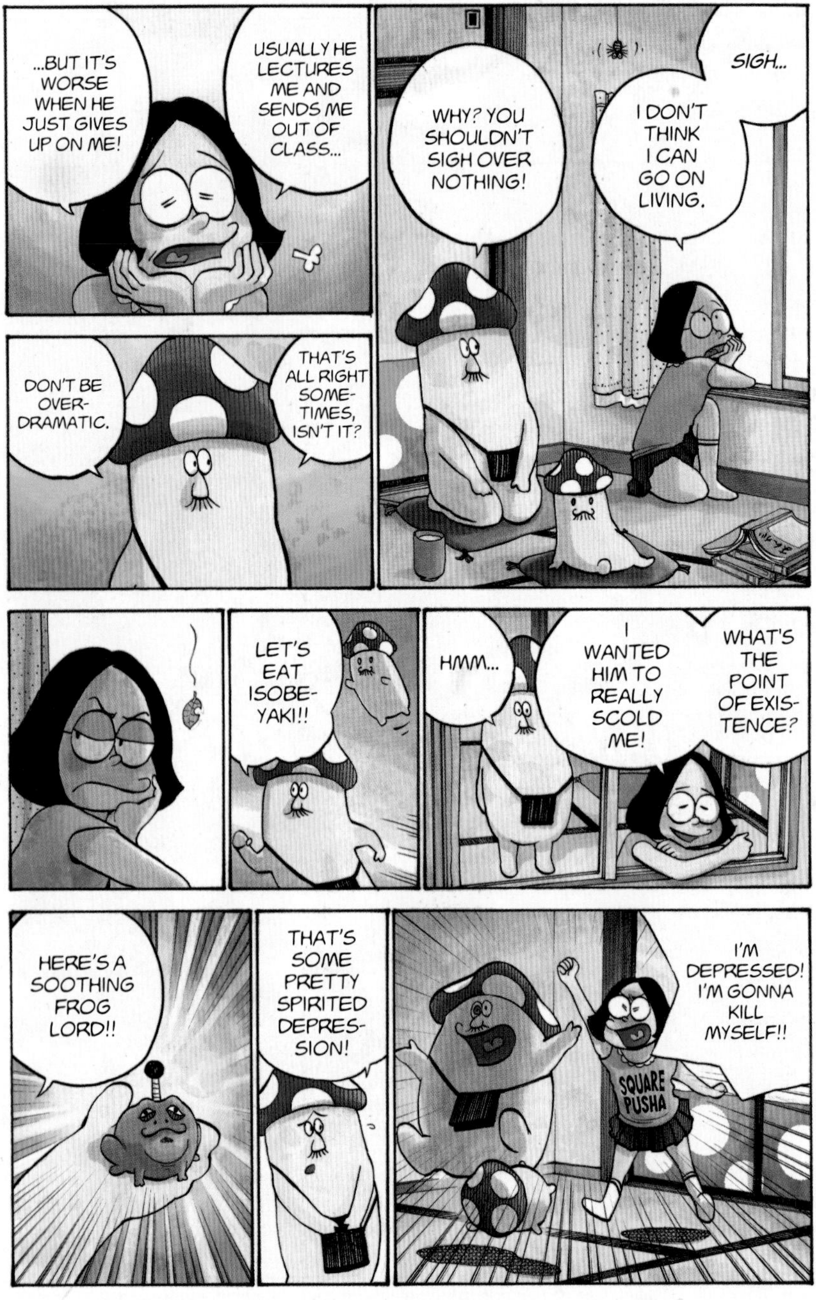
SIGH...
I DON'T THINK I CAN GO ON LIVING.
WHY? YOU SHOULDN'T SIGH OVER NOTHING!
USUALLY HE LECTURES ME AND SENDS ME OUT OF CLASS...
...BUT IT'S WORSE WHEN HE JUST GIVES UP ON ME!
THAT'S ALL RIGHT SOME-TIMES, ISN'T IT?
DON'T BE OVER-DRAMATIC.
WHAT'S THE POINT OF EXIS-TENCE?
I WANTED HIM TO REALLY SCOLD ME!
HMM...
LET'S EAT ISOBE-YAKI!!
I'M DEPRESSED! I'M GONNA KILL MYSELF!!
SQUARE PUSHA
THAT'S SOME PRETTY SPIRITED DEPRES-SION!
HERE'S A SOOTHING FROG LORD!!

SUPER-POPULAR MASTERPIECE COMEDY **ISOBEYAN** ☆Bonjiro Isofura, who just bought a boat, is waiting for your letters!

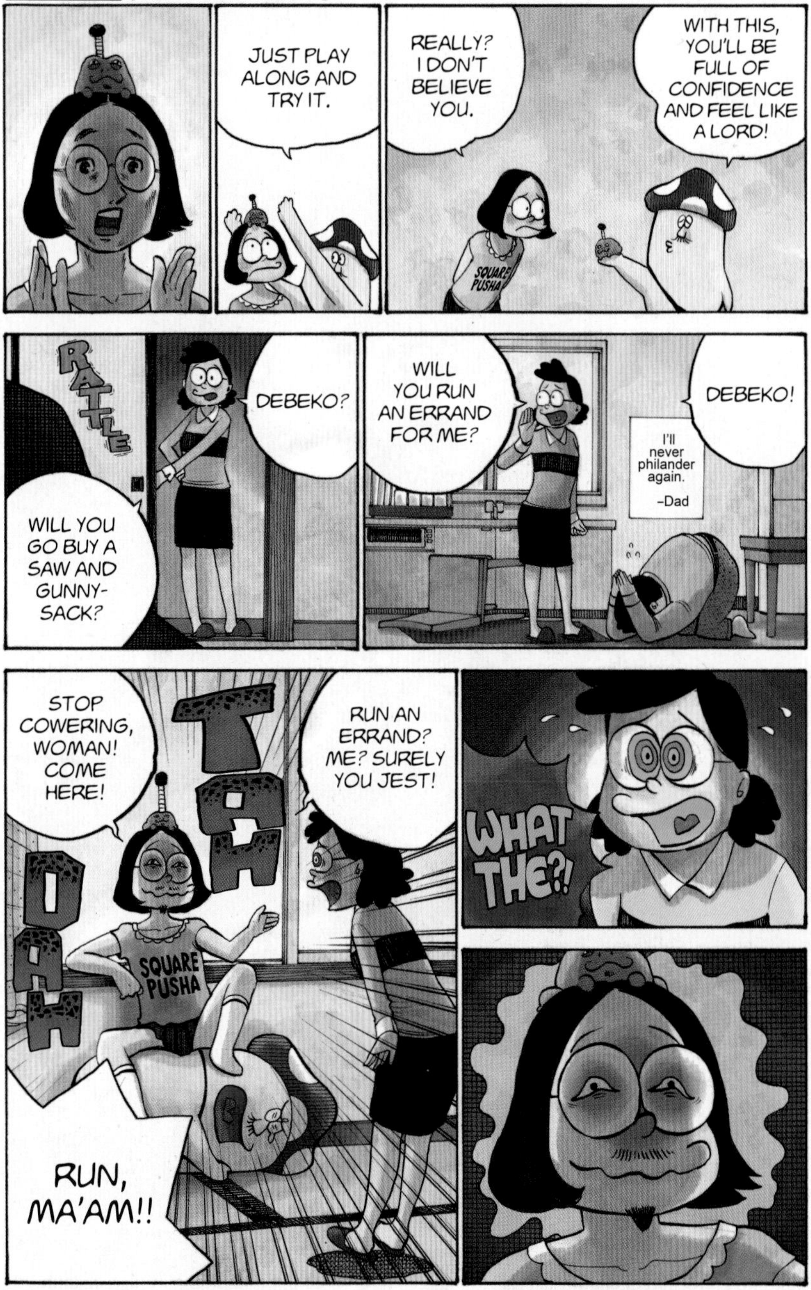
WITH THIS, YOU'LL BE FULL OF CONFIDENCE AND FEEL LIKE A LORD!
REALLY? I DON'T BELIEVE YOU.
SQUARE PUSHA
JUST PLAY ALONG AND TRY IT.
DEBEKO!
I'll never philander again. –Dad
WILL YOU RUN AN ERRAND FOR ME?
DEBEKO?
RATTLE
WILL YOU GO BUY A SAW AND GUNNY-SACK?
WHAT THE?!
RUN AN ERRAND? ME? SURELY YOU JEST!
TAH
STOP COWERING, WOMAN! COME HERE!
DAAH
SQUARE PUSHA
RUN, MA'AM!!

☞ **The look in Debeko's eyes has changed! Continued on page 162...**

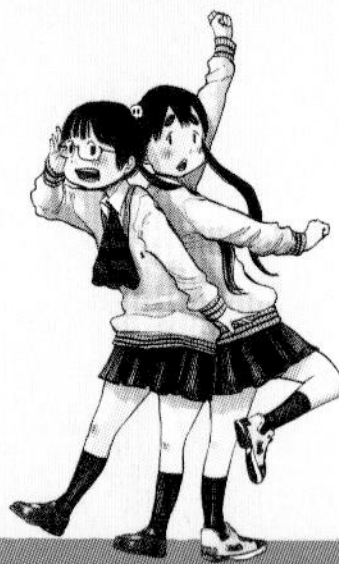

DEAD DEAD DEMON'S DEDE DEDE DESTRUCTION

3

CHAPTER 17

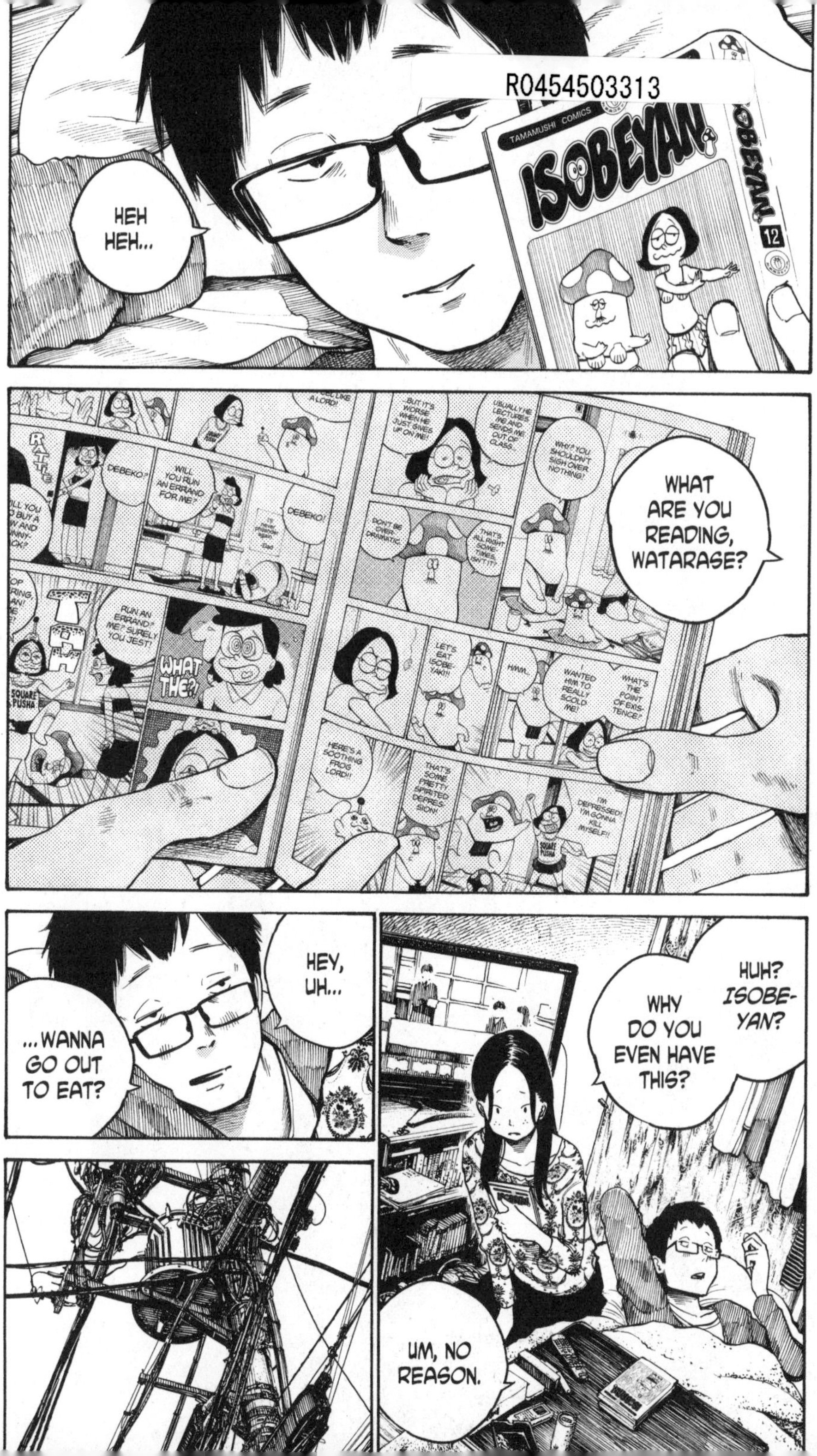
TAMAMUSHI COMICS
ISOBEYAN!
12
HEH HEH...
WHAT ARE YOU READING, WATARASE?
HUH? ISOBE-YAN?
WHY DO YOU EVEN HAVE THIS?
UM, NO REASON.
HEY, UH...
...WANNA GO OUT TO EAT?

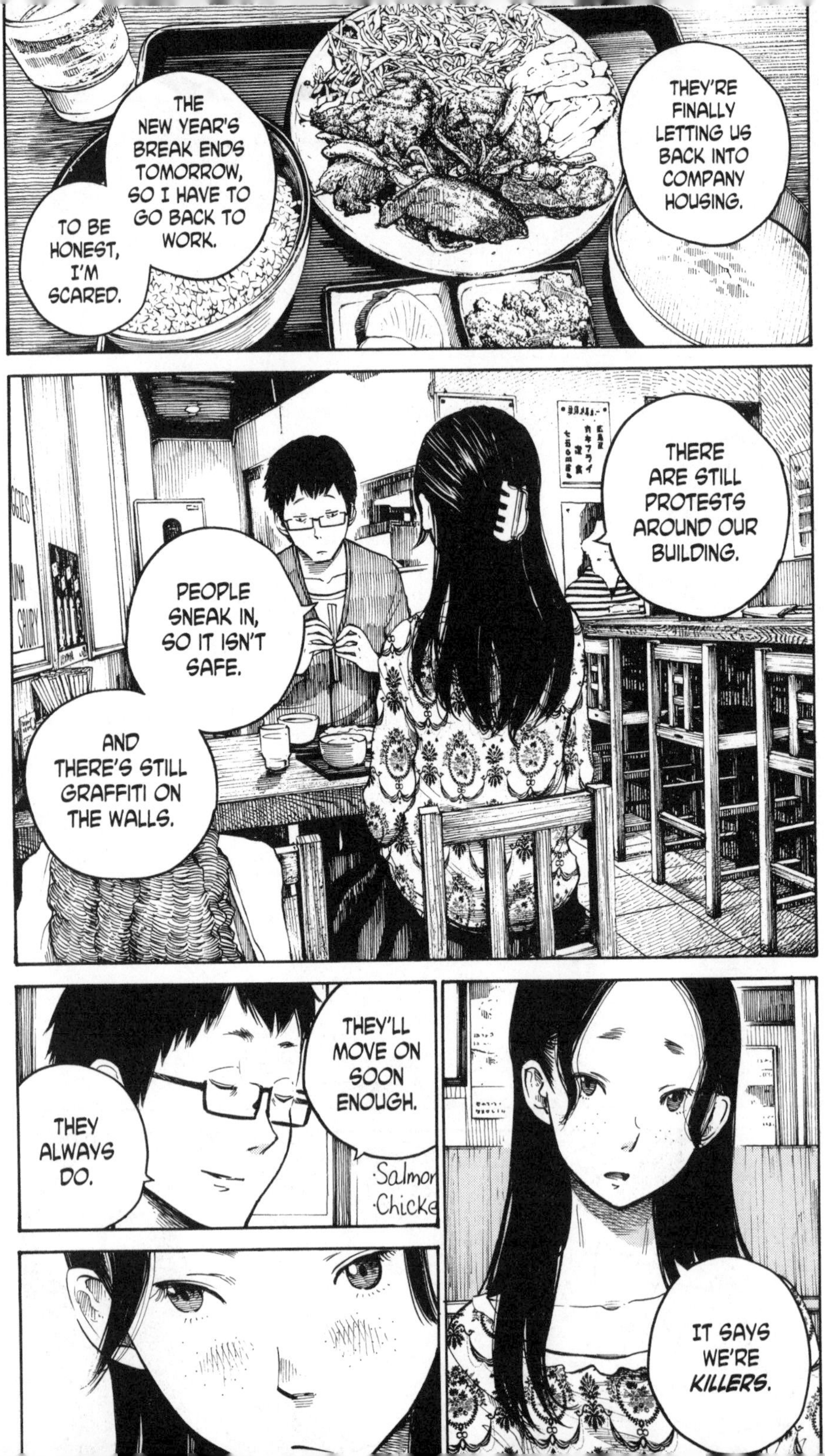
THEY'RE FINALLY LETTING US BACK INTO COMPANY HOUSING.
THE NEW YEAR'S BREAK ENDS TOMORROW, SO I HAVE TO GO BACK TO WORK.
TO BE HONEST, I'M SCARED.
THERE ARE STILL PROTESTS AROUND OUR BUILDING.
PEOPLE SNEAK IN, SO IT ISN'T SAFE.
AND THERE'S STILL GRAFFITI ON THE WALLS.
IT SAYS WE'RE *KILLERS*.
THEY'LL MOVE ON SOON ENOUGH.
THEY ALWAYS DO.

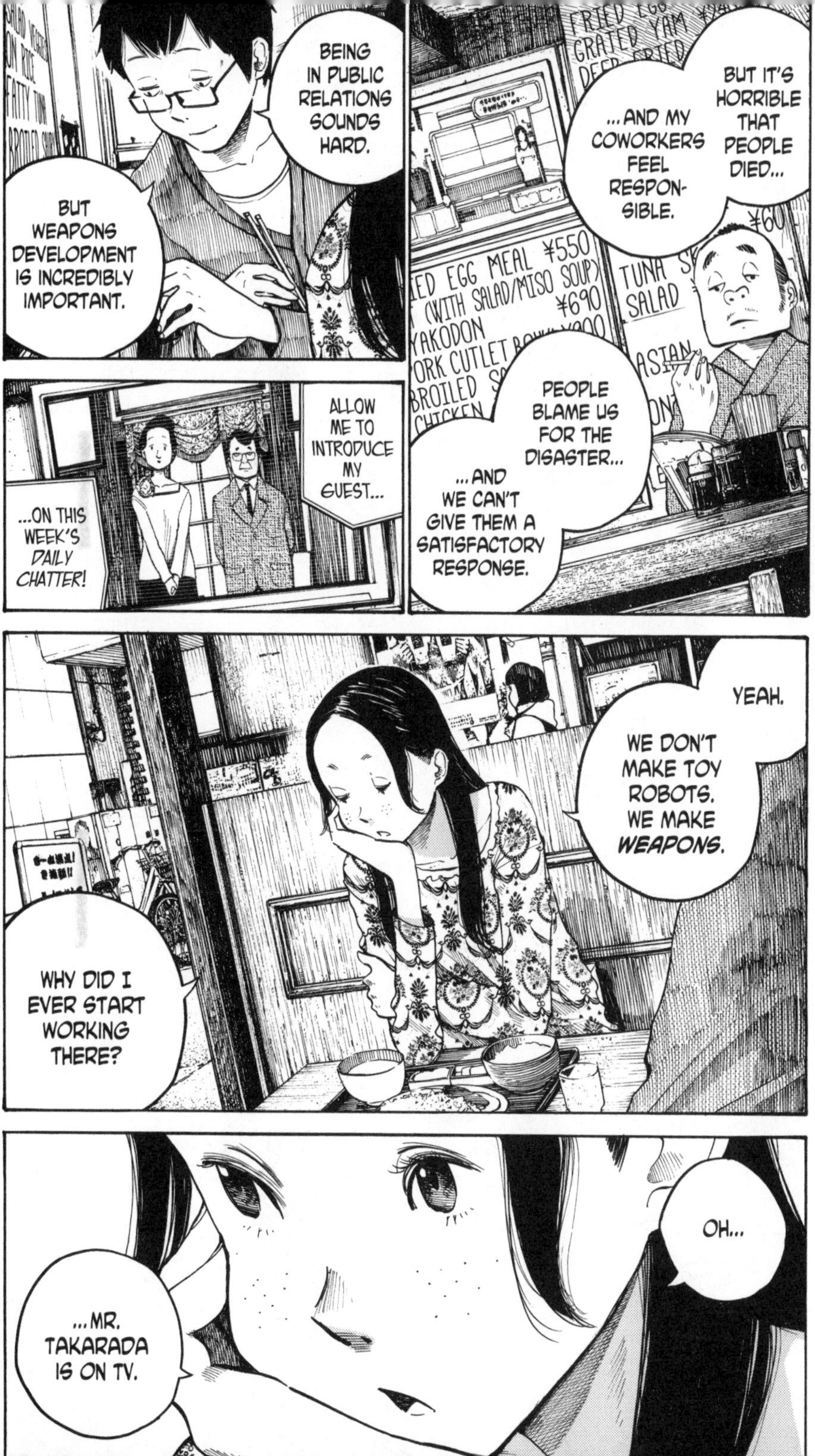
GRATED YAM
BUT IT'S HORRIBLE THAT PEOPLE DIED...
...AND MY COWORKERS FEEL RESPONSIBLE.
TUNA
SALAD
PEOPLE BLAME US FOR THE DISASTER...
...AND WE CAN'T GIVE THEM A SATISFACTORY RESPONSE.
BEING IN PUBLIC RELATIONS SOUNDS HARD.
BUT WEAPONS DEVELOPMENT IS INCREDIBLY IMPORTANT.
ALLOW ME TO INTRODUCE MY GUEST...
...ON THIS WEEK'S *DAILY CHATTER*!
YEAH.
WE DON'T MAKE TOY ROBOTS. WE MAKE ***WEAPONS***.
WHY DID I EVER START WORKING THERE?
OH...
...MR. TAKARADA IS ON TV.

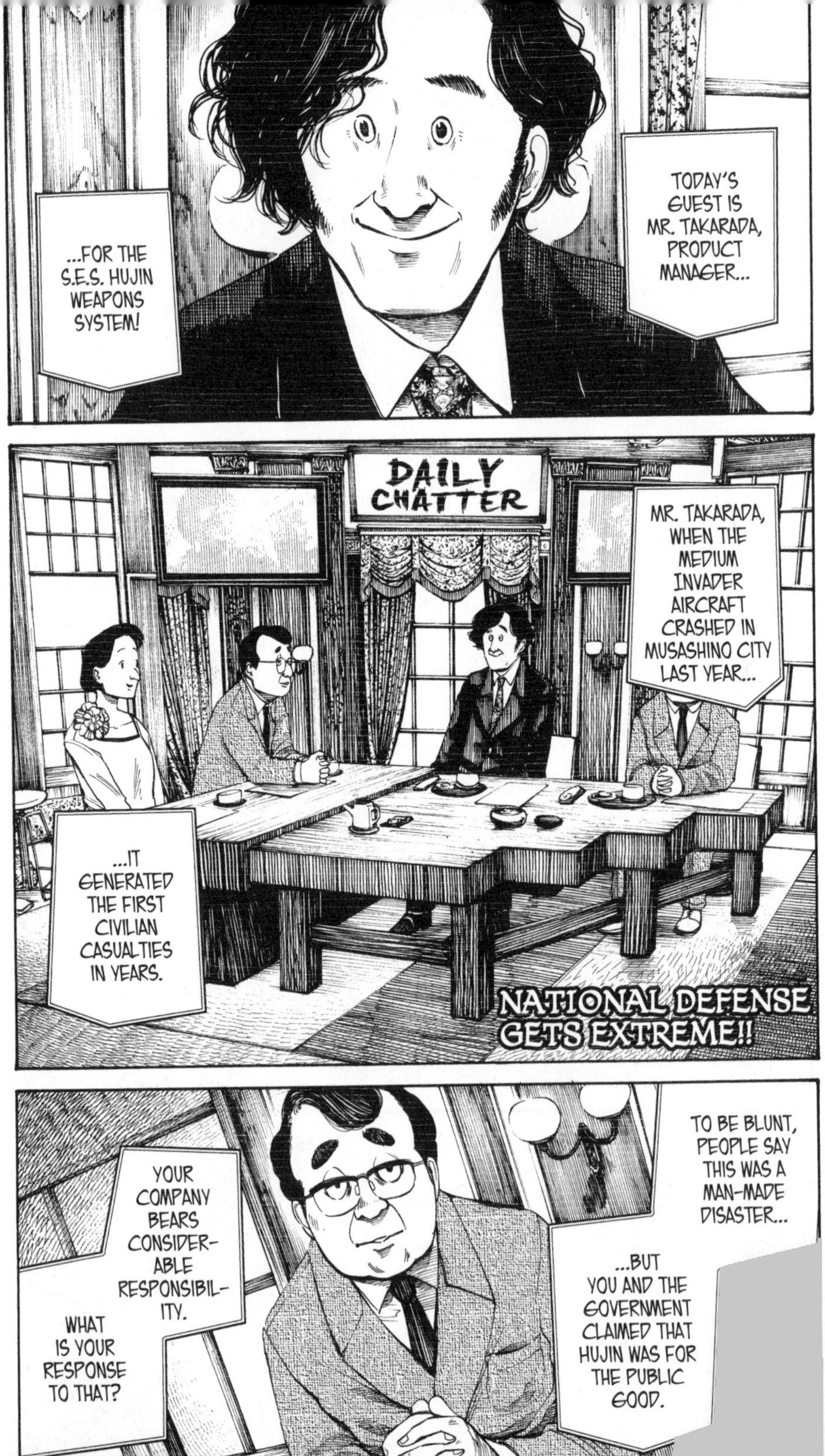
TODAY'S GUEST IS MR. TAKARADA, PRODUCT MANAGER...
...FOR THE S.E.S. HUJIN WEAPONS SYSTEM!
DAILY CHATTER
MR. TAKARADA, WHEN THE MEDIUM INVADER AIRCRAFT CRASHED IN MUSASHINO CITY LAST YEAR...
...IT GENERATED THE FIRST CIVILIAN CASUALTIES IN YEARS.
NATIONAL DEFENSE GETS EXTREME!!
TO BE BLUNT, PEOPLE SAY THIS WAS A MAN-MADE DISASTER...
...BUT YOU AND THE GOVERNMENT CLAIMED THAT HUJIN WAS FOR THE PUBLIC GOOD.
YOUR COMPANY BEARS CONSIDER-ABLE RESPONSIBIL-ITY.
WHAT IS YOUR RESPONSE TO THAT?

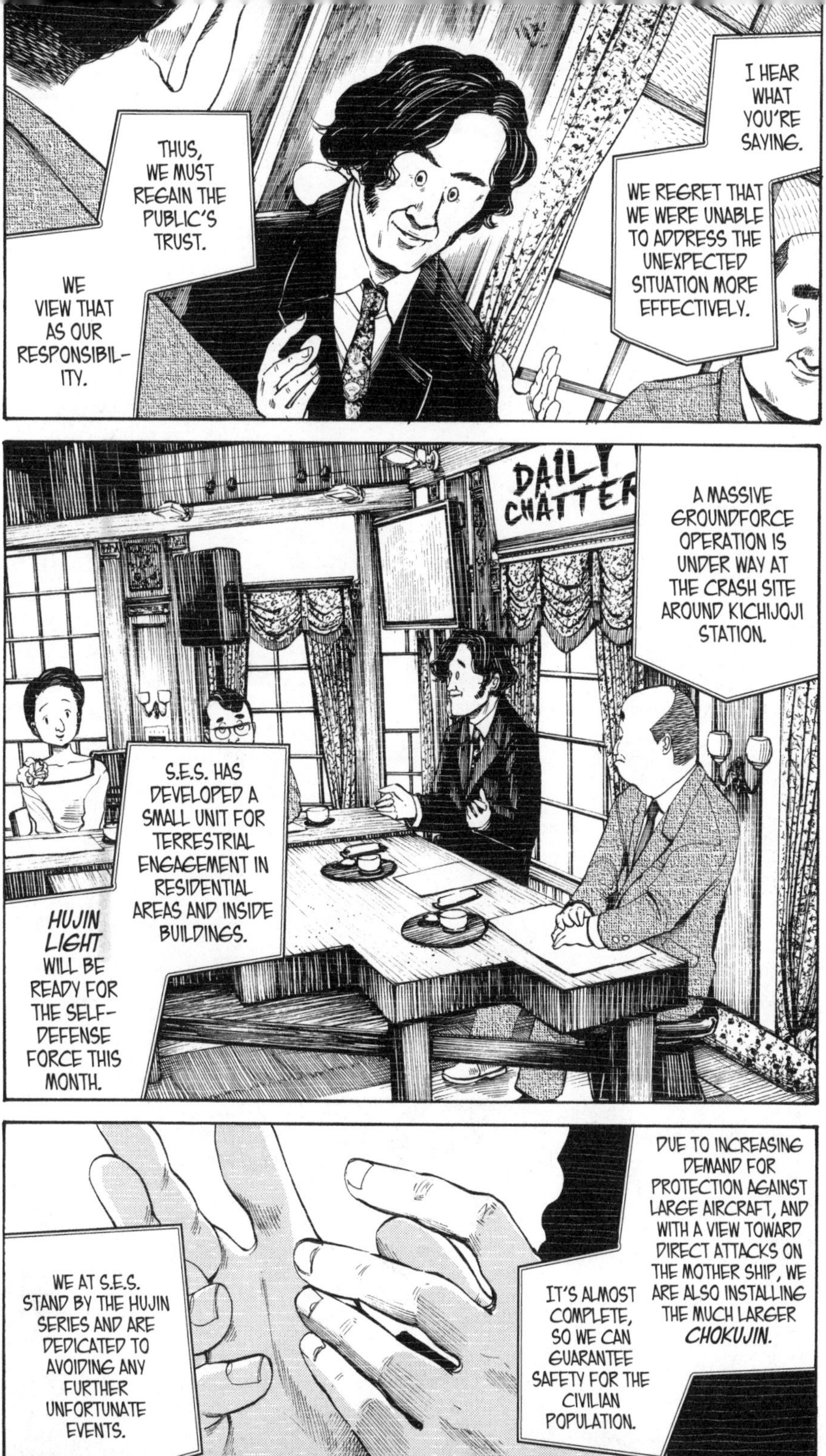
I HEAR WHAT YOU'RE SAYING.
WE REGRET THAT WE WERE UNABLE TO ADDRESS THE UNEXPECTED SITUATION MORE EFFECTIVELY.
THUS, WE MUST REGAIN THE PUBLIC'S TRUST.
WE VIEW THAT AS OUR RESPONSIBIL-ITY.
DAILY CHATTER
A MASSIVE GROUNDFORCE OPERATION IS UNDER WAY AT THE CRASH SITE AROUND KICHIJOJI STATION.
S.E.S. HAS DEVELOPED A SMALL UNIT FOR TERRESTRIAL ENGAGEMENT IN RESIDENTIAL AREAS AND INSIDE BUILDINGS.
HUJIN LIGHT WILL BE READY FOR THE SELF-DEFENSE FORCE THIS MONTH.
DUE TO INCREASING DEMAND FOR PROTECTION AGAINST LARGE AIRCRAFT, AND WITH A VIEW TOWARD DIRECT ATTACKS ON THE MOTHER SHIP, WE ARE ALSO INSTALLING THE MUCH LARGER *CHOKUJIN*.
IT'S ALMOST COMPLETE, SO WE CAN GUARANTEE SAFETY FOR THE CIVILIAN POPULATION.
WE AT S.E.S. STAND BY THE HUJIN SERIES AND ARE DEDICATED TO AVOIDING ANY FURTHER UNFORTUNATE EVENTS.

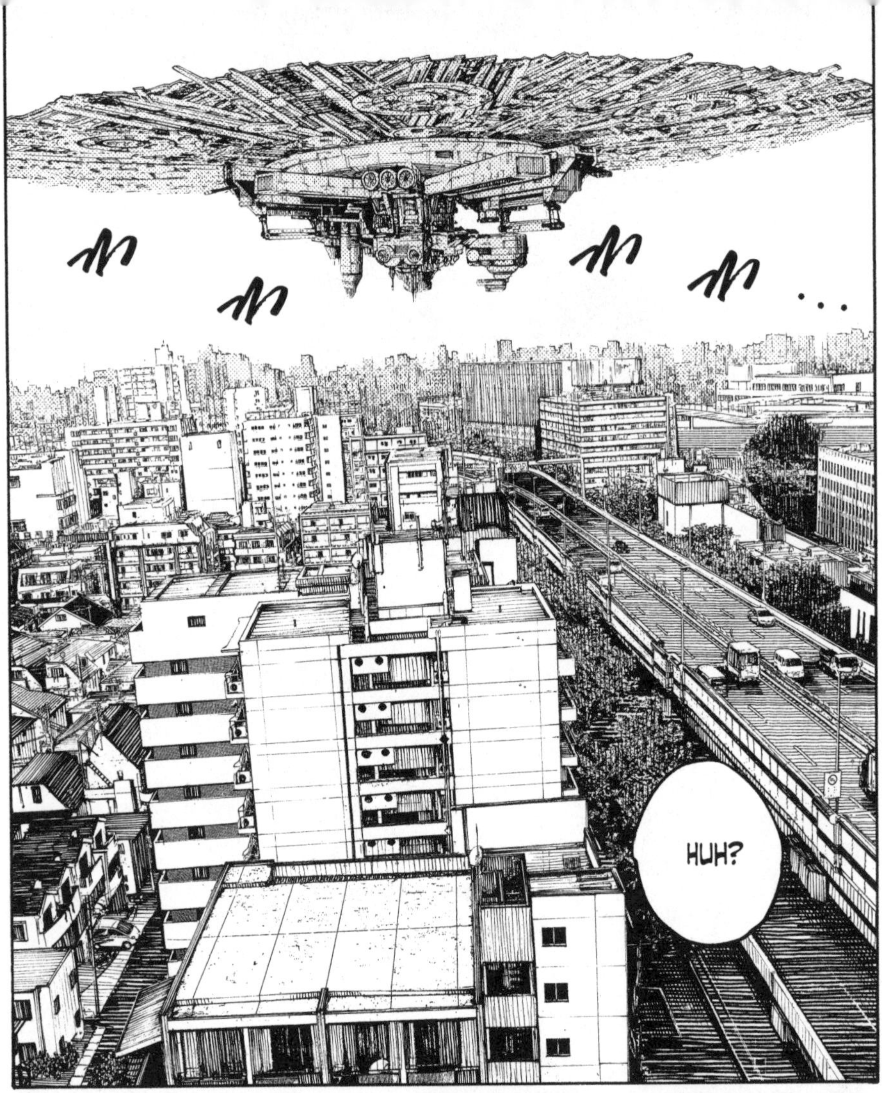
HUH?

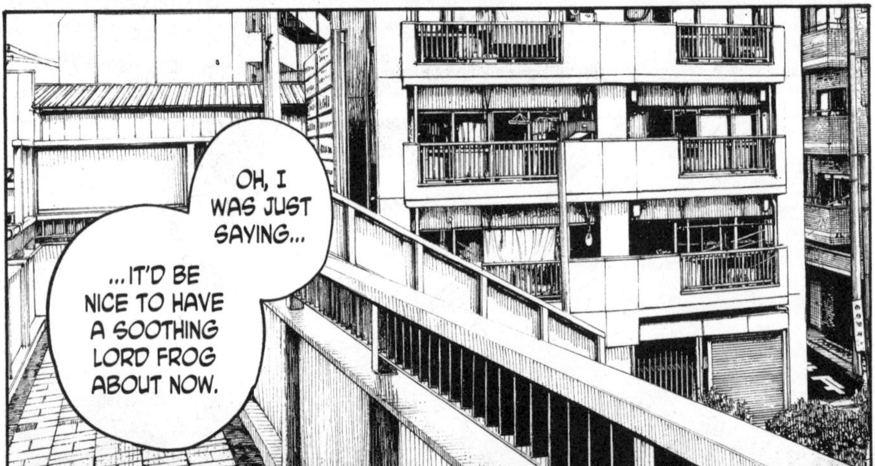
OH, I WAS JUST SAYING...
...IT'D BE NICE TO HAVE A SOOTHING LORD FROG ABOUT NOW.

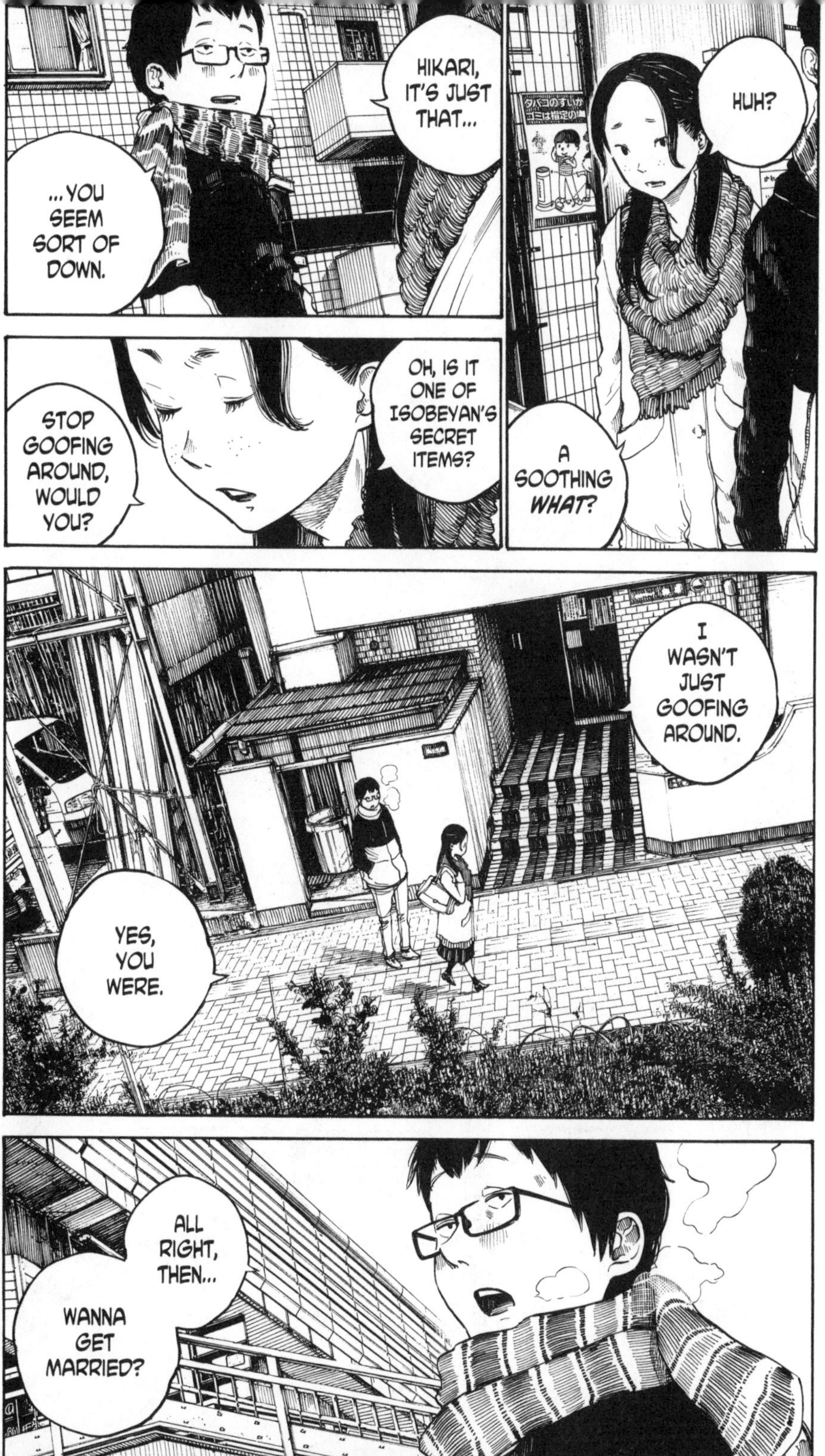
HUH?
A SOOTHING *WHAT?*
HIKARI, IT'S JUST THAT...
...YOU SEEM SORT OF DOWN.
OH, IS IT ONE OF ISOBEYAN'S SECRET ITEMS?
STOP GOOFING AROUND, WOULD YOU?
I WASN'T JUST GOOFING AROUND.
YES, YOU WERE.
ALL RIGHT, THEN...
WANNA GET MARRIED?

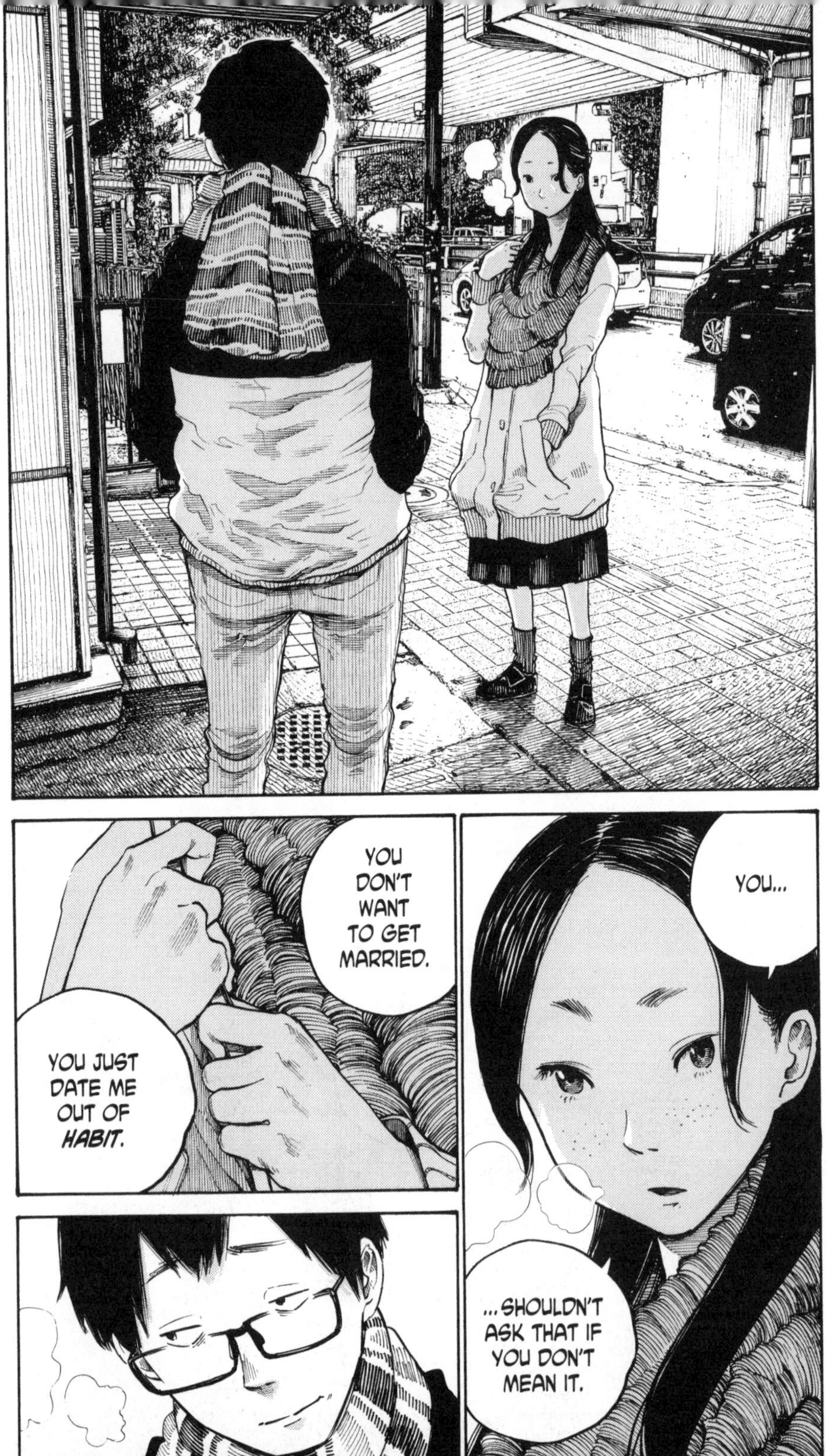
YOU...
...SHOULDN'T ASK THAT IF YOU DON'T MEAN IT.
YOU DON'T WANT TO GET MARRIED.
YOU JUST DATE ME OUT OF *HABIT*.

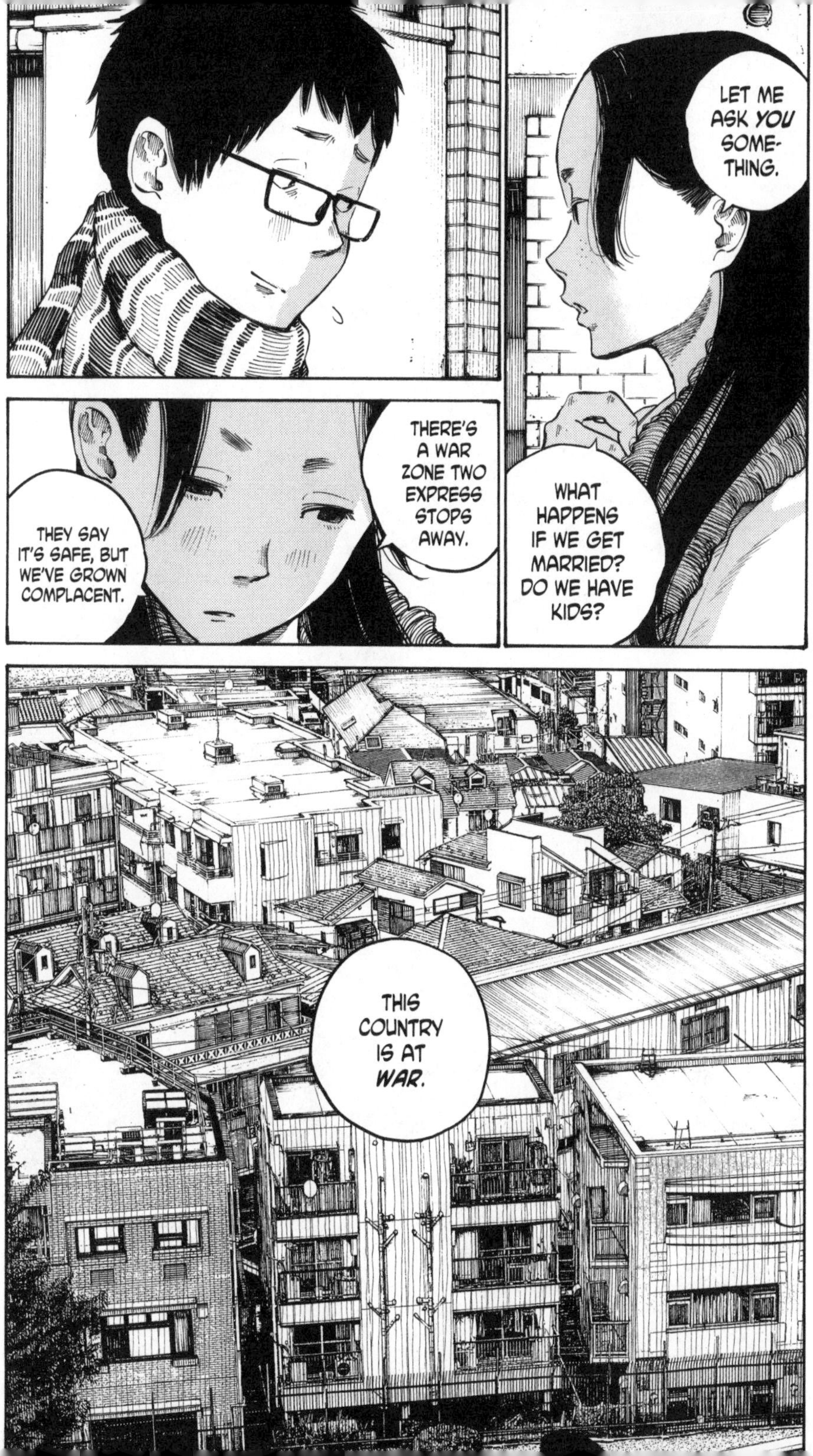
LET ME ASK YOU SOMETHING.
WHAT HAPPENS IF WE GET MARRIED? DO WE HAVE KIDS?
THERE'S A WAR ZONE TWO EXPRESS STOPS AWAY.
THEY SAY IT'S SAFE, BUT WE'VE GROWN COMPLACENT.
THIS COUNTRY IS AT WAR.

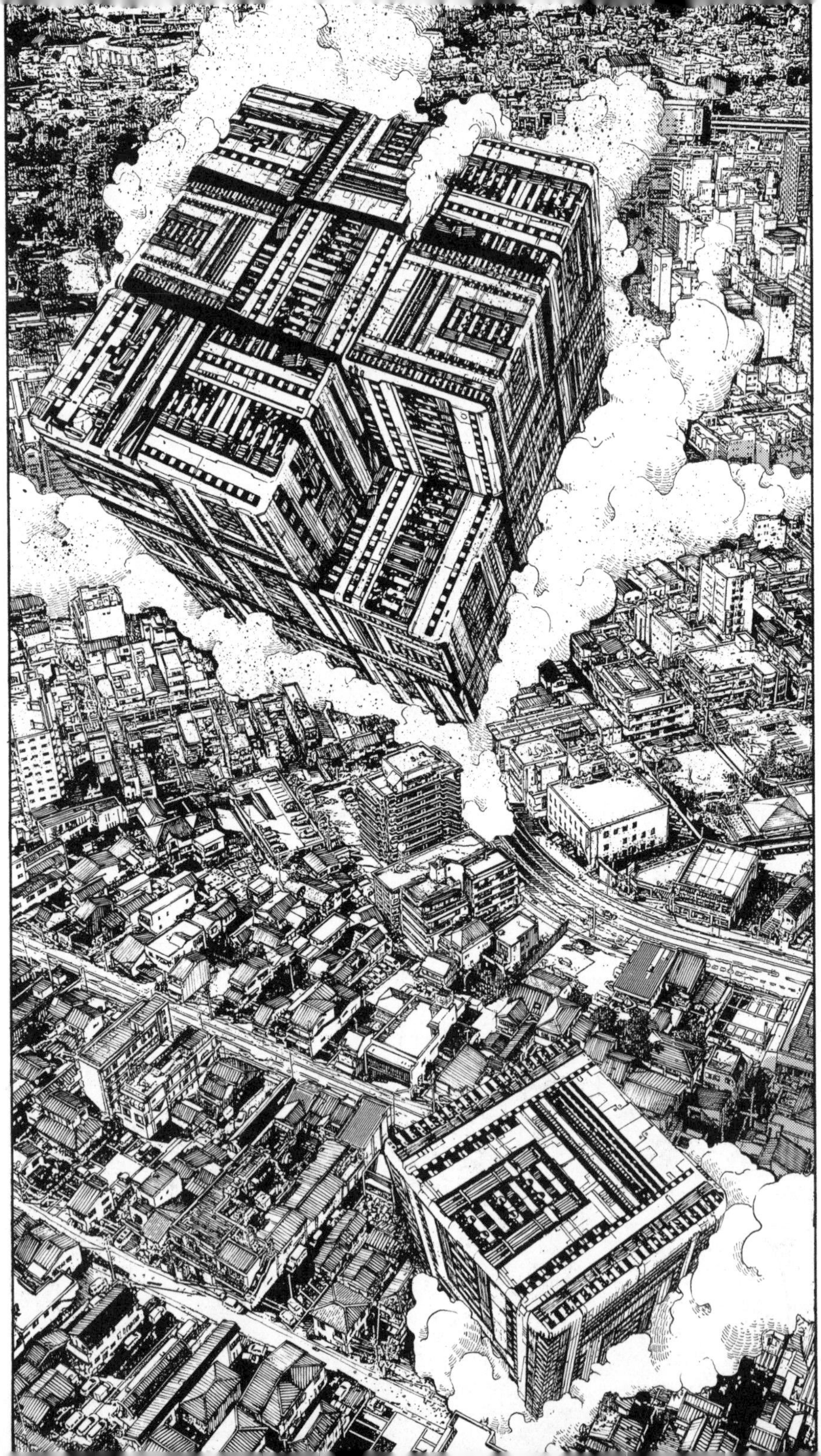

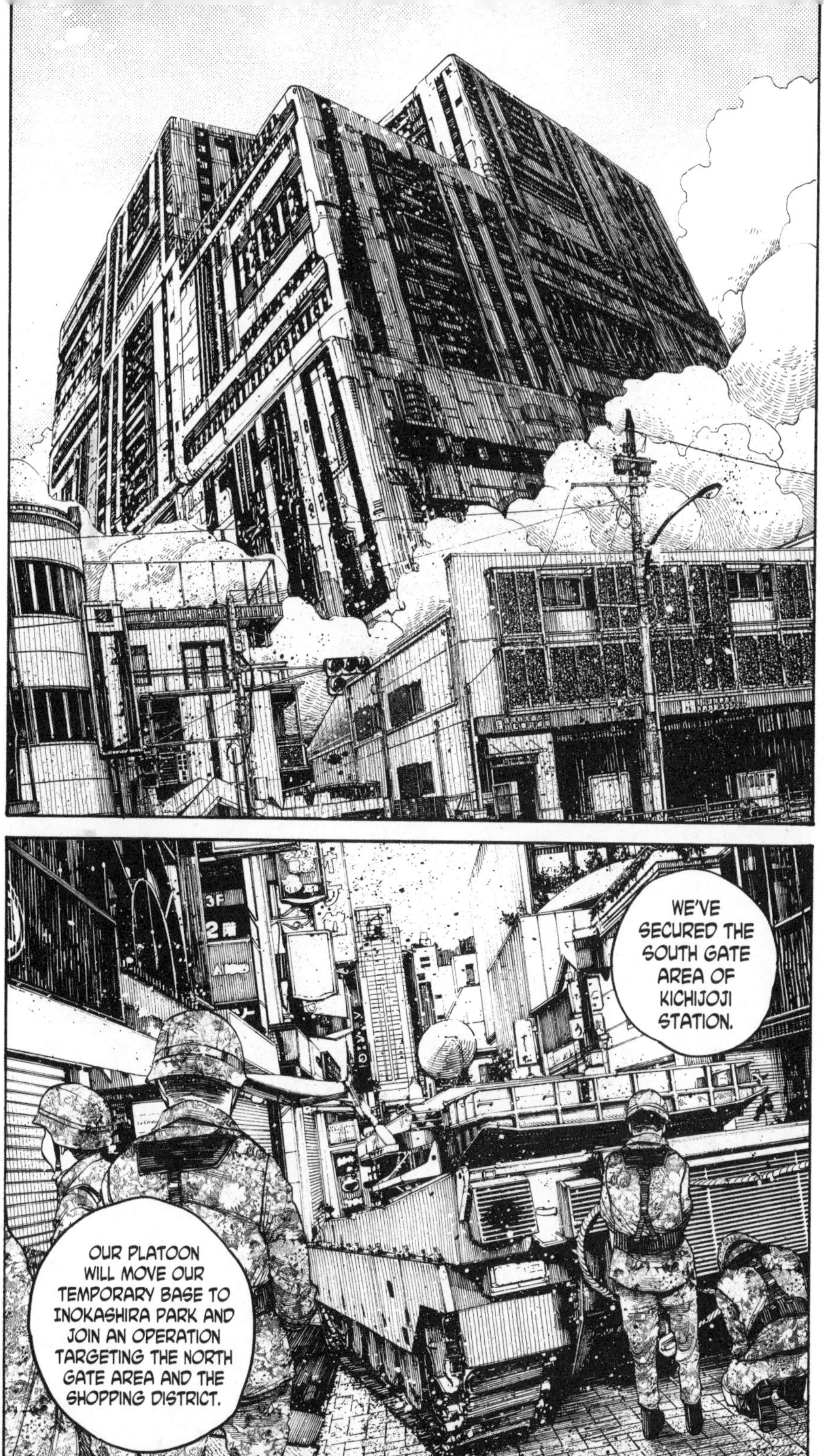
WE'VE SECURED THE SOUTH GATE AREA OF KICHIJOJI STATION.
OUR PLATOON WILL MOVE OUR TEMPORARY BASE TO INOKASHIRA PARK AND JOIN AN OPERATION TARGETING THE NORTH GATE AREA AND THE SHOPPING DISTRICT.

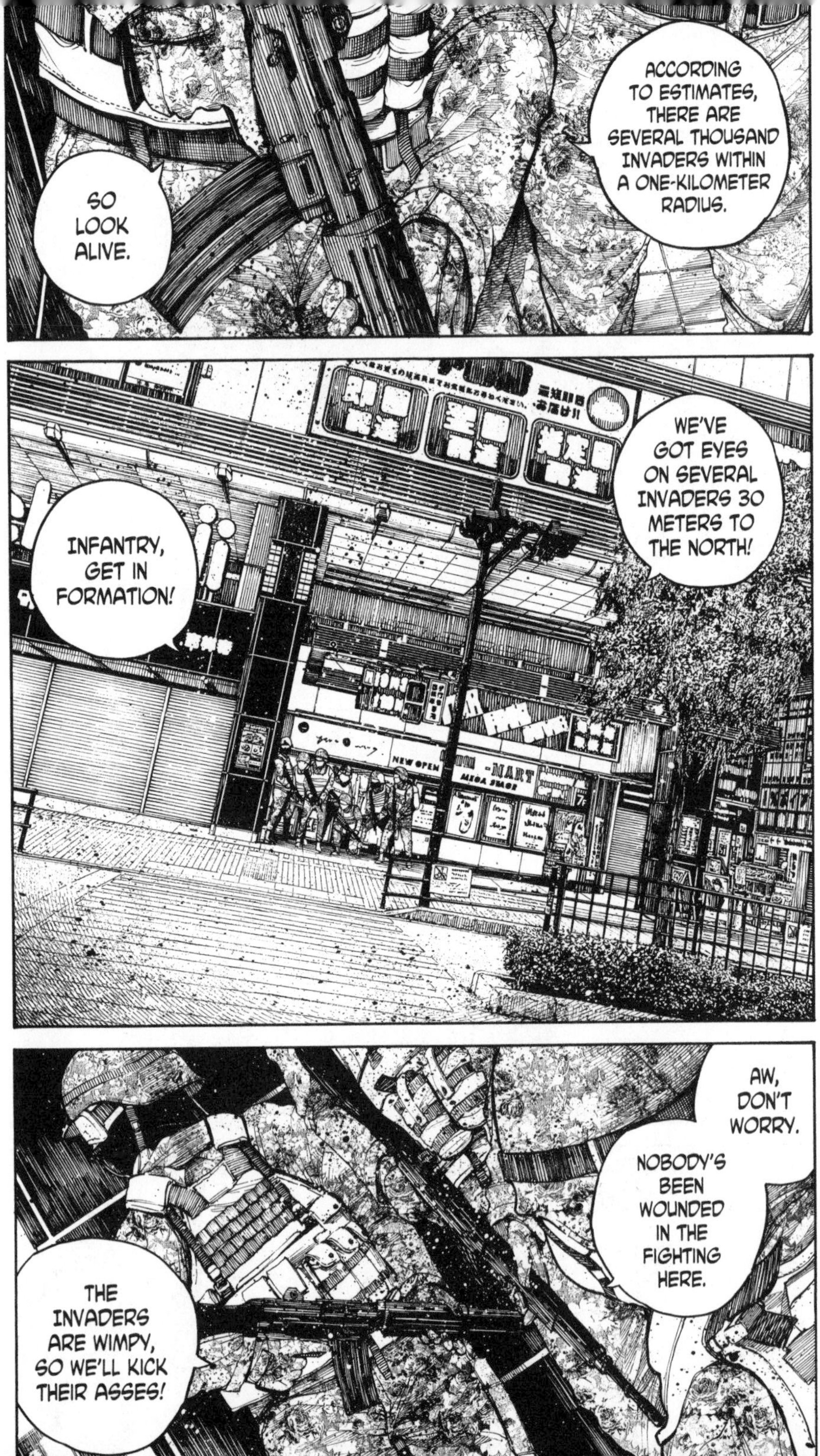
ACCORDING TO ESTIMATES, THERE ARE SEVERAL THOUSAND INVADERS WITHIN A ONE-KILOMETER RADIUS.
SO LOOK ALIVE.
WE'VE GOT EYES ON SEVERAL INVADERS 30 METERS TO THE NORTH!
INFANTRY, GET IN FORMATION!
NEW OPEN
AW, DON'T WORRY.
NOBODY'S BEEN WOUNDED IN THE FIGHTING HERE.
THE INVADERS ARE WIMPY, SO WE'LL KICK THEIR ASSES!

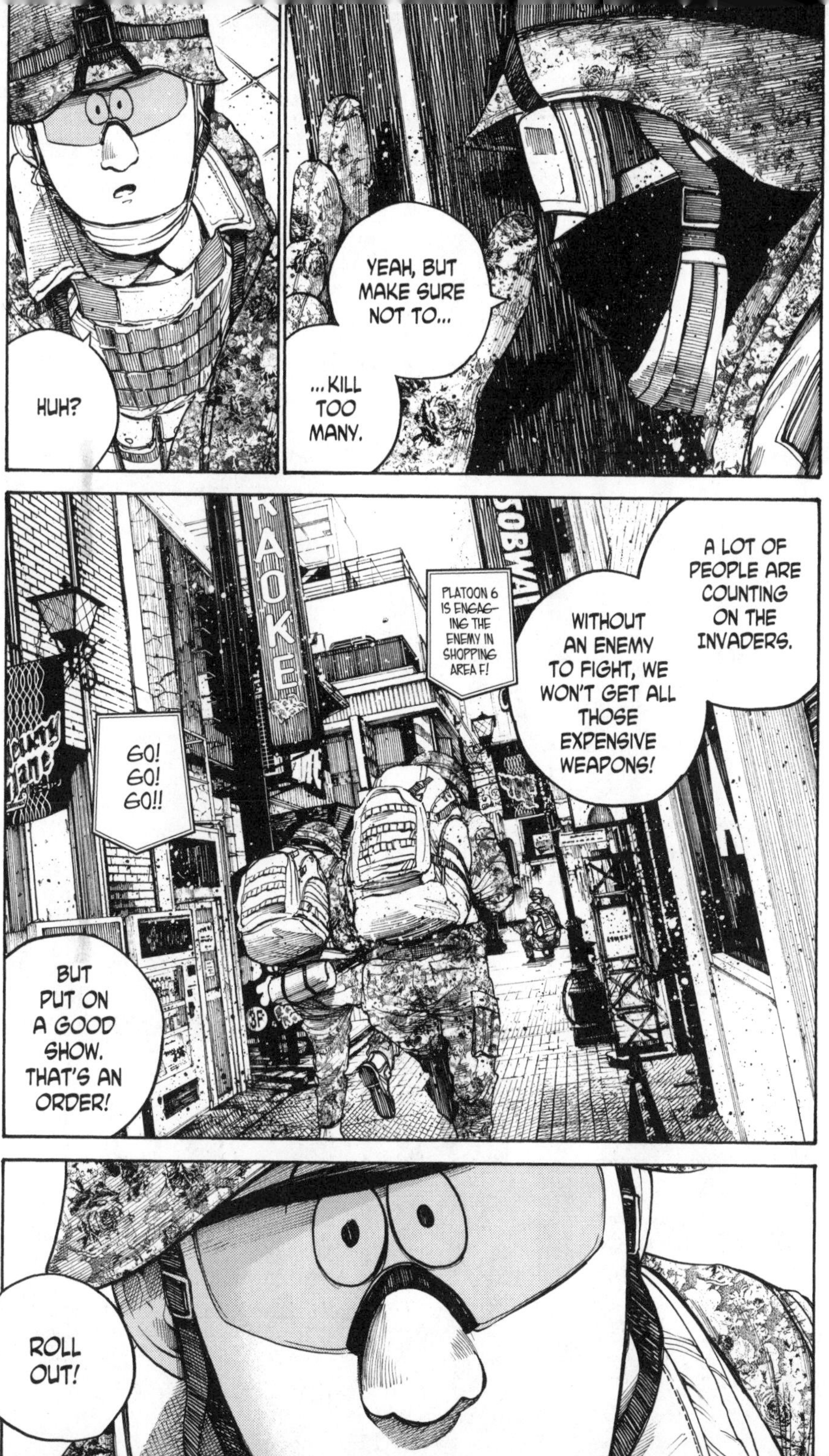
YEAH, BUT MAKE SURE NOT TO...
...KILL TOO MANY.
HUH?
A LOT OF PEOPLE ARE COUNTING ON THE INVADERS.
WITHOUT AN ENEMY TO FIGHT, WE WON'T GET ALL THOSE EXPENSIVE WEAPONS!
PLATOON 6 IS ENGAG-ING THE ENEMY IN SHOPPING AREA F!
GO! GO! GO!!
BUT PUT ON A GOOD SHOW. THAT'S AN ORDER!
ROLL OUT!

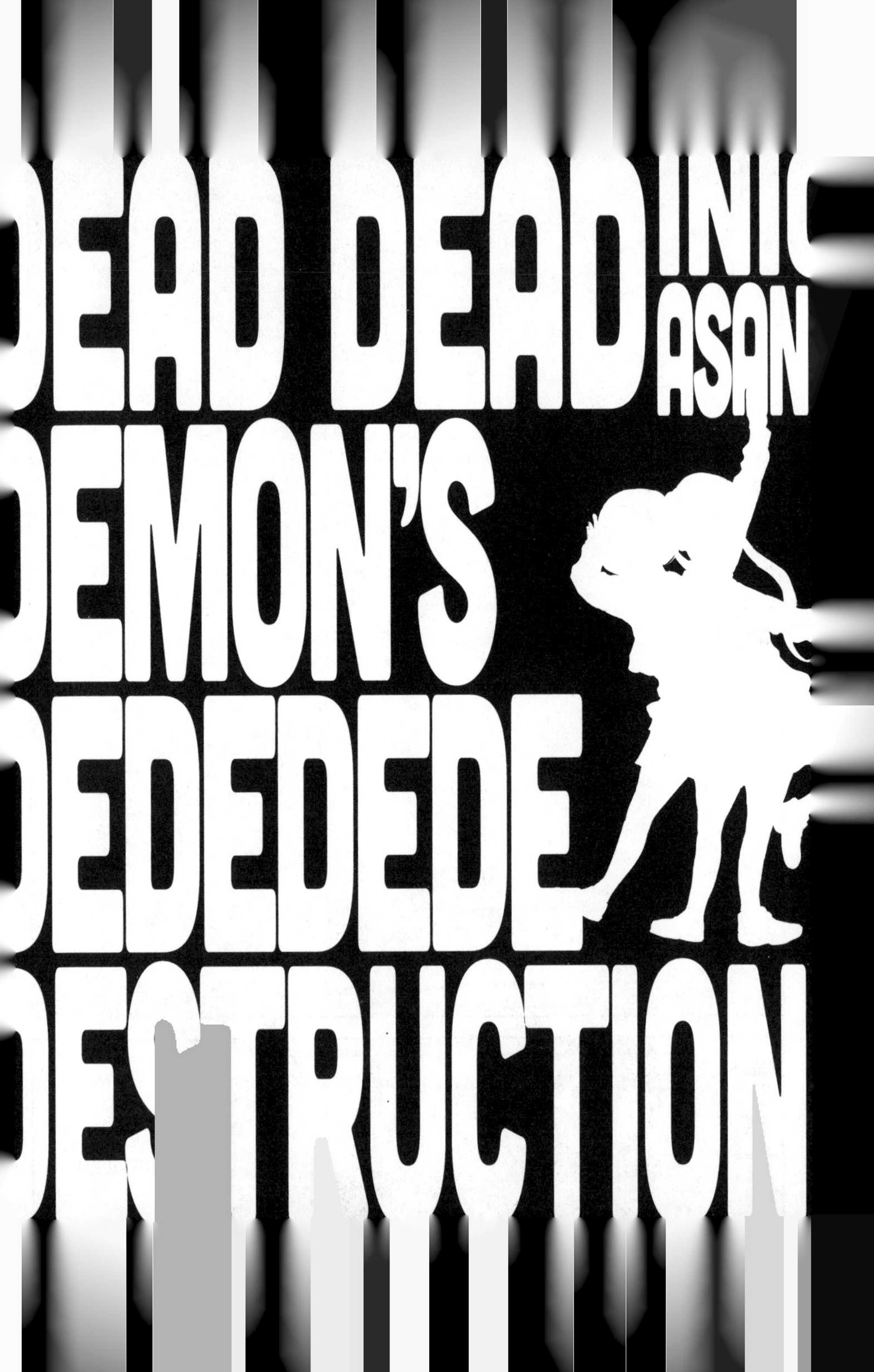
DEAD DEAD
INIO
ASAN
DEMON'S
DEDEDEDE
DESTRUCTION

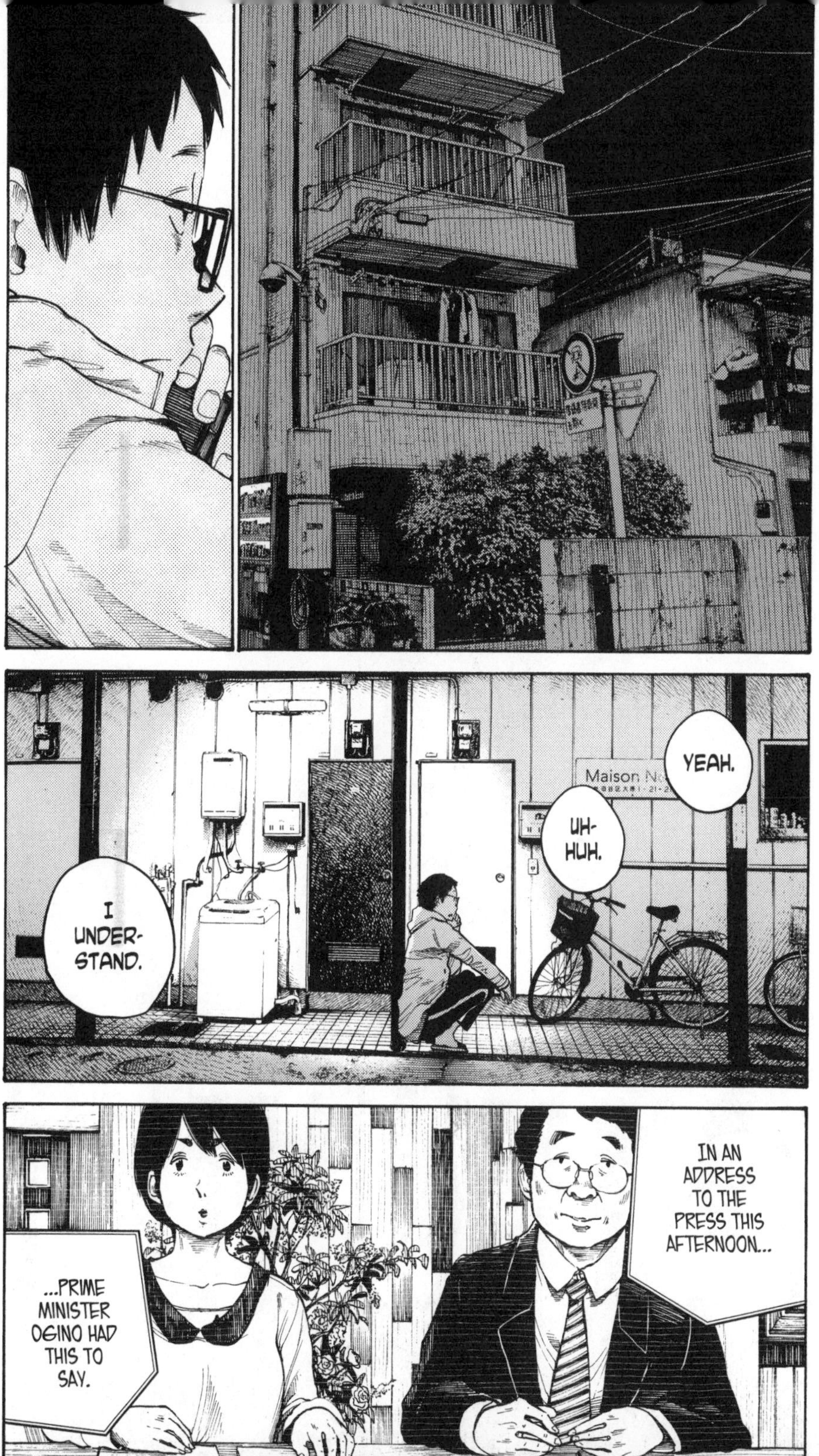
YEAH.
UH-HUH.
I UNDERSTAND.
IN AN ADDRESS TO THE PRESS THIS AFTERNOON...
...PRIME MINISTER OGINO HAD THIS TO SAY.

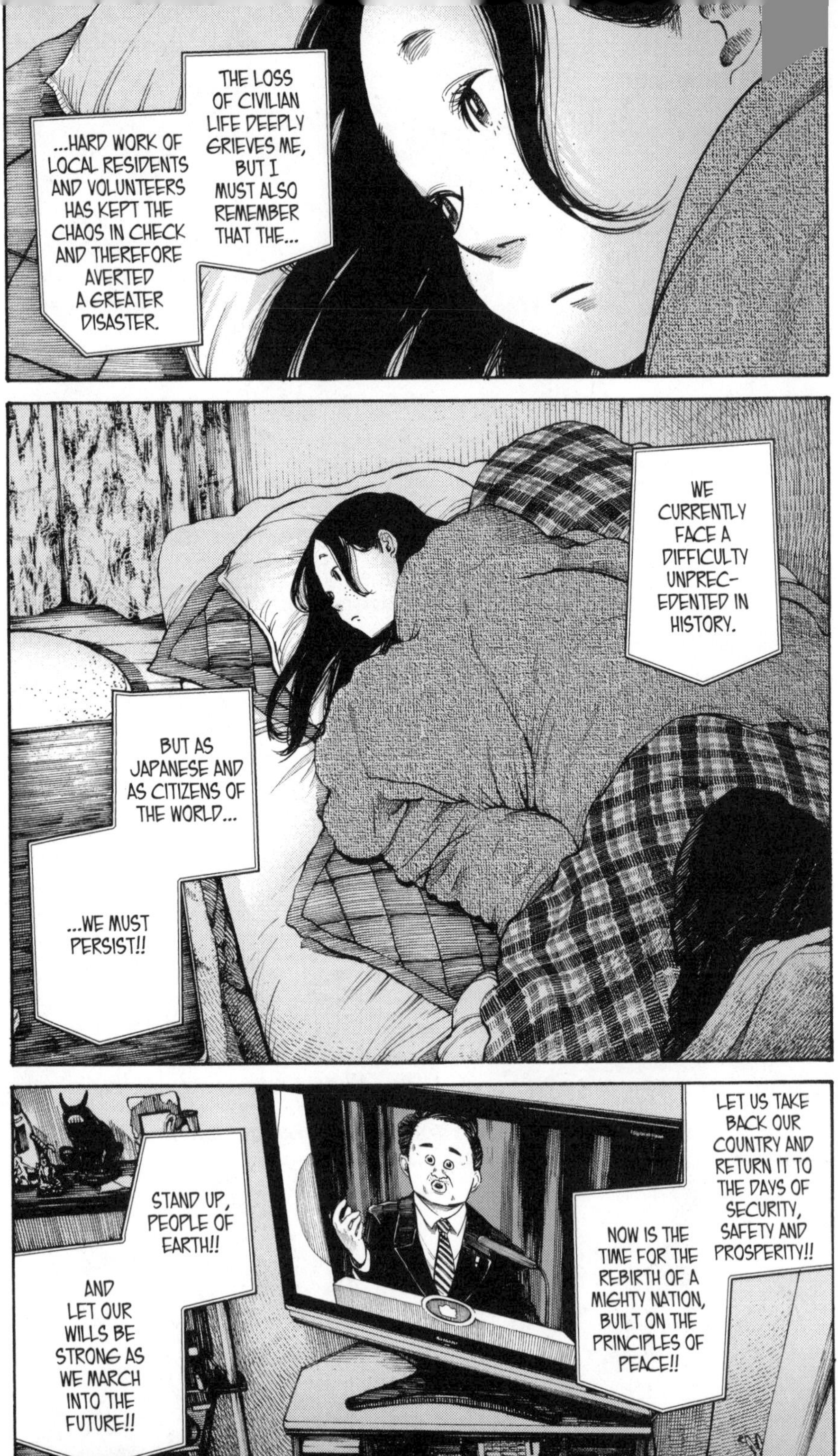
THE LOSS OF CIVILIAN LIFE DEEPLY GRIEVES ME, BUT I MUST ALSO REMEMBER THAT THE...
...HARD WORK OF LOCAL RESIDENTS AND VOLUNTEERS HAS KEPT THE CHAOS IN CHECK AND THEREFORE AVERTED A GREATER DISASTER.
WE CURRENTLY FACE A DIFFICULTY UNPREC-EDENTED IN HISTORY.
BUT AS JAPANESE AND AS CITIZENS OF THE WORLD...
...WE MUST PERSIST!!
LET US TAKE BACK OUR COUNTRY AND RETURN IT TO THE DAYS OF SECURITY, SAFETY AND PROSPERITY!!
NOW IS THE TIME FOR THE REBIRTH OF A MIGHTY NATION, BUILT ON THE PRINCIPLES OF PEACE!!
STAND UP, PEOPLE OF EARTH!!
AND LET OUR WILLS BE STRONG AS WE MARCH INTO THE FUTURE!!

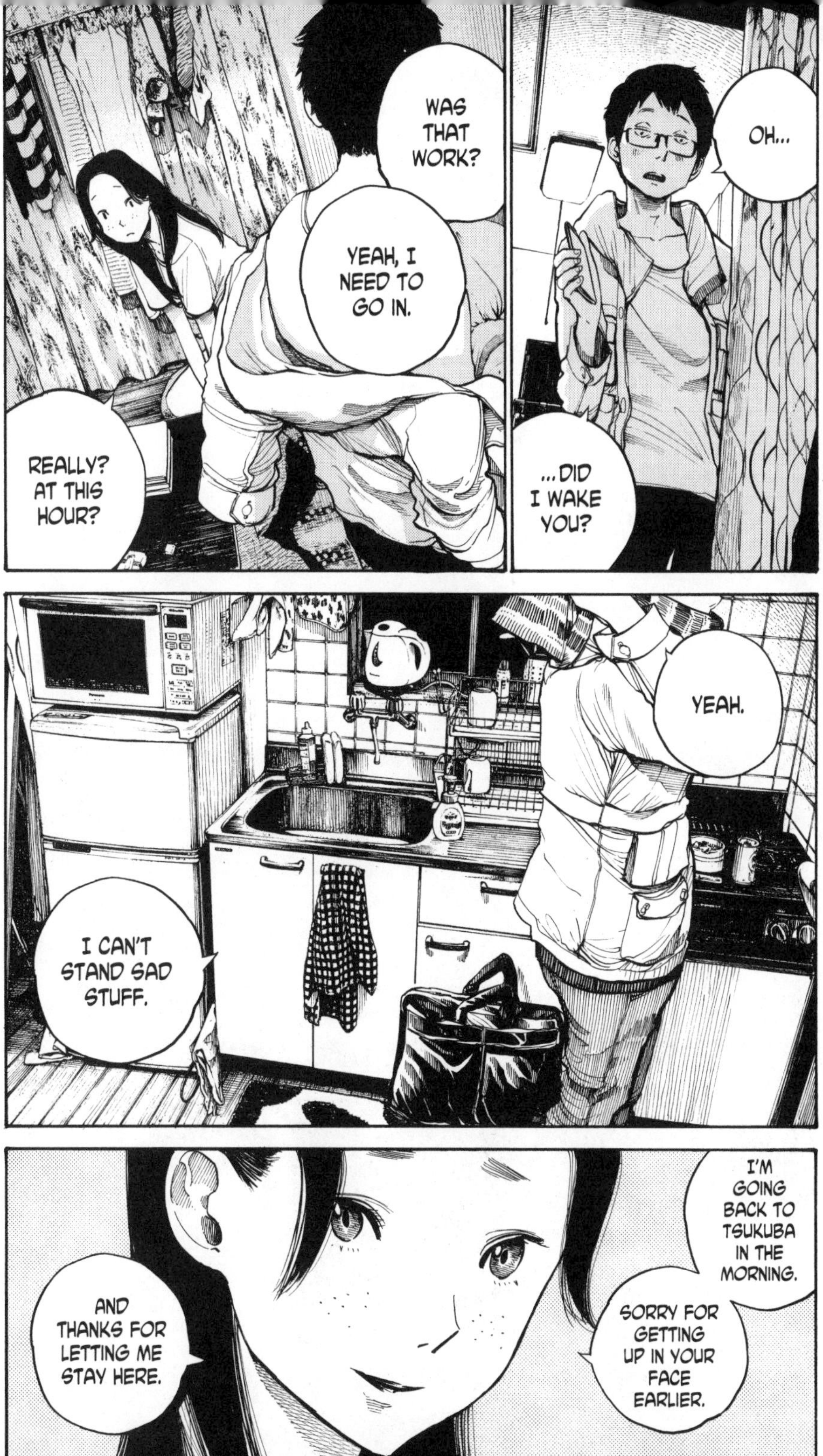
OH...
...DID I WAKE YOU?
WAS THAT WORK?
YEAH, I NEED TO GO IN.
REALLY? AT THIS HOUR?
YEAH.
I CAN'T STAND SAD STUFF.
I'M GOING BACK TO TSUKUBA IN THE MORNING.
SORRY FOR GETTING UP IN YOUR FACE EARLIER.
AND THANKS FOR LETTING ME STAY HERE.

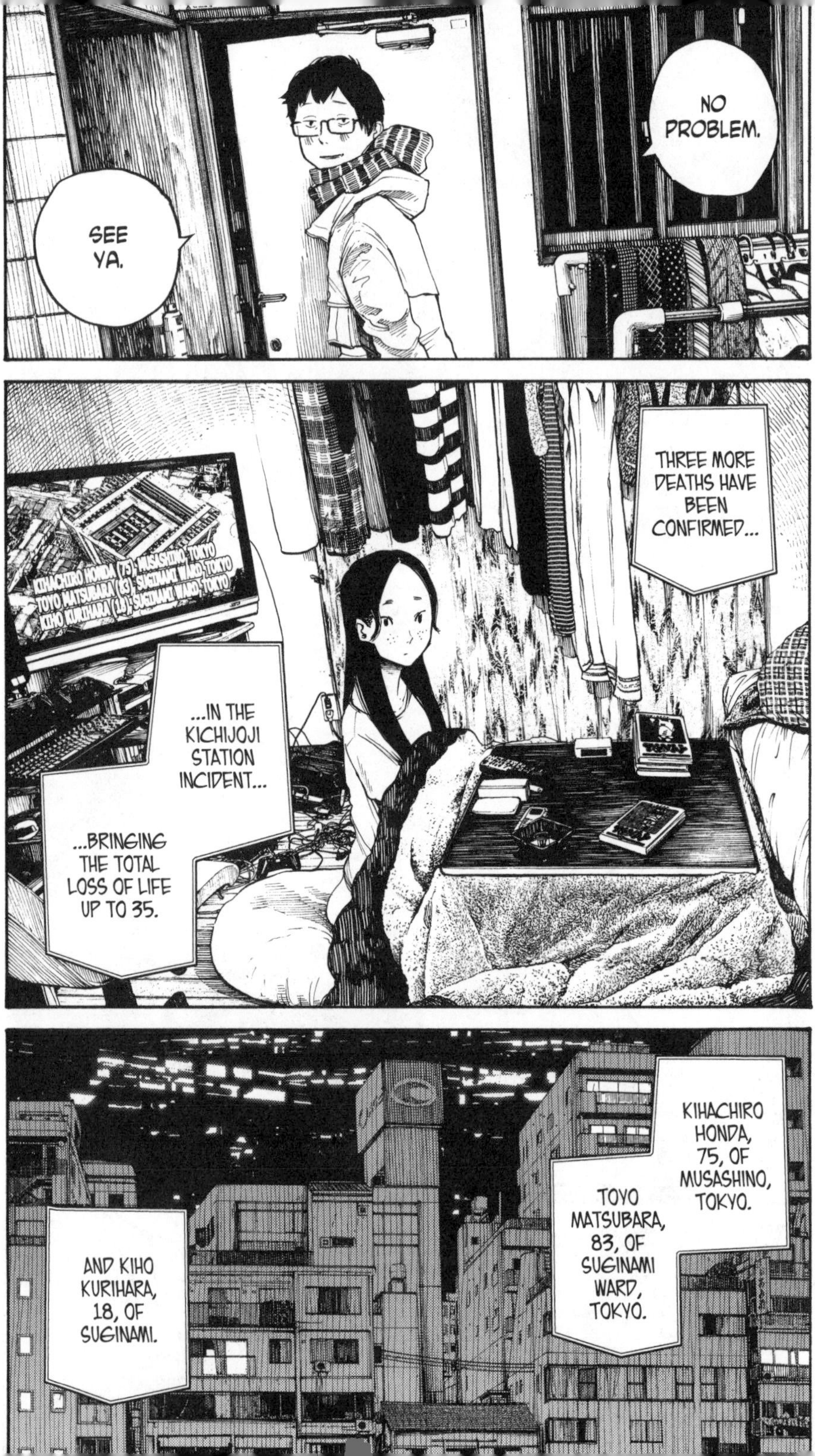
NO PROBLEM.
SEE YA.
THREE MORE DEATHS HAVE BEEN CONFIRMED...
KIHACHIRO HONDA (75), MUSASHINO, TOKYO
TOYO MATSUBARA (83), SUGINAMI WARD, TOKYO
KIHO KURIHARA (18), SUGINAMI WARD, TOKYO
...IN THE KICHIJOJI STATION INCIDENT...
...BRINGING THE TOTAL LOSS OF LIFE UP TO 35.
KIHACHIRO HONDA, 75, OF MUSASHINO, TOKYO.
TOYO MATSUBARA, 83, OF SUGINAMI WARD, TOKYO.
AND KIHO KURIHARA, 18, OF SUGINAMI.

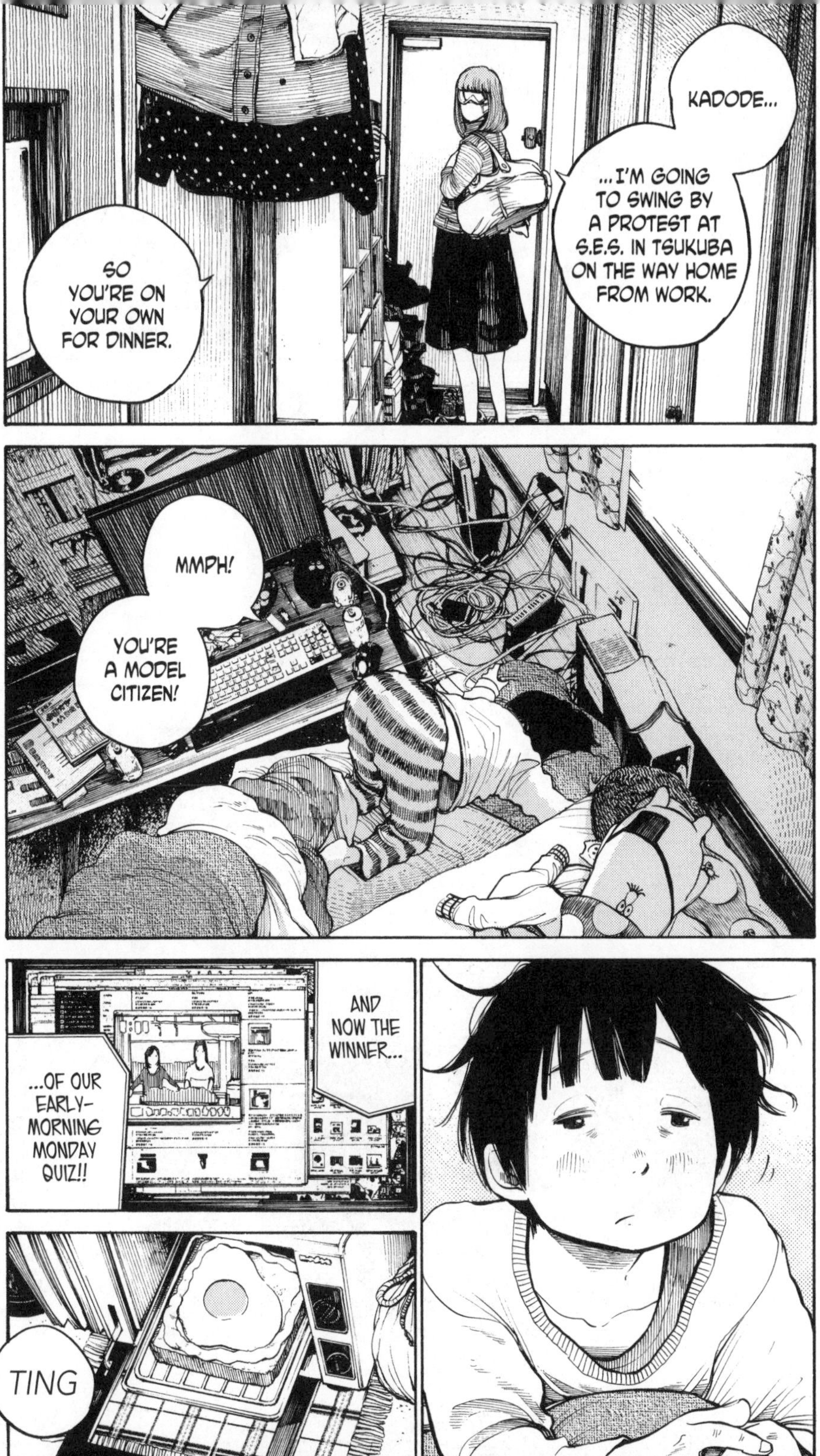
KADODE...
...I'M GOING TO SWING BY A PROTEST AT S.E.S. IN TSUKUBA ON THE WAY HOME FROM WORK.
SO YOU'RE ON YOUR OWN FOR DINNER.
MMPH!
YOU'RE A MODEL CITIZEN!
AND NOW THE WINNER...
...OF OUR EARLY-MORNING MONDAY QUIZ!!
TING

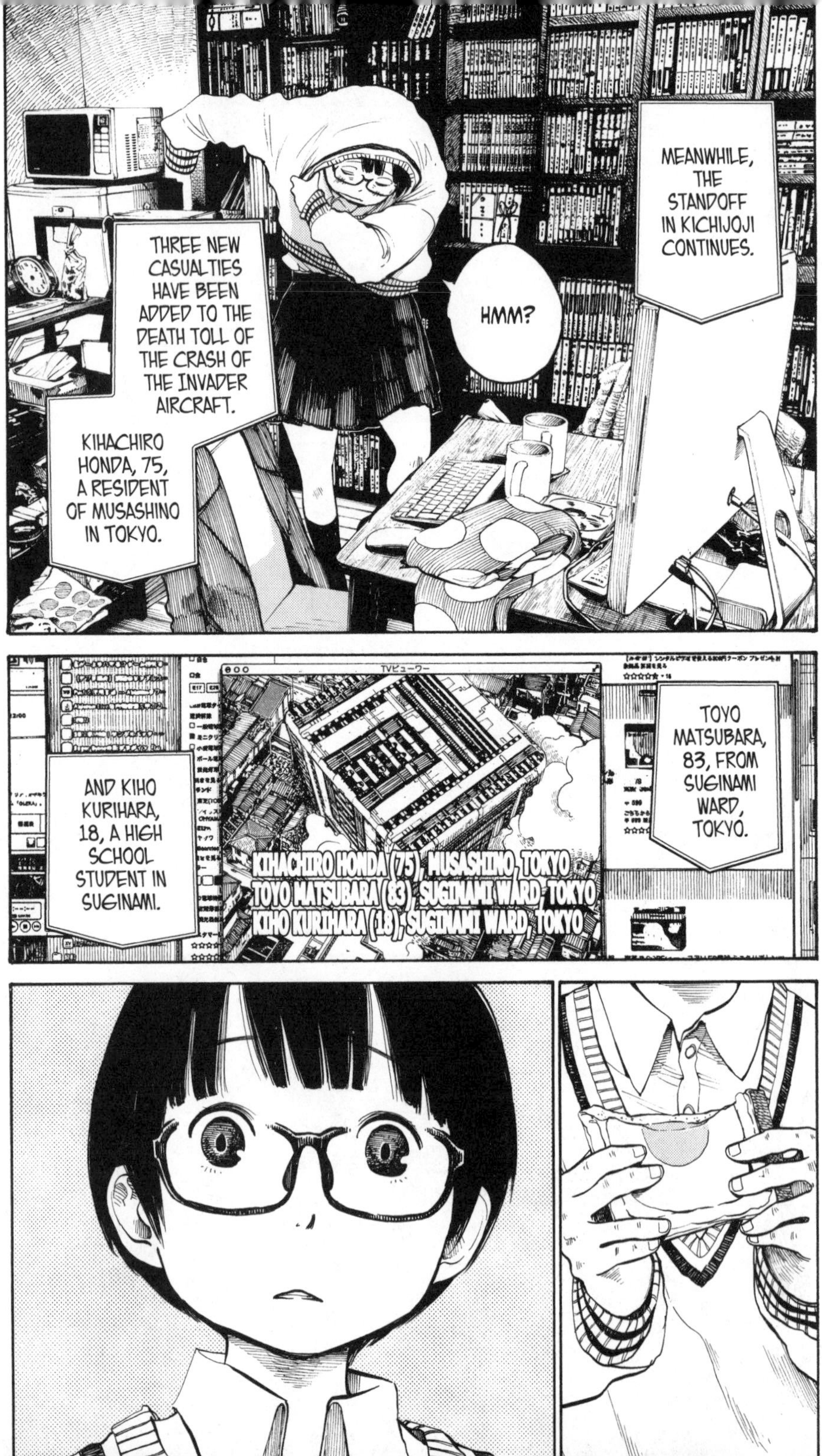
MEANWHILE, THE STANDOFF IN KICHIJOJI CONTINUES.
HMM?
THREE NEW CASUALTIES HAVE BEEN ADDED TO THE DEATH TOLL OF THE CRASH OF THE INVADER AIRCRAFT.
KIHACHIRO HONDA, 75, A RESIDENT OF MUSASHINO IN TOKYO.
TOYO MATSUBARA, 83, FROM SUGINAMI WARD, TOKYO.
TVビューワー
KIHACHIRO HONDA (75), MUSASHINO, TOKYO
TOYO MATSUBARA (83), SUGINAMI WARD, TOKYO
KIHO KURIHARA (18), SUGINAMI WARD, TOKYO
AND KIHO KURIHARA, 18, A HIGH SCHOOL STUDENT IN SUGINAMI.

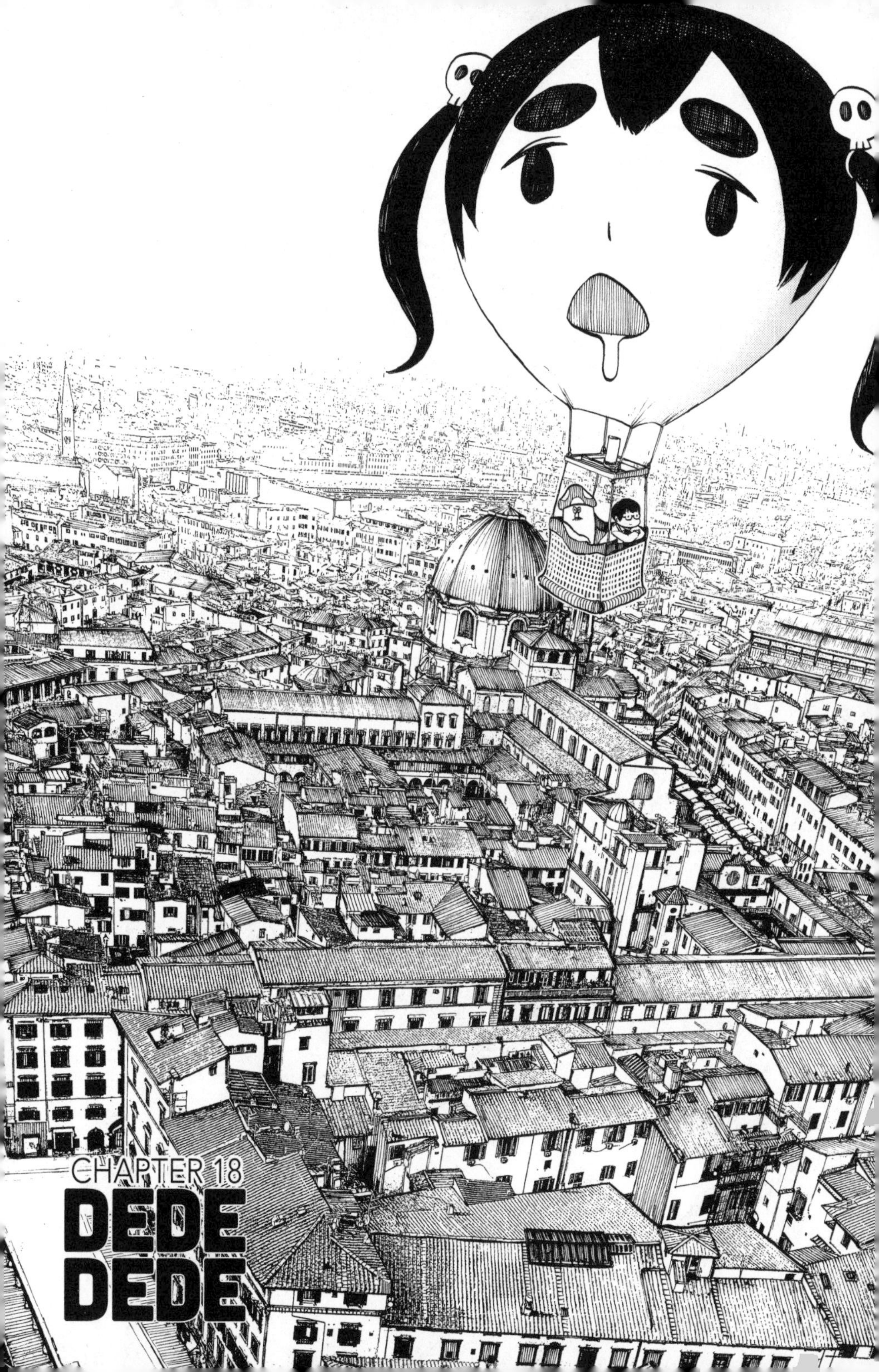
CHAPTER 18
DEDE
DEDE

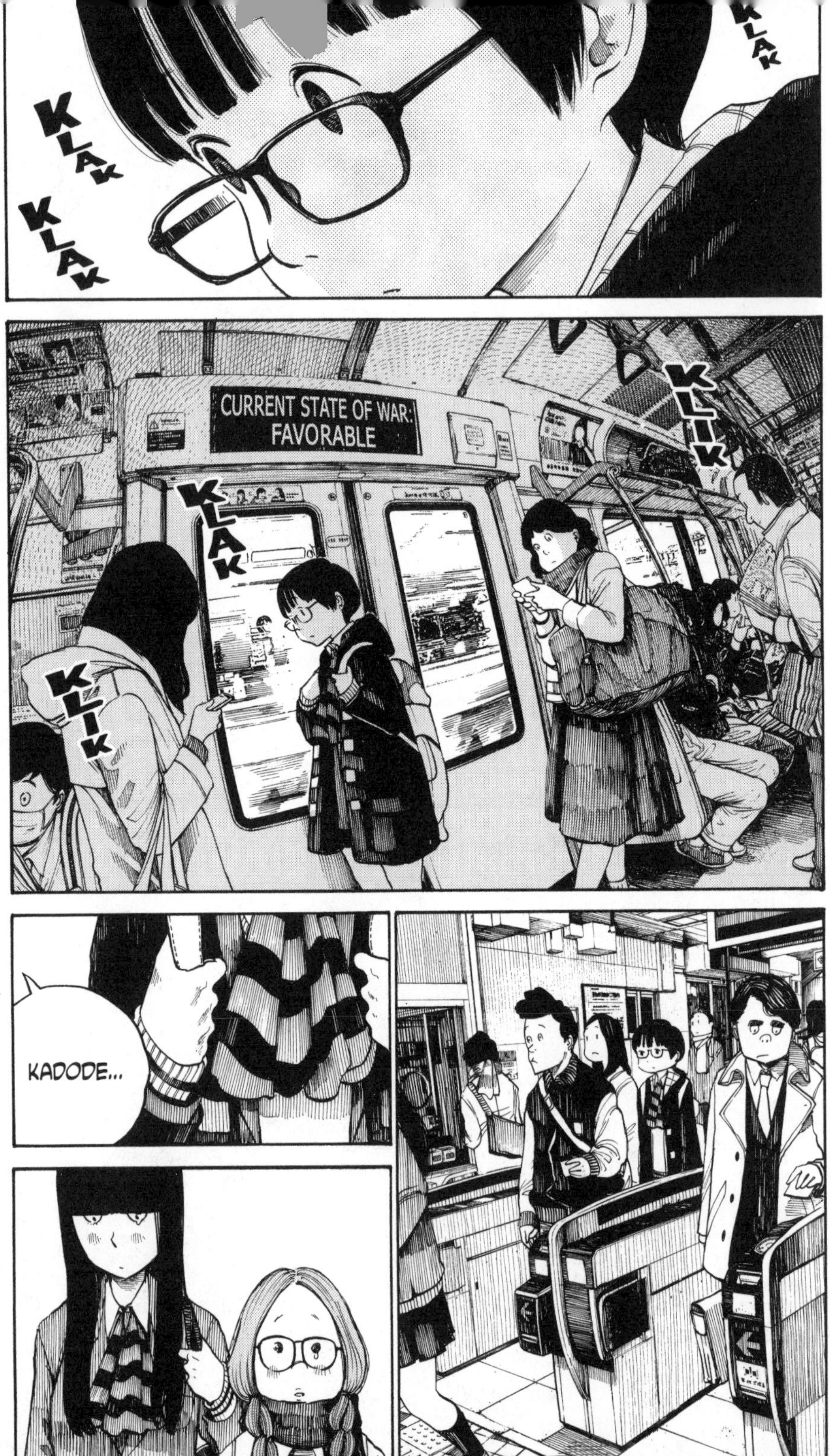
KLAK
KLAK
KLAK
CURRENT STATE OF WAR:
FAVORABLE
KLIK
KLAK
KLIK
KADODE...

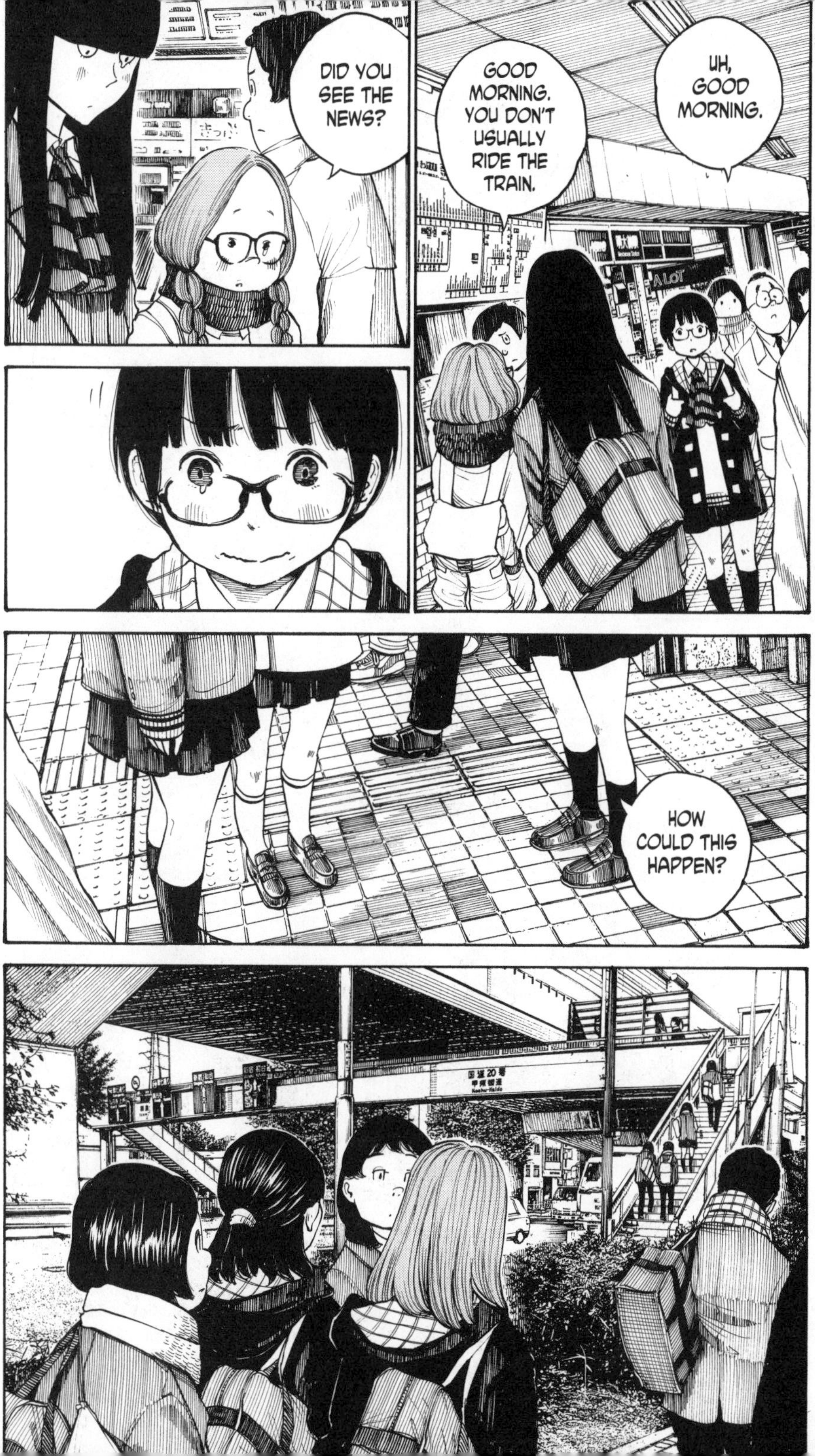
UH, GOOD MORNING.
GOOD MORNING. YOU DON'T USUALLY RIDE THE TRAIN.
DID YOU SEE THE NEWS?
HOW COULD THIS HAPPEN?

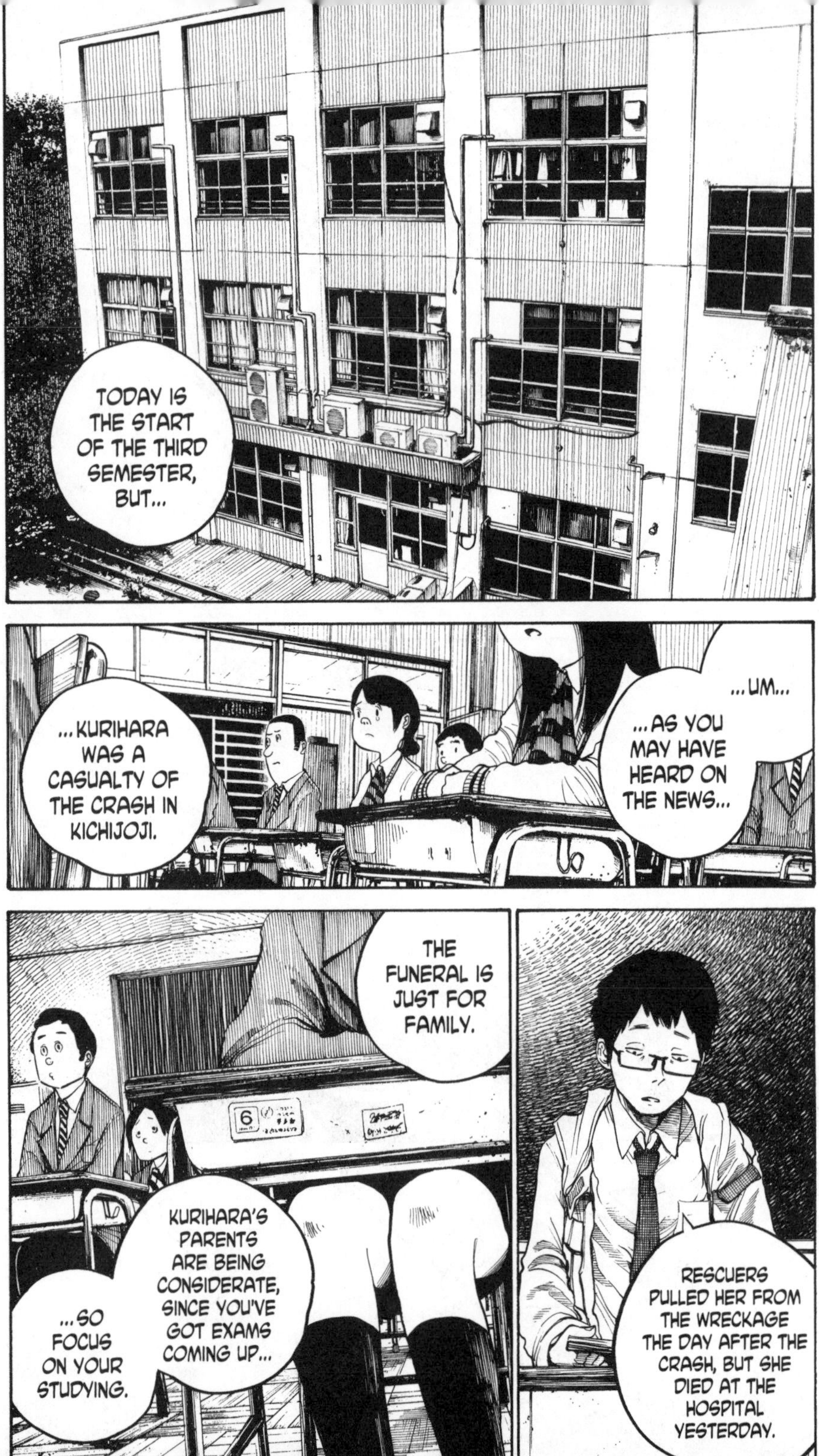
TODAY IS THE START OF THE THIRD SEMESTER, BUT...
...UM...
...AS YOU MAY HAVE HEARD ON THE NEWS...
...KURIHARA WAS A CASUALTY OF THE CRASH IN KICHIJOJI.
RESCUERS PULLED HER FROM THE WRECKAGE THE DAY AFTER THE CRASH, BUT SHE DIED AT THE HOSPITAL YESTERDAY.
THE FUNERAL IS JUST FOR FAMILY.
KURIHARA'S PARENTS ARE BEING CONSIDERATE, SINCE YOU'VE GOT EXAMS COMING UP...
...SO FOCUS ON YOUR STUDYING.

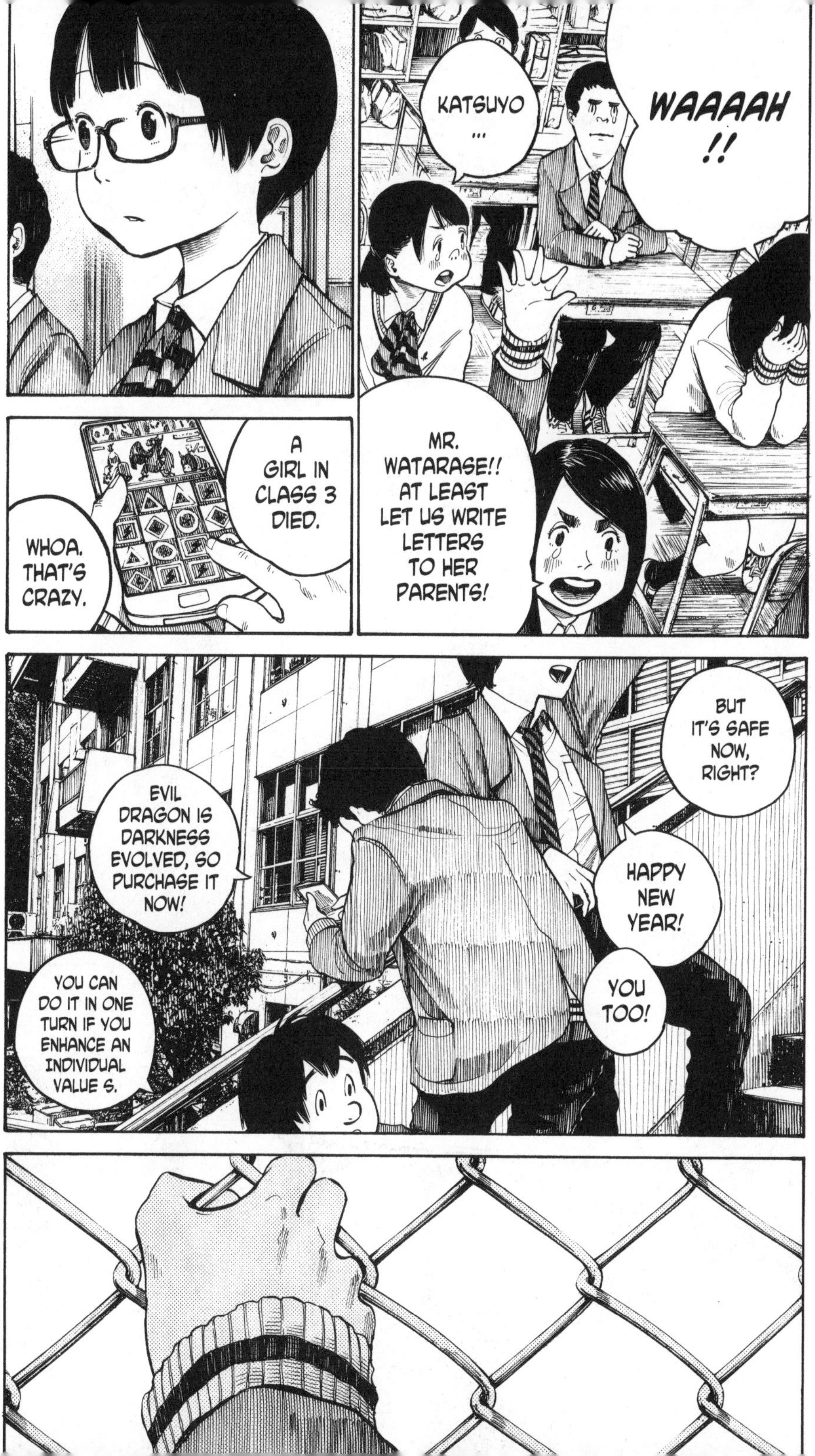
WAAAAH !!
KATSUYO ...
MR. WATARASE!! AT LEAST LET US WRITE LETTERS TO HER PARENTS!
A GIRL IN CLASS 3 DIED.
WHOA. THAT'S CRAZY.
BUT IT'S SAFE NOW, RIGHT?
HAPPY NEW YEAR!
YOU TOO!
EVIL DRAGON IS DARKNESS EVOLVED, SO PURCHASE IT NOW!
YOU CAN DO IT IN ONE TURN IF YOU ENHANCE AN INDIVIDUAL VALUE S.

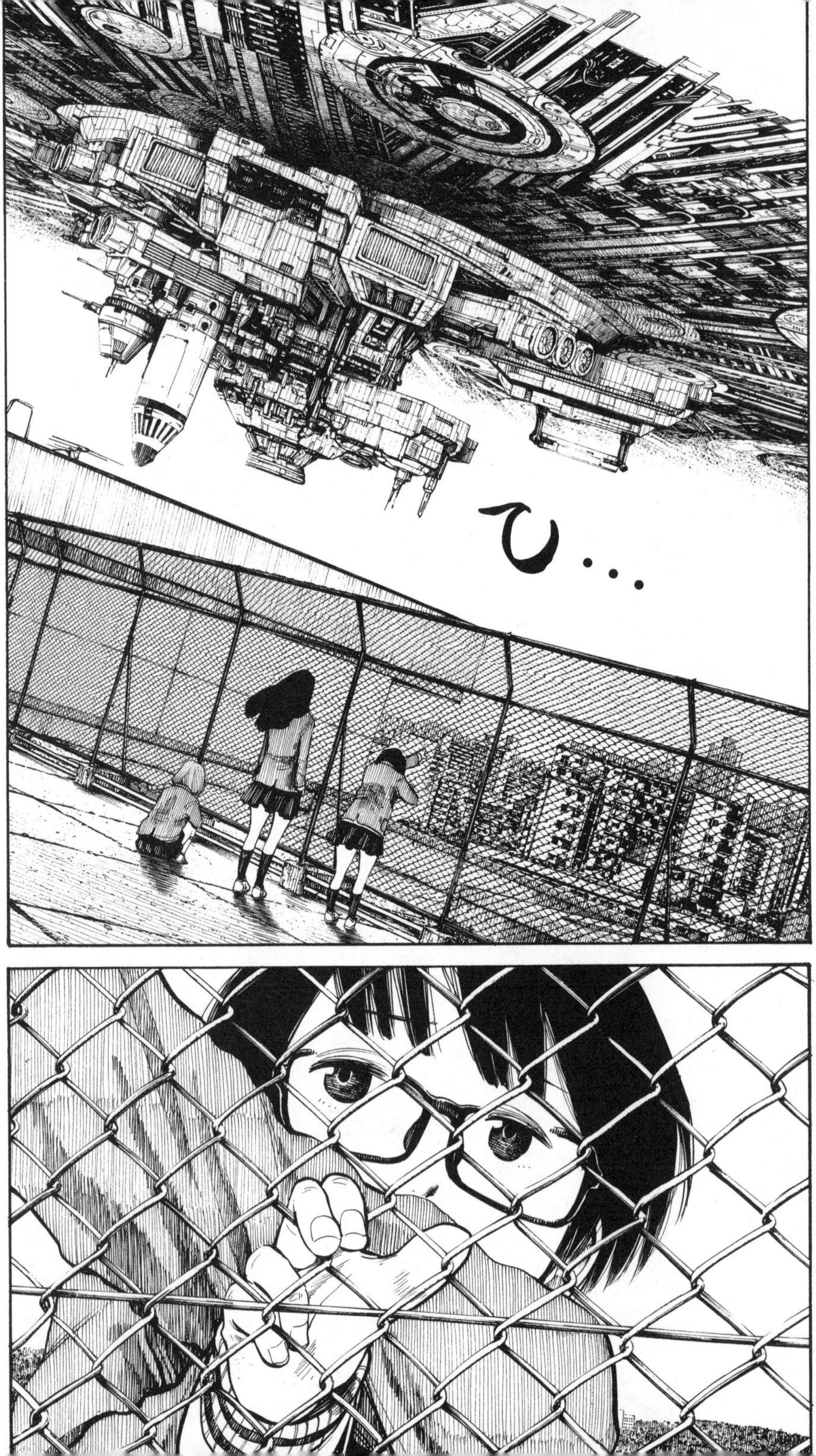
ひ…

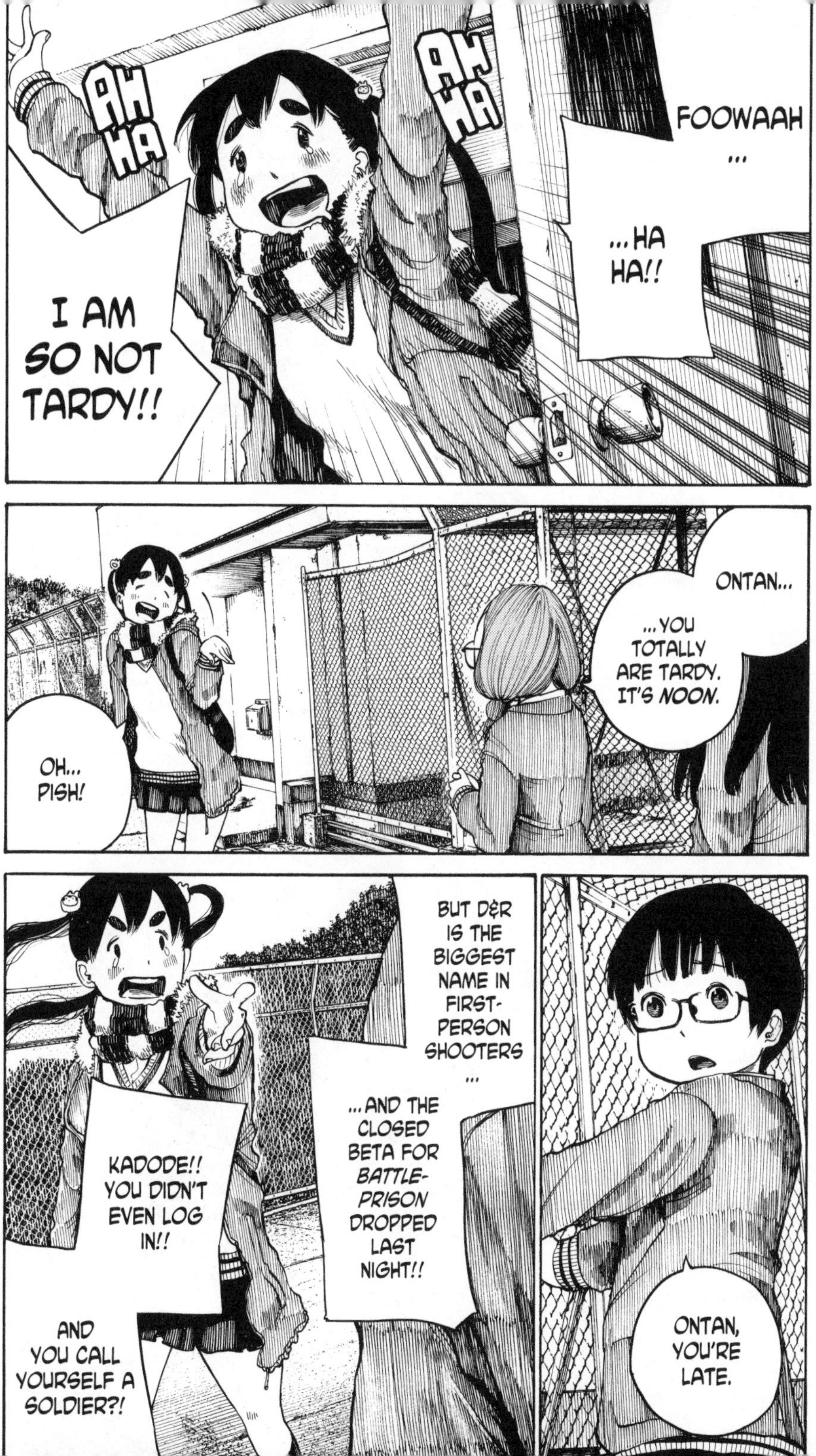
FOOWAAH ...
AH HA
AH HA
...HA HA!!
I AM SO NOT TARDY!!
ONTAN...
...YOU TOTALLY ARE TARDY. IT'S *NOON*.
OH... PISH!
ONTAN, YOU'RE LATE.
BUT D&R IS THE BIGGEST NAME IN FIRST-PERSON SHOOTERS ...
...AND THE CLOSED BETA FOR *BATTLE-PRISON* DROPPED LAST NIGHT!!
KADODE!! YOU DIDN'T EVEN LOG IN!!
AND YOU CALL YOURSELF A SOLDIER?!

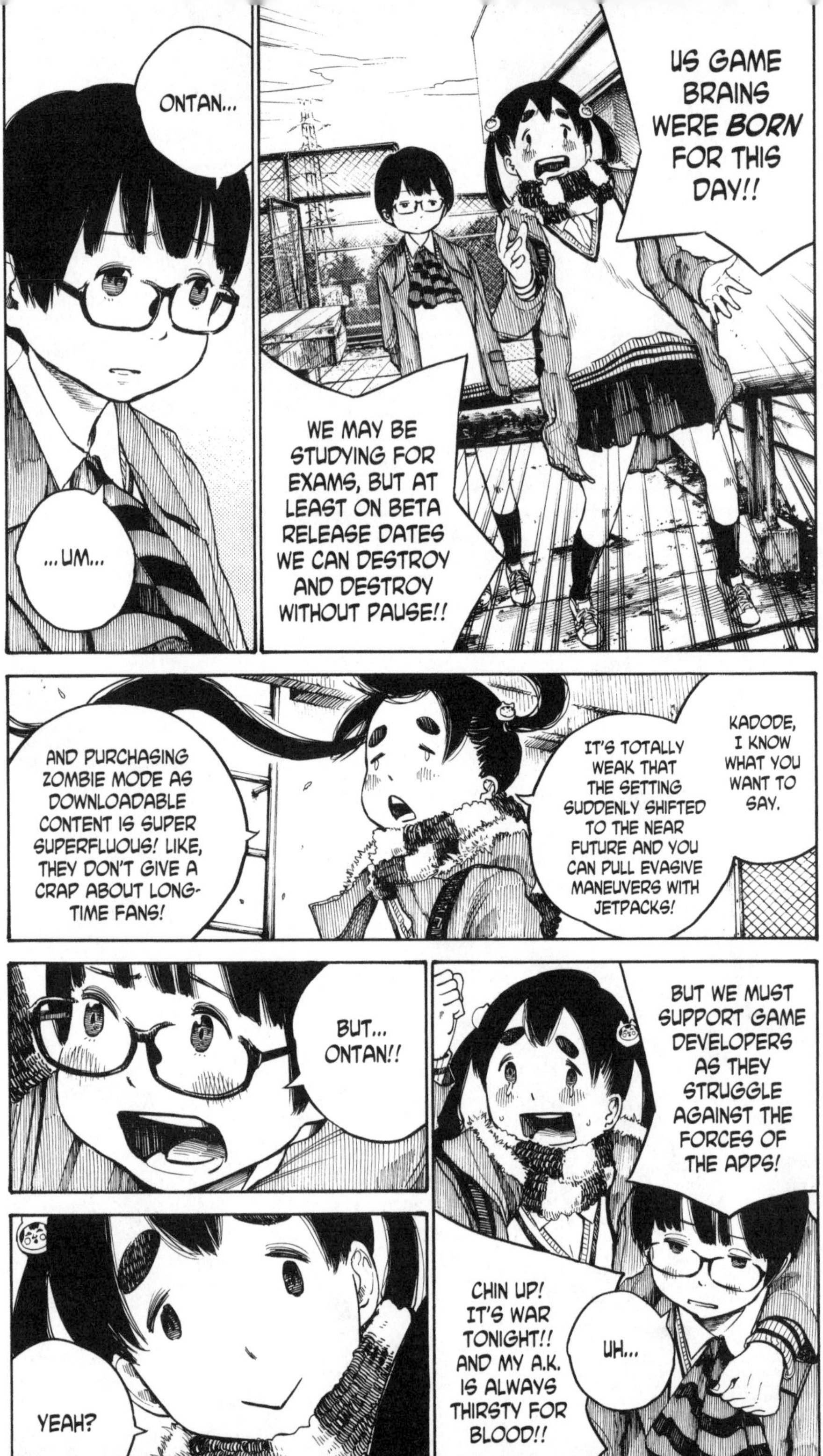
US GAME BRAINS WERE *BORN* FOR THIS DAY!!
WE MAY BE STUDYING FOR EXAMS, BUT AT LEAST ON BETA RELEASE DATES WE CAN DESTROY AND DESTROY WITHOUT PAUSE!!
ONTAN...
...UM...
KADODE, I KNOW WHAT YOU WANT TO SAY.
IT'S TOTALLY WEAK THAT THE SETTING SUDDENLY SHIFTED TO THE NEAR FUTURE AND YOU CAN PULL EVASIVE MANEUVERS WITH JETPACKS!
AND PURCHASING ZOMBIE MODE AS DOWNLOADABLE CONTENT IS SUPER SUPERFLUOUS! LIKE, THEY DON'T GIVE A CRAP ABOUT LONG-TIME FANS!
BUT WE MUST SUPPORT GAME DEVELOPERS AS THEY STRUGGLE AGAINST THE FORCES OF THE APPS!
UH...
CHIN UP! IT'S WAR TONIGHT!! AND MY A.K. IS ALWAYS THIRSTY FOR BLOOD!!
BUT... ONTAN!!
YEAH?

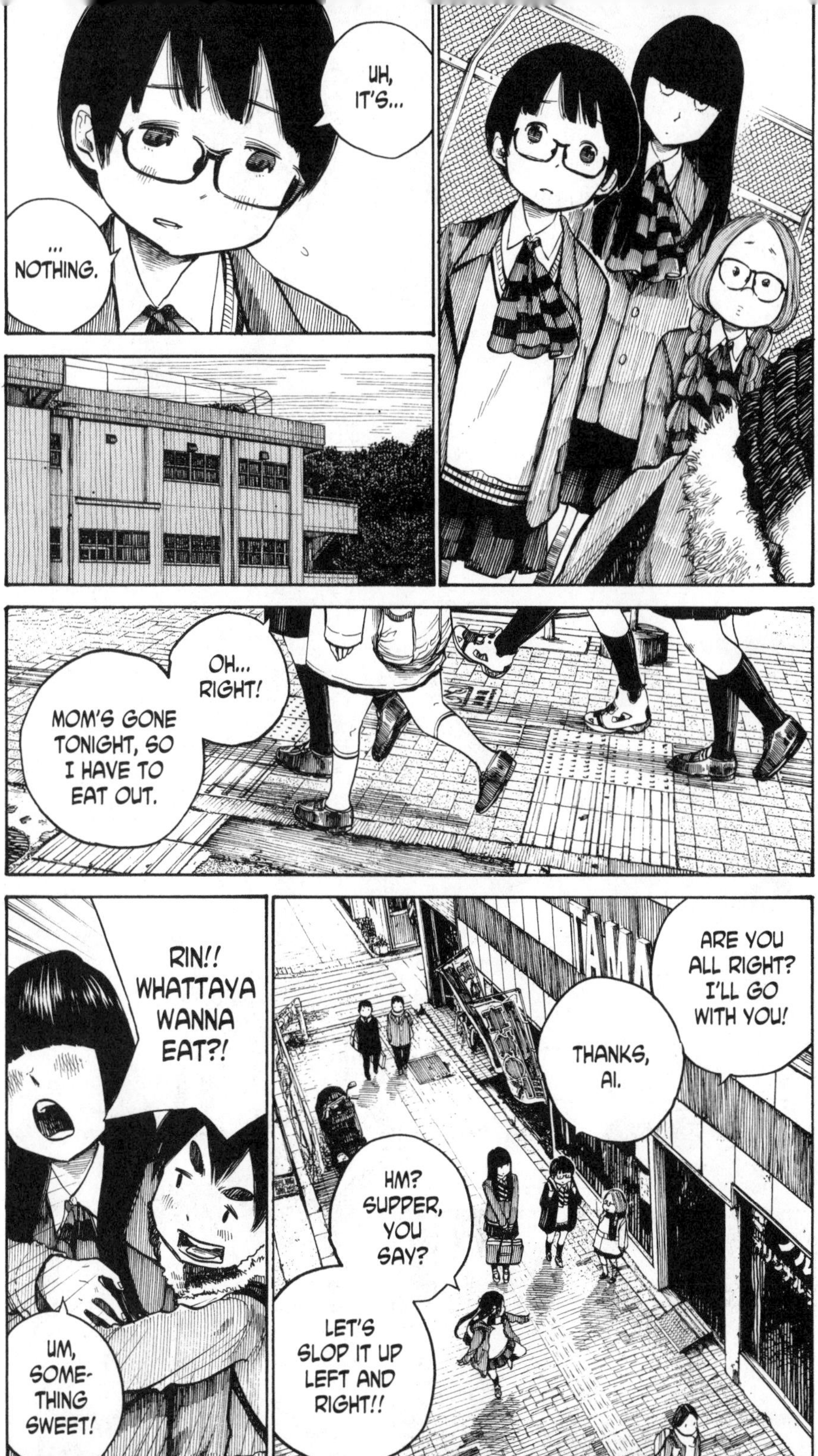
UH, IT'S...
... NOTHING.
OH... RIGHT!
MOM'S GONE TONIGHT, SO I HAVE TO EAT OUT.
ARE YOU ALL RIGHT? I'LL GO WITH YOU!
THANKS, AI.
HM? SUPPER, YOU SAY?
LET'S SLOP IT UP LEFT AND RIGHT!!
RIN!! WHATTAYA WANNA EAT?!
UM, SOME-THING SWEET!

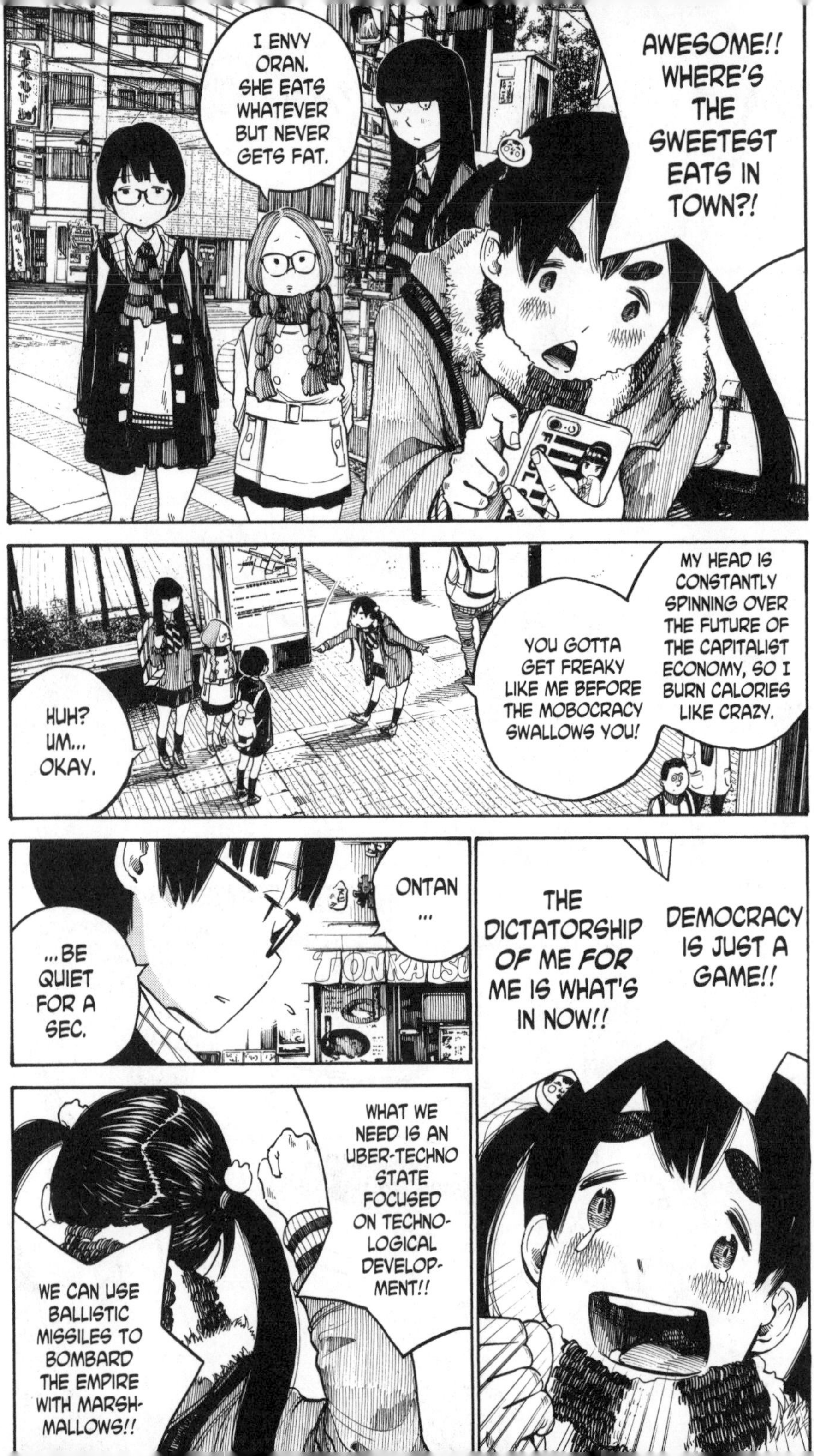
AWESOME!! WHERE'S THE SWEETEST EATS IN TOWN?!
I ENVY ORAN. SHE EATS WHATEVER BUT NEVER GETS FAT.
MY HEAD IS CONSTANTLY SPINNING OVER THE FUTURE OF THE CAPITALIST ECONOMY, SO I BURN CALORIES LIKE CRAZY.
YOU GOTTA GET FREAKY LIKE ME BEFORE THE MOBOCRACY SWALLOWS YOU!
HUH? UM... OKAY.
DEMOCRACY IS JUST A GAME!!
THE DICTATORSHIP OF ME *FOR* ME IS WHAT'S IN NOW!!
ONTAN ...
...BE QUIET FOR A SEC.
TONKATSU
WHAT WE NEED IS AN UBER-TECHNO STATE FOCUSED ON TECHNOLOGICAL DEVELOPMENT!!
WE CAN USE BALLISTIC MISSILES TO BOMBARD THE EMPIRE WITH MARSHMALLOWS!!

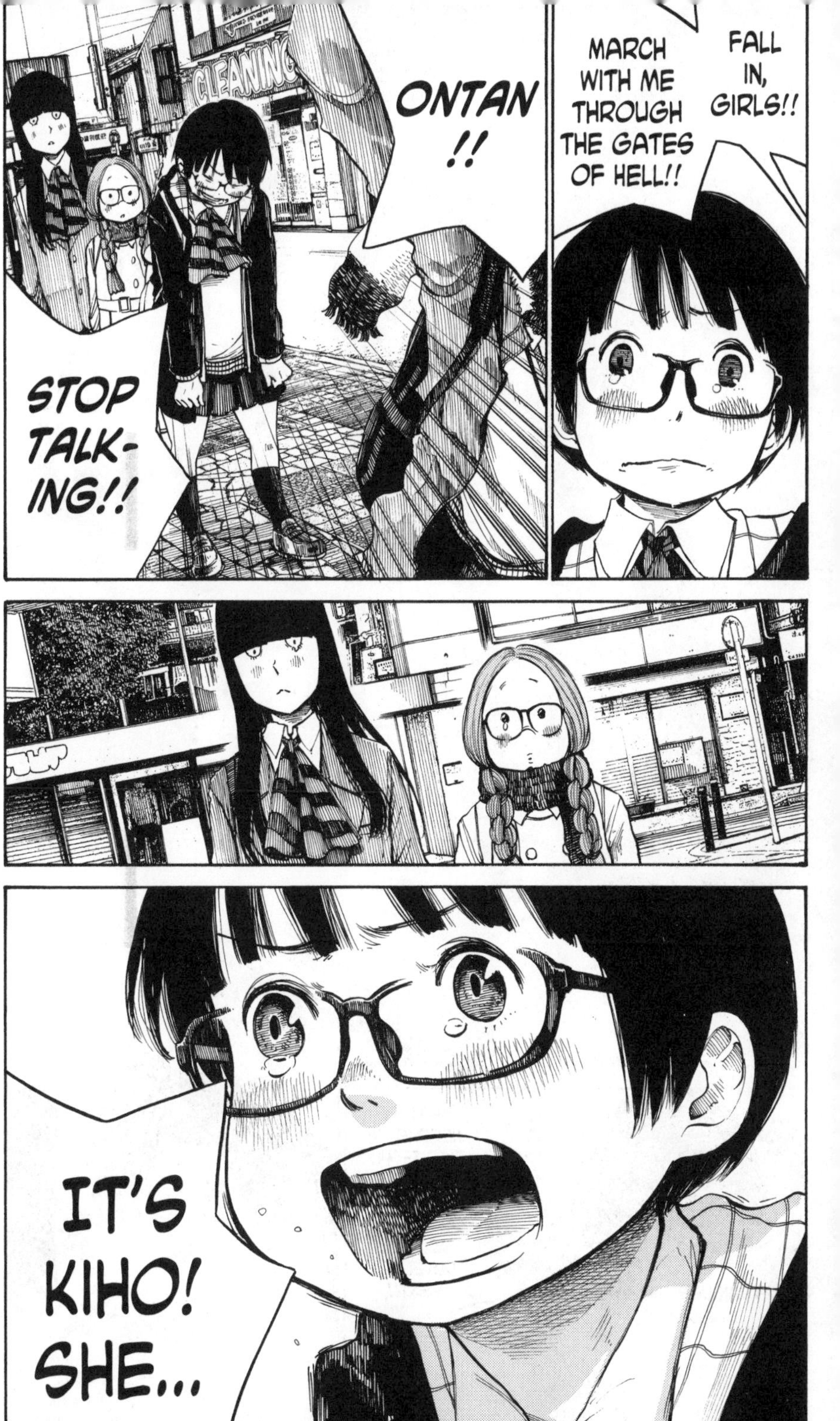
FALL IN, GIRLS!!
MARCH WITH ME THROUGH THE GATES OF HELL!!
ONTAN !!
STOP TALKING!!
IT'S KIHO! SHE...

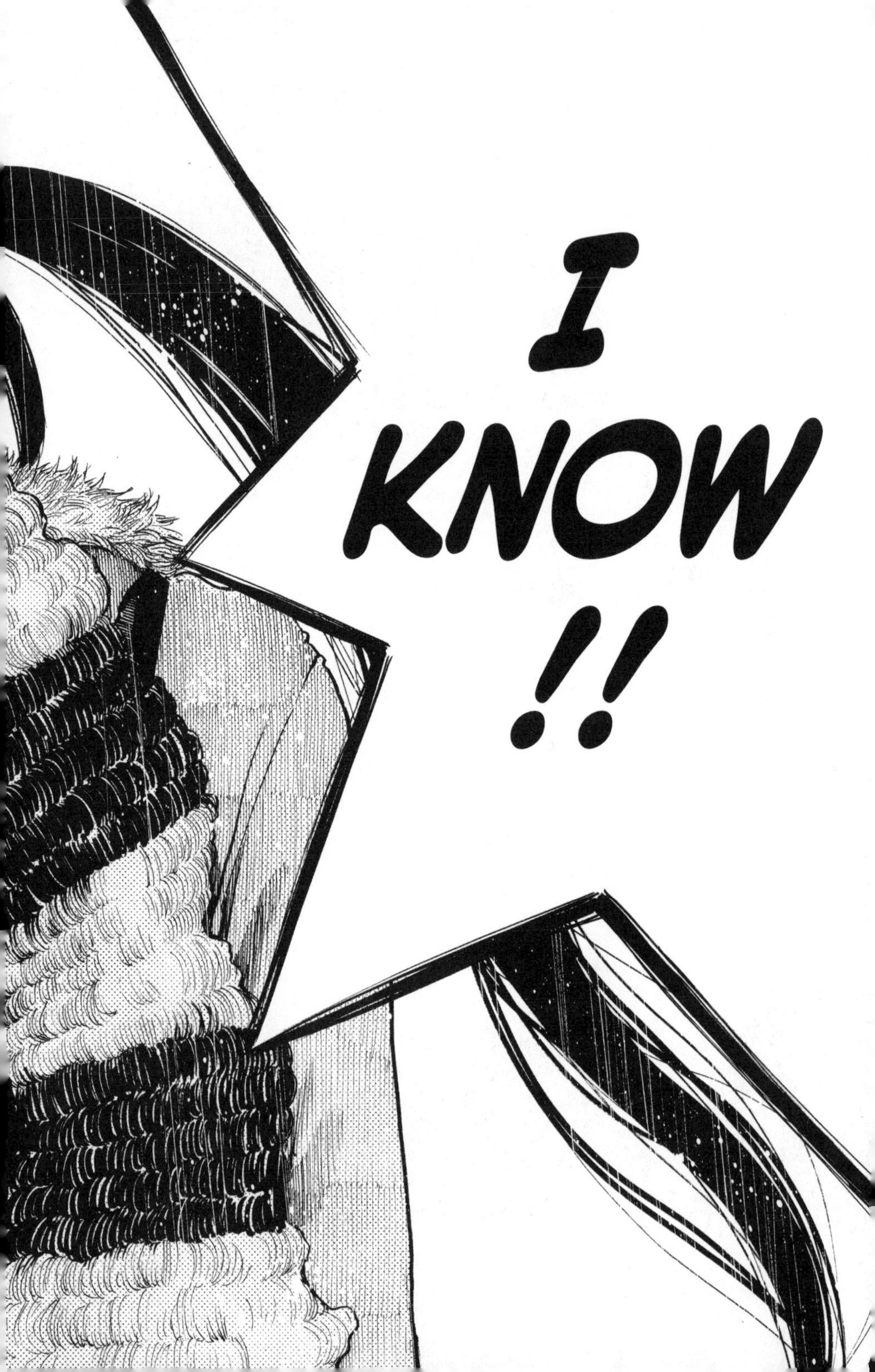
I KNOW!!

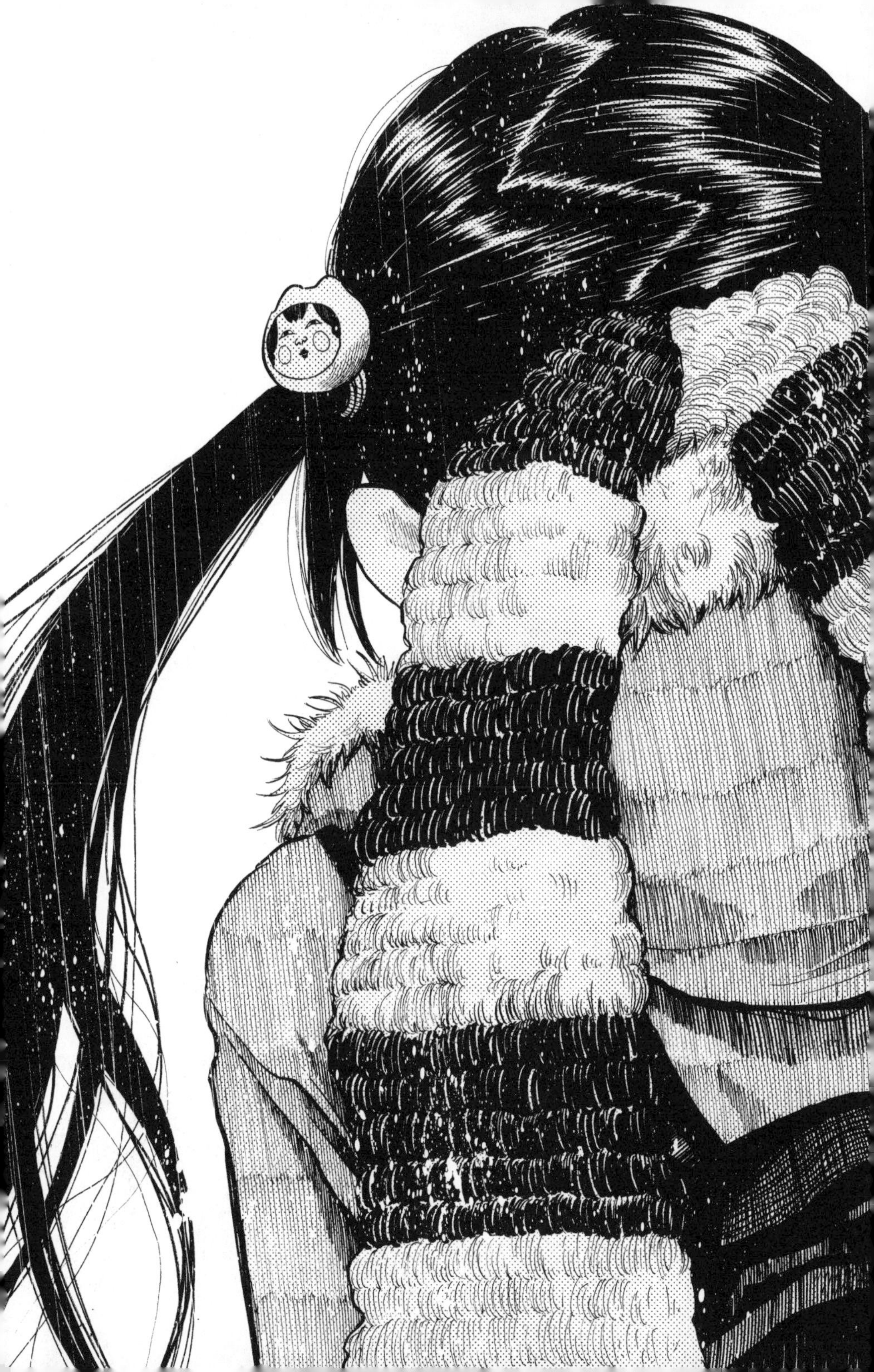

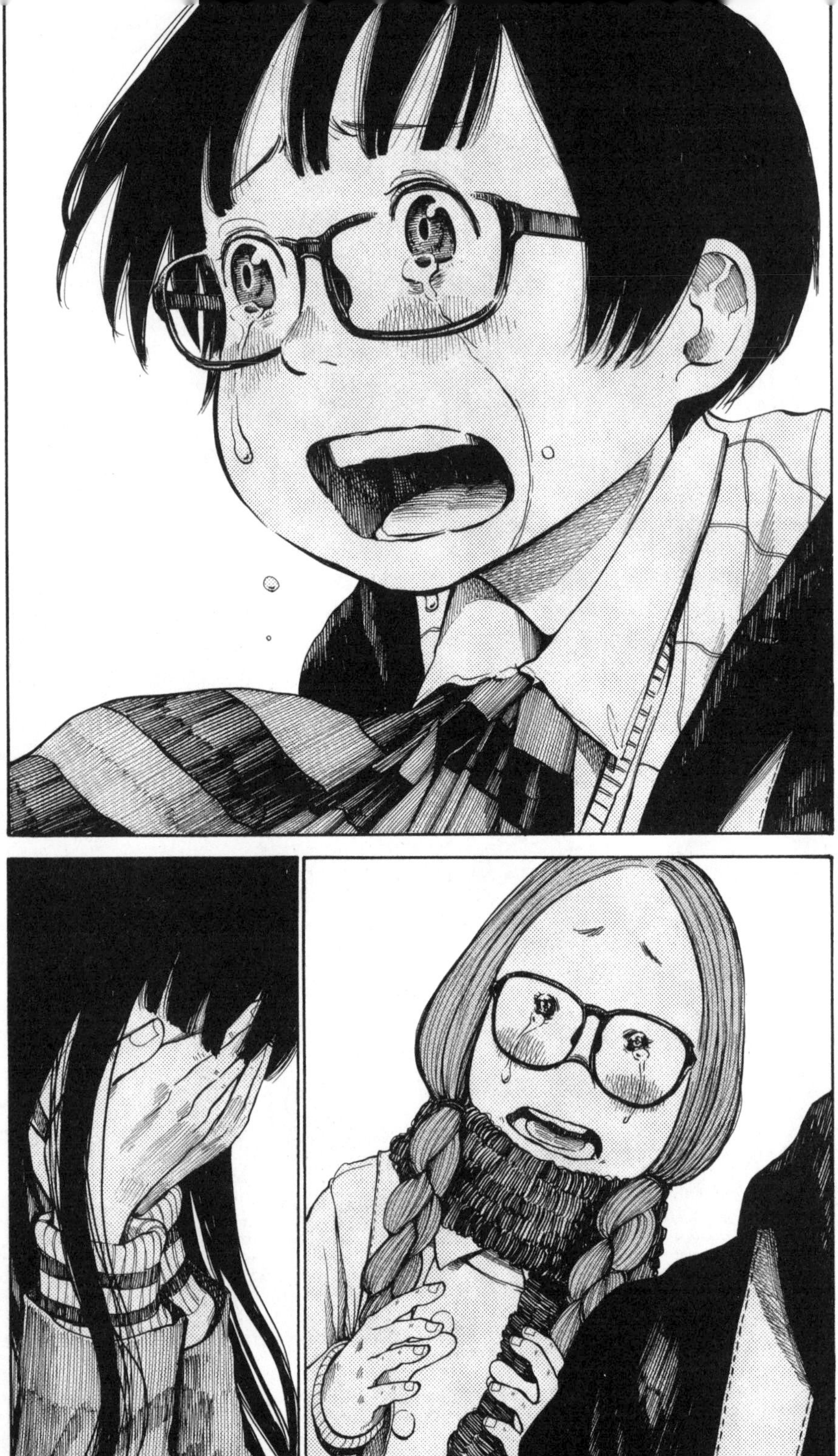

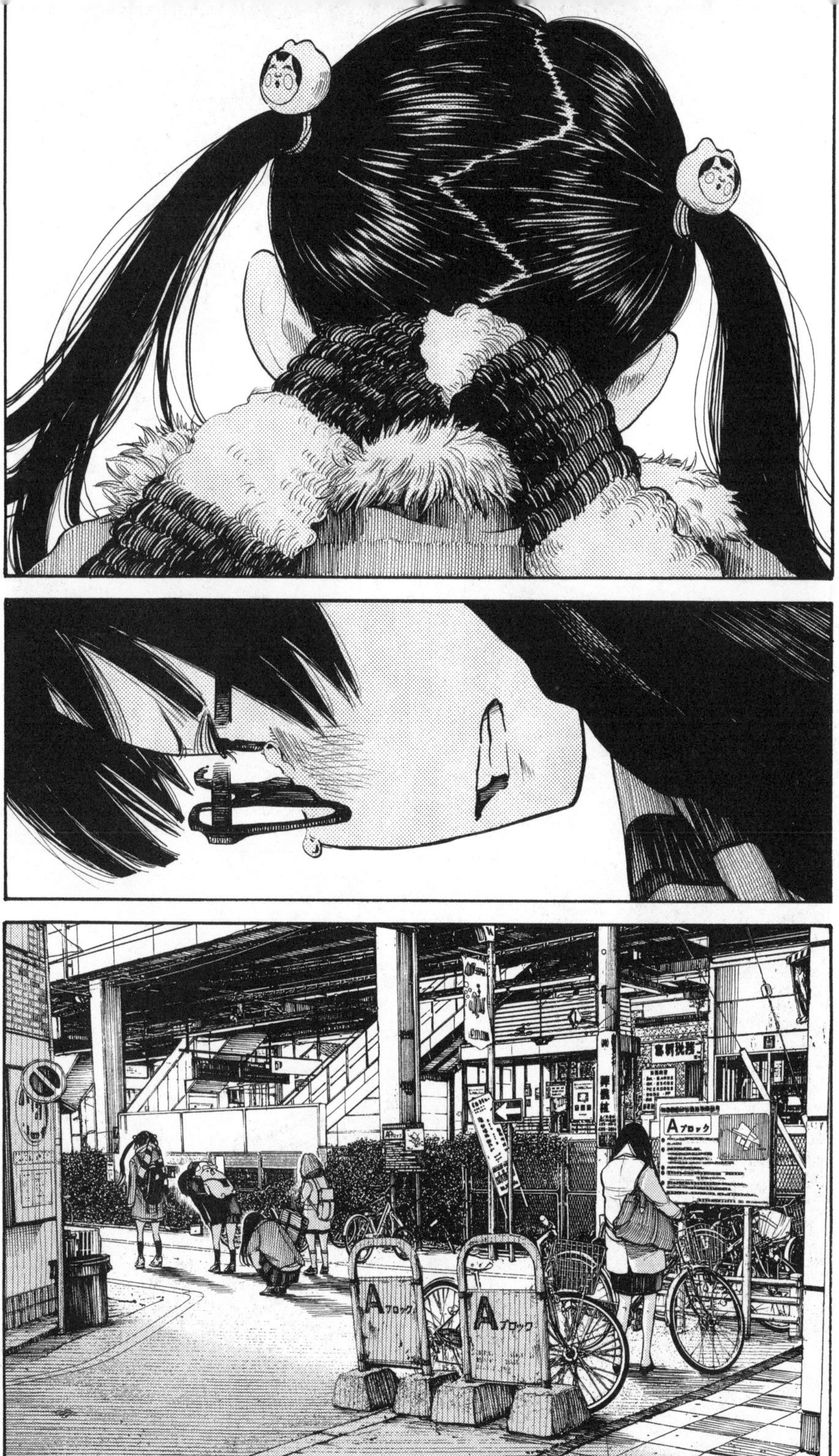
Aブロック
Aブロック
Aブロック

A PROPOSAL WAS BROUGHT BEFORE THE DIET TODAY...

...TO REVISE THE BASIC LAW FOR COUNTER-MEASURES AGAINST INVADERS.

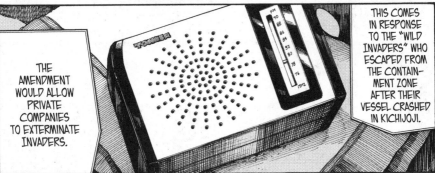

THIS COMES IN RESPONSE TO THE "WILD INVADERS" WHO ESCAPED FROM THE CONTAINMENT ZONE AFTER THEIR VESSEL CRASHED IN KICHIJOJI.

THE AMENDMENT WOULD ALLOW PRIVATE COMPANIES TO EXTERMINATE INVADERS.

PRIME MINISTER OGINO...

...HAS EXPRESSED HIS DESIRE FOR SWIFT PASSAGE OF THE BILL.

HUMAN RIGHTS GROUPS HAVE OBJECTED, CLAIMING THAT THE INVADERS ARE INTELLIGENT BEINGS AND THE BILL VIOLATES THEIR RIGHTS.

A SMALL PROTEST IS BEING HELD OUTSIDE THE DIET IN REACTION.

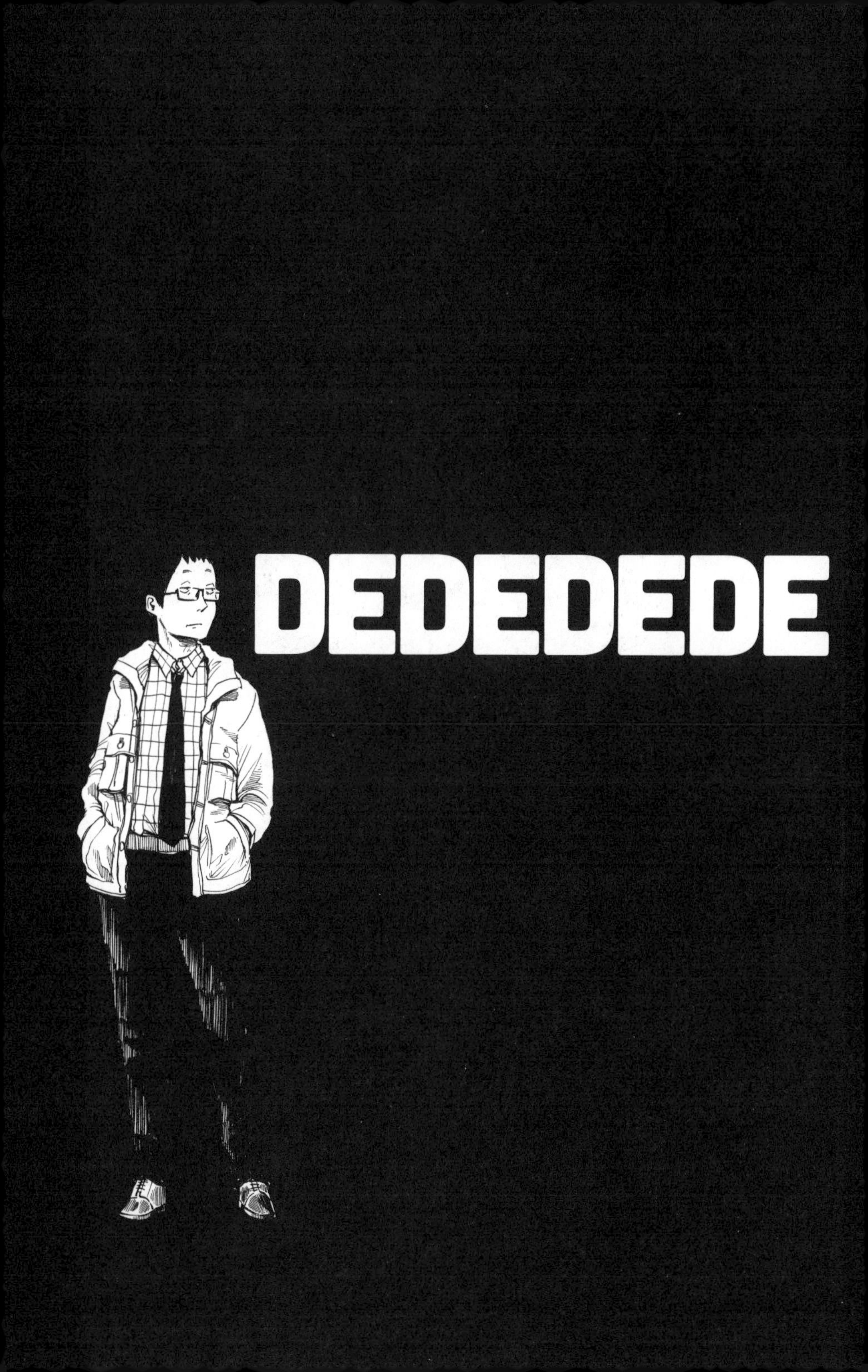
DEDEDEDE

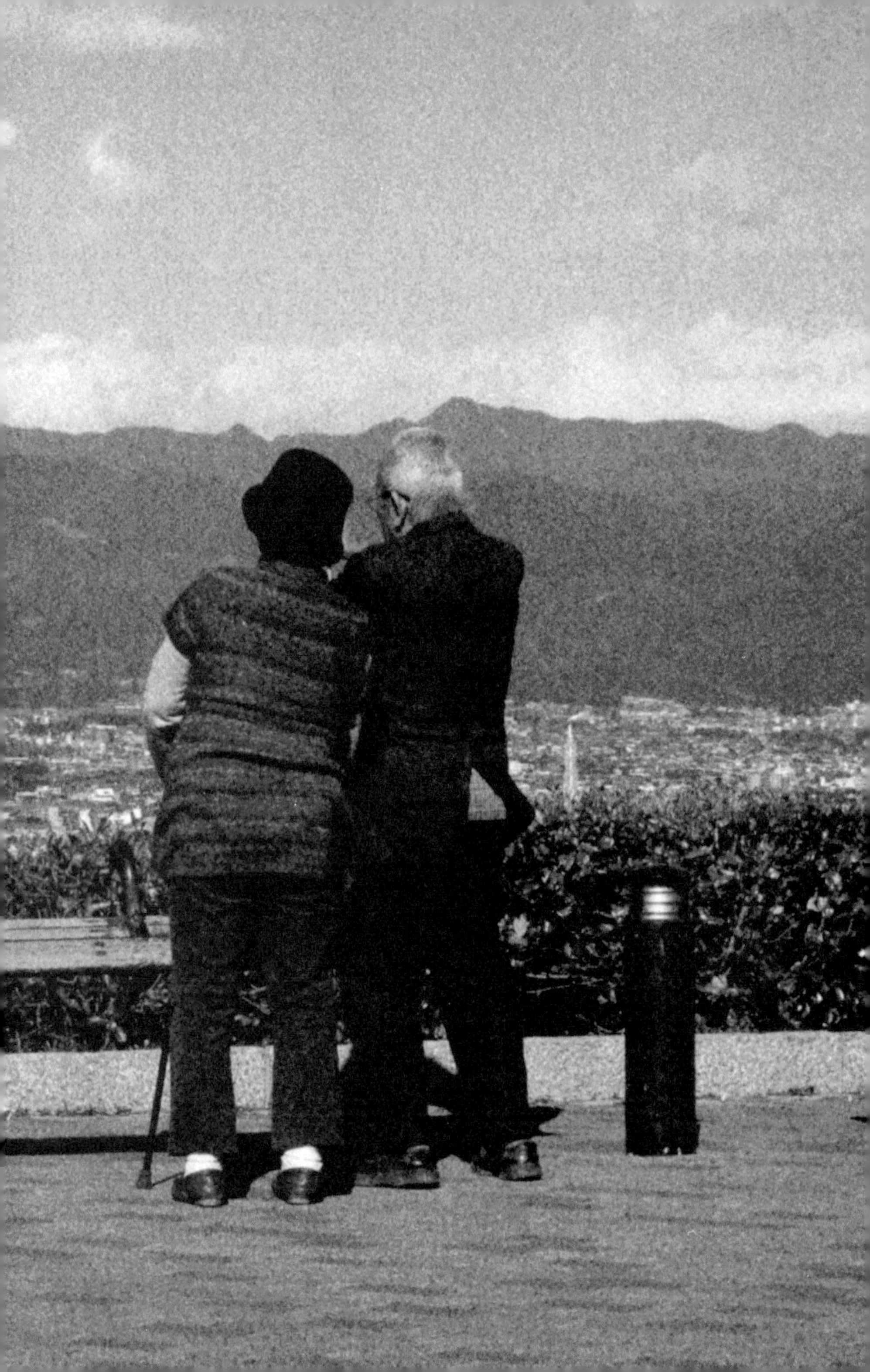

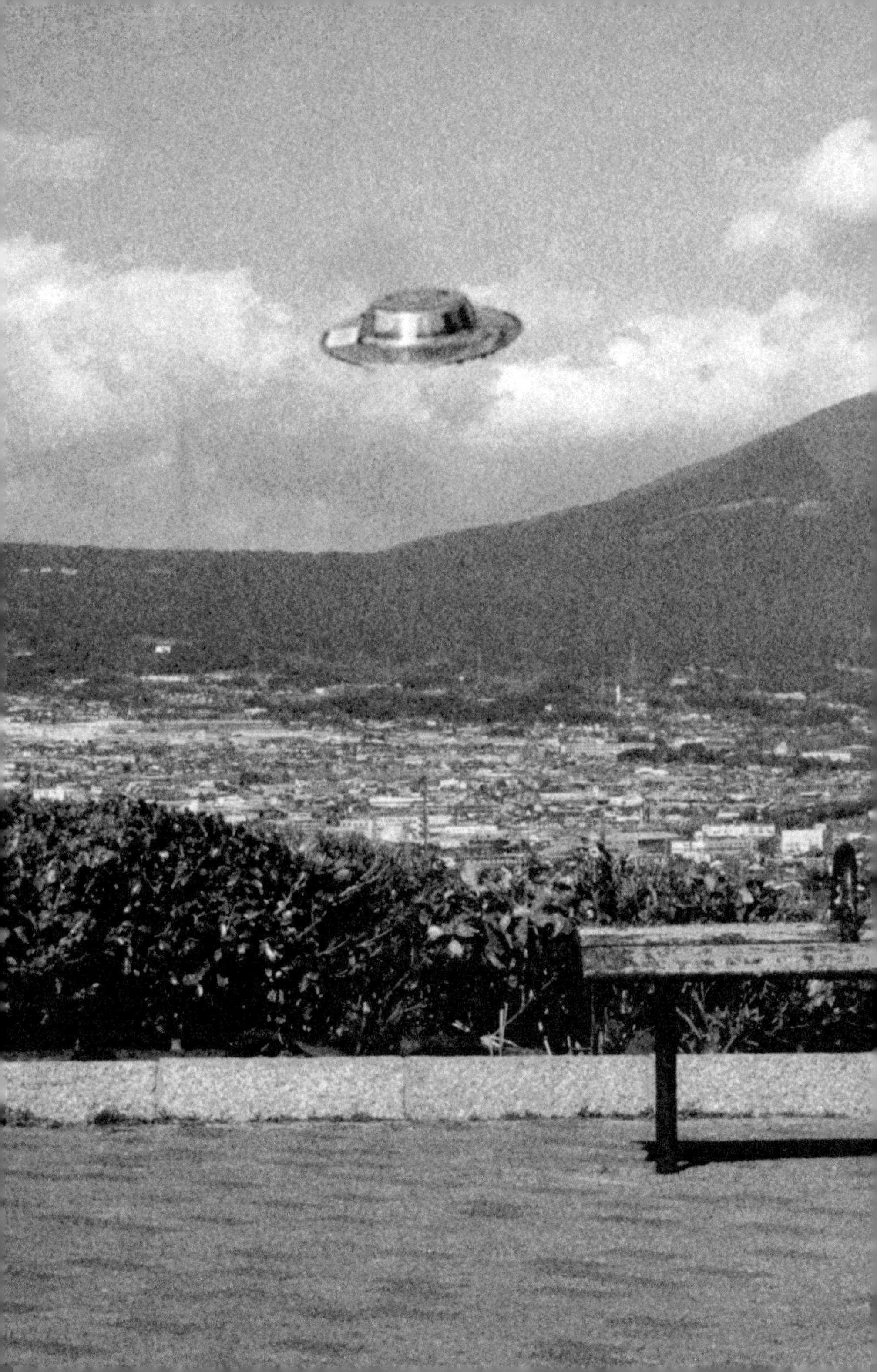

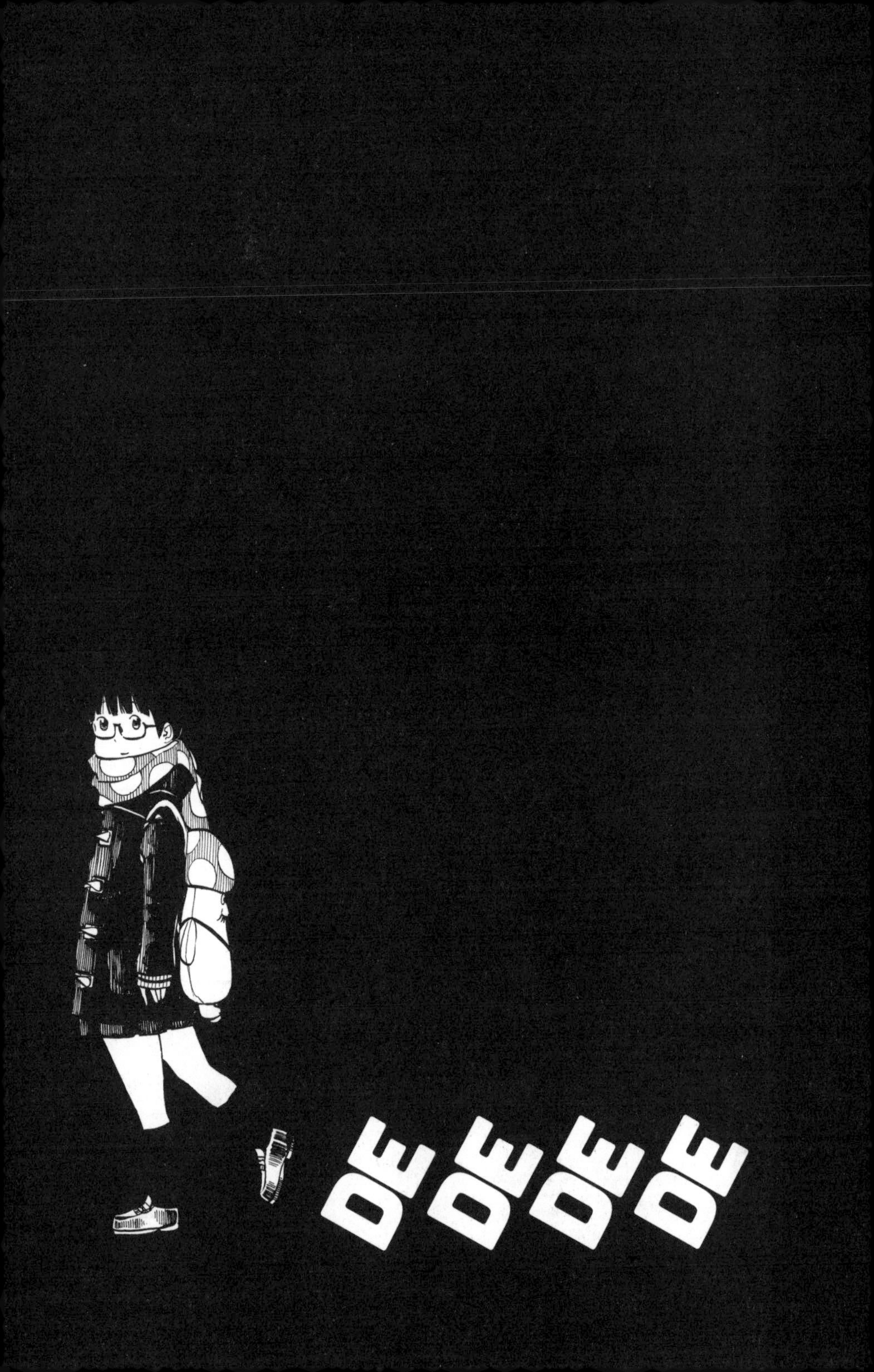
DE DE DE DE

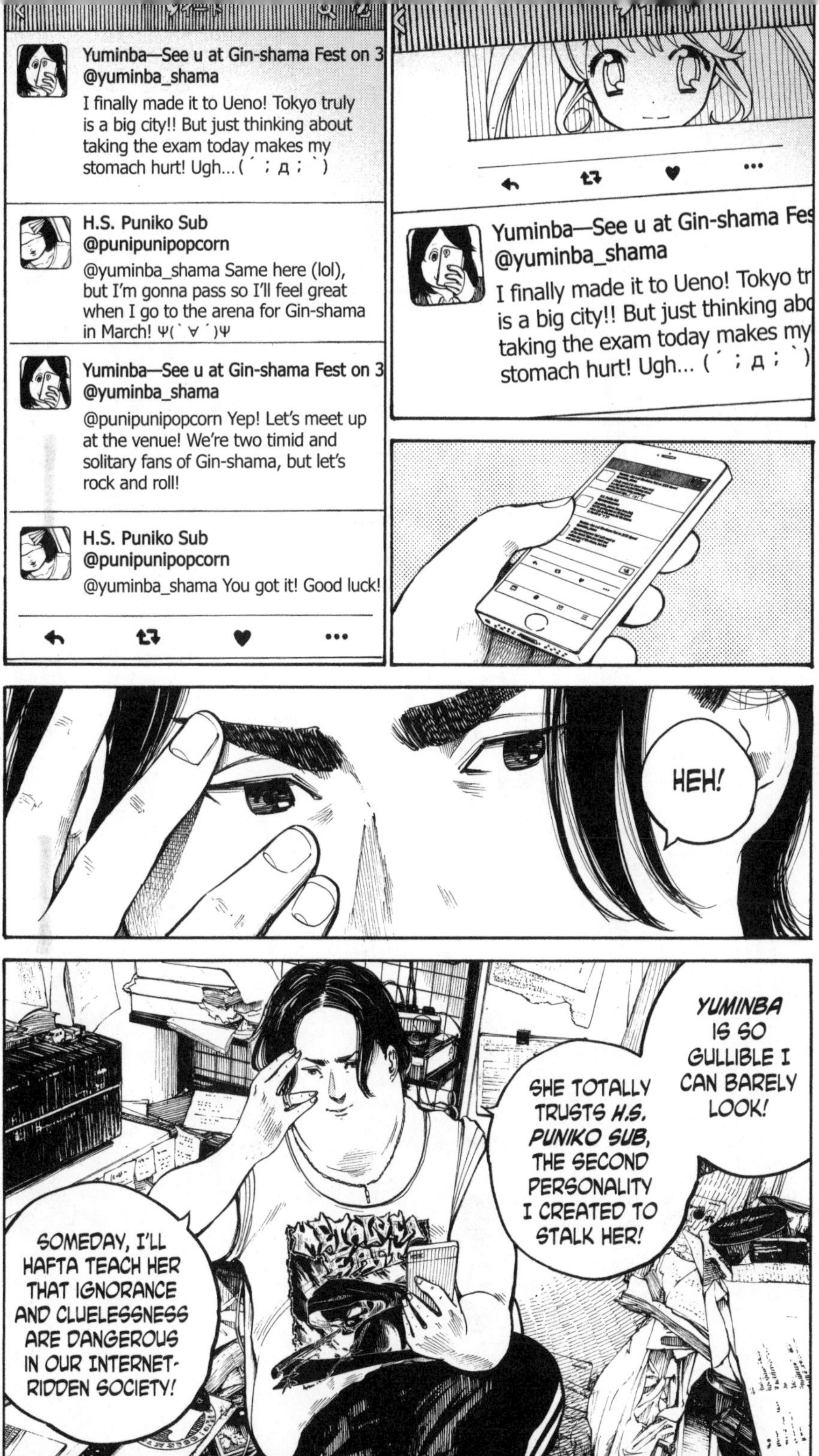
Yuminba—See u at Gin-shama Fes
@yuminba_shama
I finally made it to Ueno! Tokyo tr
is a big city!! But just thinking abo
taking the exam today makes my
stomach hurt! Ugh... (´ ; д ; `)
Yuminba—See u at Gin-shama Fest on 3
@yuminba_shama
I finally made it to Ueno! Tokyo truly is a big city!! But just thinking about taking the exam today makes my stomach hurt! Ugh... (´ ; д ; `)
H.S. Puniko Sub
@punipunipopcorn
@yuminba_shama Same here (lol), but I'm gonna pass so I'll feel great when I go to the arena for Gin-shama in March! Ψ(`∀´)Ψ
Yuminba—See u at Gin-shama Fest on 3
@yuminba_shama
@punipunipopcorn Yep! Let's meet up at the venue! We're two timid and solitary fans of Gin-shama, but let's rock and roll!
H.S. Puniko Sub
@punipunipopcorn
@yuminba_shama You got it! Good luck!
HEH!
YUMINBA IS SO GULLIBLE I CAN BARELY LOOK!
SHE TOTALLY TRUSTS *H.S. PUNIKO SUB*, THE SECOND PERSONALITY I CREATED TO STALK HER!
SOMEDAY, I'LL HAFTA TEACH HER THAT IGNORANCE AND CLUELESSNESS ARE DANGEROUS IN OUR INTERNET-RIDDEN SOCIETY!

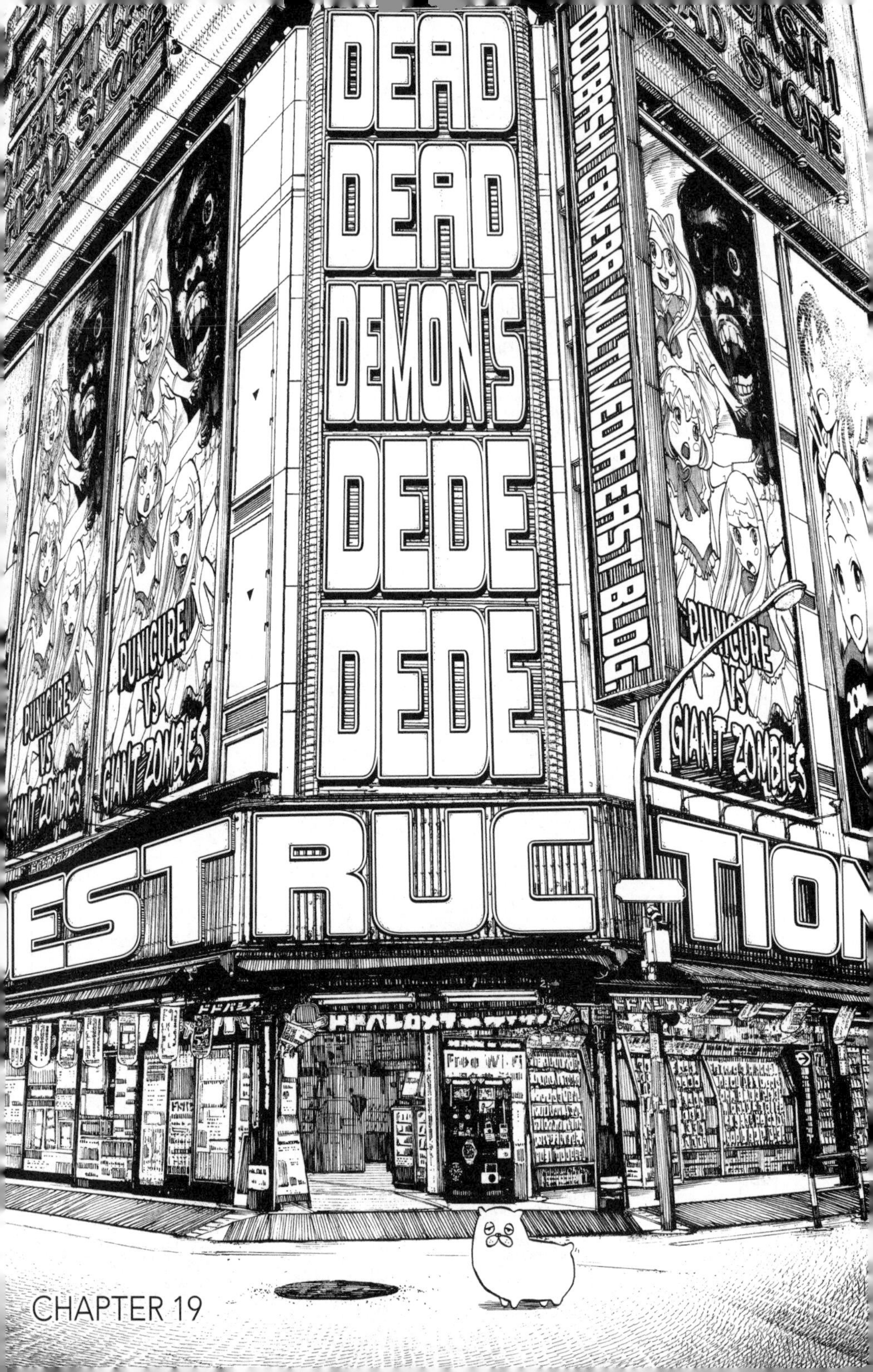
DEAD DEAD DEMON'S DEDEDEDE DESTRUCTION
PUNICURE VS GIANT ZOMBIES
PUNICURE VS GIANT ZOMBIES
PUNICURE VS GIANT ZOMBIES
YODOBASHI CAMERA MULTIMEDIA EAST BLDG.
YODOBASHI STORE
HEAD STORE

CHAPTER 19

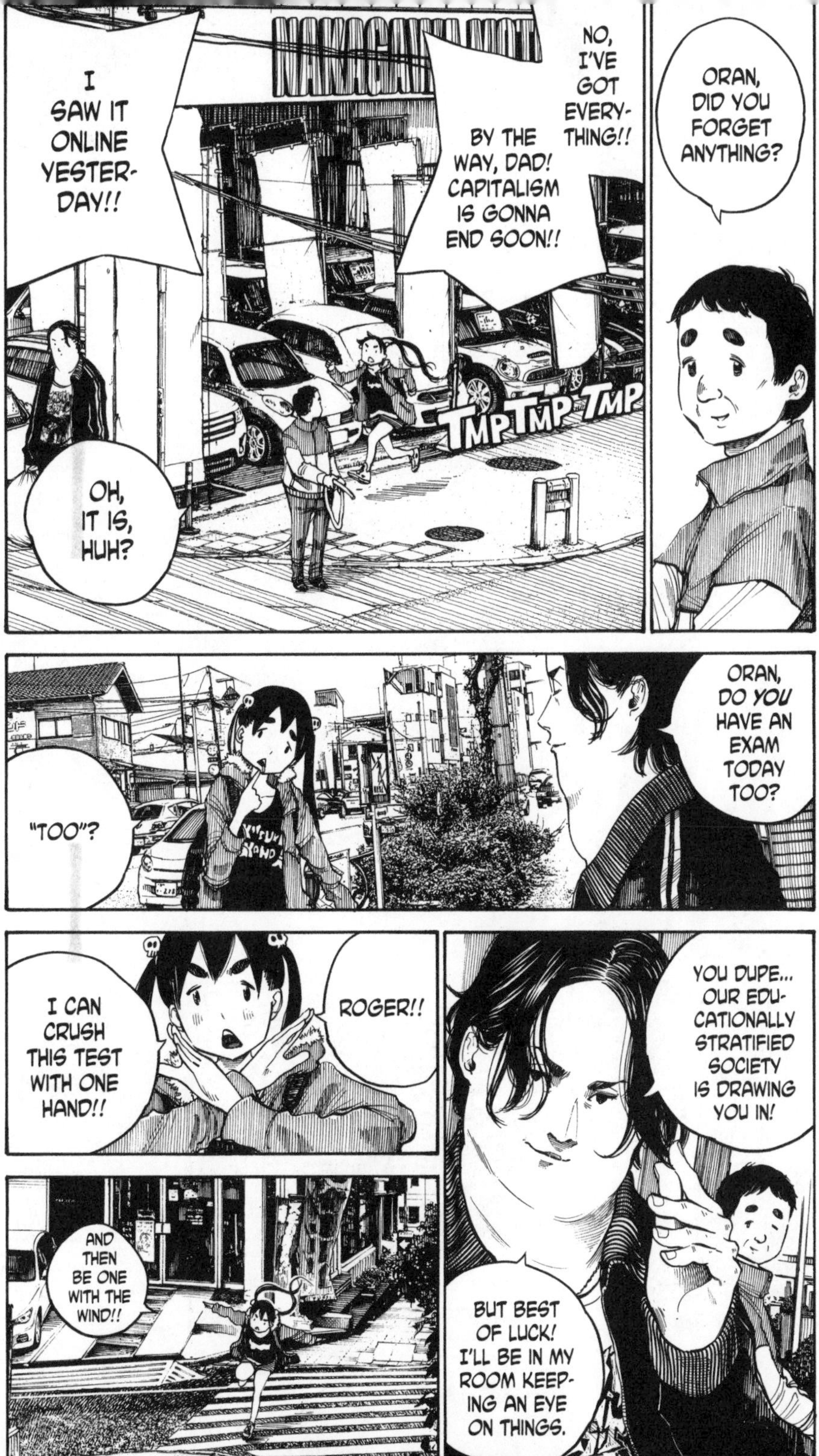
ORAN, DID YOU FORGET ANYTHING?
NO, I'VE GOT EVERYTHING!!
BY THE WAY, DAD! CAPITALISM IS GONNA END SOON!!
I SAW IT ONLINE YESTERDAY!!
TMP TMP TMP
OH, IT IS, HUH?
ORAN, DO *YOU* HAVE AN EXAM TODAY TOO?
"TOO"?
YOU DUPE... OUR EDUCATIONALLY STRATIFIED SOCIETY IS DRAWING YOU IN!
BUT BEST OF LUCK! I'LL BE IN MY ROOM KEEPING AN EYE ON THINGS.
ROGER!!
I CAN CRUSH THIS TEST WITH ONE HAND!!
AND THEN BE ONE WITH THE WIND!!

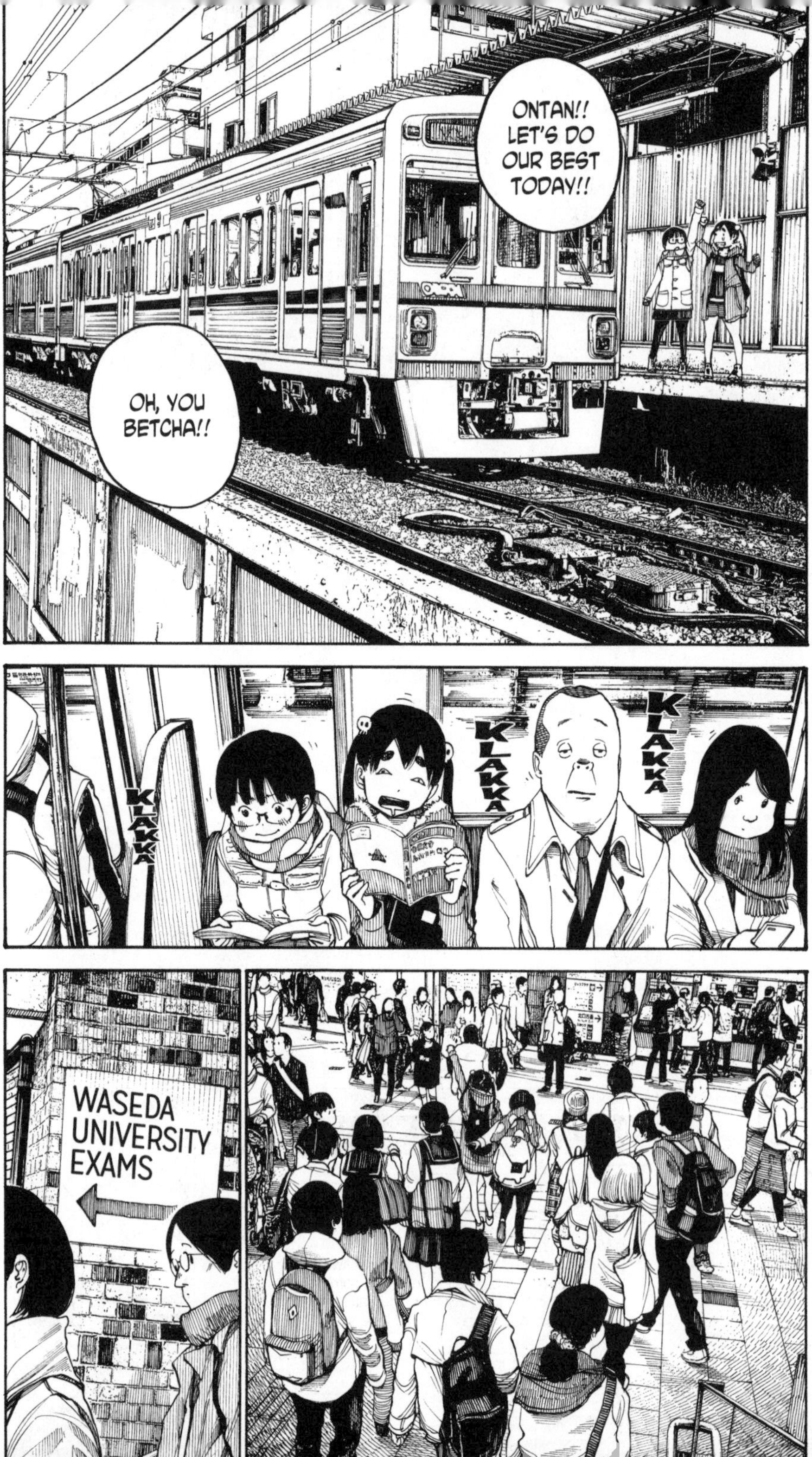
ONTAN!! LET'S DO OUR BEST TODAY!!
OH, YOU BETCHA!!
KLAKKA
KLAKKA
KLAKKA
WASEDA UNIVERSITY EXAMS

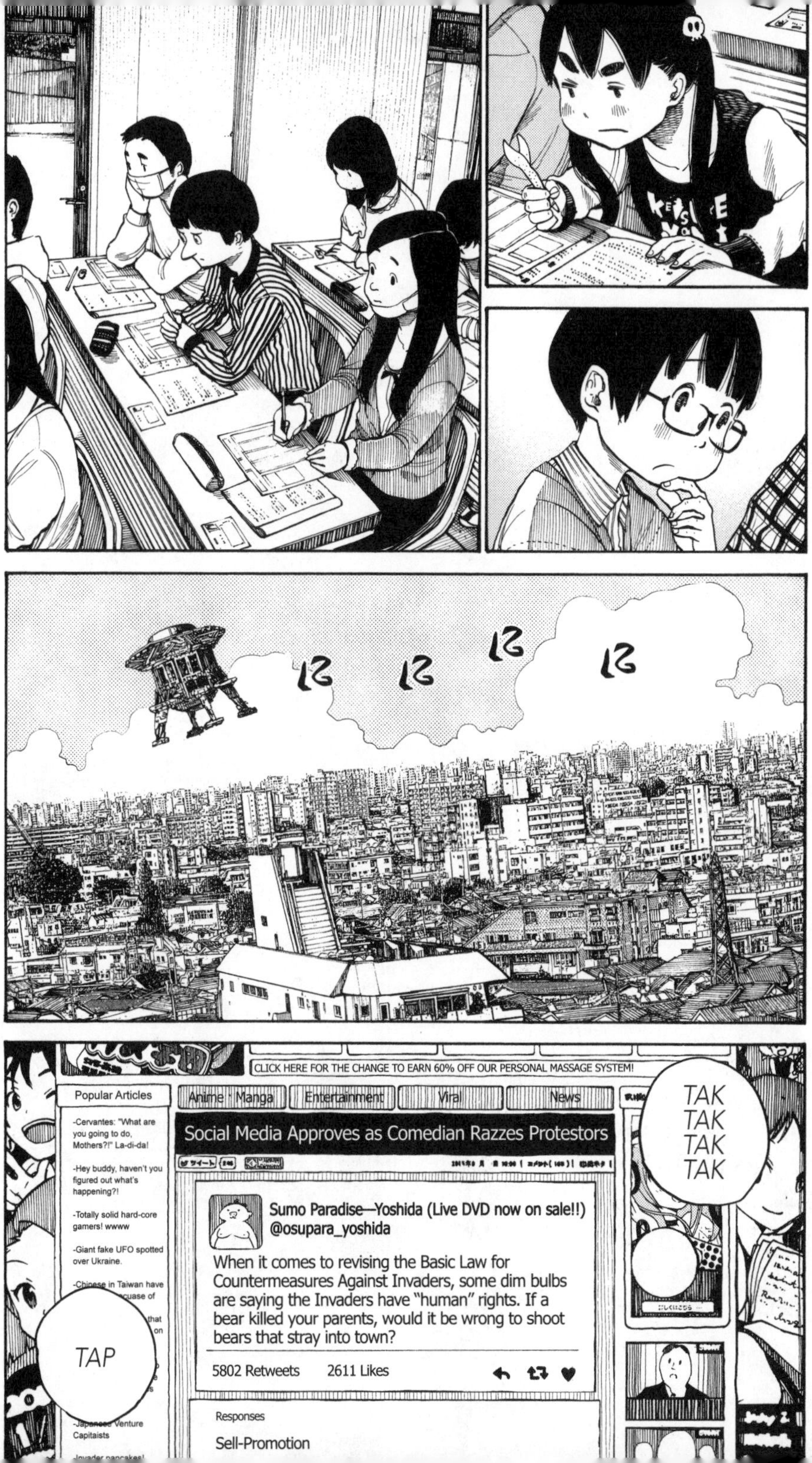
TAK TAK TAK TAK
CLICK HERE FOR THE CHANGE TO EARN 60% OFF OUR PERSONAL MASSAGE SYSTEM!
Popular Articles
-Cervantes: "What are you going to do, Mothers?!" La-di-da!
-Hey buddy, haven't you figured out what's happening?!
-Totally solid hard-core gamers! wwww
-Giant fake UFO spotted over Ukraine.
-Chinese in Taiwan have
-Japanese Venture Capitaists
-Invader pancakes!
Anime · Manga
Entertainment
Viral
News
Social Media Approves as Comedian Razzes Protestors
Sumo Paradise—Yoshida (Live DVD now on sale!!)
@osupara_yoshida
When it comes to revising the Basic Law for Countermeasures Against Invaders, some dim bulbs are saying the Invaders have "human" rights. If a bear killed your parents, would it be wrong to shoot bears that stray into town?
5802 Retweets
2611 Likes
Responses
Sell-Promotion
TAP

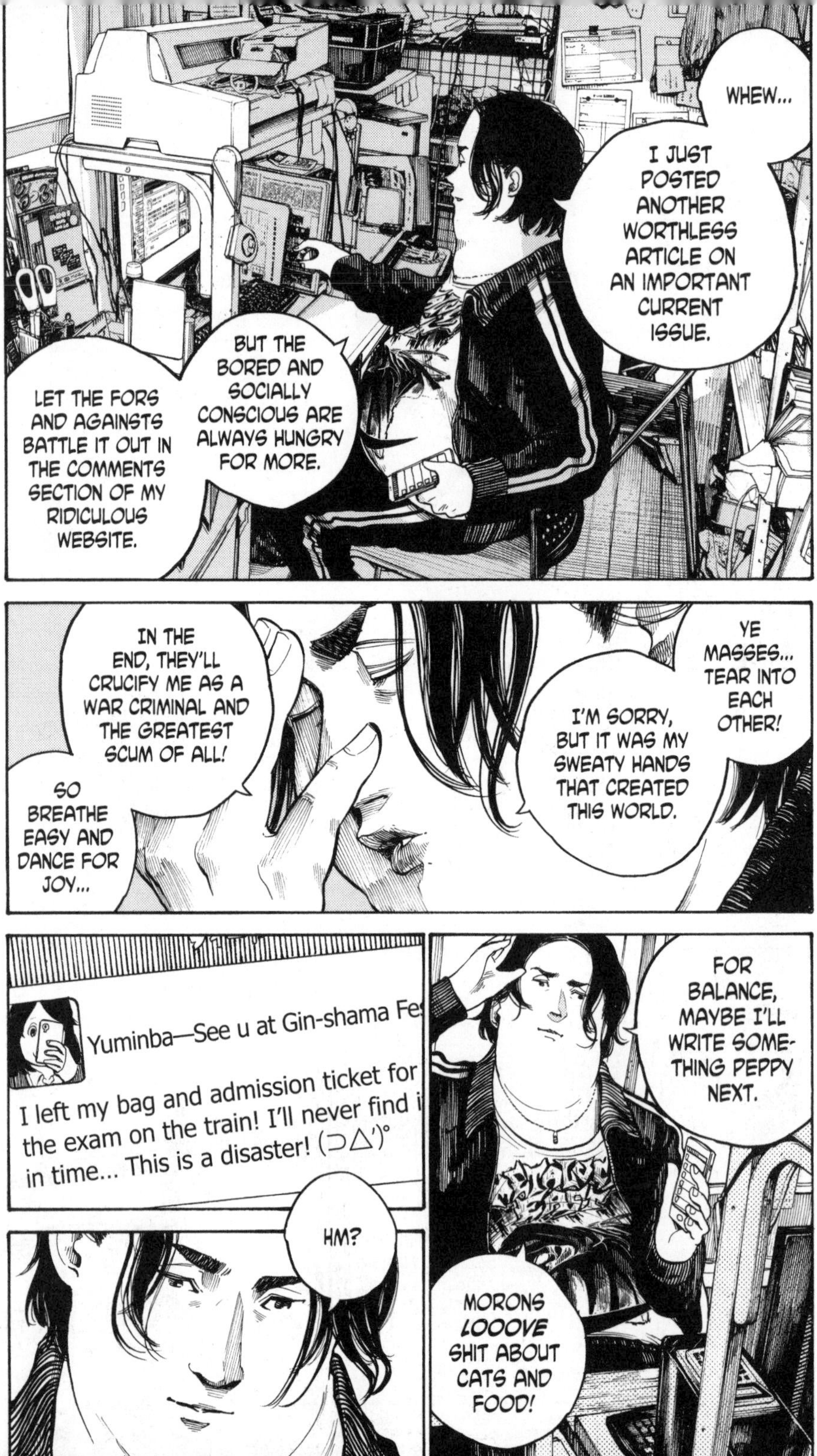
WHEW...
I JUST POSTED ANOTHER WORTHLESS ARTICLE ON AN IMPORTANT CURRENT ISSUE.
BUT THE BORED AND SOCIALLY CONSCIOUS ARE ALWAYS HUNGRY FOR MORE.
LET THE FORS AND AGAINSTS BATTLE IT OUT IN THE COMMENTS SECTION OF MY RIDICULOUS WEBSITE.
YE MASSES... TEAR INTO EACH OTHER!
I'M SORRY, BUT IT WAS MY SWEATY HANDS THAT CREATED THIS WORLD.
IN THE END, THEY'LL CRUCIFY ME AS A WAR CRIMINAL AND THE GREATEST SCUM OF ALL!
SO BREATHE EASY AND DANCE FOR JOY...
FOR BALANCE, MAYBE I'LL WRITE SOME-THING PEPPY NEXT.
MORONS *LOOOVE* SHIT ABOUT CATS AND FOOD!
Yuminba—See u at Gin-shama Fes
I left my bag and admission ticket for the exam on the train! I'll never find i in time... This is a disaster! (⊃△')°
HM?

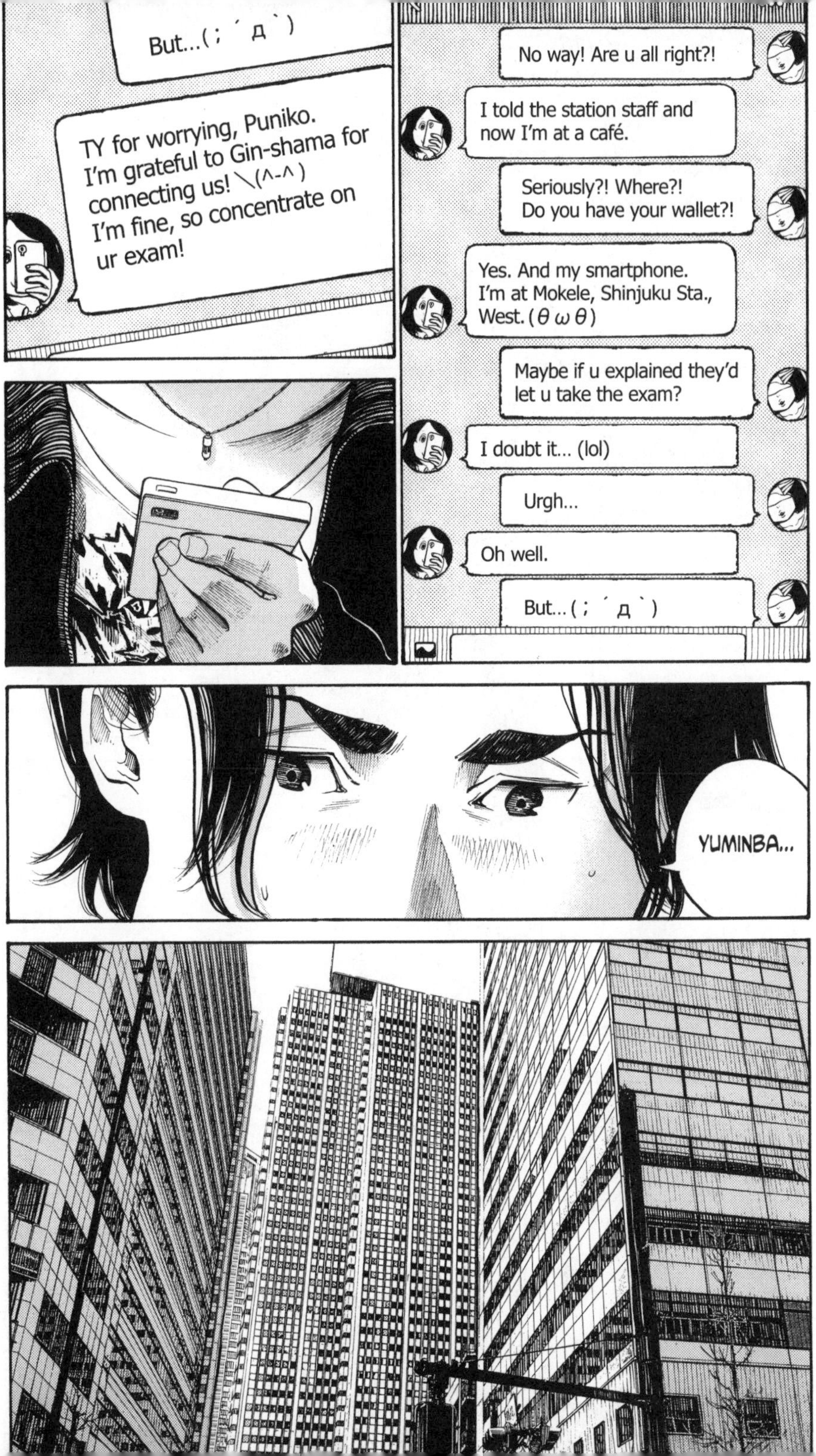

No way! Are u all right?!
I told the station staff and now I'm at a café.
Seriously?! Where?! Do you have your wallet?!
Yes. And my smartphone. I'm at Mokele, Shinjuku Sta., West. (θωθ)
Maybe if u explained they'd let u take the exam?
I doubt it... (lol)
Urgh...
Oh well.
But... (; ´ д `)
But... (; ´ д `)
TY for worrying, Puniko. I'm grateful to Gin-shama for connecting us! ＼(^-^) I'm fine, so concentrate on ur exam!
YUMINBA...

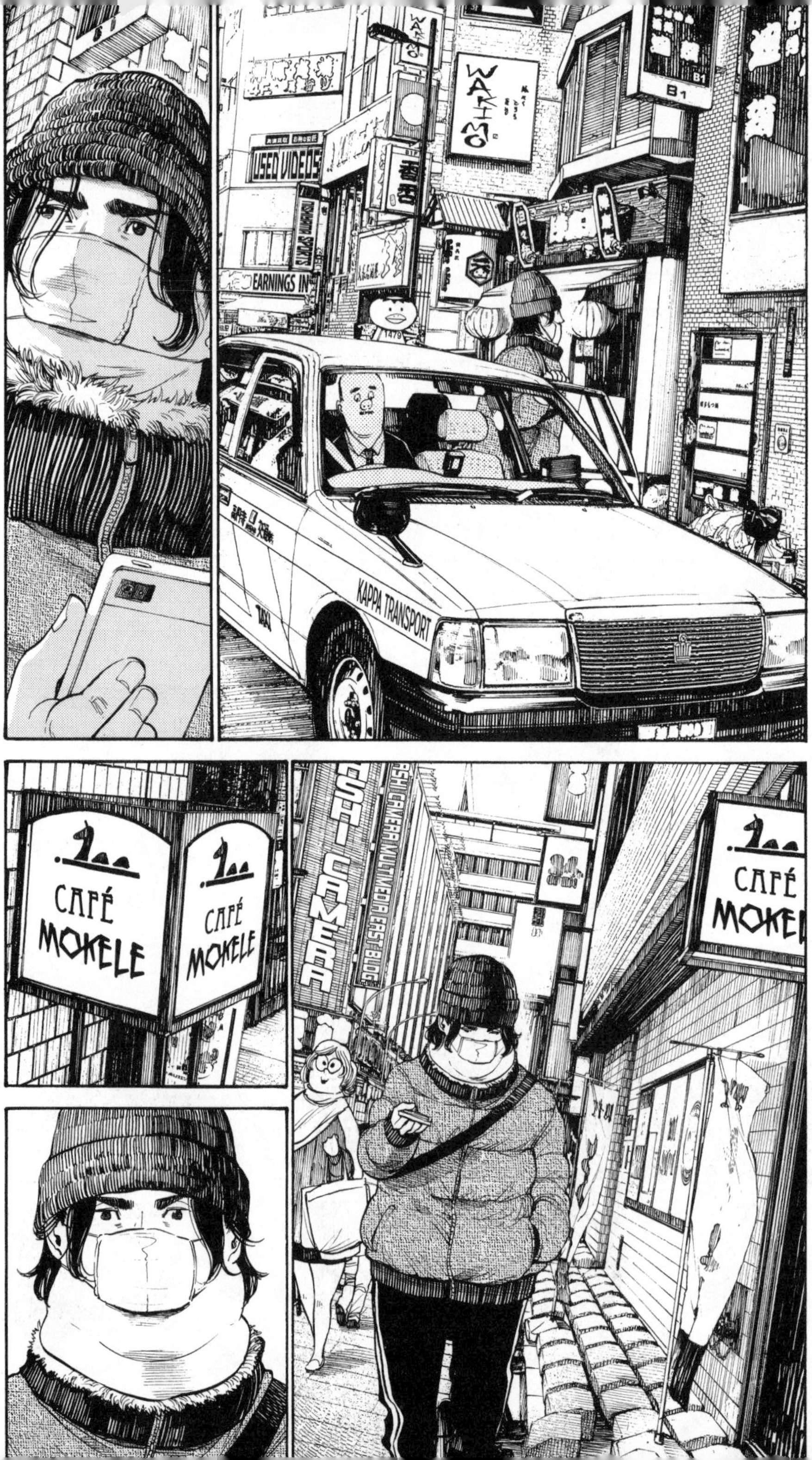
WAKIMO
B1
USED VIDEOS
KAPPA TRANSPORT
TAXI
CAFÉ MOKELE
CAMERA
CAFÉ MOKELE
CAFÉ MOKELE

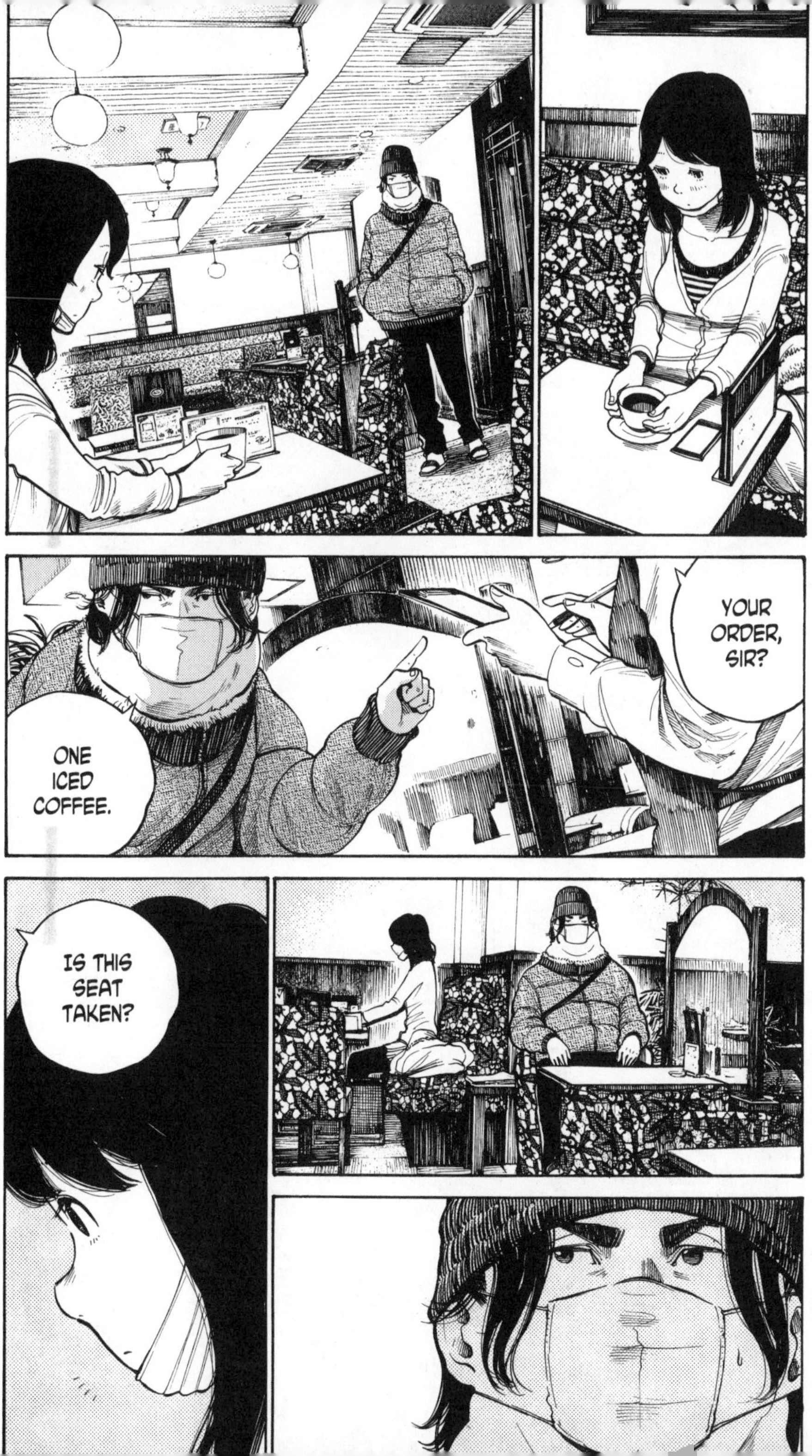
YOUR ORDER, SIR?
ONE ICED COFFEE.
IS THIS SEAT TAKEN?

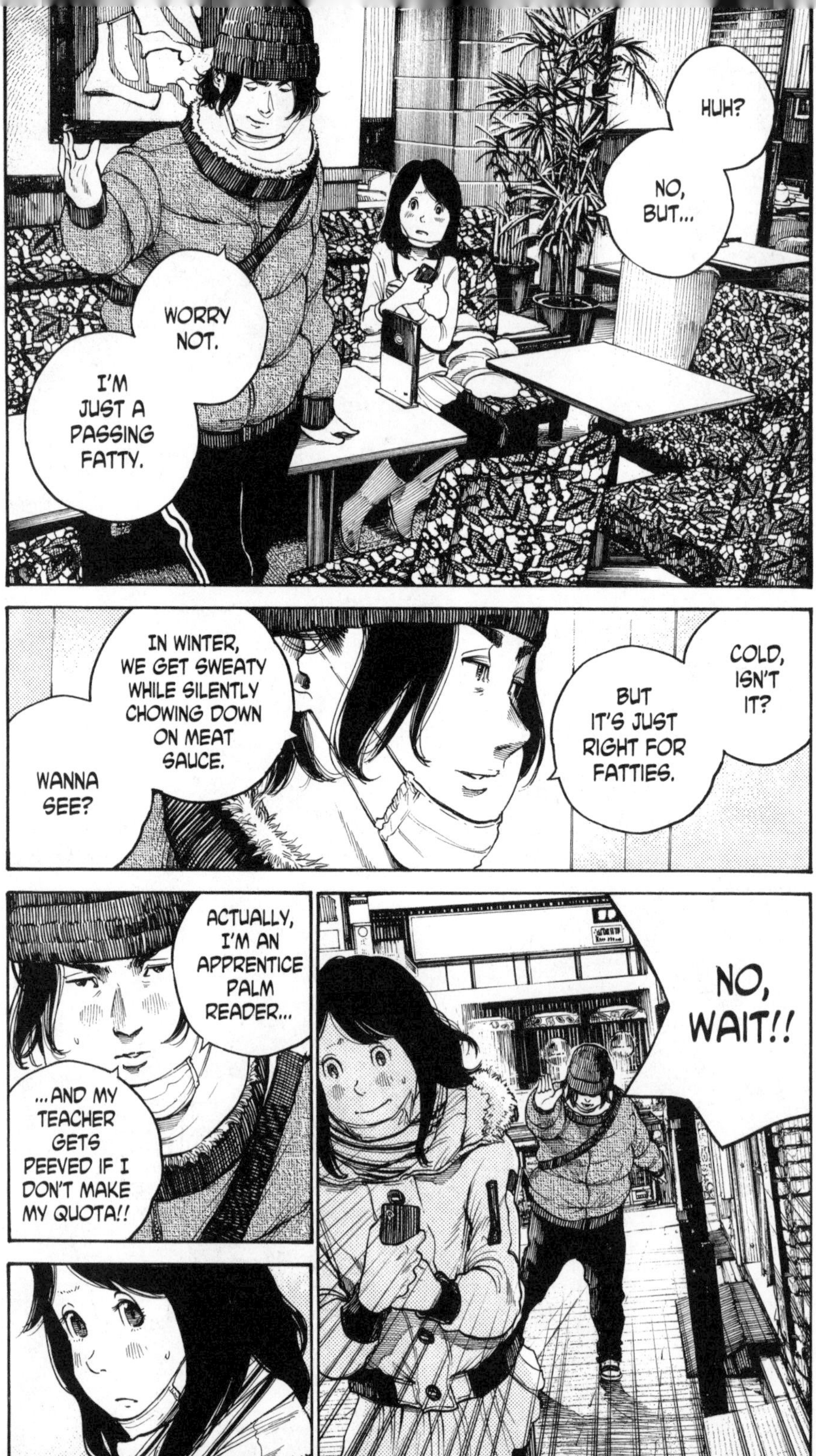
HUH?
NO, BUT...
WORRY NOT.
I'M JUST A PASSING FATTY.
COLD, ISN'T IT?
BUT IT'S JUST RIGHT FOR FATTIES.
IN WINTER, WE GET SWEATY WHILE SILENTLY CHOWING DOWN ON MEAT SAUCE.
WANNA SEE?
NO, WAIT!!
ACTUALLY, I'M AN APPRENTICE PALM READER...
...AND MY TEACHER GETS PEEVED IF I DON'T MAKE MY QUOTA!!

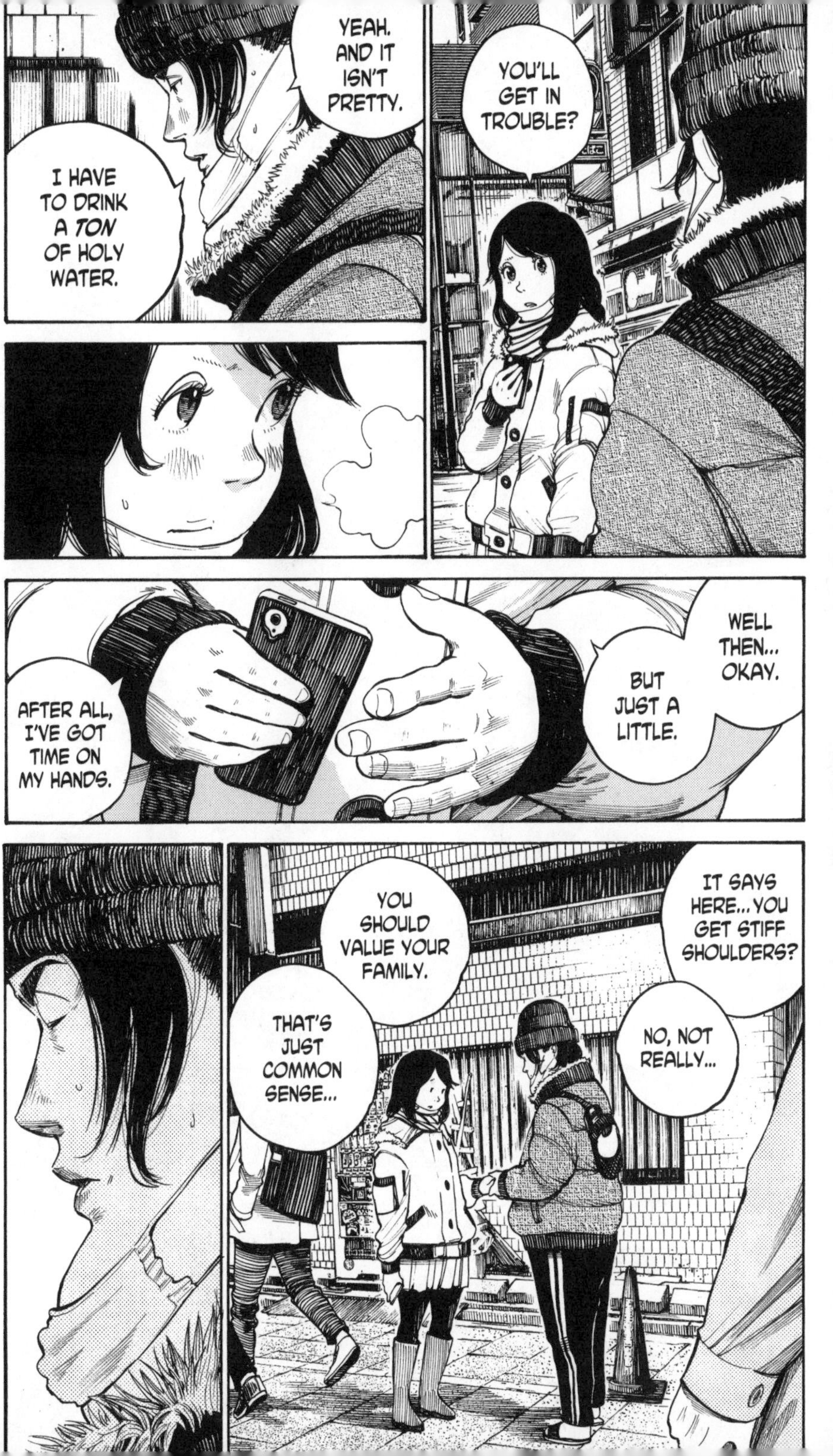
YOU'LL GET IN TROUBLE?
YEAH. AND IT ISN'T PRETTY.
I HAVE TO DRINK A *TON* OF HOLY WATER.
WELL THEN... OKAY.
BUT JUST A LITTLE.
AFTER ALL, I'VE GOT TIME ON MY HANDS.
IT SAYS HERE...YOU GET STIFF SHOULDERS?
NO, NOT REALLY...
YOU SHOULD VALUE YOUR FAMILY.
THAT'S JUST COMMON SENSE...

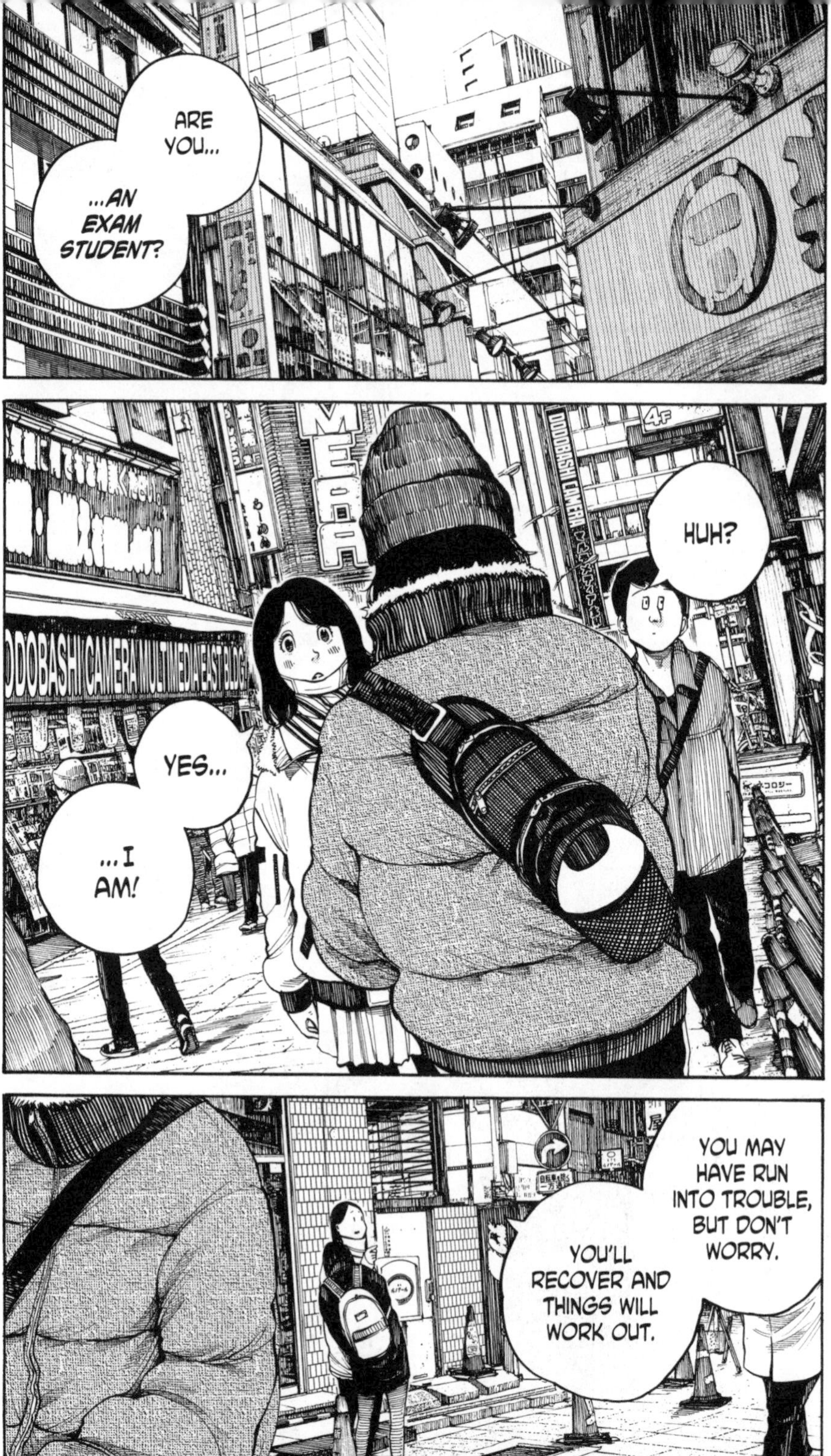
ARE YOU...
...AN EXAM STUDENT?
HUH?
YES...
...I AM!
YOU MAY HAVE RUN INTO TROUBLE, BUT DON'T WORRY.
YOU'LL RECOVER AND THINGS WILL WORK OUT.

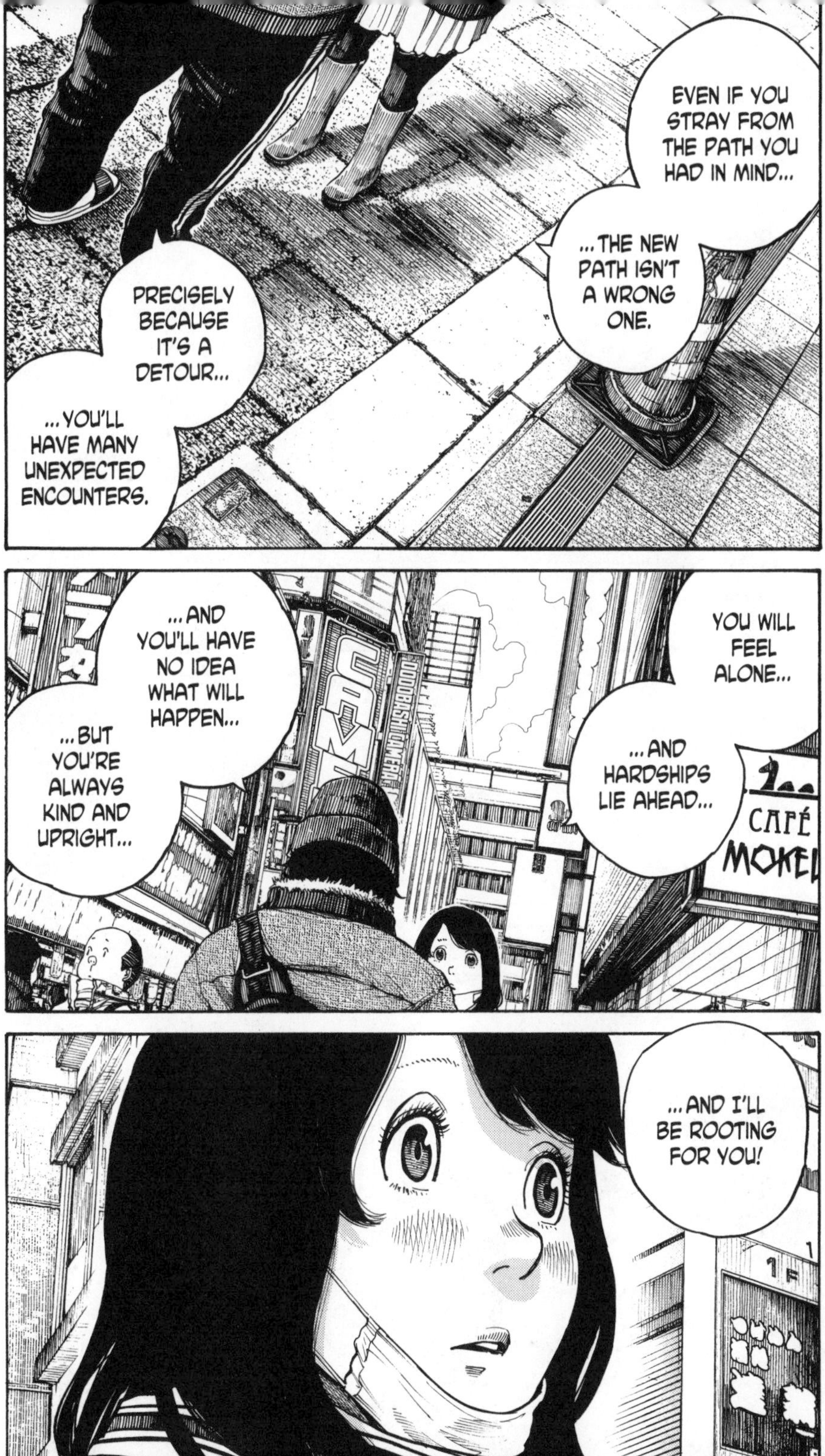
EVEN IF YOU STRAY FROM THE PATH YOU HAD IN MIND...
...THE NEW PATH ISN'T A WRONG ONE.
PRECISELY BECAUSE IT'S A DETOUR...
...YOU'LL HAVE MANY UNEXPECTED ENCOUNTERS.
YOU WILL FEEL ALONE...
...AND HARDSHIPS LIE AHEAD...
CAFÉ
...AND YOU'LL HAVE NO IDEA WHAT WILL HAPPEN...
...BUT YOU'RE ALWAYS KIND AND UPRIGHT...
...AND I'LL BE ROOTING FOR YOU!

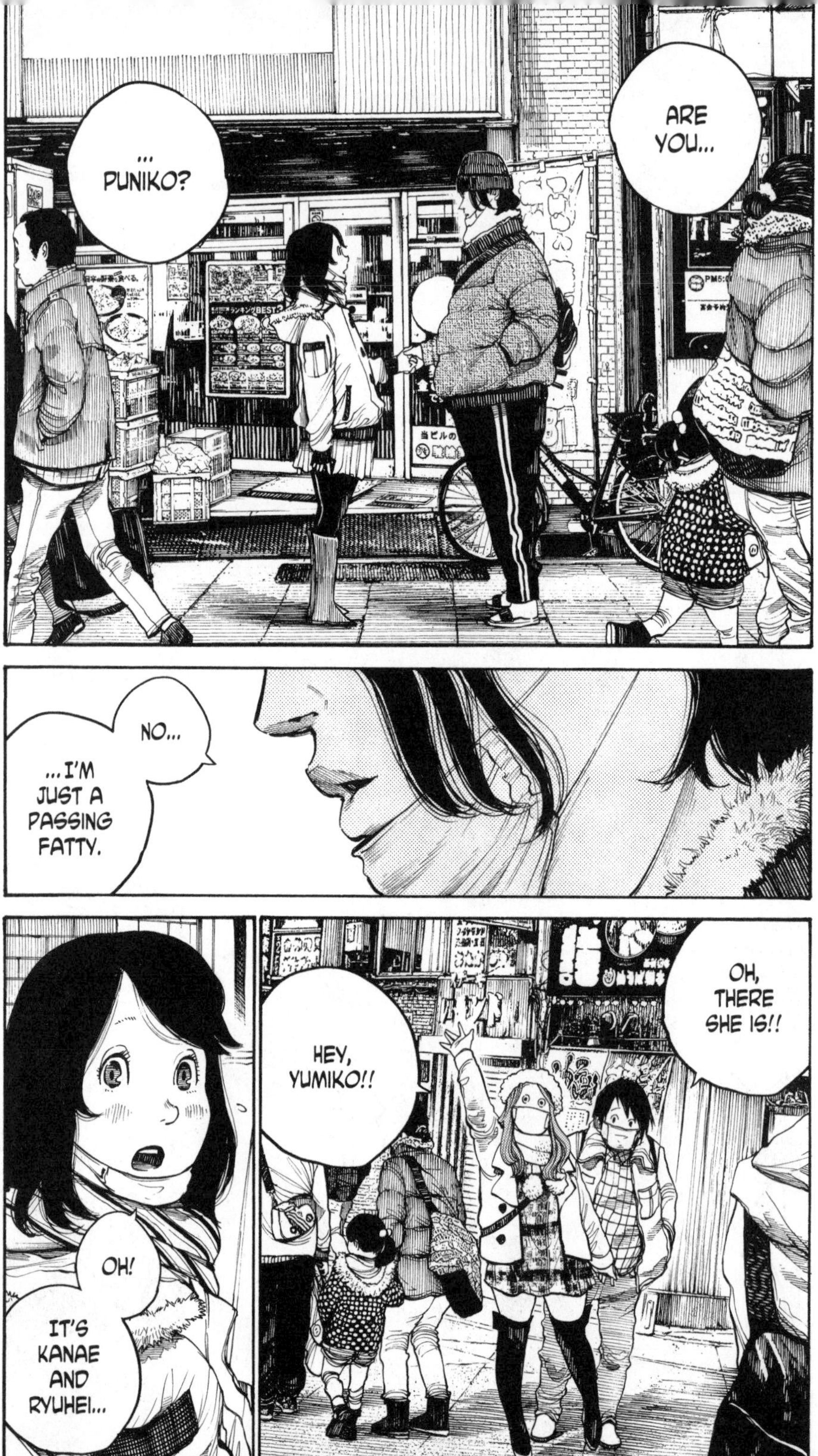
ARE YOU...
... PUNIKO?
NO...
...I'M JUST A PASSING FATTY.
OH, THERE SHE IS!!
HEY, YUMIKO!!
OH!
IT'S KANAE AND RYUHEI...

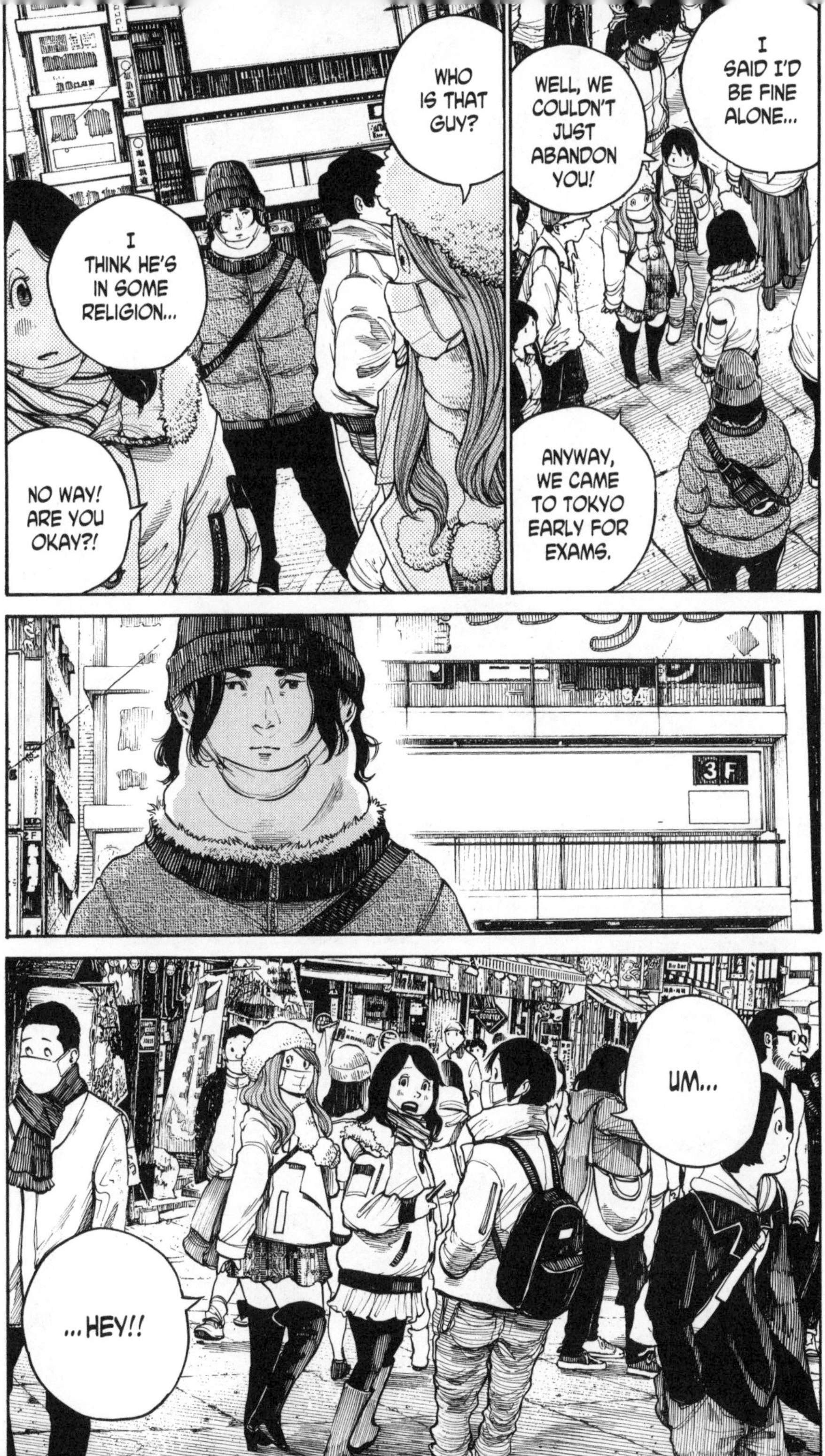

I SAID I'D BE FINE ALONE...
WELL, WE COULDN'T JUST ABANDON YOU!
ANYWAY, WE CAME TO TOKYO EARLY FOR EXAMS.
WHO IS THAT GUY?
I THINK HE'S IN SOME RELIGION...
NO WAY! ARE YOU OKAY?!
3F
UM...
...HEY!!

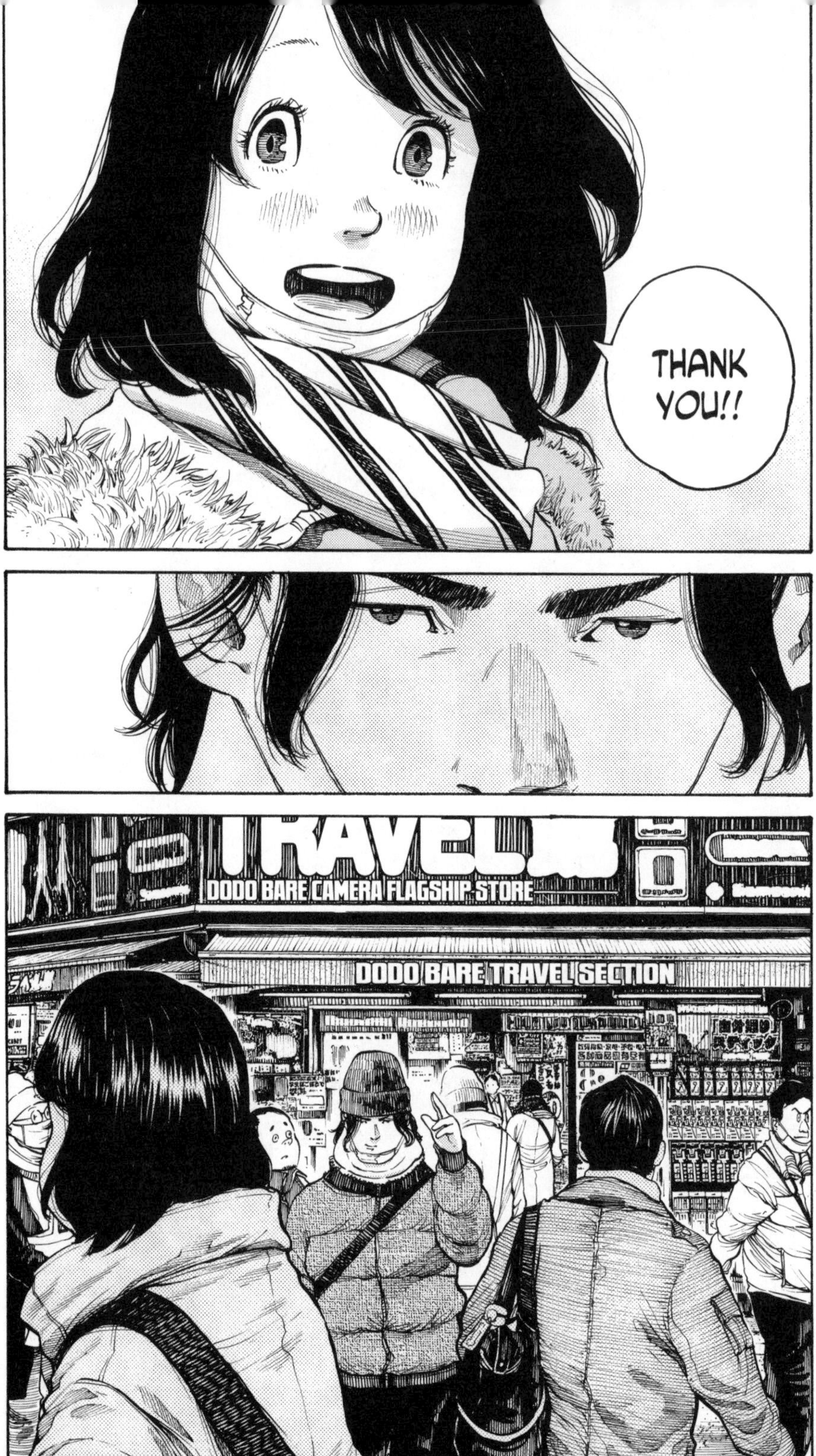
THANK YOU!!
DODO BARE CAMERA FLAGSHIP STORE
DODO BARE TRAVEL SECTION

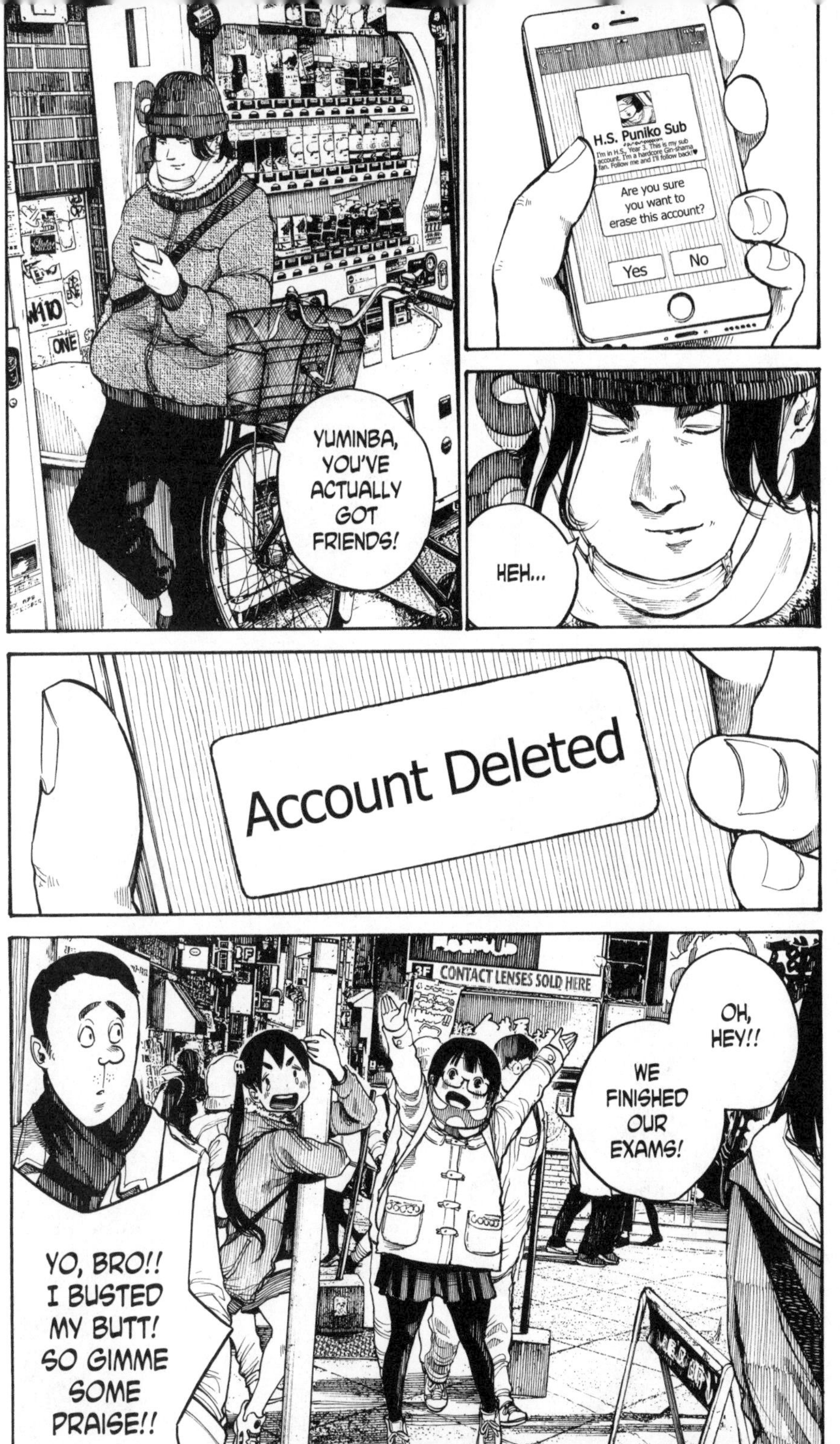
H.S. Puniko Sub
I'm in H.S. Year 3. This is my sub account. I'm a hardcore Gin-shama fan. Follow me and I'll follow back!♥
Are you sure you want to erase this account?
Yes
No
HEH...
YUMINBA, YOU'VE ACTUALLY GOT FRIENDS!
Account Deleted
CONTACT LENSES SOLD HERE
OH, HEY!!
WE FINISHED OUR EXAMS!
YO, BRO!! I BUSTED MY BUTT! SO GIMME SOME PRAISE!!

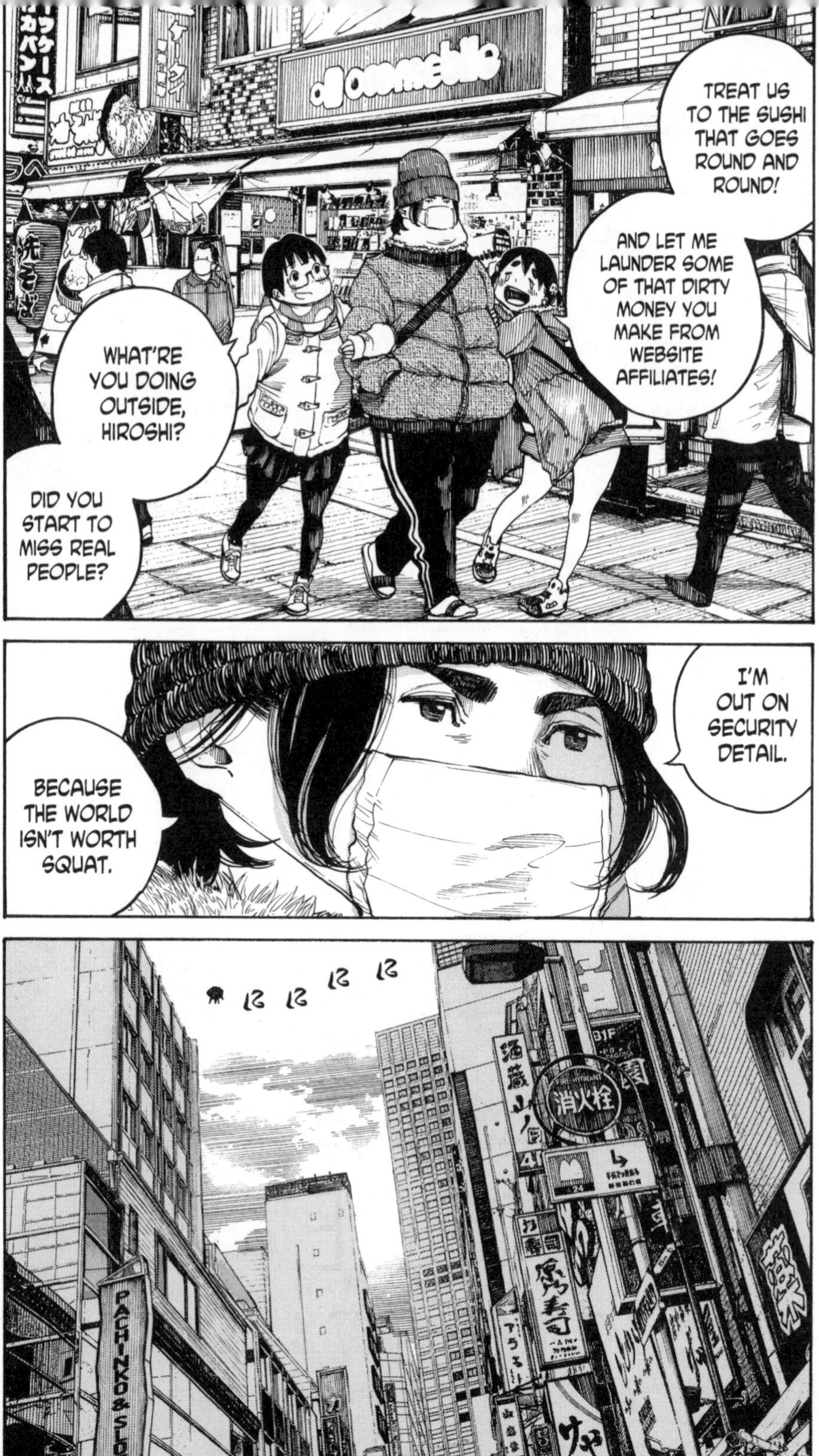
TREAT US TO THE SUSHI THAT GOES ROUND AND ROUND!
AND LET ME LAUNDER SOME OF THAT DIRTY MONEY YOU MAKE FROM WEBSITE AFFILIATES!
WHAT'RE YOU DOING OUTSIDE, HIROSHI?
DID YOU START TO MISS REAL PEOPLE?
I'M OUT ON SECURITY DETAIL.
BECAUSE THE WORLD ISN'T WORTH SQUAT.
消火栓
PACHINKO

DEAD DEAD DEMON'S

CHAPTER 20

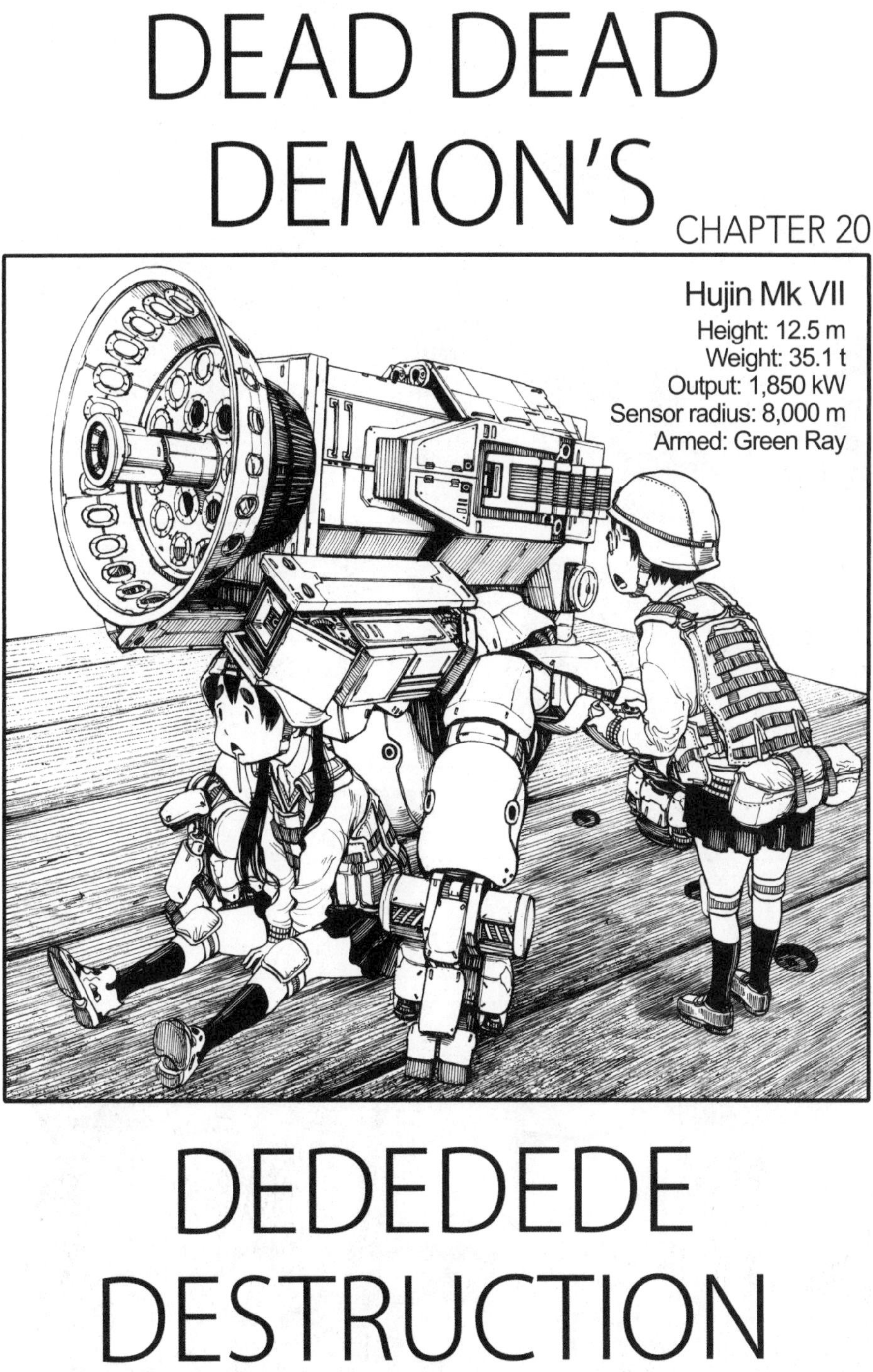
Hujin Mk VII
Height: 12.5 m
Weight: 35.1 t
Output: 1,850 kW
Sensor radius: 8,000 m
Armed: Green Ray

DEDEDEDE DESTRUCTION

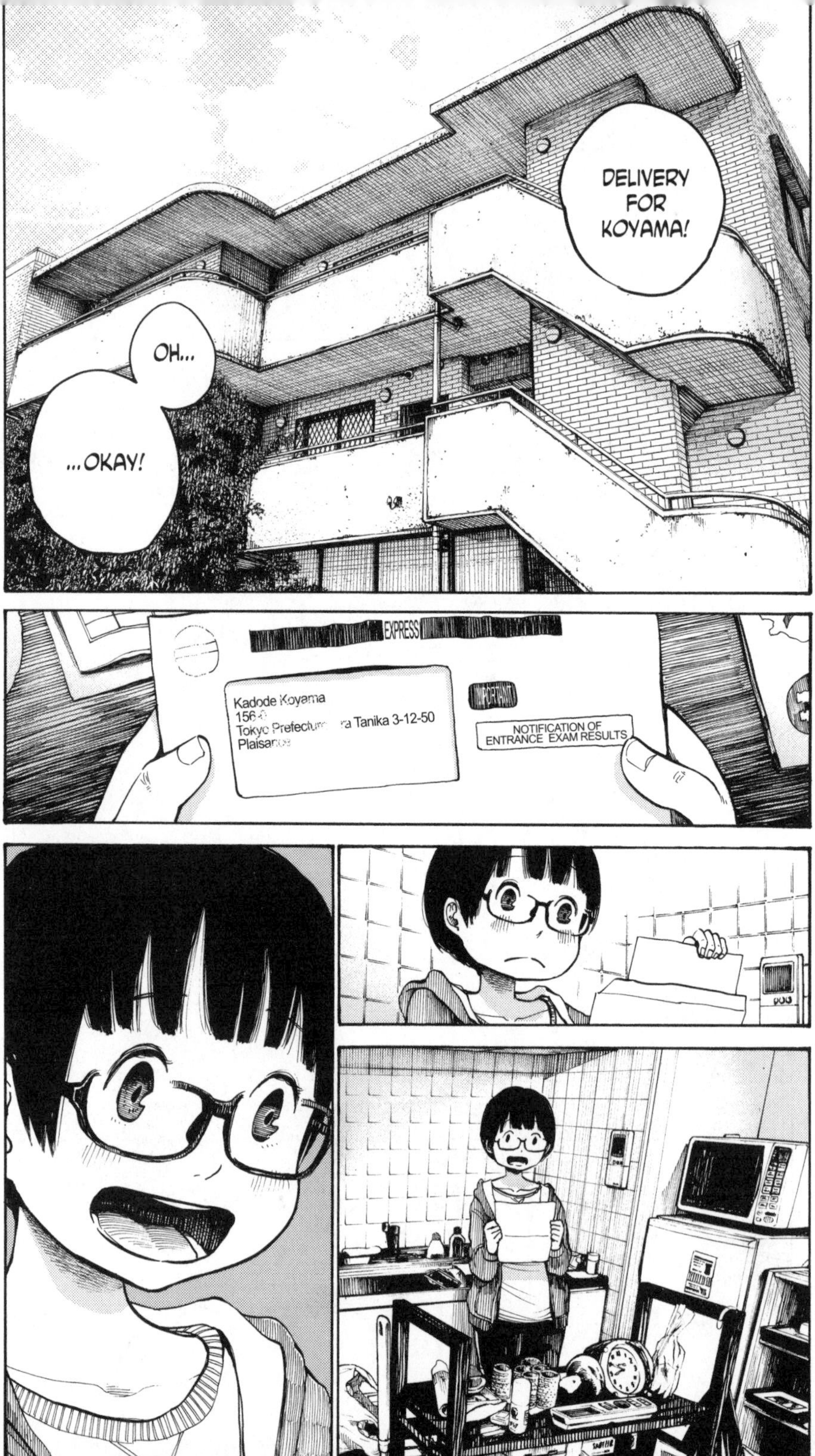
DELIVERY FOR KOYAMA!
OH...
...OKAY!
[redacted] EXPRESS [redacted]
Kadode Koyama
156-0
Tokyo Prefectu ra Tanika 3-12-50
Plaisan
IMPORTANT
NOTIFICATION OF ENTRANCE EXAM RESULTS

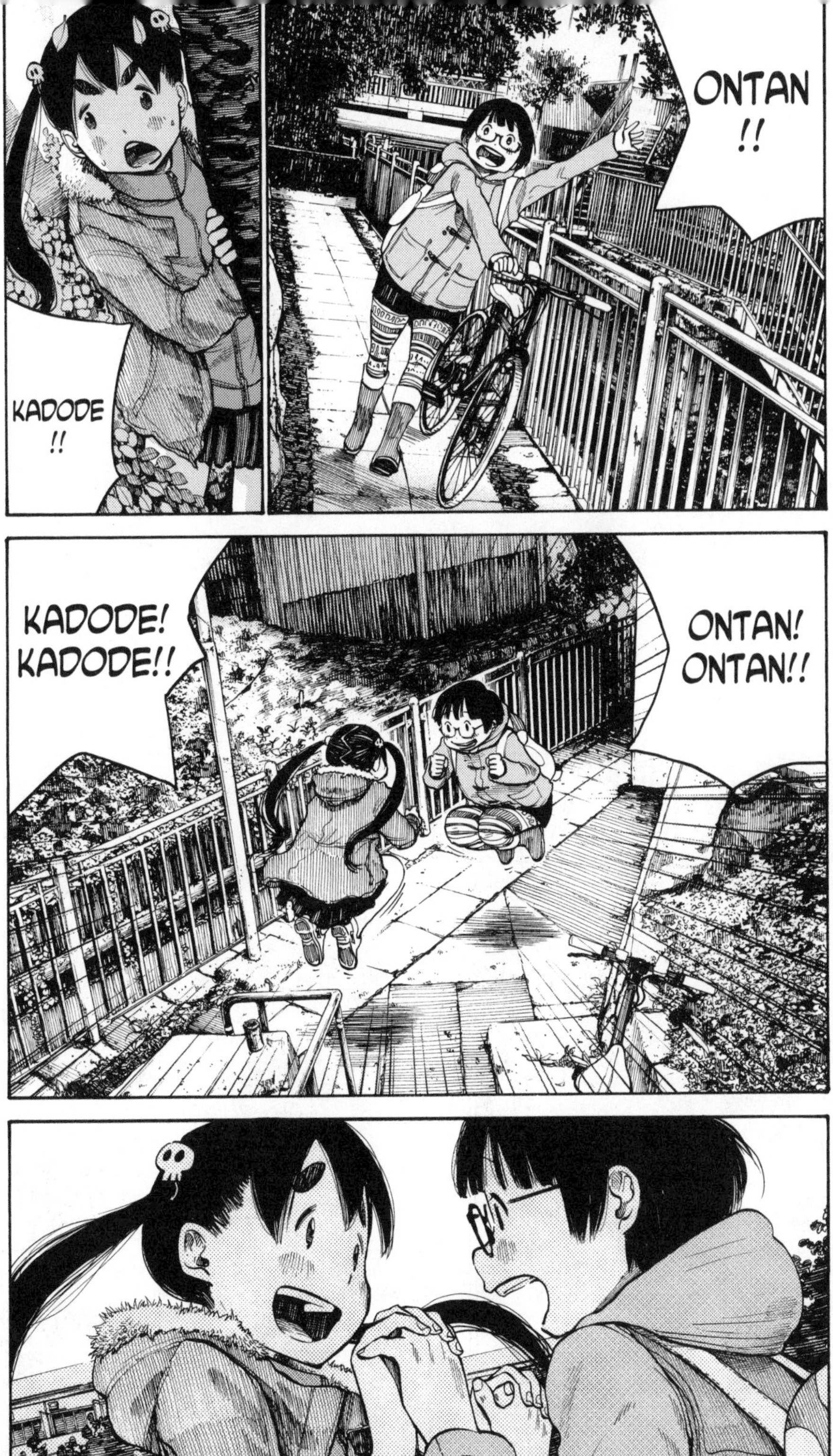
ONTAN !!
KADODE !!
ONTAN! ONTAN!!
KADODE! KADODE!!

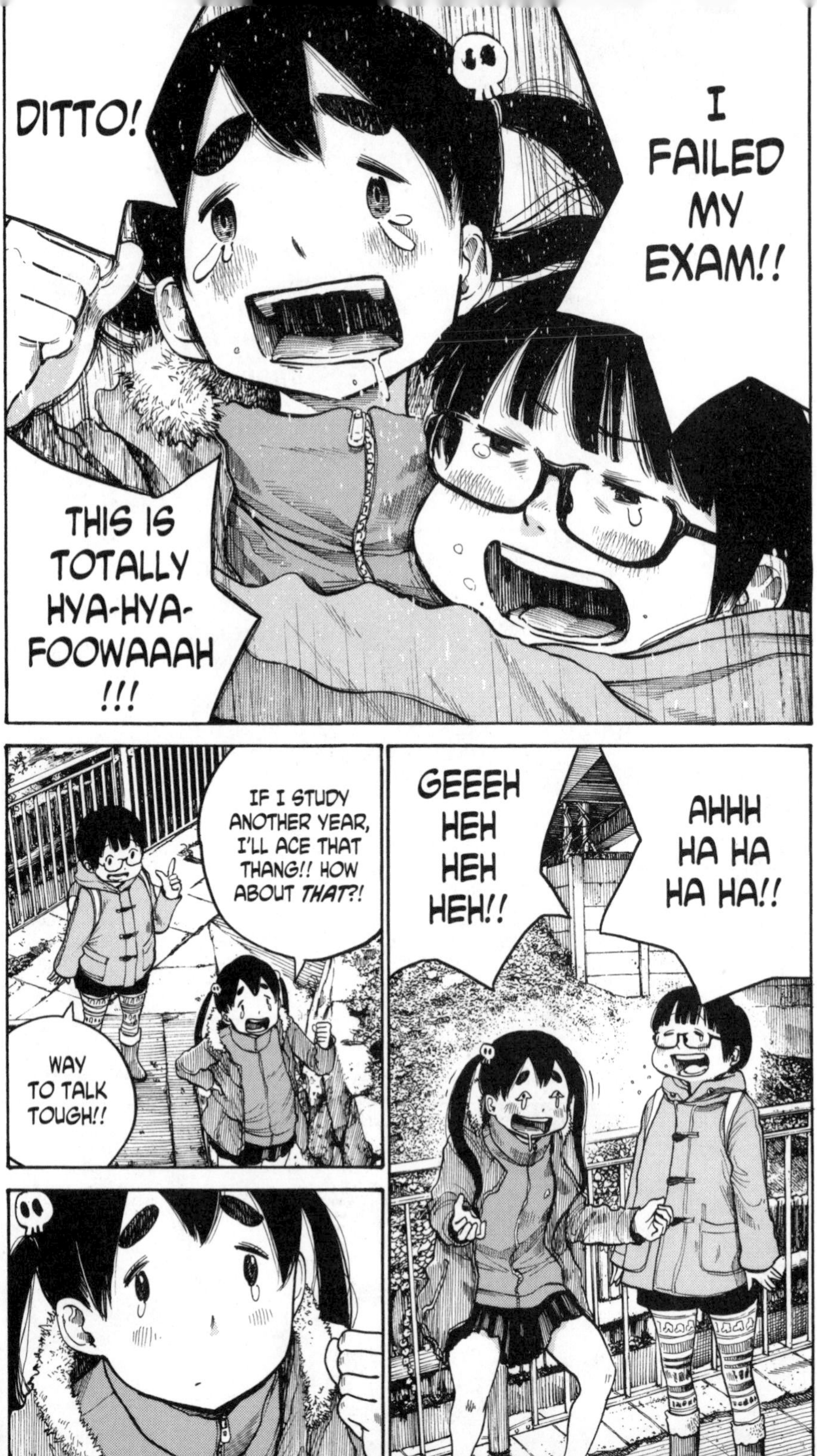
I FAILED MY EXAM!!
DITTO!
THIS IS TOTALLY HYA-HYA-FOOWAAAH!!!
AHHH HA HA HA HA!!
GEEEH HEH HEH HEH!!
IF I STUDY ANOTHER YEAR, I'LL ACE THAT THANG!! HOW ABOUT *THAT*?!
WAY TO TALK TOUGH!!

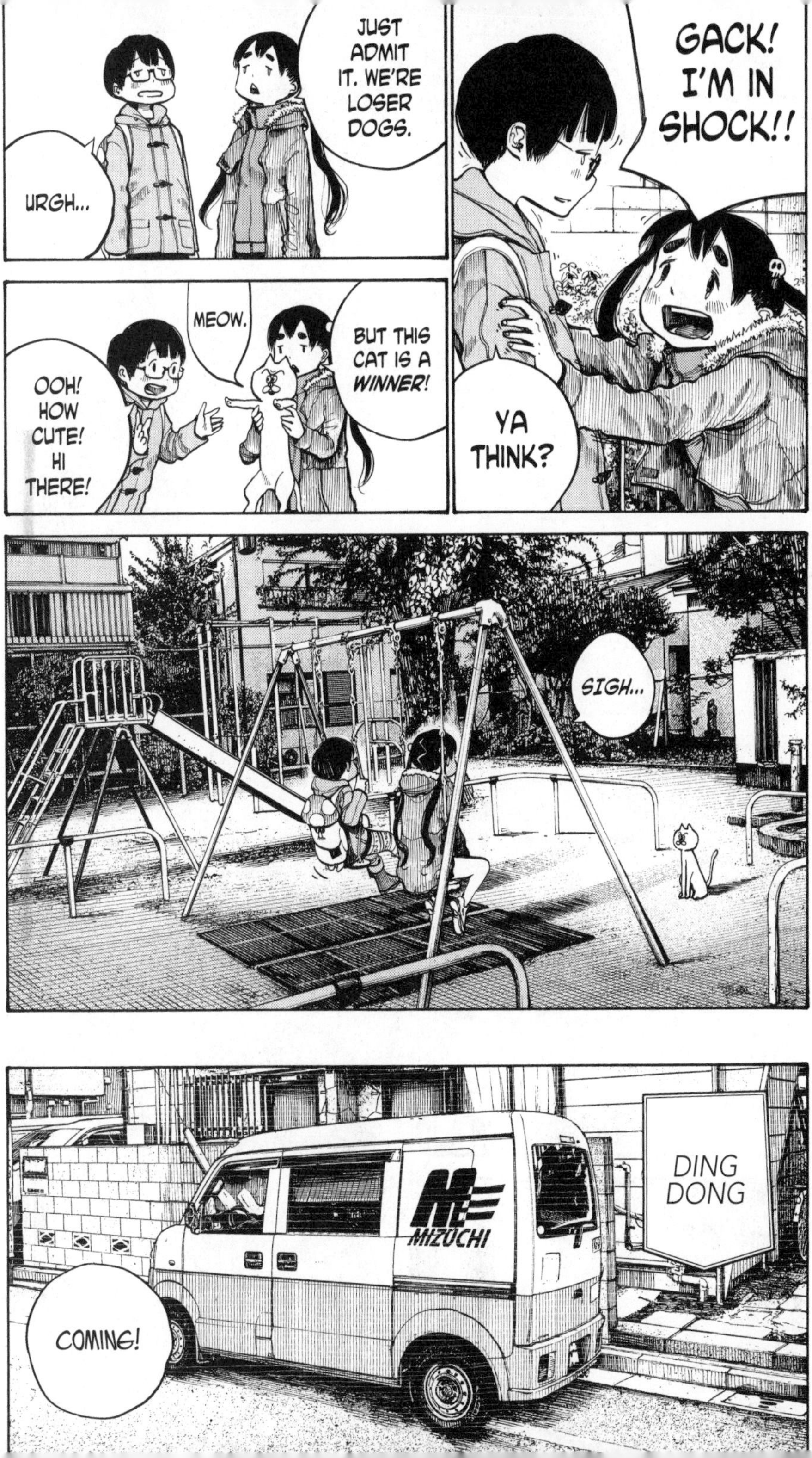
GACK! I'M IN SHOCK!!
YA THINK?
JUST ADMIT IT. WE'RE LOSER DOGS.
URGH...
BUT THIS CAT IS A *WINNER*!
MEOW.
OOH! HOW CUTE! HI THERE!
SIGH...
DING DONG
MIZUCHI
COMING!

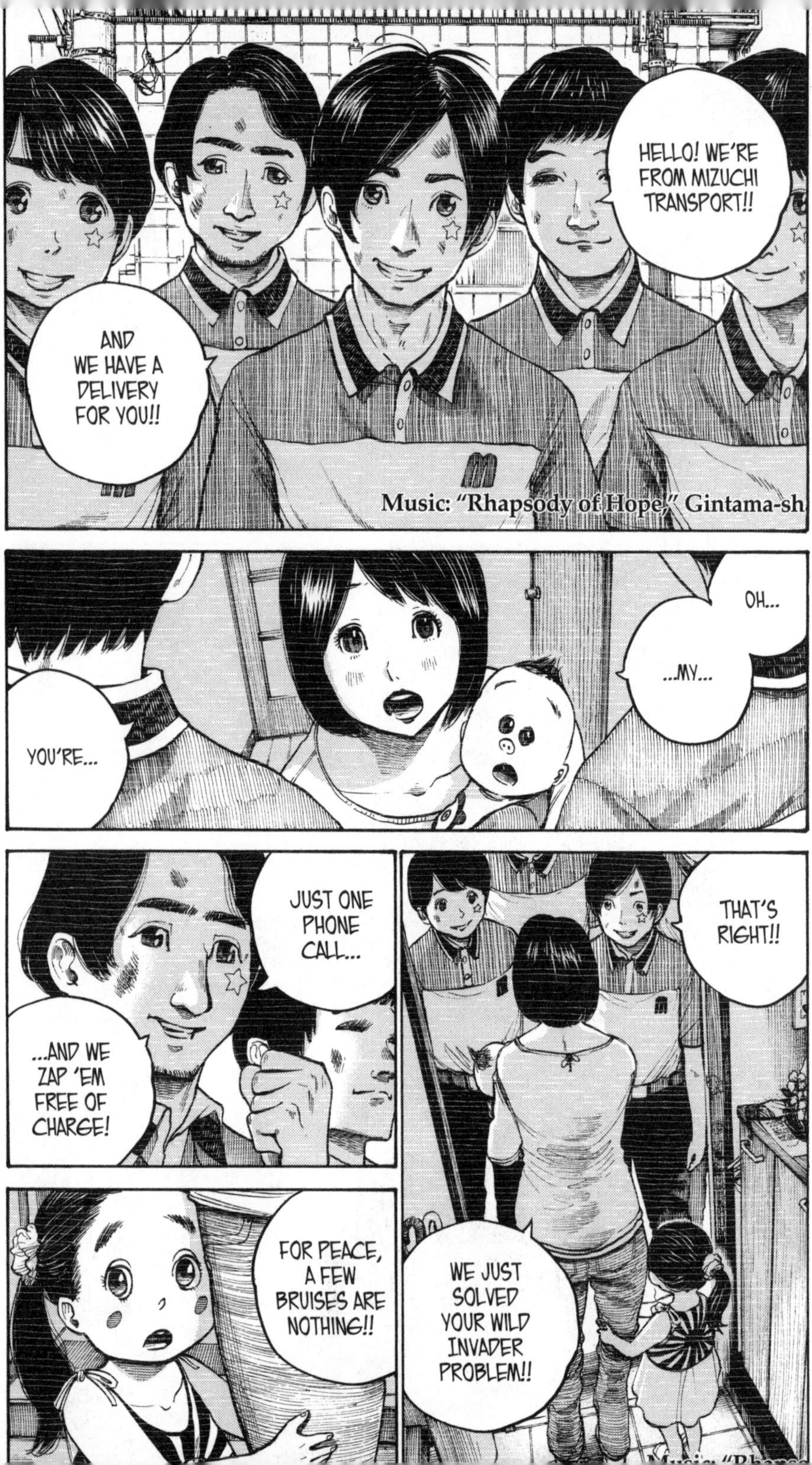
HELLO! WE'RE FROM MIZUCHI TRANSPORT!!
AND WE HAVE A DELIVERY FOR YOU!!
Music: "Rhapsody of Hope," Gintama-sh
OH...
...MY...
YOU'RE...
THAT'S RIGHT!!
WE JUST SOLVED YOUR WILD INVADER PROBLEM!!
JUST ONE PHONE CALL...
...AND WE ZAP 'EM FREE OF CHARGE!
FOR PEACE, A FEW BRUISES ARE NOTHING!!

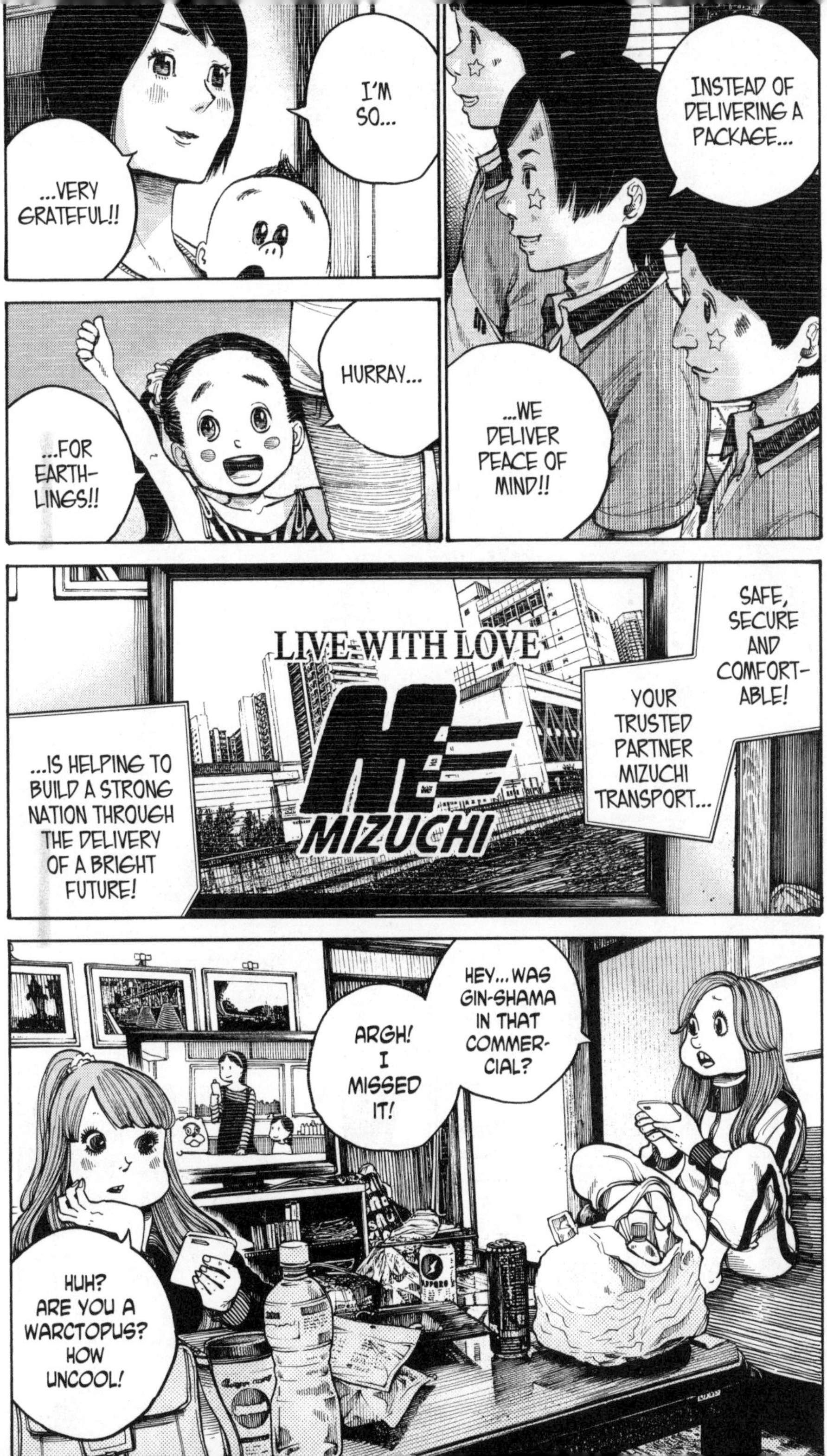

INSTEAD OF DELIVERING A PACKAGE...
...WE DELIVER PEACE OF MIND!!
I'M SO...
...VERY GRATEFUL!!
HURRAY...
...FOR EARTH-LINGS!!
SAFE, SECURE AND COMFORT-ABLE!
YOUR TRUSTED PARTNER MIZUCHI TRANSPORT...
LIVE WITH LOVE
MIZUCHI
...IS HELPING TO BUILD A STRONG NATION THROUGH THE DELIVERY OF A BRIGHT FUTURE!
HEY...WAS GIN-SHAMA IN THAT COMMER-CIAL?
ARGH! I MISSED IT!
HUH? ARE YOU A WARCTOPUS? HOW UNCOOL!

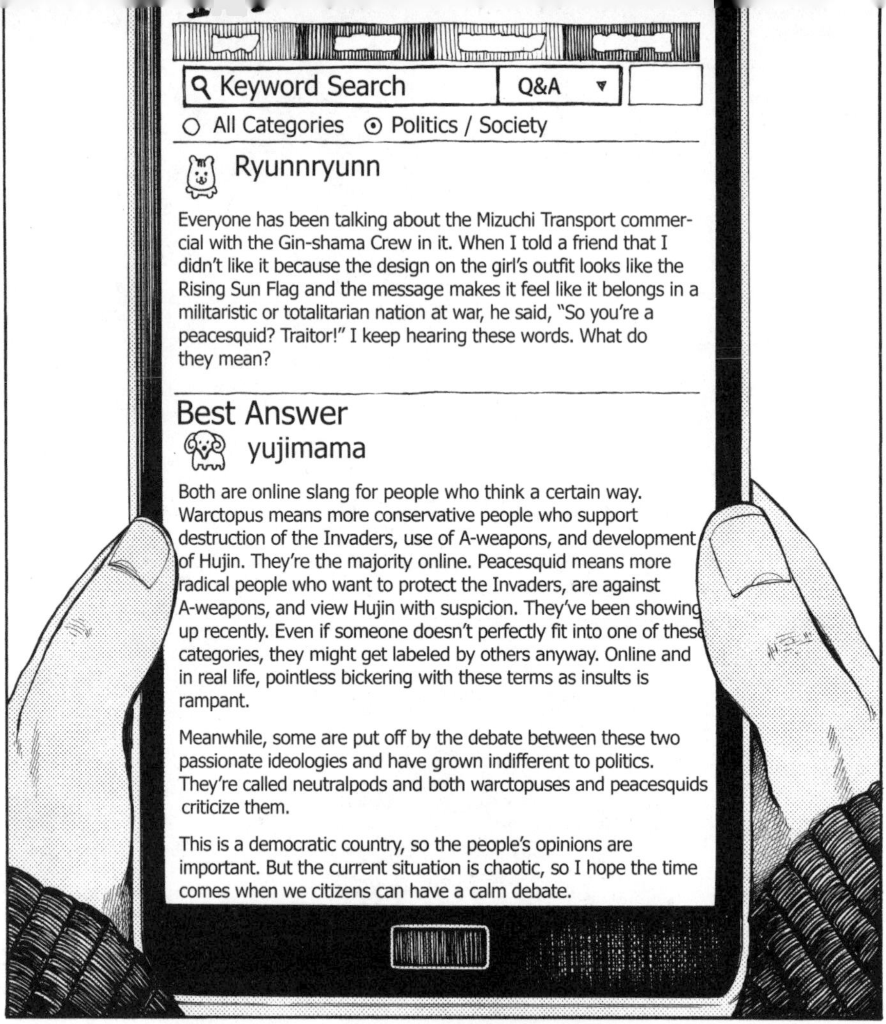
Keyword Search
Q&A
All Categories
Politics / Society
Ryunnryunn
Everyone has been talking about the Mizuchi Transport commercial with the Gin-shama Crew in it. When I told a friend that I didn't like it because the design on the girl's outfit looks like the Rising Sun Flag and the message makes it feel like it belongs in a militaristic or totalitarian nation at war, he said, "So you're a peacesquid? Traitor!" I keep hearing these words. What do they mean?
Best Answer
yujimama
Both are online slang for people who think a certain way. Warctopus means more conservative people who support destruction of the Invaders, use of A-weapons, and development of Hujin. They're the majority online. Peacesquid means more radical people who want to protect the Invaders, are against A-weapons, and view Hujin with suspicion. They've been showing up recently. Even if someone doesn't perfectly fit into one of these categories, they might get labeled by others anyway. Online and in real life, pointless bickering with these terms as insults is rampant.
Meanwhile, some are put off by the debate between these two passionate ideologies and have grown indifferent to politics. They're called neutralpods and both warctopuses and peacesquids criticize them.
This is a democratic country, so the people's opinions are important. But the current situation is chaotic, so I hope the time comes when we citizens can have a calm debate.

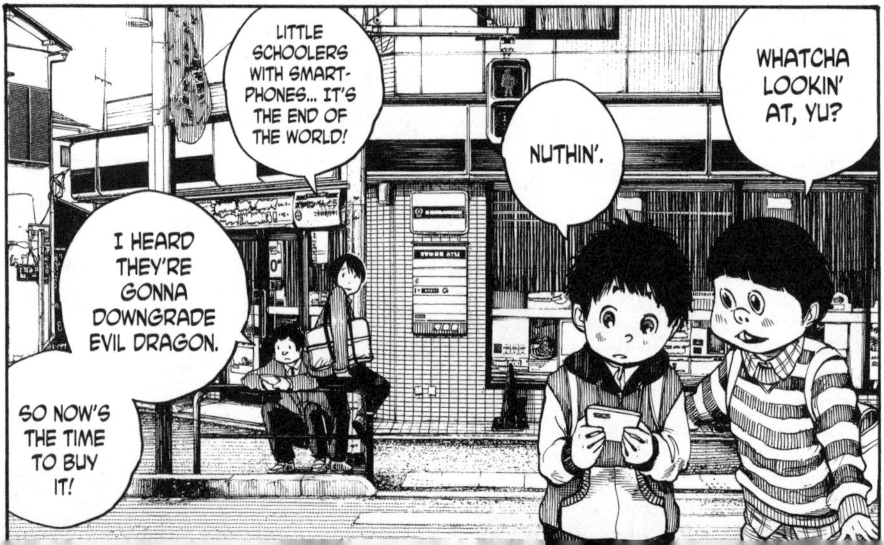
WHATCHA LOOKIN' AT, YU?
NUTHIN'.
LITTLE SCHOOLERS WITH SMART-PHONES... IT'S THE END OF THE WORLD!
I HEARD THEY'RE GONNA DOWNGRADE EVIL DRAGON.
SO NOW'S THE TIME TO BUY IT!

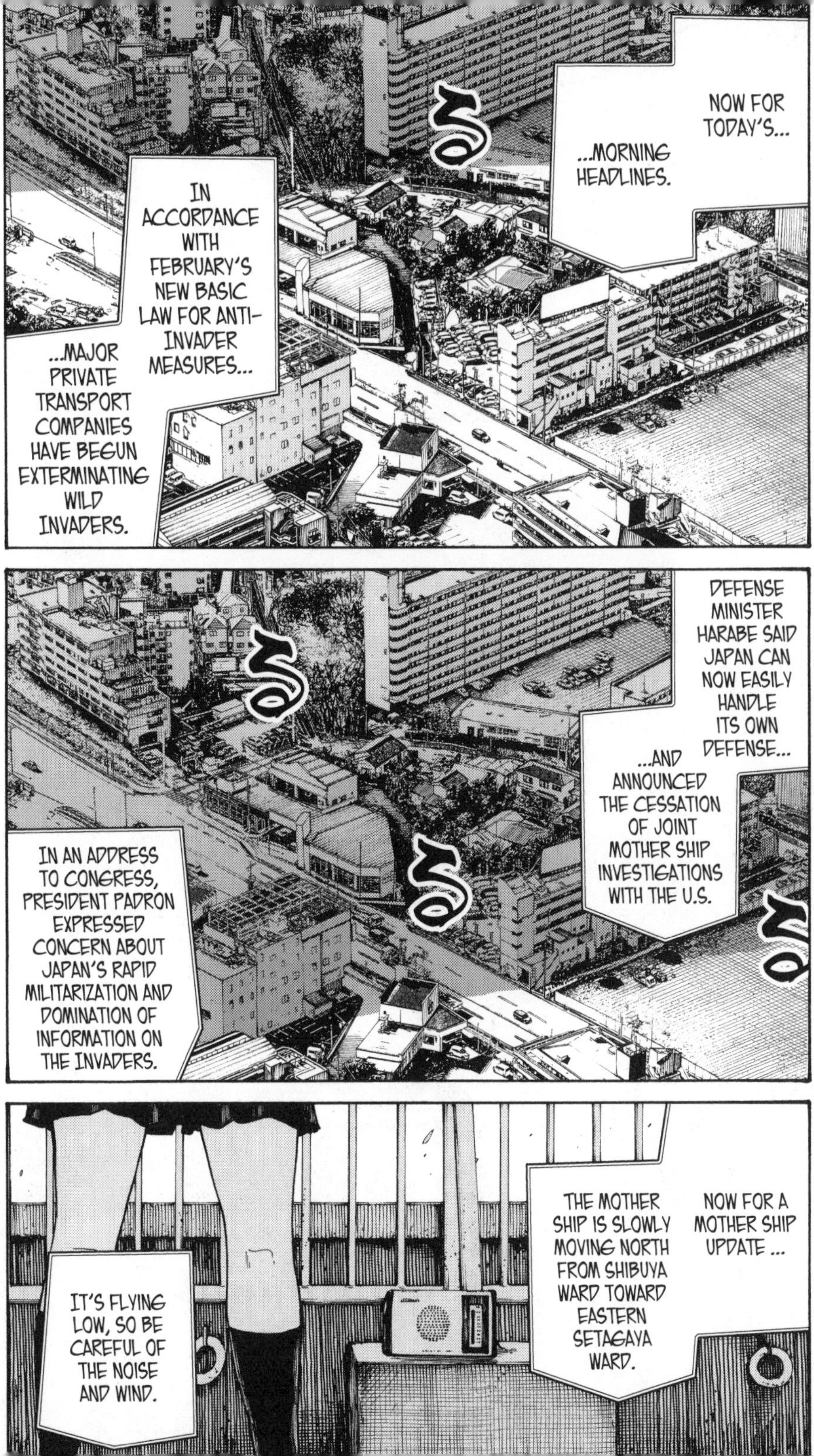
NOW FOR TODAY'S...
...MORNING HEADLINES.
IN ACCORDANCE WITH FEBRUARY'S NEW BASIC LAW FOR ANTI-INVADER MEASURES...
...MAJOR PRIVATE TRANSPORT COMPANIES HAVE BEGUN EXTERMINATING WILD INVADERS.
DEFENSE MINISTER HARABE SAID JAPAN CAN NOW EASILY HANDLE ITS OWN DEFENSE...
...AND ANNOUNCED THE CESSATION OF JOINT MOTHER SHIP INVESTIGATIONS WITH THE U.S.
IN AN ADDRESS TO CONGRESS, PRESIDENT PADRON EXPRESSED CONCERN ABOUT JAPAN'S RAPID MILITARIZATION AND DOMINATION OF INFORMATION ON THE INVADERS.
NOW FOR A MOTHER SHIP UPDATE ...
THE MOTHER SHIP IS SLOWLY MOVING NORTH FROM SHIBUYA WARD TOWARD EASTERN SETAGAYA WARD.
IT'S FLYING LOW, SO BE CAREFUL OF THE NOISE AND WIND.

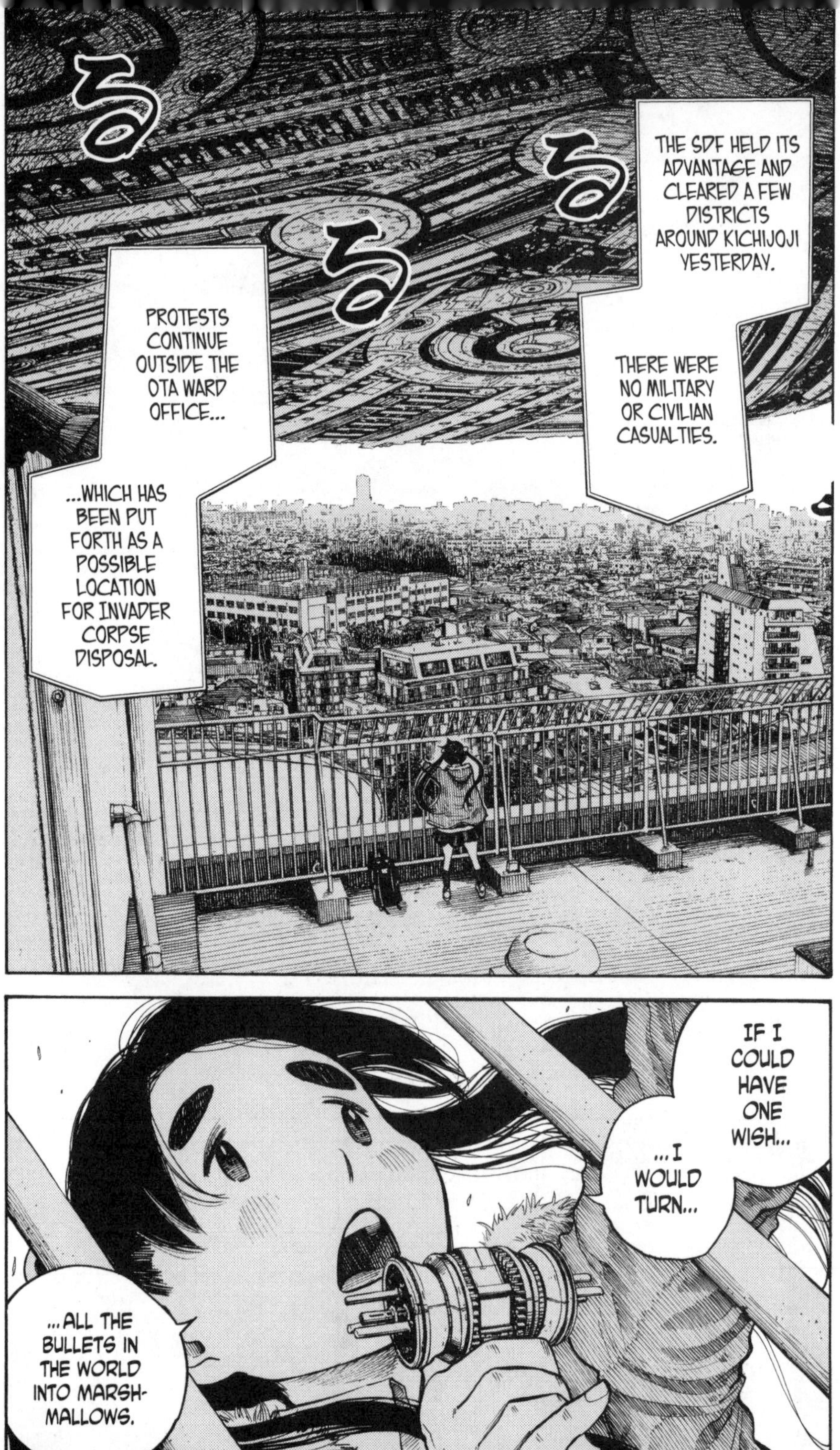
THE SDF HELD ITS ADVANTAGE AND CLEARED A FEW DISTRICTS AROUND KICHIJOJI YESTERDAY.
THERE WERE NO MILITARY OR CIVILIAN CASUALTIES.
PROTESTS CONTINUE OUTSIDE THE OTA WARD OFFICE...
...WHICH HAS BEEN PUT FORTH AS A POSSIBLE LOCATION FOR INVADER CORPSE DISPOSAL.
IF I COULD HAVE ONE WISH...
...I WOULD TURN...
...ALL THE BULLETS IN THE WORLD INTO MARSH-MALLOWS.

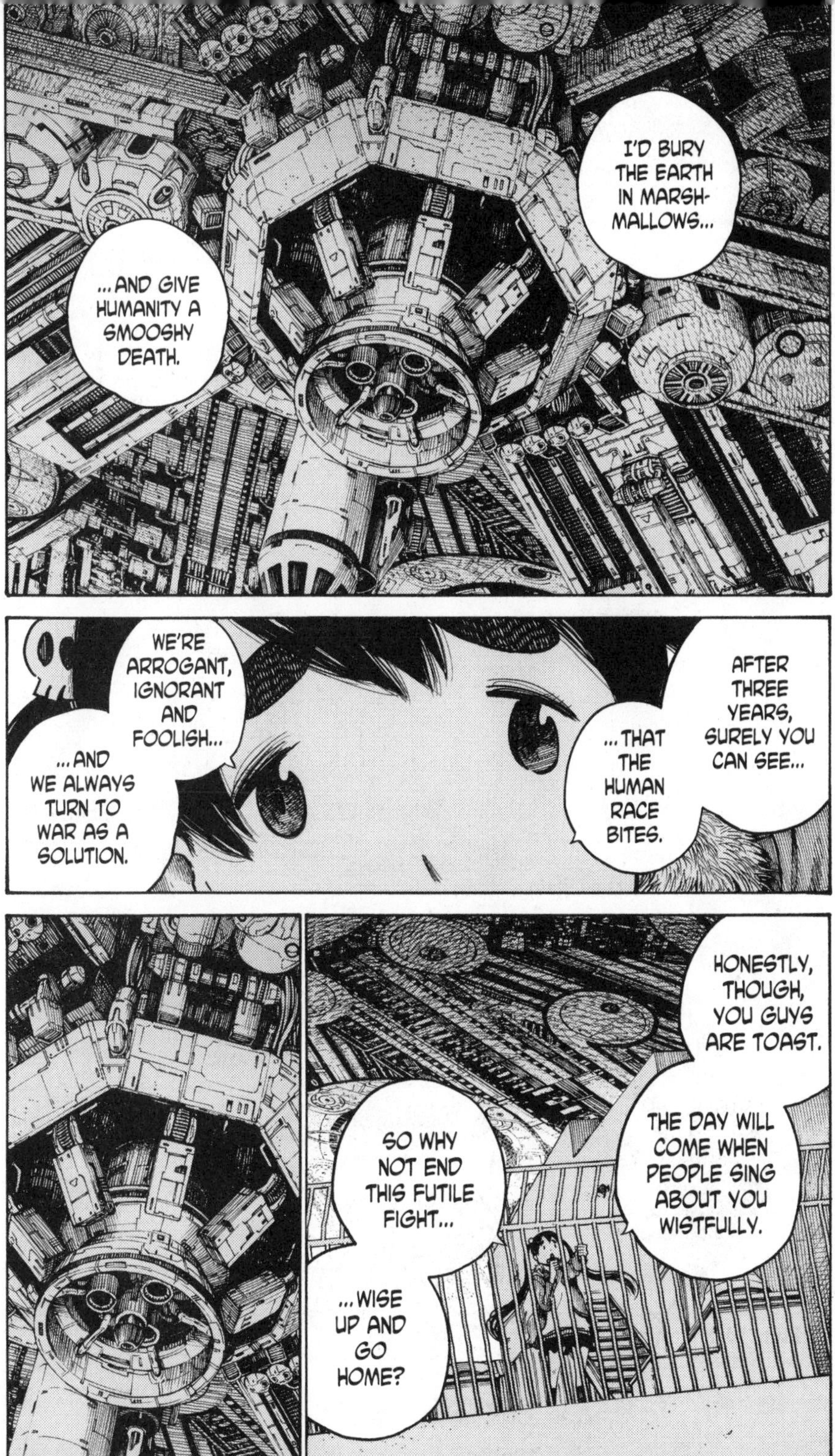
I'D BURY THE EARTH IN MARSH-MALLOWS...
...AND GIVE HUMANITY A SMOOSHY DEATH.
AFTER THREE YEARS, SURELY YOU CAN SEE...
...THAT THE HUMAN RACE BITES.
WE'RE ARROGANT, IGNORANT AND FOOLISH...
...AND WE ALWAYS TURN TO WAR AS A SOLUTION.
HONESTLY, THOUGH, YOU GUYS ARE TOAST.
THE DAY WILL COME WHEN PEOPLE SING ABOUT YOU WISTFULLY.
SO WHY NOT END THIS FUTILE FIGHT...
...WISE UP AND GO HOME?

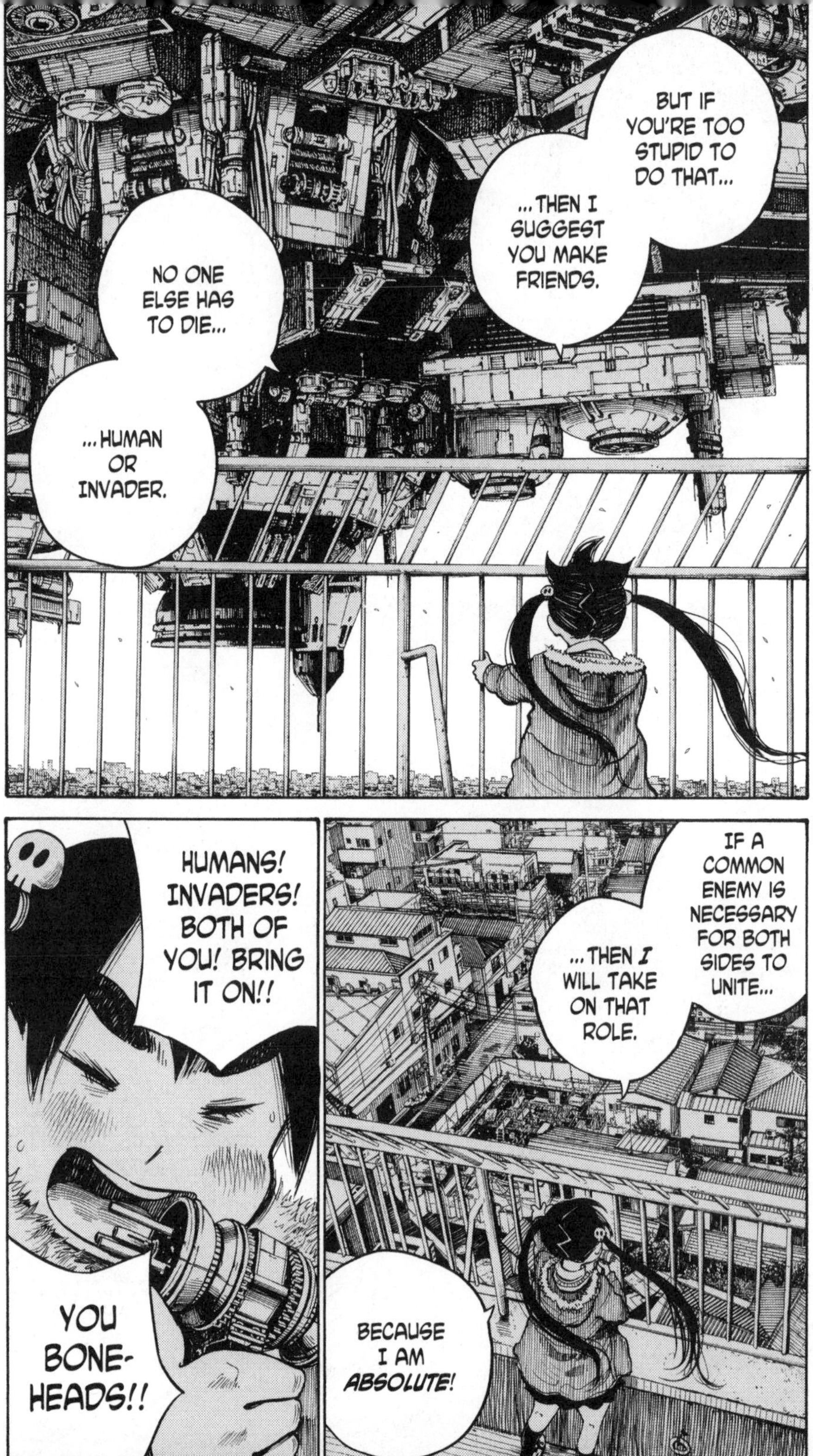
BUT IF YOU'RE TOO STUPID TO DO THAT...
...THEN I SUGGEST YOU MAKE FRIENDS.
NO ONE ELSE HAS TO DIE...
...HUMAN OR INVADER.
IF A COMMON ENEMY IS NECESSARY FOR BOTH SIDES TO UNITE...
...THEN *I* WILL TAKE ON THAT ROLE.
BECAUSE I AM *ABSOLUTE*!
HUMANS! INVADERS! BOTH OF YOU! BRING IT ON!!
YOU BONE-HEADS!!

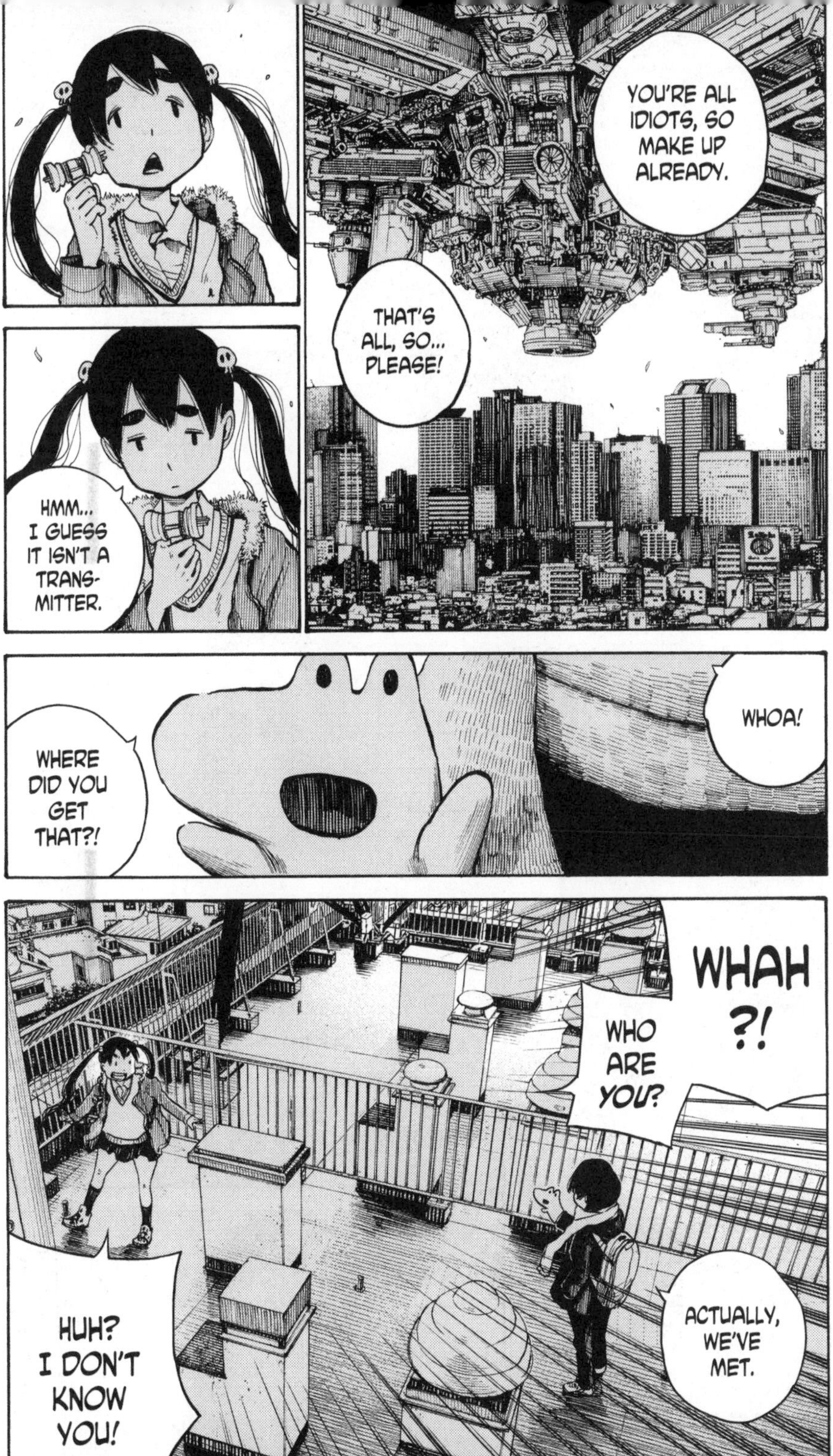
YOU'RE ALL IDIOTS, SO MAKE UP ALREADY.
THAT'S ALL, SO... PLEASE!
HMM... I GUESS IT ISN'T A TRANSMITTER.
WHOA!
WHERE DID YOU GET THAT?!
WHAH ?!
WHO ARE YOU?
ACTUALLY, WE'VE MET.
HUH? I DON'T KNOW YOU!

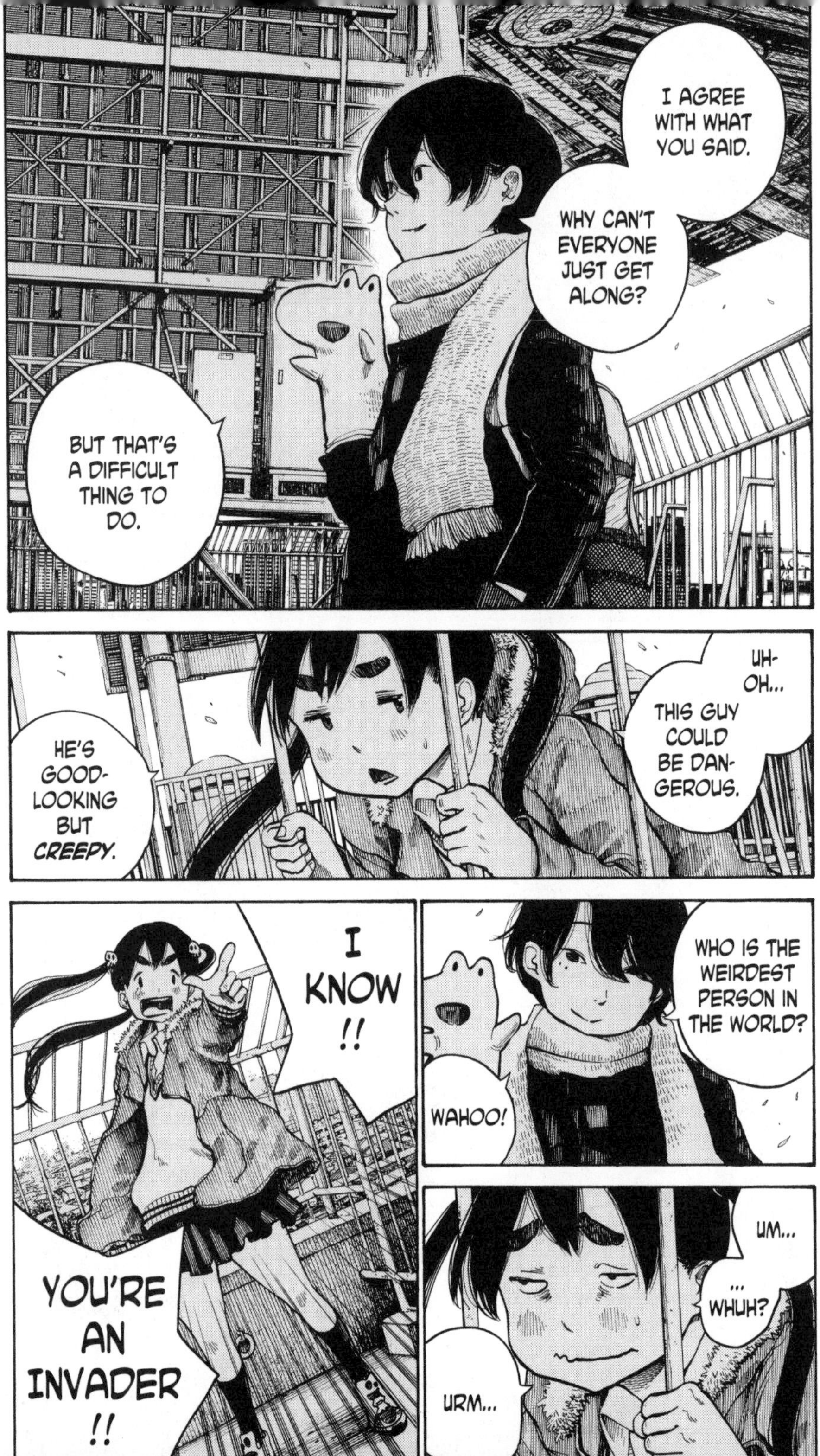
I AGREE WITH WHAT YOU SAID.
WHY CAN'T EVERYONE JUST GET ALONG?
BUT THAT'S A DIFFICULT THING TO DO.
UH-OH... THIS GUY COULD BE DAN-GEROUS.
HE'S GOOD-LOOKING BUT *CREEPY*.
WHO IS THE WEIRDEST PERSON IN THE WORLD?
WAHOO!
UM...
... WHUH?
URM...
I KNOW !!
YOU'RE AN INVADER !!

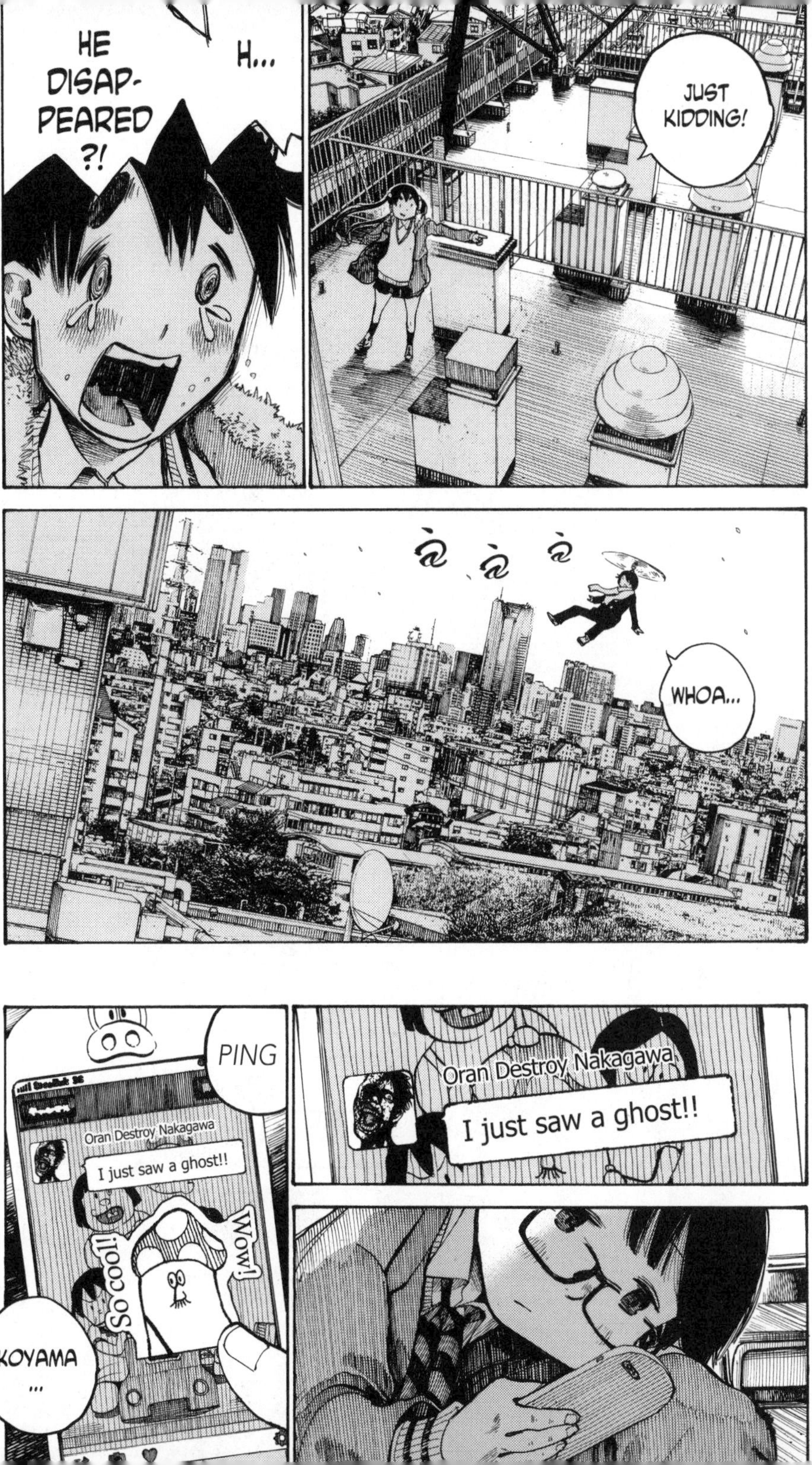
JUST KIDDING!
H...
HE DISAP- PEARED ?!
WHOA...
Oran Destroy Nakagawa
I just saw a ghost!!
PING
Oran Destroy Nakagawa
I just saw a ghost!!
Wow!
So cool!!
KOYAMA ...

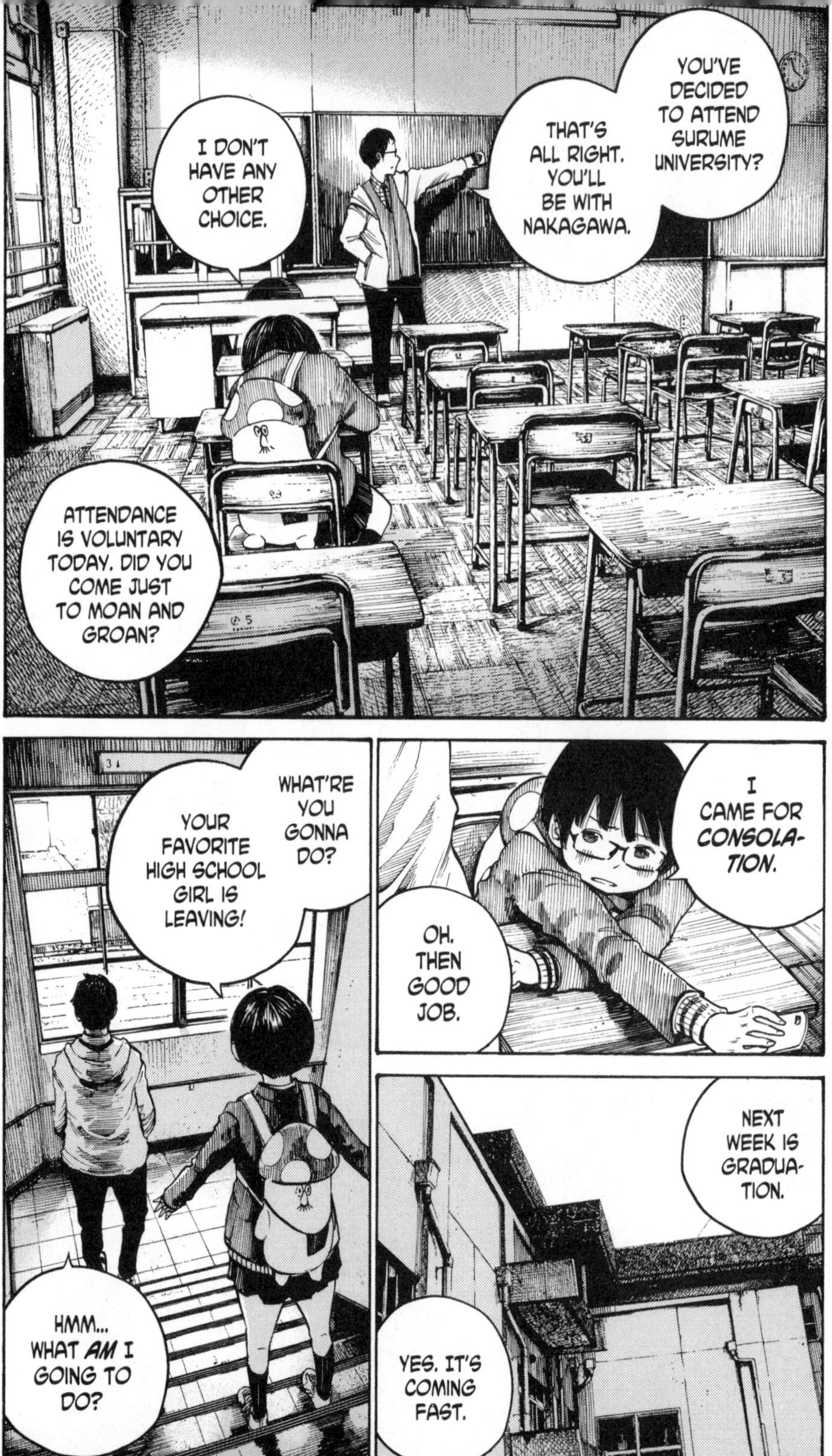
YOU'VE DECIDED TO ATTEND SURUME UNIVERSITY?
I DON'T HAVE ANY OTHER CHOICE.
THAT'S ALL RIGHT. YOU'LL BE WITH NAKAGAWA.
ATTENDANCE IS VOLUNTARY TODAY. DID YOU COME JUST TO MOAN AND GROAN?
I CAME FOR *CONSOLATION.*
OH. THEN GOOD JOB.
NEXT WEEK IS GRADUATION.
YES. IT'S COMING FAST.
YOUR FAVORITE HIGH SCHOOL GIRL IS LEAVING! WHAT'RE YOU GONNA DO?
HMM... WHAT *AM* I GOING TO DO?

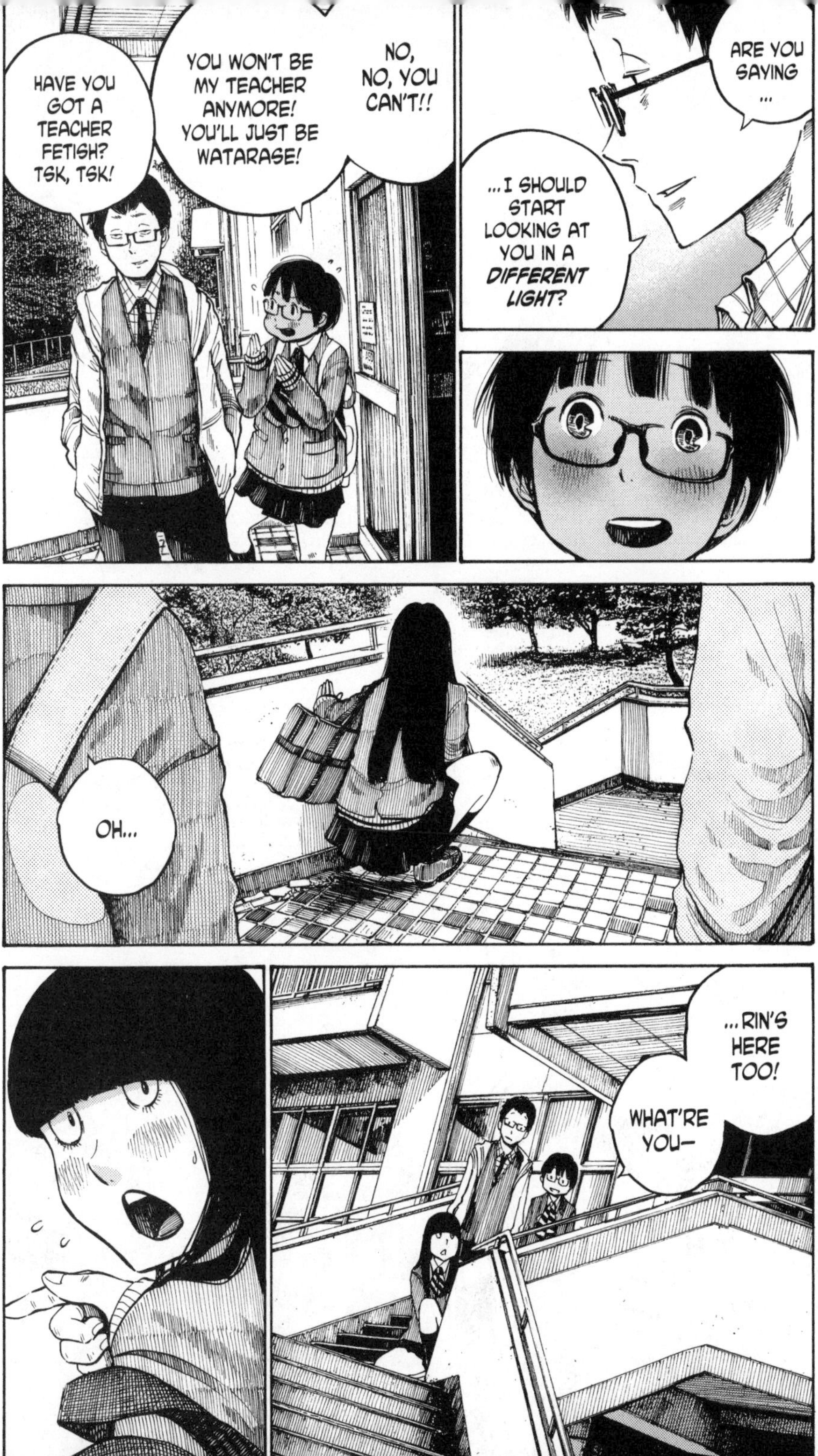
ARE YOU SAYING ...
...I SHOULD START LOOKING AT YOU IN A *DIFFERENT LIGHT?*
NO, NO, YOU CAN'T!!
YOU WON'T BE MY TEACHER ANYMORE! YOU'LL JUST BE WATARASE!
HAVE YOU GOT A TEACHER FETISH? TSK, TSK!
OH...
...RIN'S HERE TOO!
WHAT'RE YOU—

WHAT'S UP?

UM...

...UH...

I KNOW THIS IS SUDDEN...

...SO I'M SORRY, BUT...

HUH?

...WILL YOU GO ON A DATE WITH ME?

IF YOU DON'T MIND, NEXT WEEK...

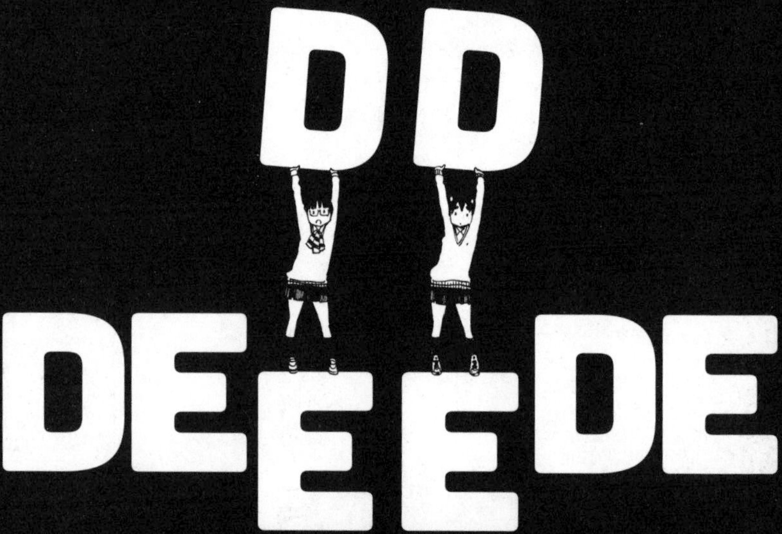
DD
DEEEDE

CHAPTER 21

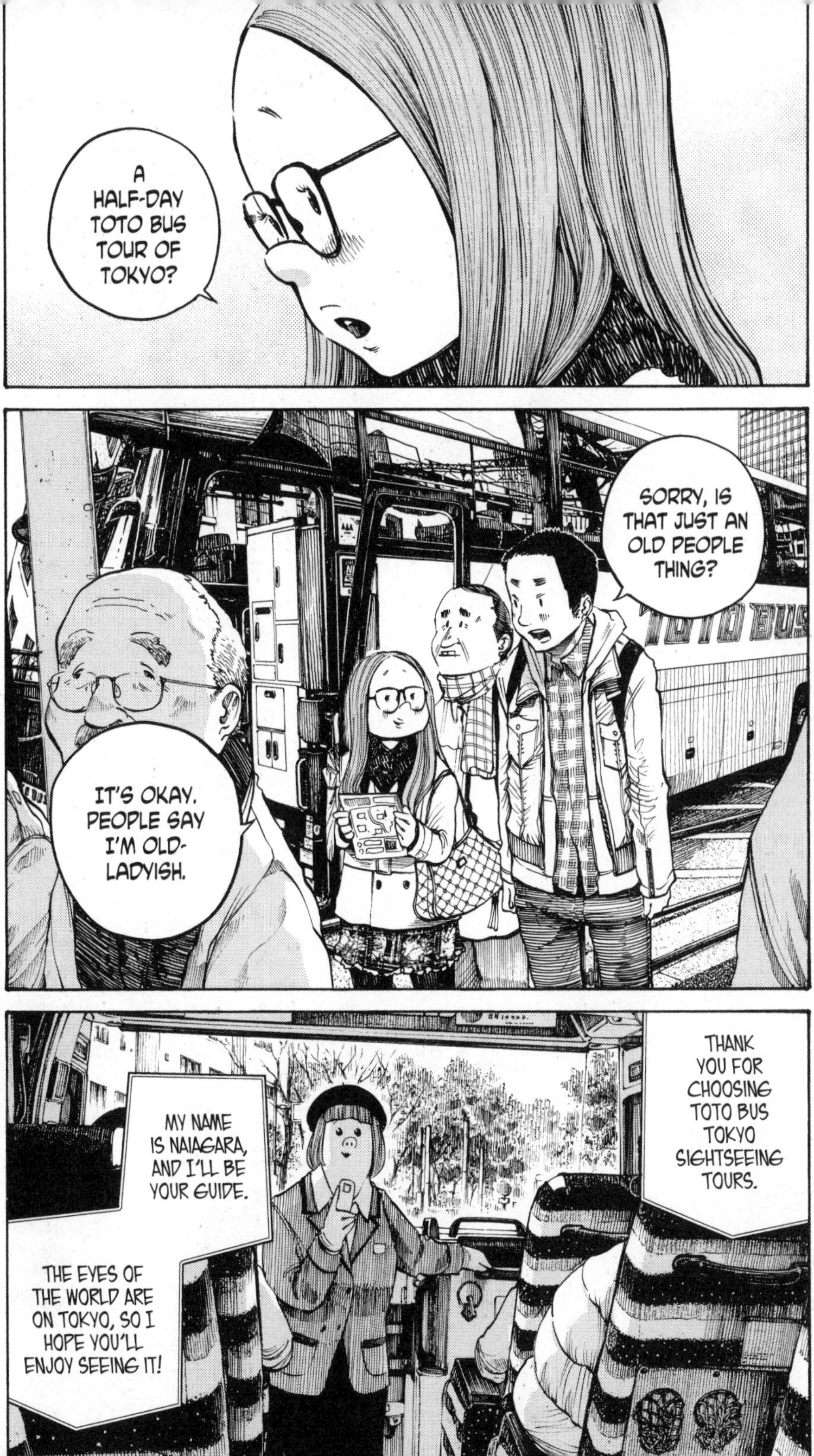
A HALF-DAY TOTO BUS TOUR OF TOKYO?
SORRY, IS THAT JUST AN OLD PEOPLE THING?
TOTO BUS
IT'S OKAY. PEOPLE SAY I'M OLD-LADYISH.
THANK YOU FOR CHOOSING TOTO BUS TOKYO SIGHTSEEING TOURS.
MY NAME IS NAIAGARA, AND I'LL BE YOUR GUIDE.
THE EYES OF THE WORLD ARE ON TOKYO, SO I HOPE YOU'LL ENJOY SEEING IT!

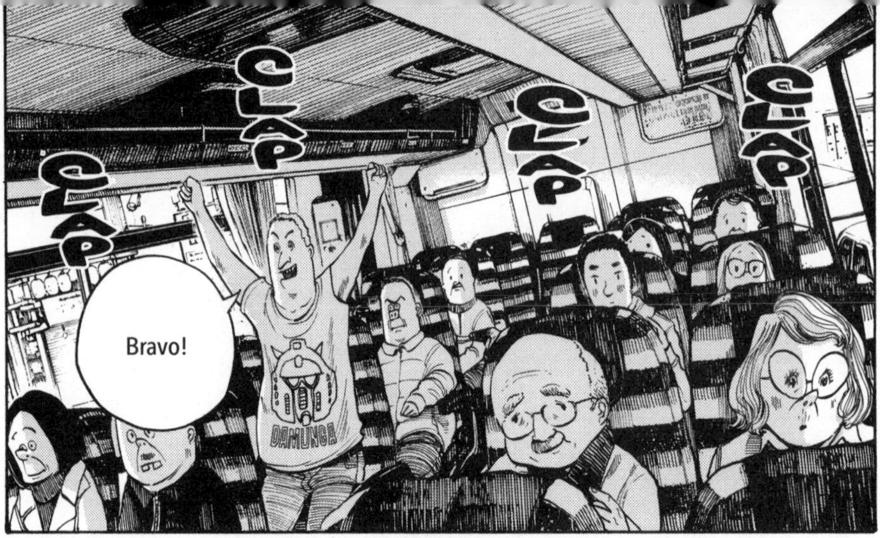
CLAP
CLAP
CLAP
CLAP
Bravo!

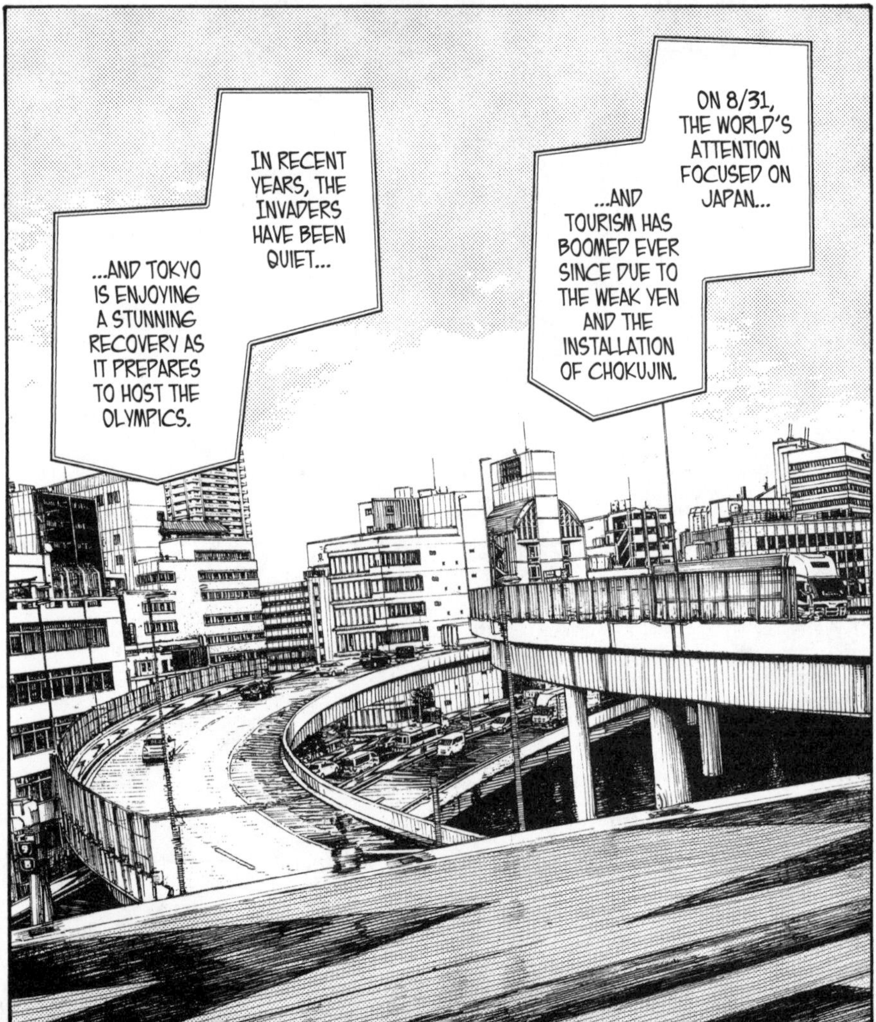
ON 8/31, THE WORLD'S ATTENTION FOCUSED ON JAPAN...
...AND TOURISM HAS BOOMED EVER SINCE DUE TO THE WEAK YEN AND THE INSTALLATION OF CHOKUJIN.
IN RECENT YEARS, THE INVADERS HAVE BEEN QUIET...
...AND TOKYO IS ENJOYING A STUNNING RECOVERY AS IT PREPARES TO HOST THE OLYMPICS.

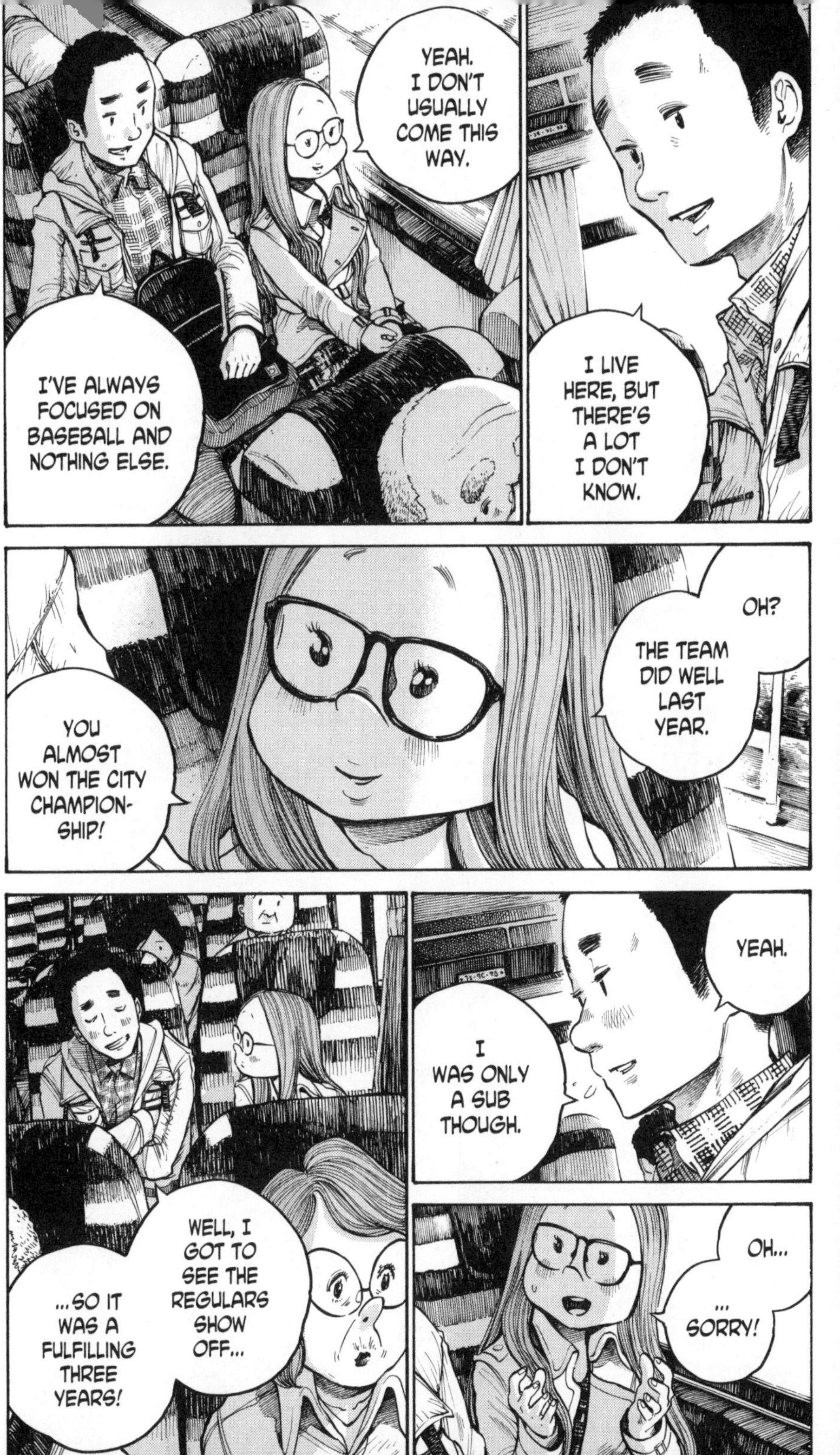
I LIVE HERE, BUT THERE'S A LOT I DON'T KNOW.
YEAH. I DON'T USUALLY COME THIS WAY.
I'VE ALWAYS FOCUSED ON BASEBALL AND NOTHING ELSE.
OH?
THE TEAM DID WELL LAST YEAR.
YOU ALMOST WON THE CITY CHAMPION-SHIP!
YEAH.
I WAS ONLY A SUB THOUGH.
OH...
... SORRY!
WELL, I GOT TO SEE THE REGULARS SHOW OFF...
...SO IT WAS A FULFILLING THREE YEARS!

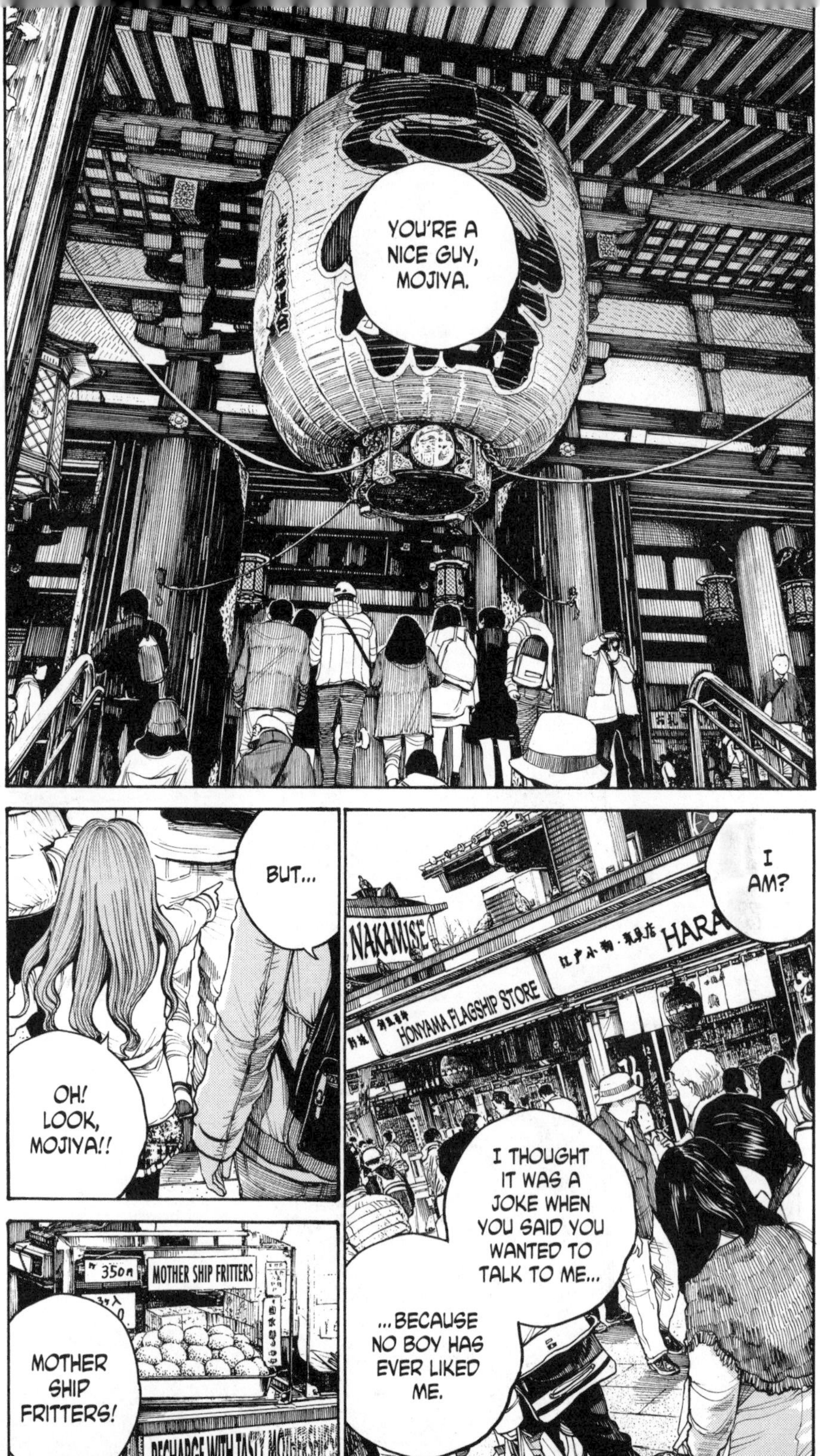
YOU'RE A NICE GUY, MOJIYA.
I AM?
NAKAMISE
HONYAMA FLAGSHIP STORE
I THOUGHT IT WAS A JOKE WHEN YOU SAID YOU WANTED TO TALK TO ME...
...BECAUSE NO BOY HAS EVER LIKED ME.
BUT...
OH! LOOK, MOJIYA!!
MOTHER SHIP FRITTERS
MOTHER SHIP FRITTERS!
RECHARGE WITH TASTY

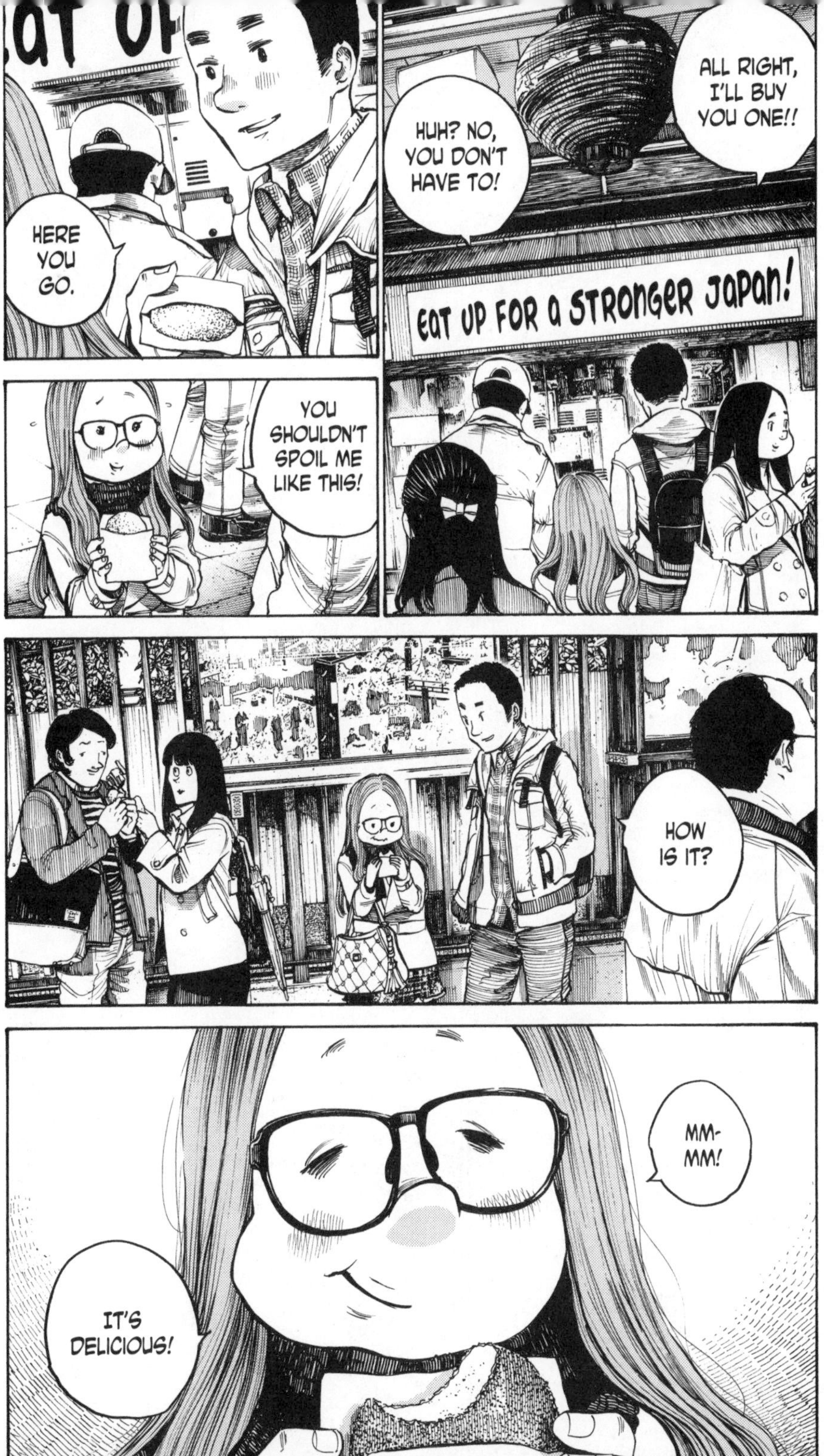
ALL RIGHT, I'LL BUY YOU ONE!!
HUH? NO, YOU DON'T HAVE TO!
EAT UP FOR A STRONGER JAPAN!
HERE YOU GO.
YOU SHOULDN'T SPOIL ME LIKE THIS!
HOW IS IT?
MM-MM!
IT'S DELICIOUS!

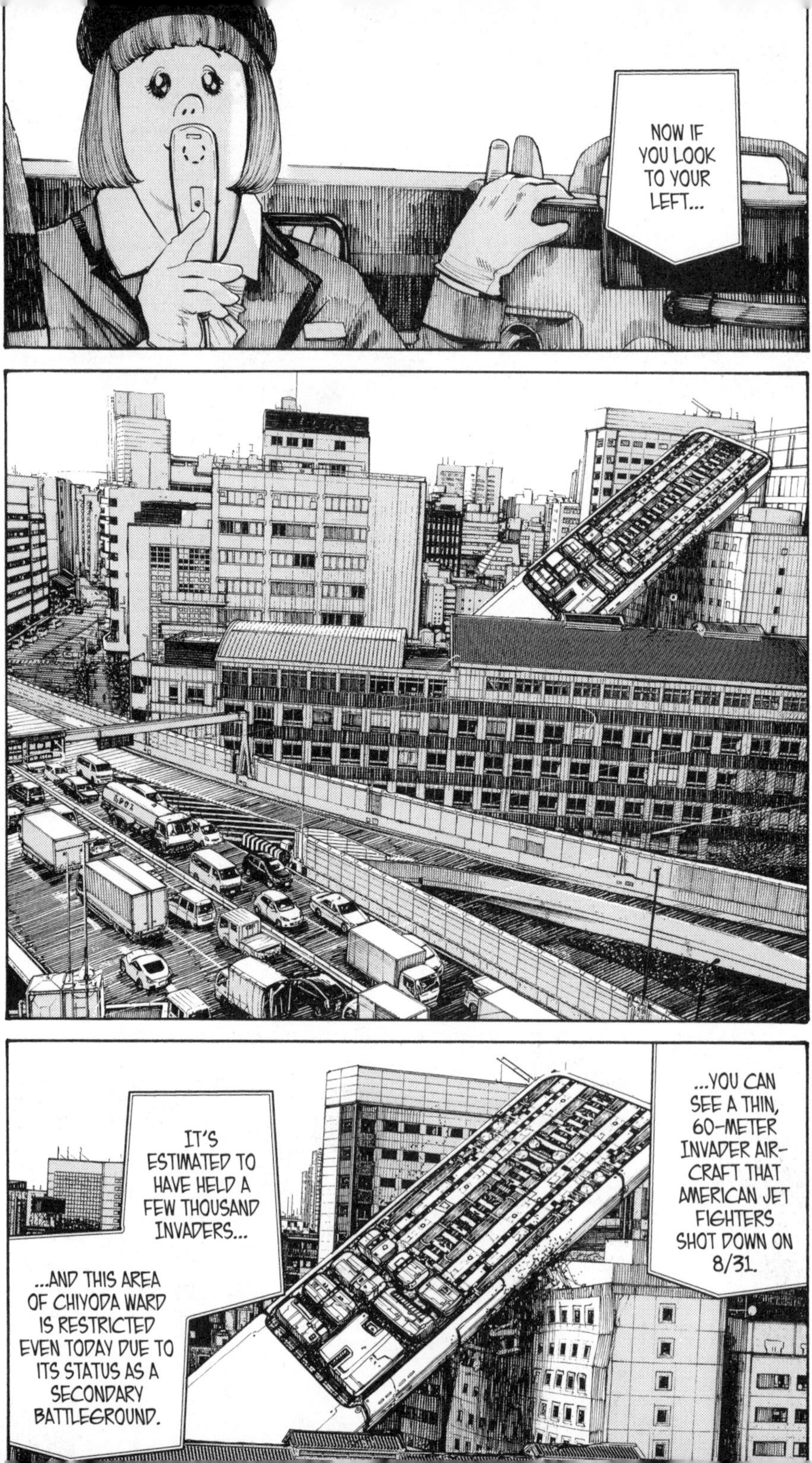
NOW IF YOU LOOK TO YOUR LEFT...
...YOU CAN SEE A THIN, 60-METER INVADER AIR-CRAFT THAT AMERICAN JET FIGHTERS SHOT DOWN ON 8/31.
IT'S ESTIMATED TO HAVE HELD A FEW THOUSAND INVADERS...
...AND THIS AREA OF CHIYODA WARD IS RESTRICTED EVEN TODAY DUE TO ITS STATUS AS A SECONDARY BATTLEGROUND.

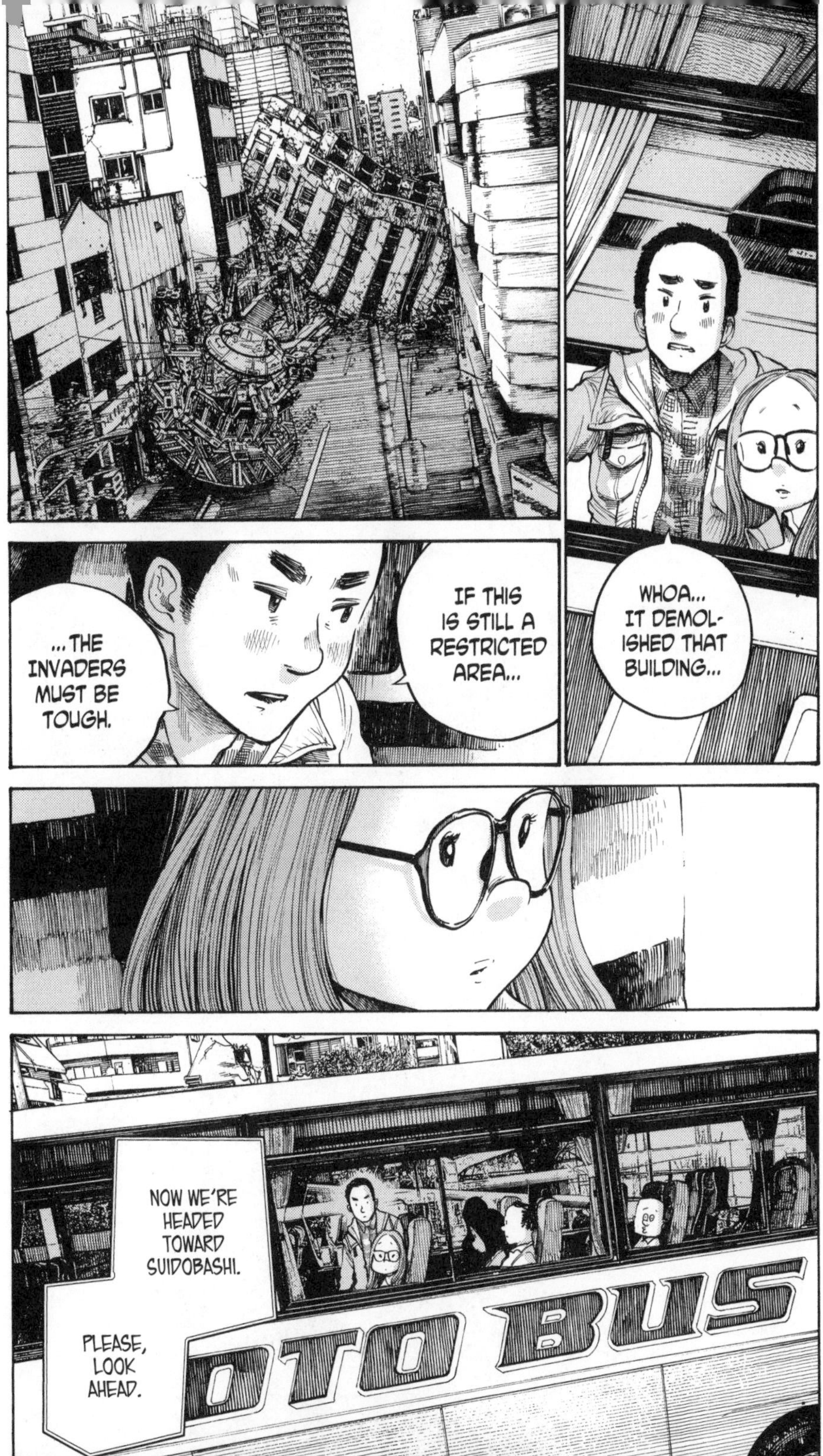
WHOA... IT DEMOL-ISHED THAT BUILDING...
IF THIS IS STILL A RESTRICTED AREA...
...THE INVADERS MUST BE TOUGH.
NOW WE'RE HEADED TOWARD SUIDOBASHI.
PLEASE, LOOK AHEAD.
OTO BUS

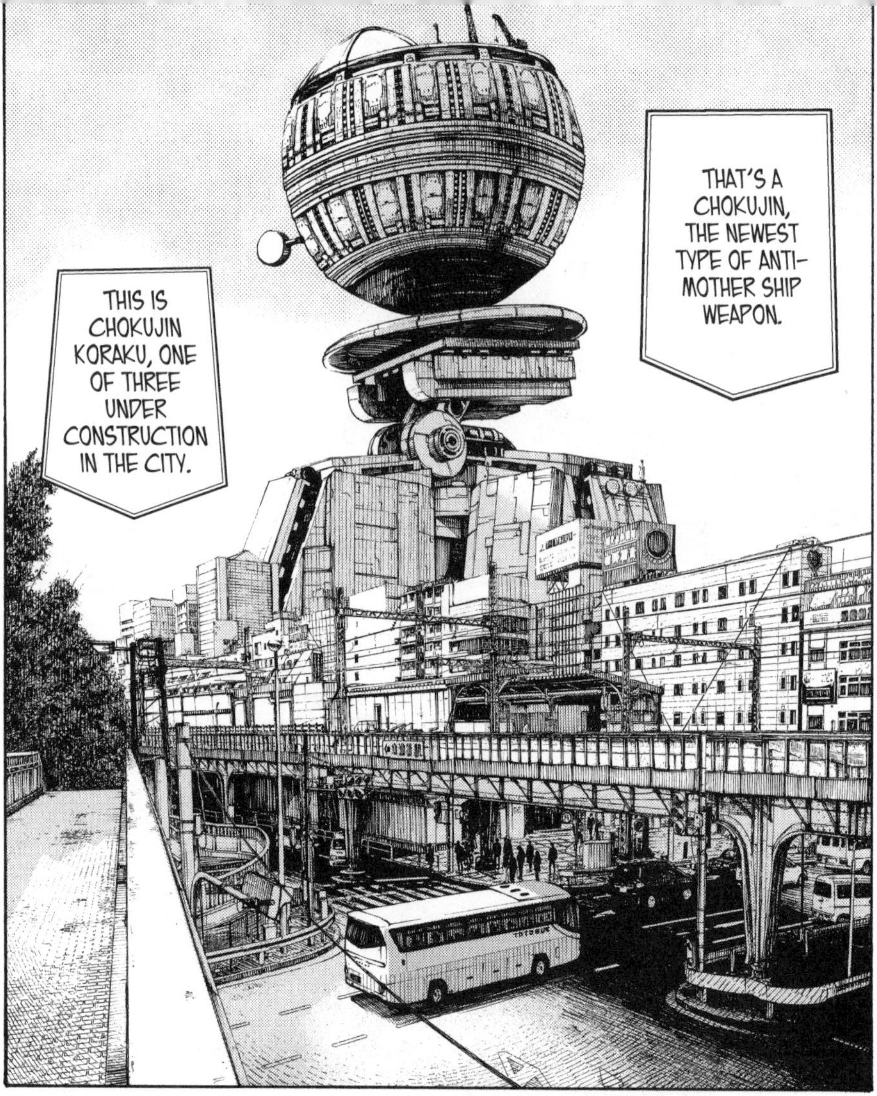
THAT'S A CHOKUJIN, THE NEWEST TYPE OF ANTI-MOTHER SHIP WEAPON.
THIS IS CHOKUJIN KORAKU, ONE OF THREE UNDER CONSTRUCTION IN THE CITY.

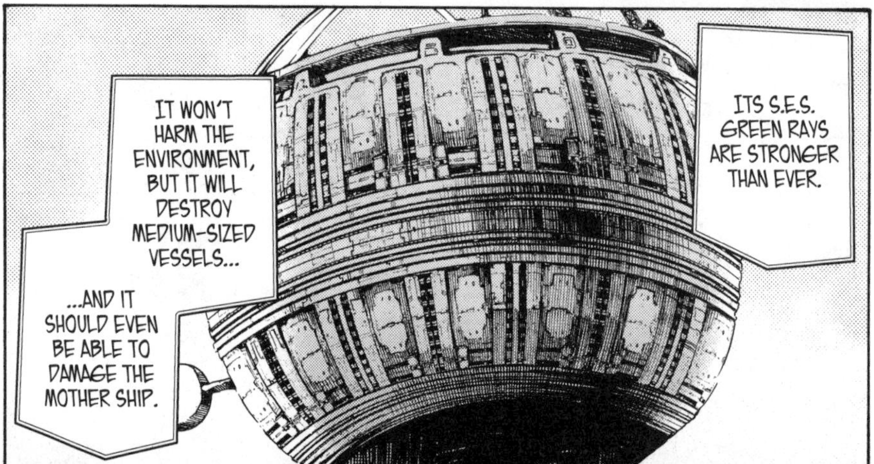
ITS S.E.S. GREEN RAYS ARE STRONGER THAN EVER.
IT WON'T HARM THE ENVIRONMENT, BUT IT WILL DESTROY MEDIUM-SIZED VESSELS...
...AND IT SHOULD EVEN BE ABLE TO DAMAGE THE MOTHER SHIP.

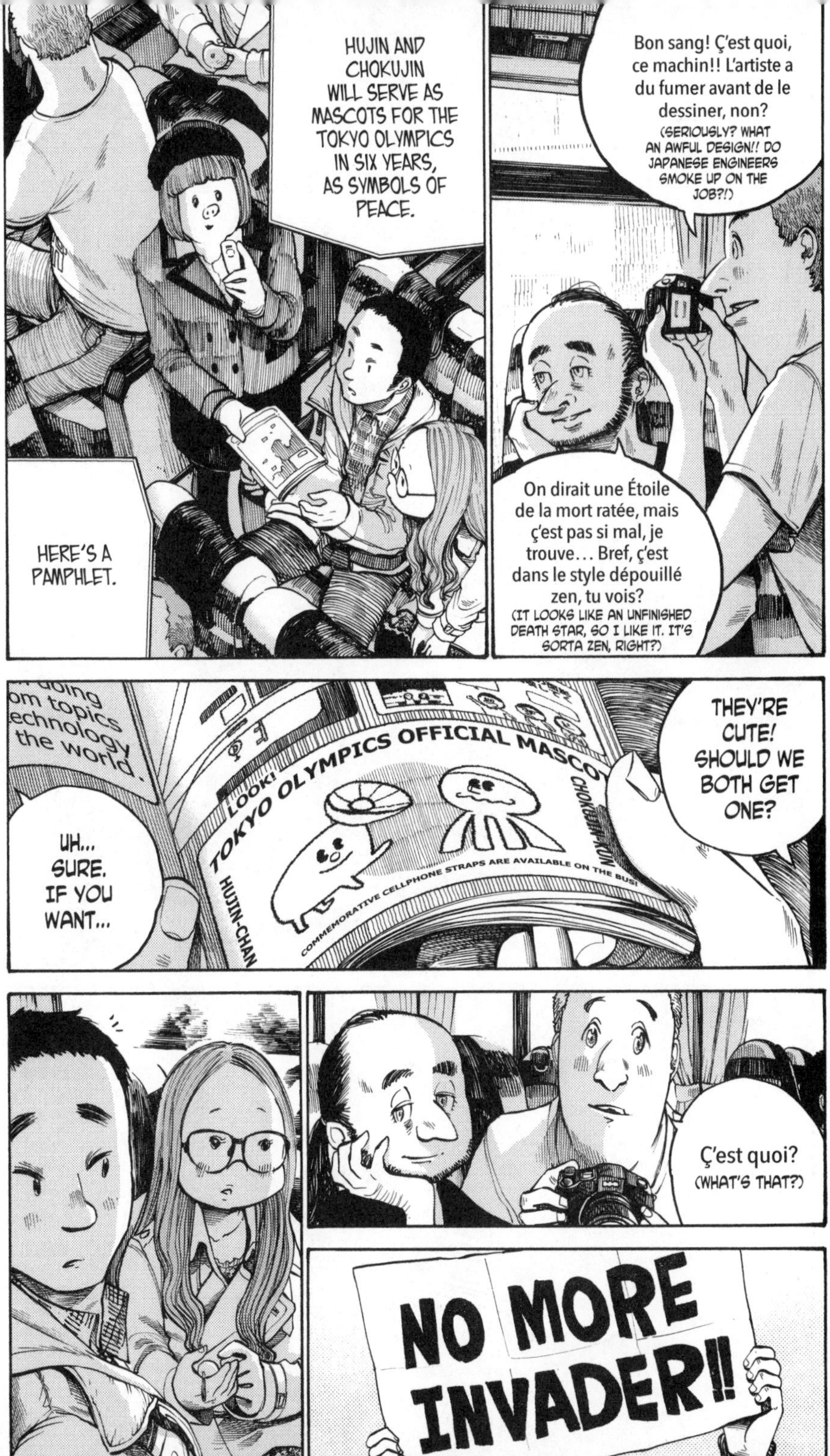
Bon sang! Ç'est quoi, ce machin!! L'artiste a du fumer avant de le dessiner, non?
(SERIOUSLY? WHAT AN AWFUL DESIGN!! DO JAPANESE ENGINEERS SMOKE UP ON THE JOB?!)
On dirait une Étoile de la mort ratée, mais ç'est pas si mal, je trouve… Bref, ç'est dans le style dépouillé zen, tu vois?
(IT LOOKS LIKE AN UNFINISHED DEATH STAR, SO I LIKE IT. IT'S SORTA ZEN, RIGHT?)
HUJIN AND CHOKUJIN WILL SERVE AS MASCOTS FOR THE TOKYO OLYMPICS IN SIX YEARS, AS SYMBOLS OF PEACE.
HERE'S A PAMPHLET.
THEY'RE CUTE! SHOULD WE BOTH GET ONE?
LOOK!
TOKYO OLYMPICS OFFICIAL MASCO
COMMEMORATIVE CELLPHONE STRAPS ARE AVAILABLE ON THE BUS!
HUJIN-CHAN
UH... SURE. IF YOU WANT...
Ç'est quoi?
(WHAT'S THAT?)
NO MORE INVADER!!

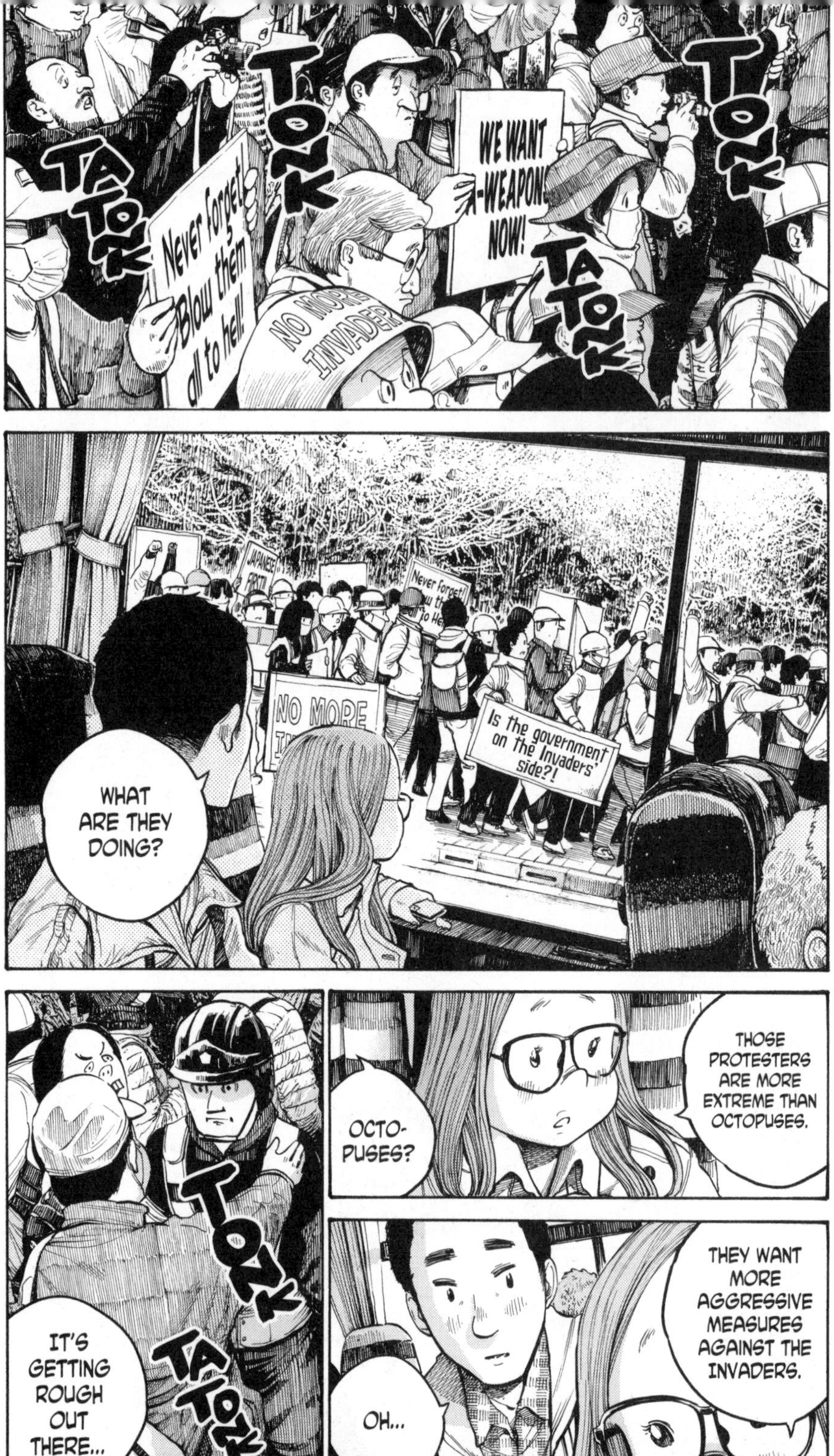
TONK
TONK
WE WANT A-WEAPONS NOW!
TATONK
Never forget! Blow them all to hell!
NO MORE INVADER
TATONK
JAPANESE FIRST!!
Never forget!
NO MORE
Is the government on the Invaders' side?!
WHAT ARE THEY DOING?
THOSE PROTESTERS ARE MORE EXTREME THAN OCTOPUSES.
OCTO-PUSES?
THEY WANT MORE AGGRESSIVE MEASURES AGAINST THE INVADERS.
OH...
TONK
TATONK
IT'S GETTING ROUGH OUT THERE...

SAVE OUR CHILDREN FROM THE [...]ERS!!

FOR A BRIGHT FUTURE!

[...]ERS GO HOME!

WE WANT WEAPONS [...]

DOWN WITH A GOVERNMENT THAT SACRIFICES ITS PEOPLE!!

STOP WEAPONIZ[...] OF OUR [...]

[...]ANT [...] JAPAN FIRST!!

[...]ORE NO MORE [...]DERI INVAD[...]

IS THE GOVERNMENT ON THE INVADER[...]?!

GRAH

TONK TA TONK

GRAH

TONK TA TONK

GRAH

OH...

[...]WN WITH A GOVERNMENT
THAT SACRIFICES [...]

IT'S TOO BAD ABOUT KURIHARA.

YOU GIRLS ALWAYS LOOKED LIKE YOU WERE HAVING FUN.

THAT PHOTO IS FROM OUR GRADUATION TRIP. I WONDER WHO GAVE IT TO THEM?

YEAH...

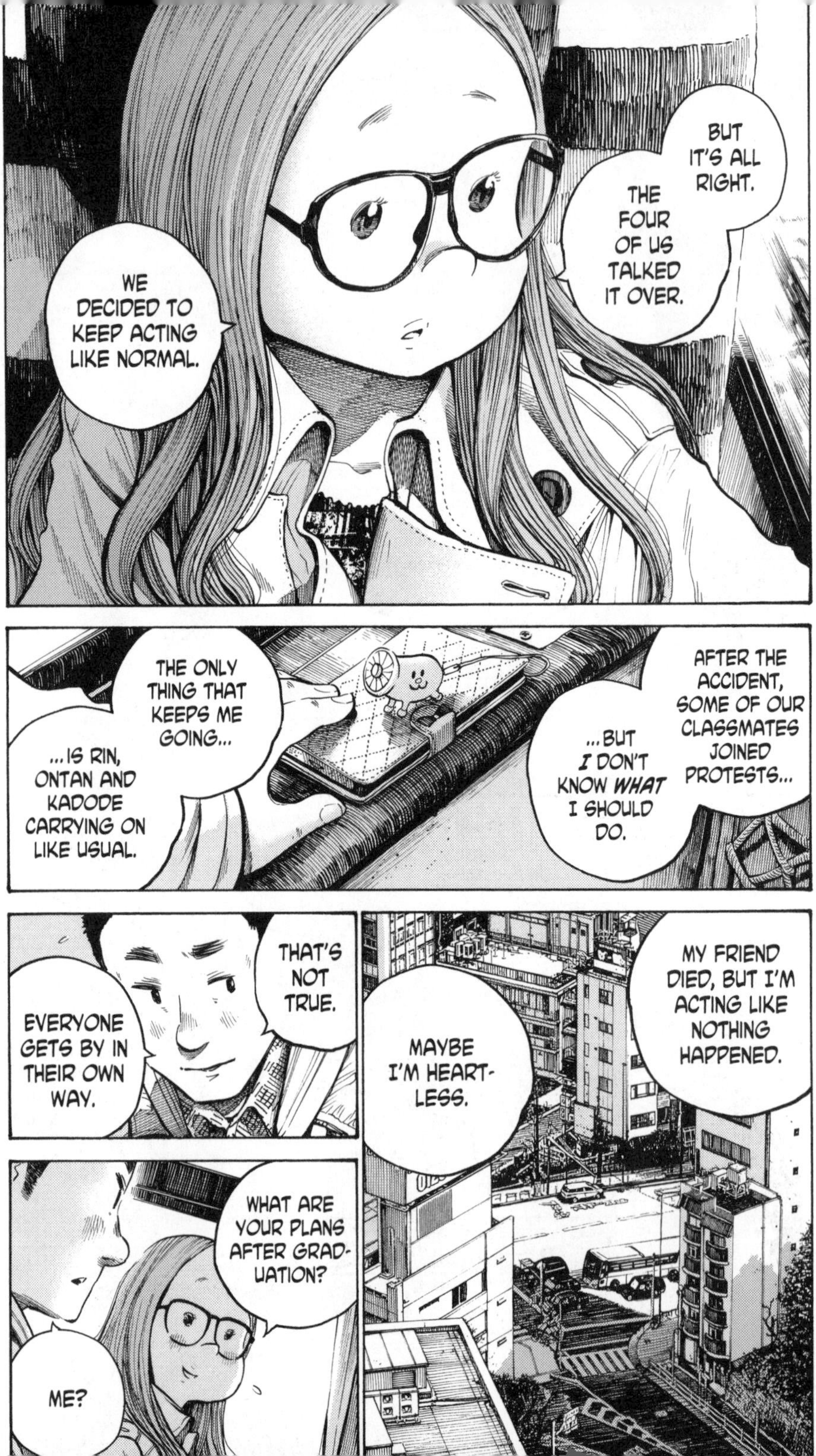
BUT IT'S ALL RIGHT.
THE FOUR OF US TALKED IT OVER.
WE DECIDED TO KEEP ACTING LIKE NORMAL.
AFTER THE ACCIDENT, SOME OF OUR CLASSMATES JOINED PROTESTS...
...BUT *I* DON'T KNOW *WHAT* I SHOULD DO.
THE ONLY THING THAT KEEPS ME GOING...
...IS RIN, ONTAN AND KADODE CARRYING ON LIKE USUAL.
MY FRIEND DIED, BUT I'M ACTING LIKE NOTHING HAPPENED.
MAYBE I'M HEART-LESS.
THAT'S NOT TRUE.
EVERYONE GETS BY IN THEIR OWN WAY.
WHAT ARE YOUR PLANS AFTER GRAD-UATION?
ME?

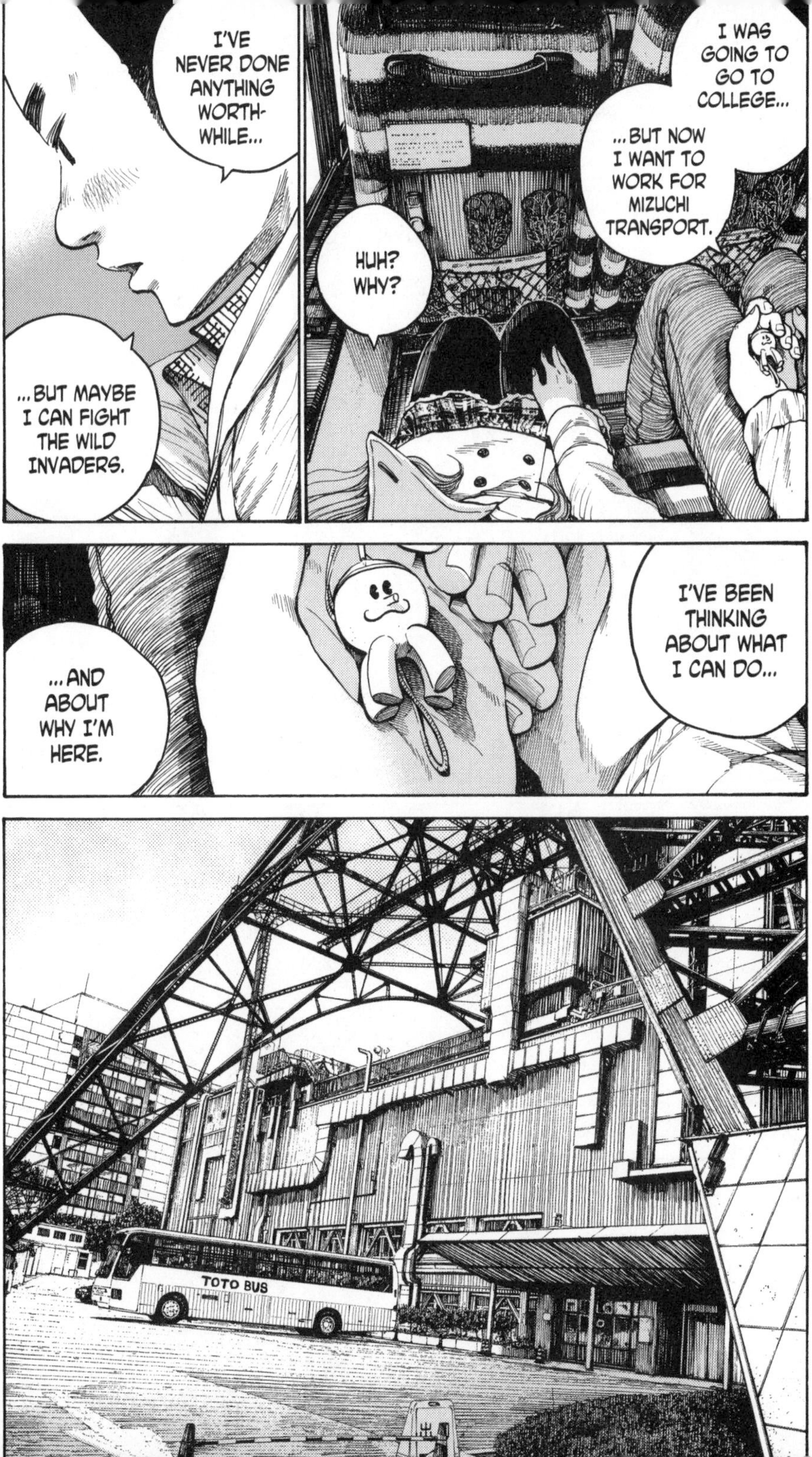
I WAS GOING TO GO TO COLLEGE...
...BUT NOW I WANT TO WORK FOR MIZUCHI TRANSPORT.
HUH? WHY?
I'VE NEVER DONE ANYTHING WORTH-WHILE...
...BUT MAYBE I CAN FIGHT THE WILD INVADERS.
I'VE BEEN THINKING ABOUT WHAT I CAN DO...
...AND ABOUT WHY I'M HERE.
TOTO BUS

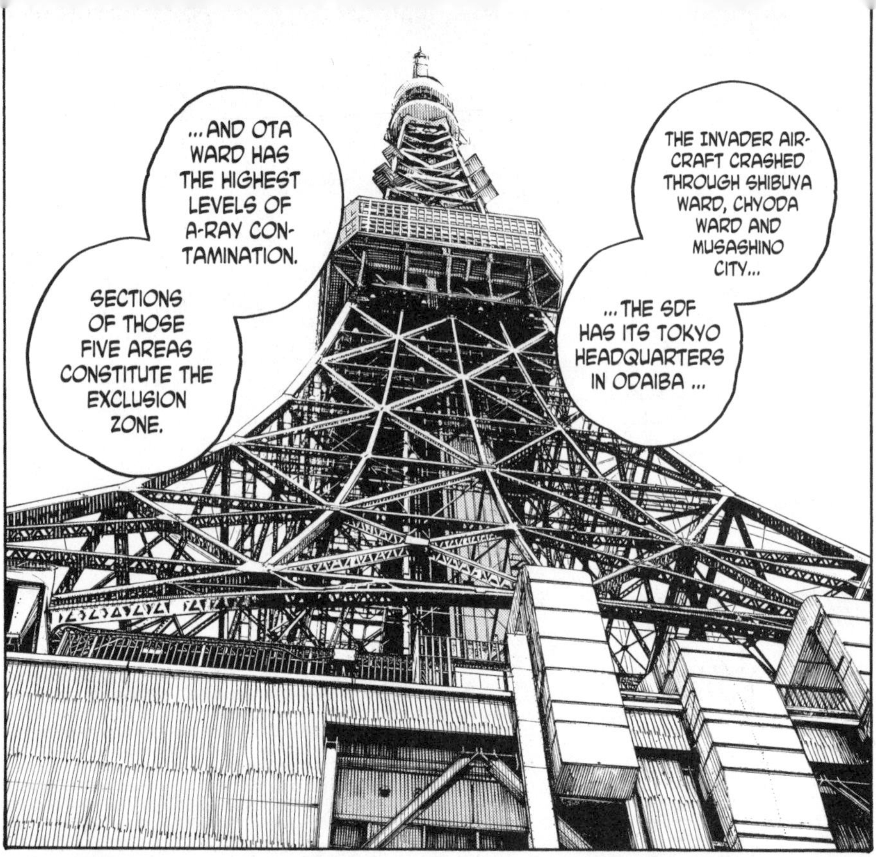
THE INVADER AIR-CRAFT CRASHED THROUGH SHIBUYA WARD, CHYODA WARD AND MUSASHINO CITY...
...THE SDF HAS ITS TOKYO HEADQUARTERS IN ODAIBA ...
...AND OTA WARD HAS THE HIGHEST LEVELS OF A-RAY CON-TAMINATION.
SECTIONS OF THOSE FIVE AREAS CONSTITUTE THE EXCLUSION ZONE.

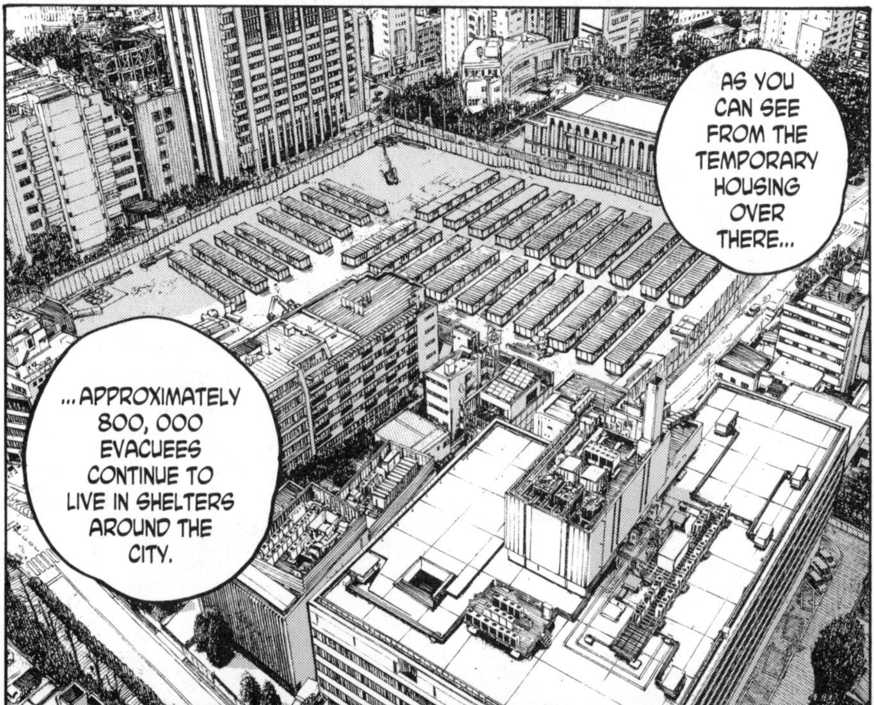
AS YOU CAN SEE FROM THE TEMPORARY HOUSING OVER THERE...
...APPROXIMATELY 800, 000 EVACUEES CONTINUE TO LIVE IN SHELTERS AROUND THE CITY.

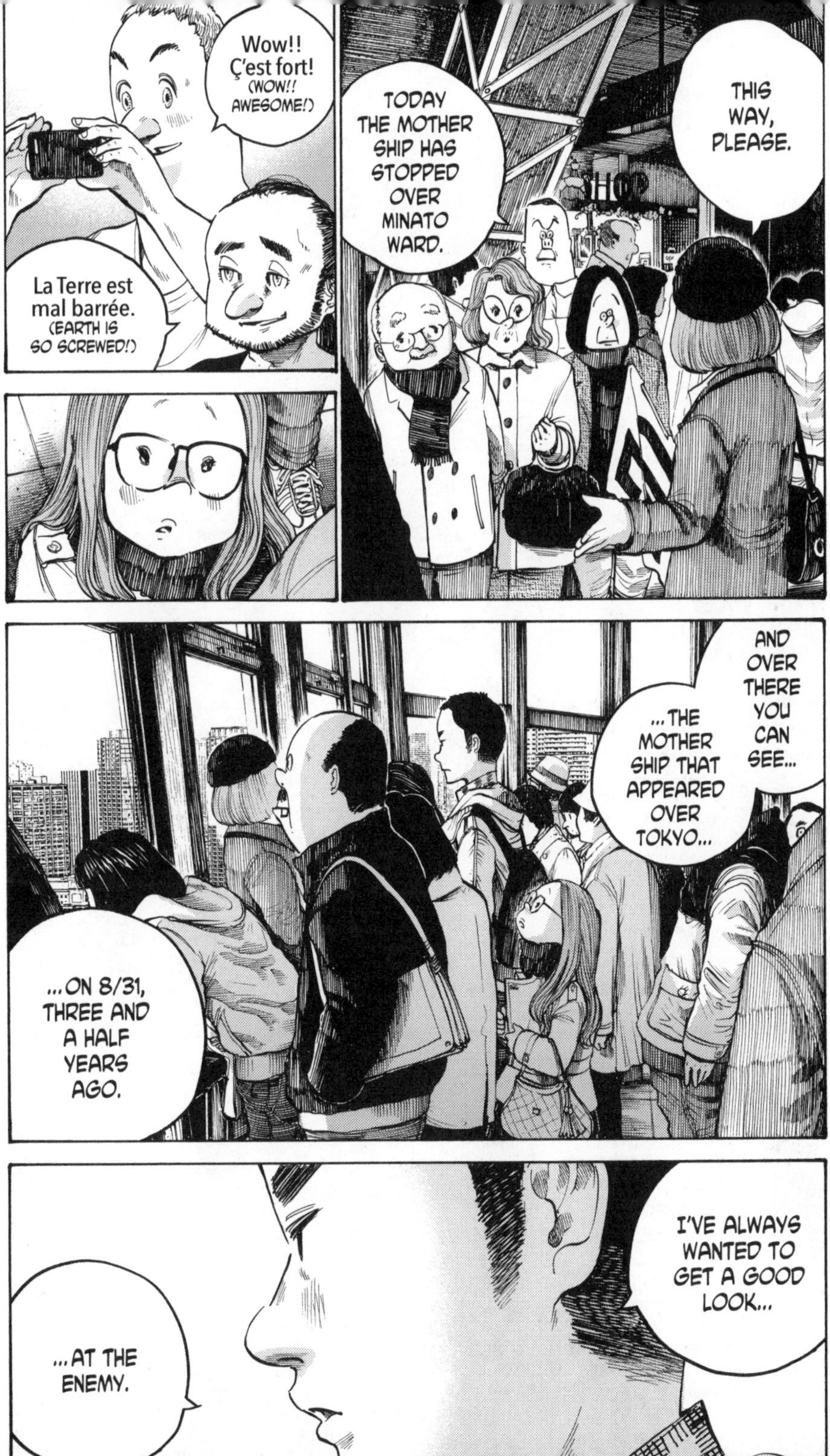
THIS WAY, PLEASE.
TODAY THE MOTHER SHIP HAS STOPPED OVER MINATO WARD.
Wow!! Ç'est fort! (WOW!! AWESOME!)
La Terre est mal barrée. (EARTH IS SO SCREWED!)
AND OVER THERE YOU CAN SEE...
...THE MOTHER SHIP THAT APPEARED OVER TOKYO...
...ON 8/31, THREE AND A HALF YEARS AGO.
I'VE ALWAYS WANTED TO GET A GOOD LOOK...
...AT THE ENEMY.

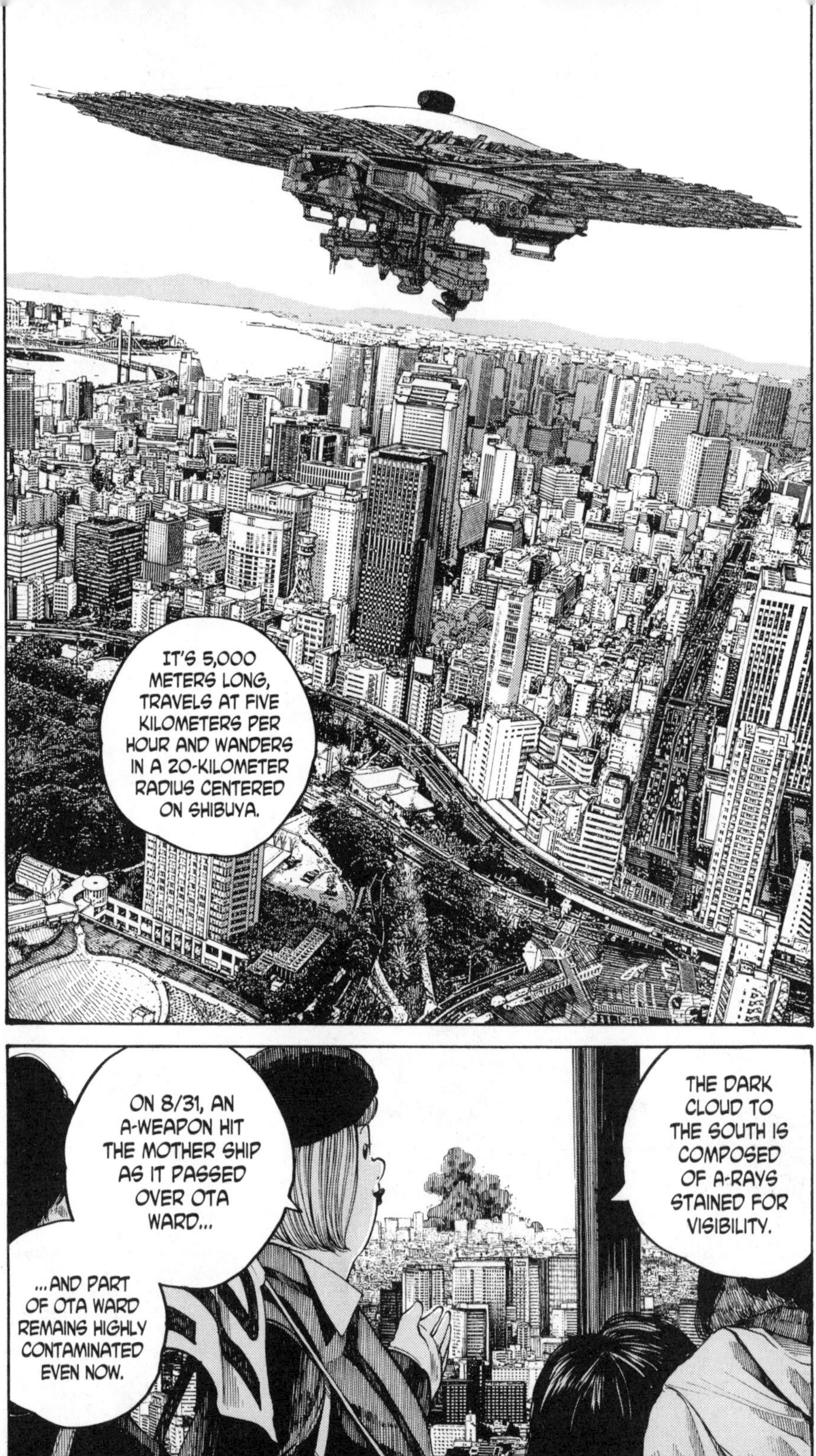
IT'S 5,000 METERS LONG, TRAVELS AT FIVE KILOMETERS PER HOUR AND WANDERS IN A 20-KILOMETER RADIUS CENTERED ON SHIBUYA.
THE DARK CLOUD TO THE SOUTH IS COMPOSED OF A-RAYS STAINED FOR VISIBILITY.
ON 8/31, AN A-WEAPON HIT THE MOTHER SHIP AS IT PASSED OVER OTA WARD...
...AND PART OF OTA WARD REMAINS HIGHLY CONTAMINATED EVEN NOW.

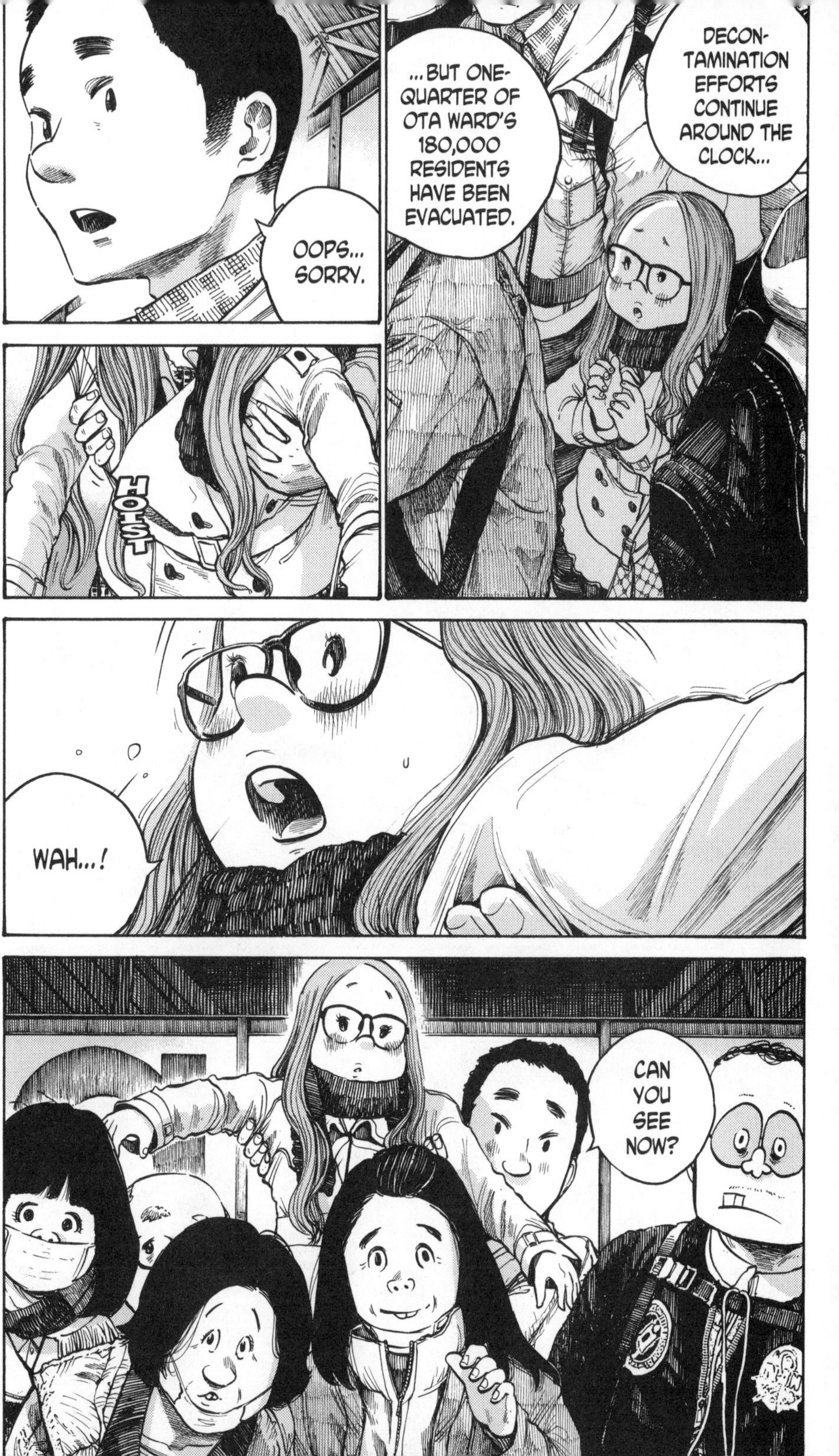
DECON-TAMINATION EFFORTS CONTINUE AROUND THE CLOCK...
...BUT ONE-QUARTER OF OTA WARD'S 180,000 RESIDENTS HAVE BEEN EVACUATED.
OOPS... SORRY.
HOIST
WAH...!
CAN YOU SEE NOW?

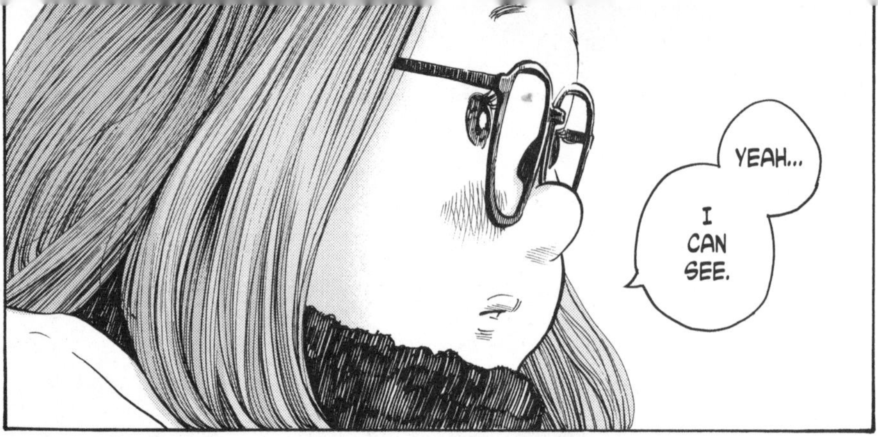
YEAH...
I CAN SEE.

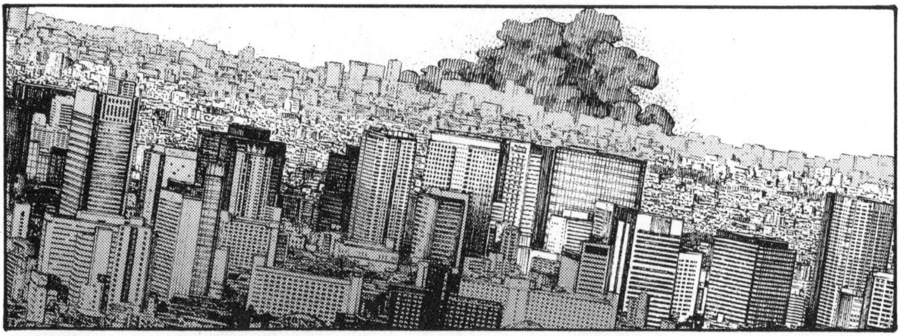

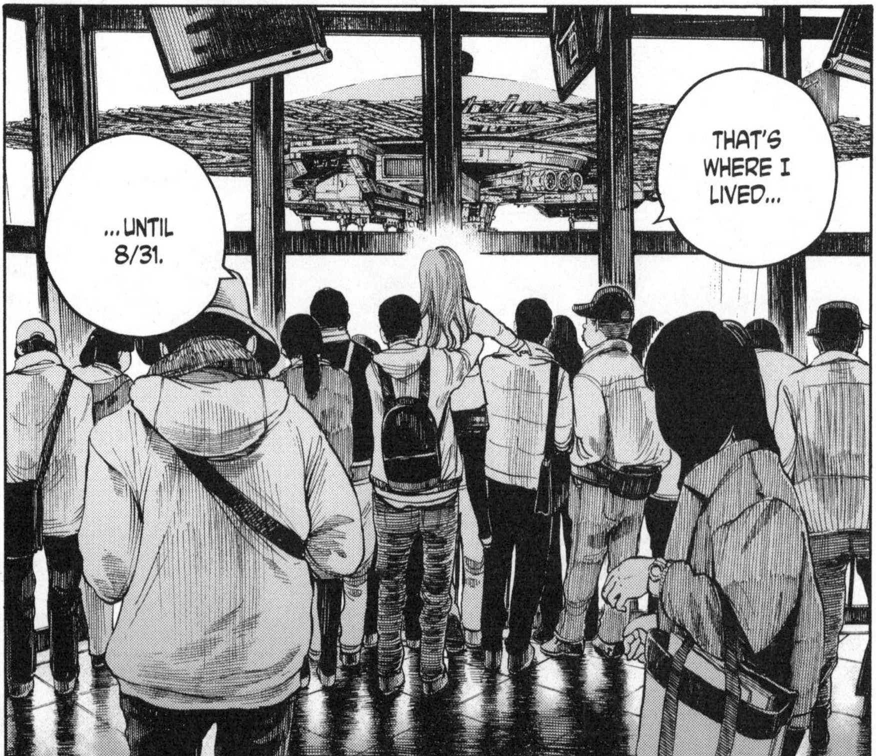
THAT'S WHERE I LIVED...
...UNTIL 8/31.

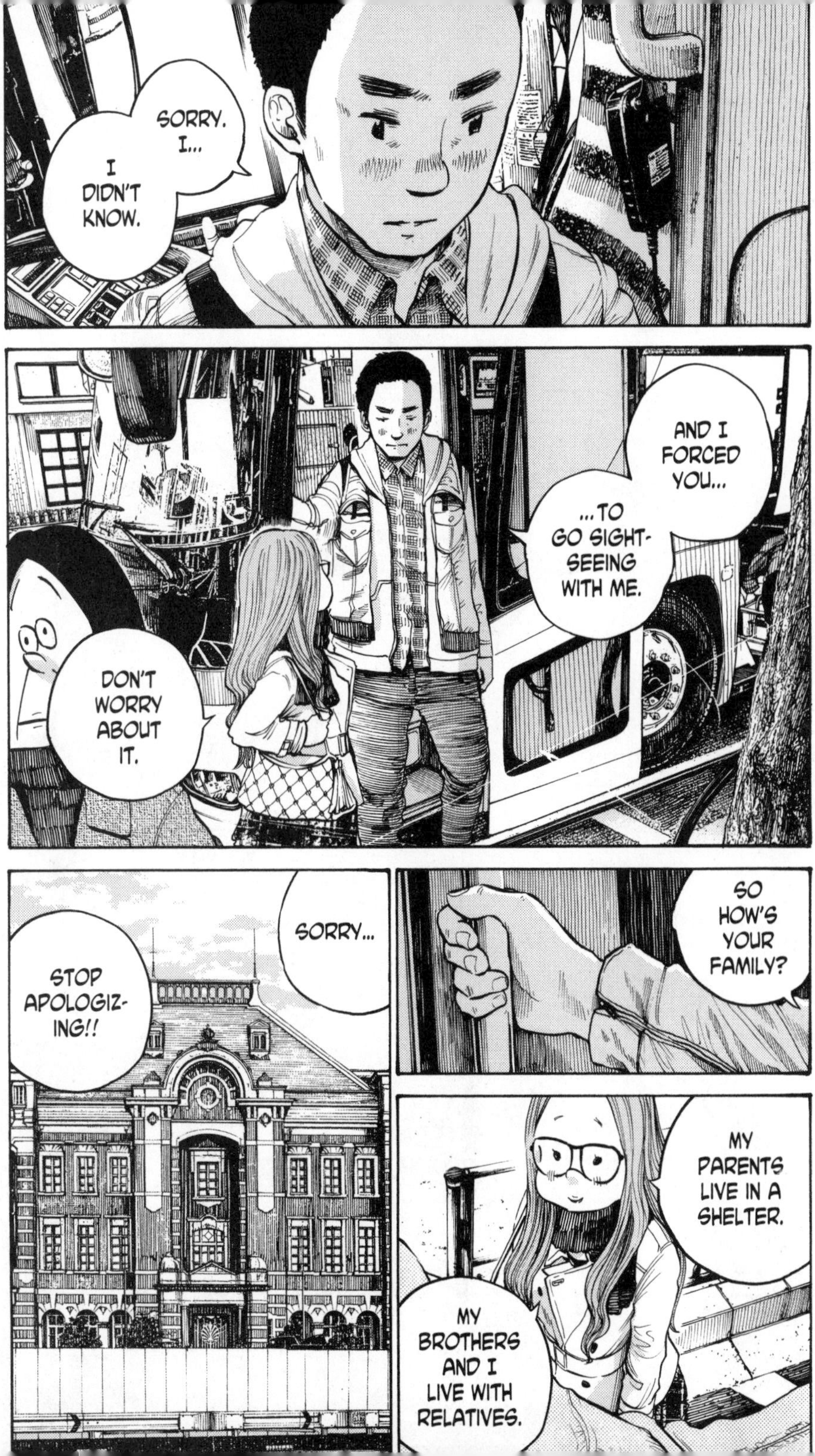
SORRY. I...
I DIDN'T KNOW.
AND I FORCED YOU...
...TO GO SIGHT-SEEING WITH ME.
DON'T WORRY ABOUT IT.
SO HOW'S YOUR FAMILY?
MY PARENTS LIVE IN A SHELTER.
MY BROTHERS AND I LIVE WITH RELATIVES.
SORRY...
STOP APOLOGIZING!!

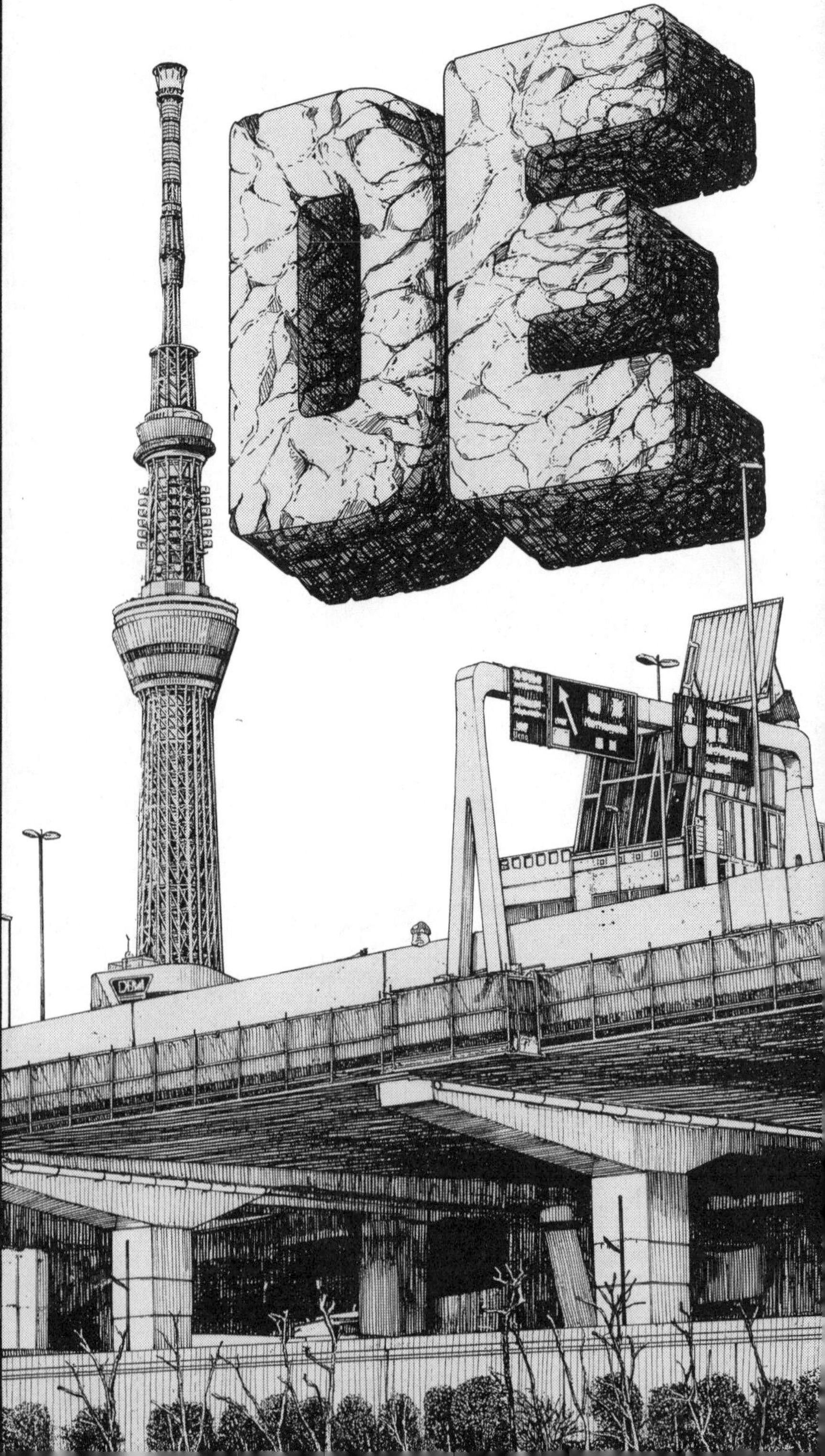

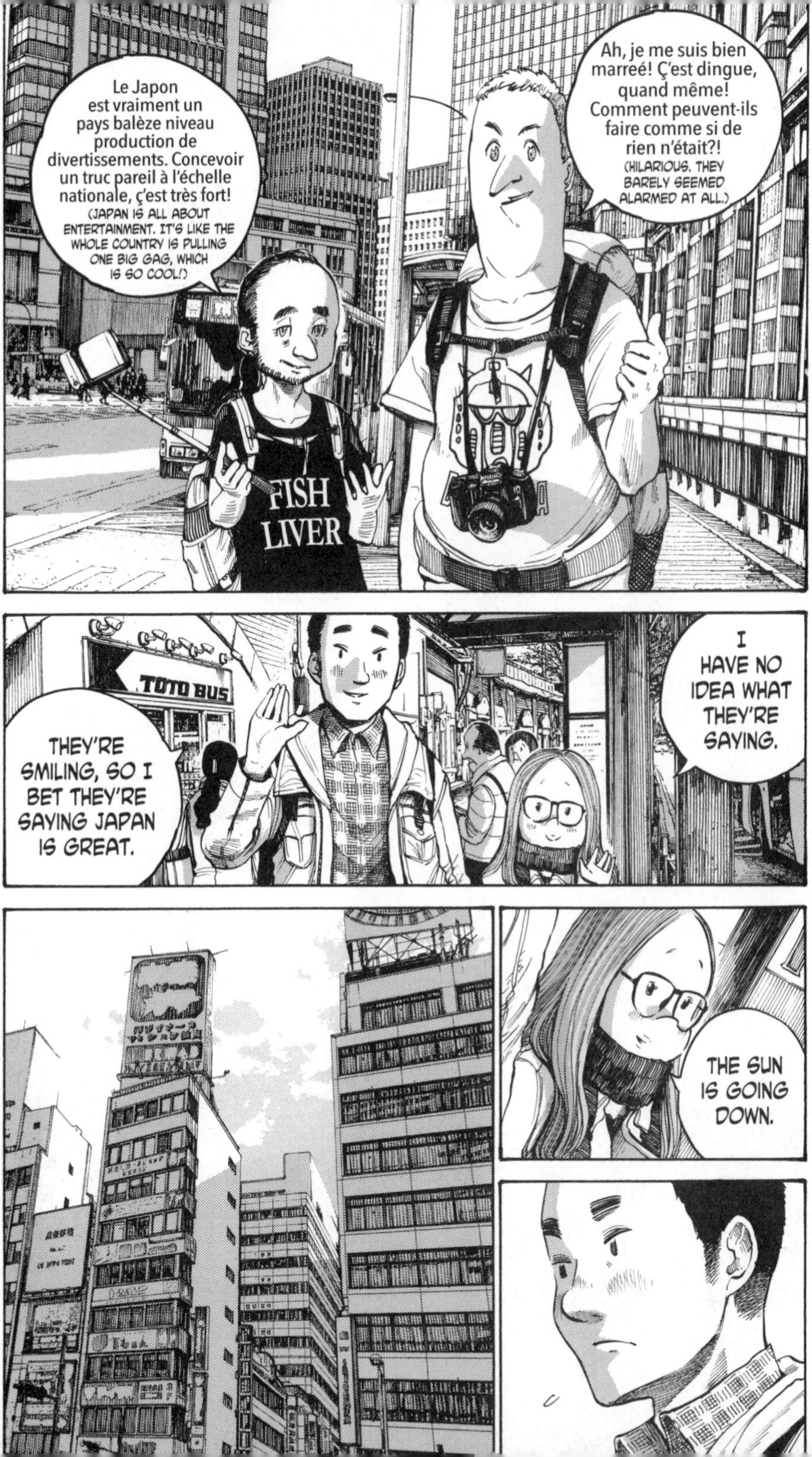
Ah, je me suis bien marreé! Ç'est dingue, quand même! Comment peuvent-ils faire comme si de rien n'était?!
(HILARIOUS. THEY BARELY SEEMED ALARMED AT ALL.)
Le Japon est vraiment un pays balèze niveau production de divertissements. Concevoir un truc pareil à l'échelle nationale, ç'est très fort!
(JAPAN IS ALL ABOUT ENTERTAINMENT. IT'S LIKE THE WHOLE COUNTRY IS PULLING ONE BIG GAG, WHICH IS SO COOL!)
FISH LIVER
I HAVE NO IDEA WHAT THEY'RE SAYING.
TOTO BUS
THEY'RE SMILING, SO I BET THEY'RE SAYING JAPAN IS GREAT.
THE SUN IS GOING DOWN.

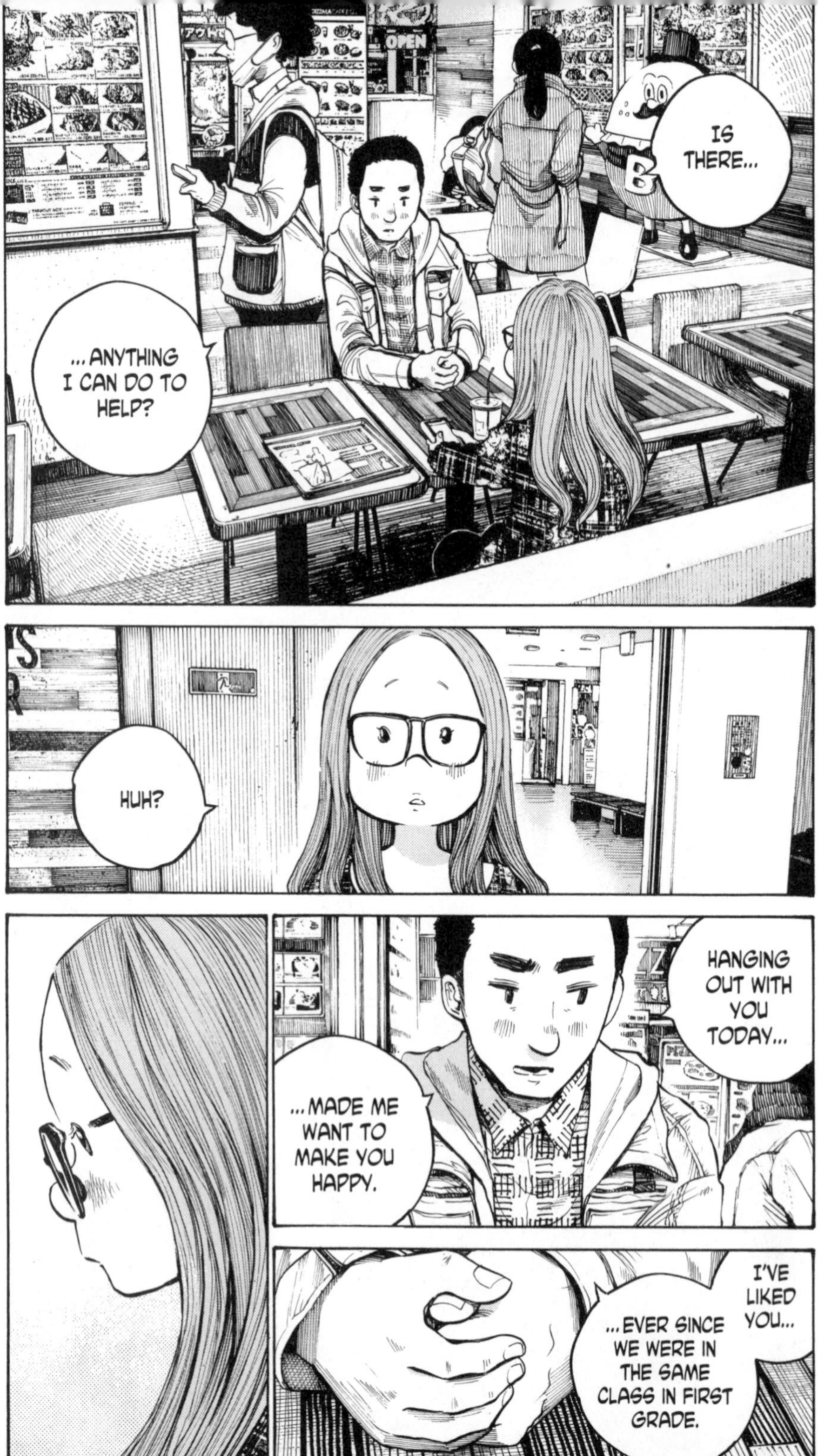
OPEN
IS THERE...
...ANYTHING I CAN DO TO HELP?
HUH?
HANGING OUT WITH YOU TODAY...
...MADE ME WANT TO MAKE YOU HAPPY.
I'VE LIKED YOU...
...EVER SINCE WE WERE IN THE SAME CLASS IN FIRST GRADE.

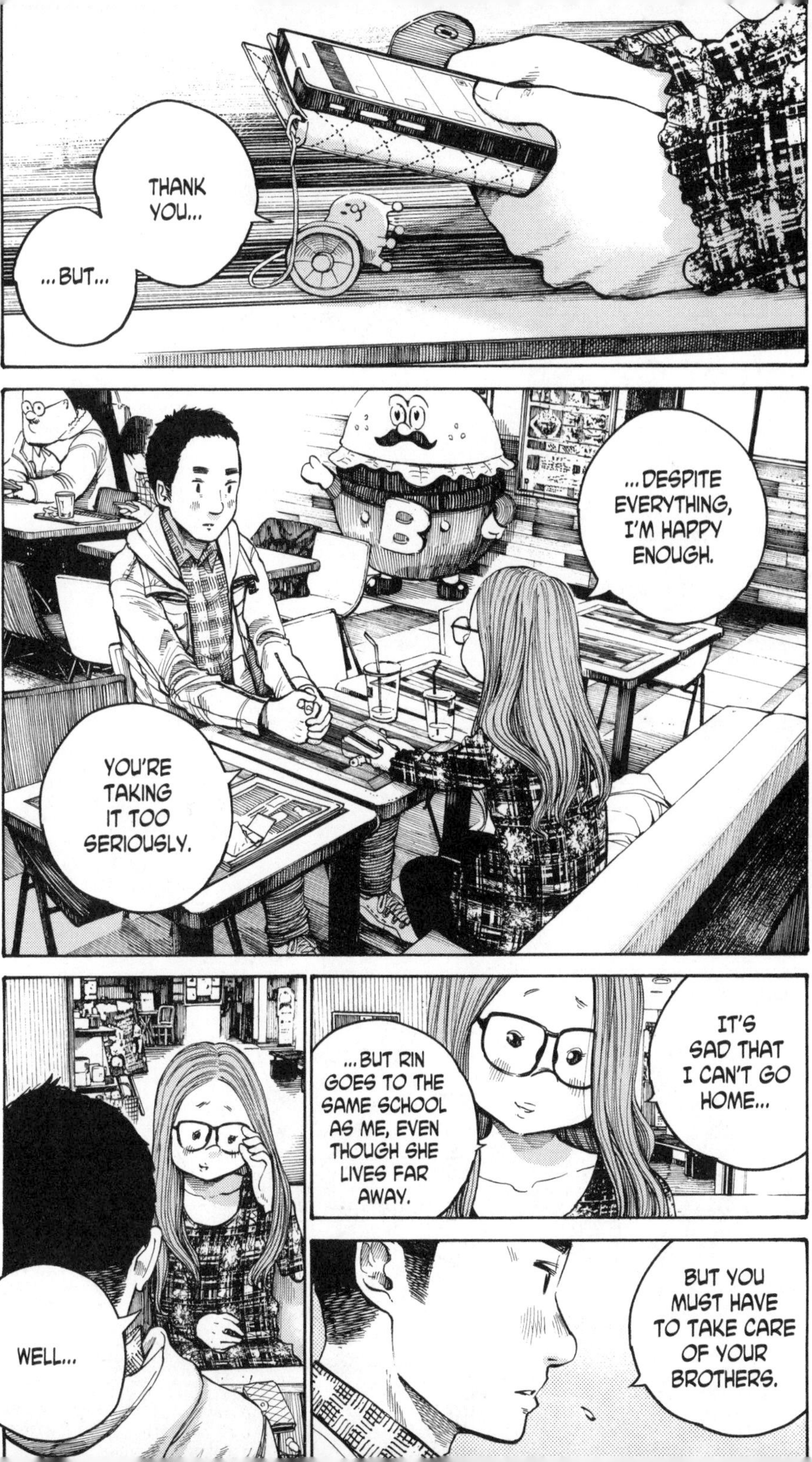
THANK YOU...
...BUT...
...DESPITE EVERYTHING, I'M HAPPY ENOUGH.
YOU'RE TAKING IT TOO SERIOUSLY.
IT'S SAD THAT I CAN'T GO HOME...
...BUT RIN GOES TO THE SAME SCHOOL AS ME, EVEN THOUGH SHE LIVES FAR AWAY.
BUT YOU MUST HAVE TO TAKE CARE OF YOUR BROTHERS.
WELL...

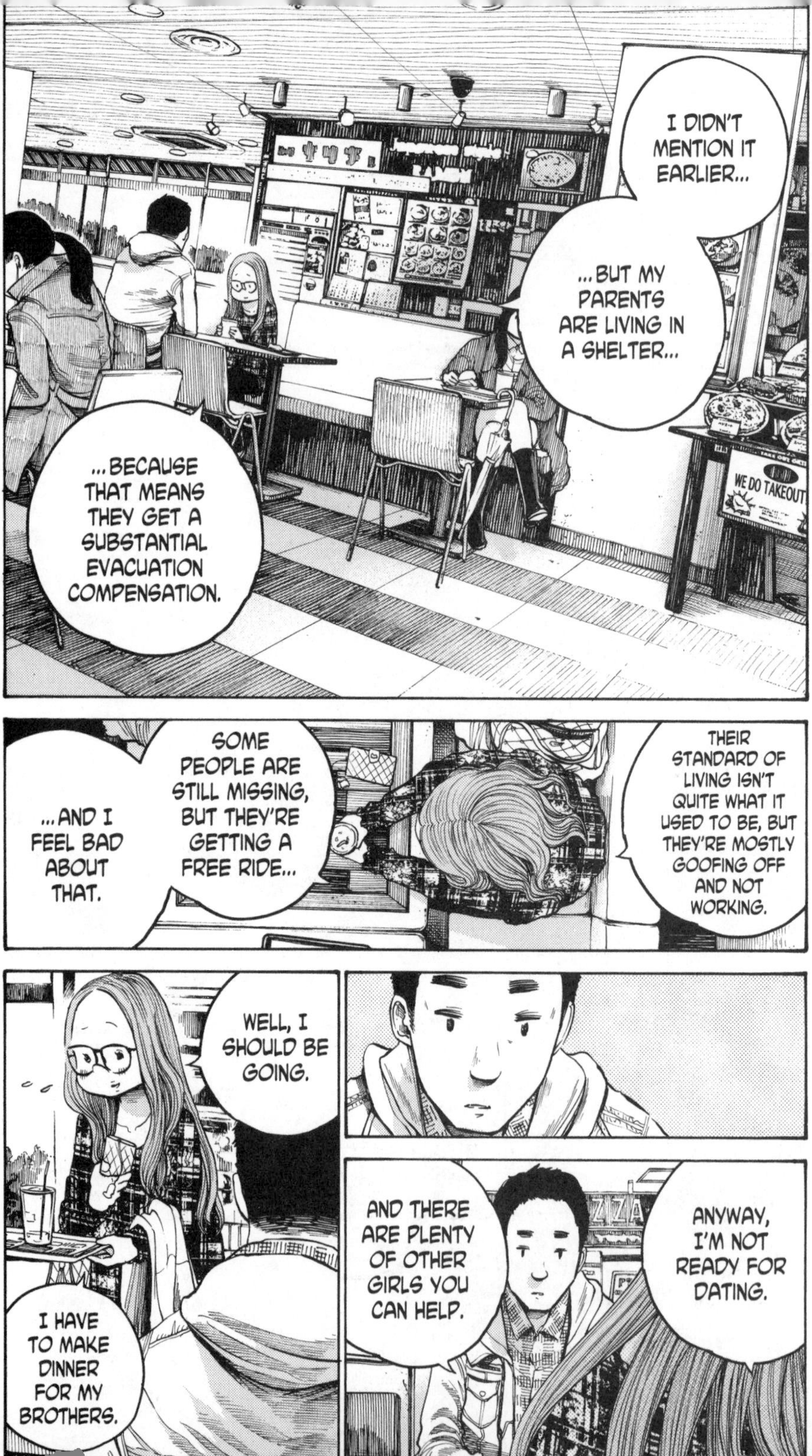
I DIDN'T MENTION IT EARLIER...
...BUT MY PARENTS ARE LIVING IN A SHELTER...
WE DO TAKEOUT
...BECAUSE THAT MEANS THEY GET A SUBSTANTIAL EVACUATION COMPENSATION.
THEIR STANDARD OF LIVING ISN'T QUITE WHAT IT USED TO BE, BUT THEY'RE MOSTLY GOOFING OFF AND NOT WORKING.
SOME PEOPLE ARE STILL MISSING, BUT THEY'RE GETTING A FREE RIDE...
...AND I FEEL BAD ABOUT THAT.
ANYWAY, I'M NOT READY FOR DATING.
AND THERE ARE PLENTY OF OTHER GIRLS YOU CAN HELP.
WELL, I SHOULD BE GOING.
I HAVE TO MAKE DINNER FOR MY BROTHERS.

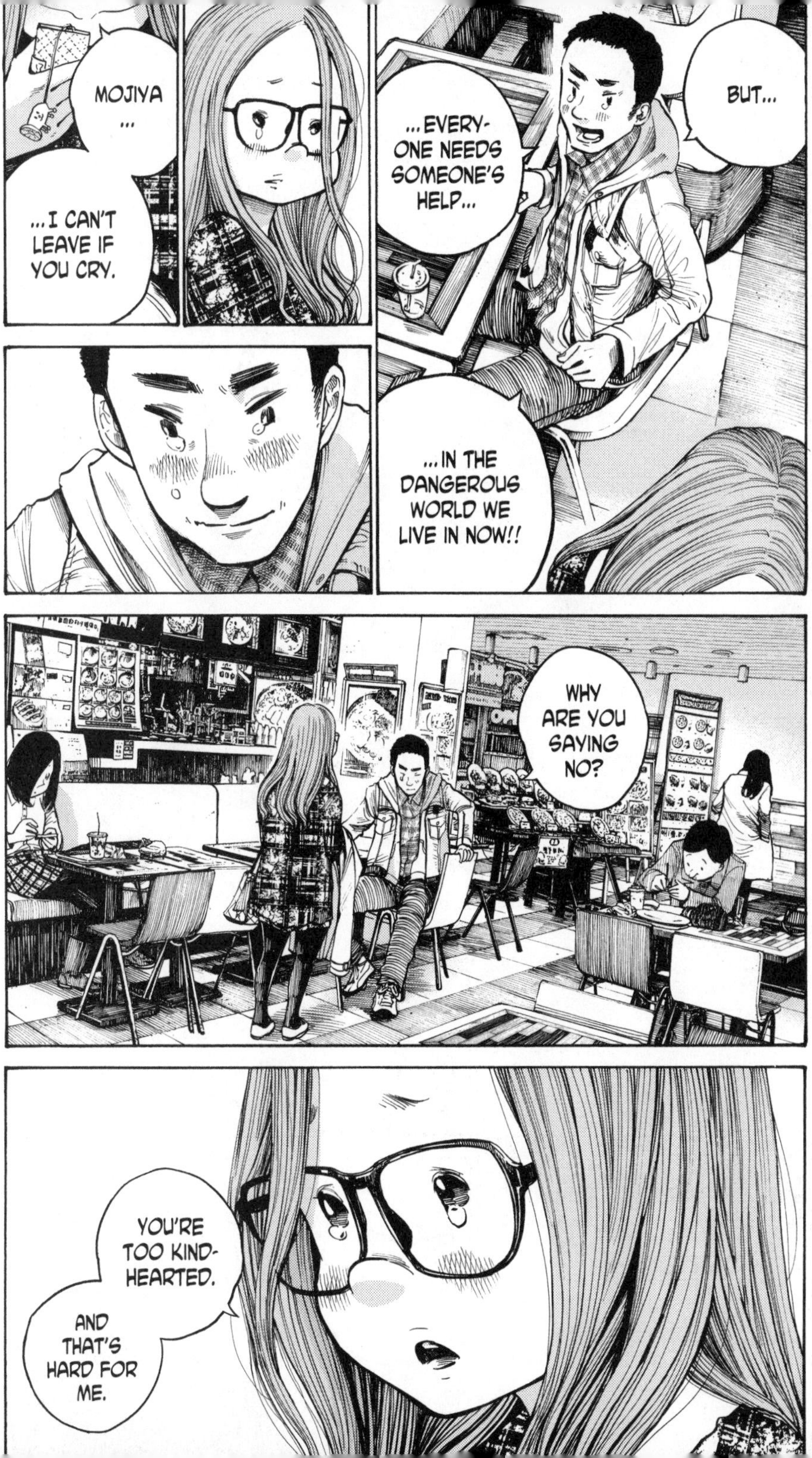
BUT...
...EVERY-ONE NEEDS SOMEONE'S HELP...
...IN THE DANGEROUS WORLD WE LIVE IN NOW!!
MOJIYA...
...I CAN'T LEAVE IF YOU CRY.
WHY ARE YOU SAYING NO?
YOU'RE TOO KIND-HEARTED.
AND THAT'S HARD FOR ME.

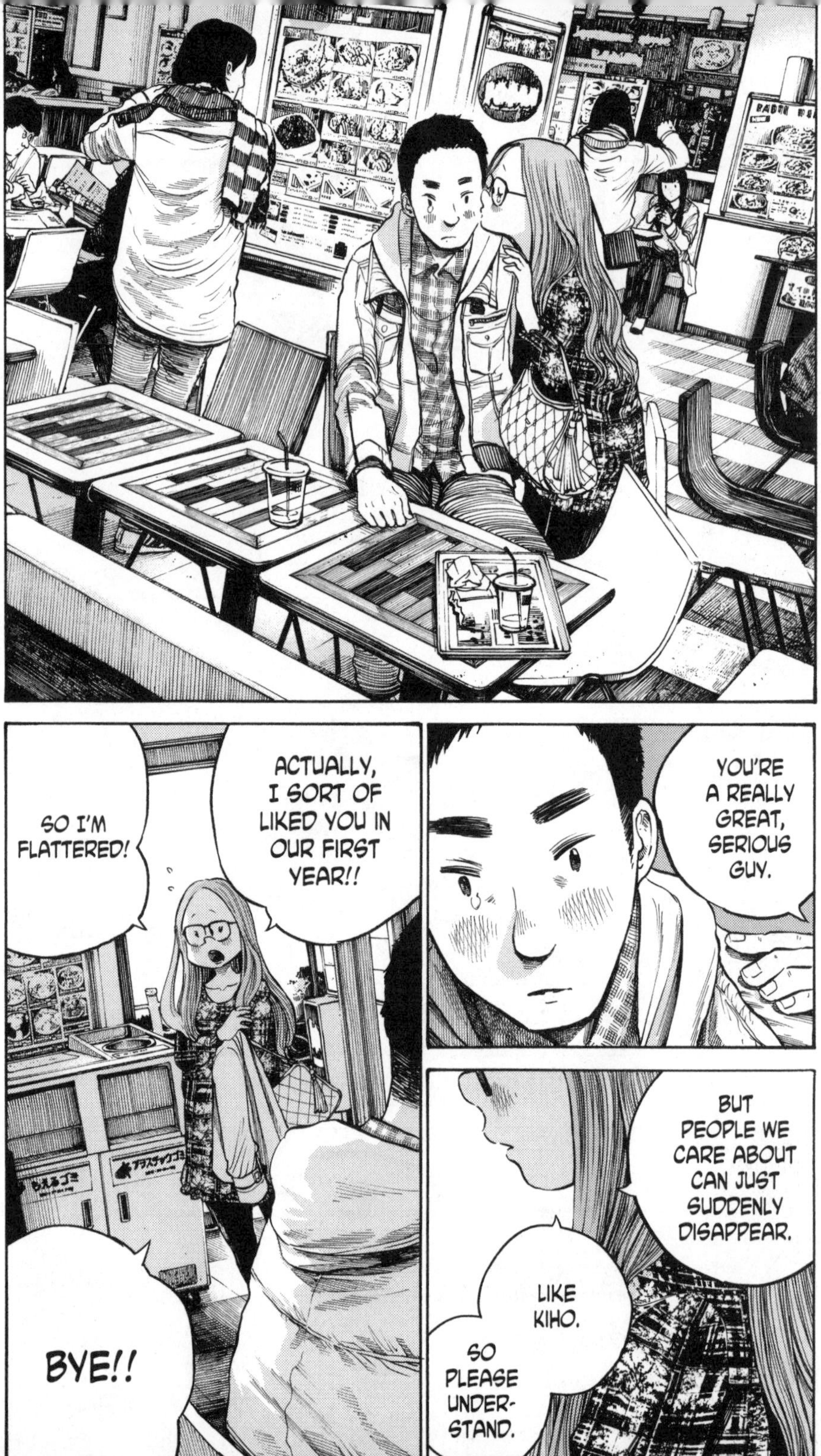
YOU'RE A REALLY GREAT, SERIOUS GUY.
BUT PEOPLE WE CARE ABOUT CAN JUST SUDDENLY DISAPPEAR.
LIKE KIHO.
SO PLEASE UNDER-STAND.
ACTUALLY, I SORT OF LIKED YOU IN OUR FIRST YEAR!!
SO I'M FLATTERED!
BYE!!

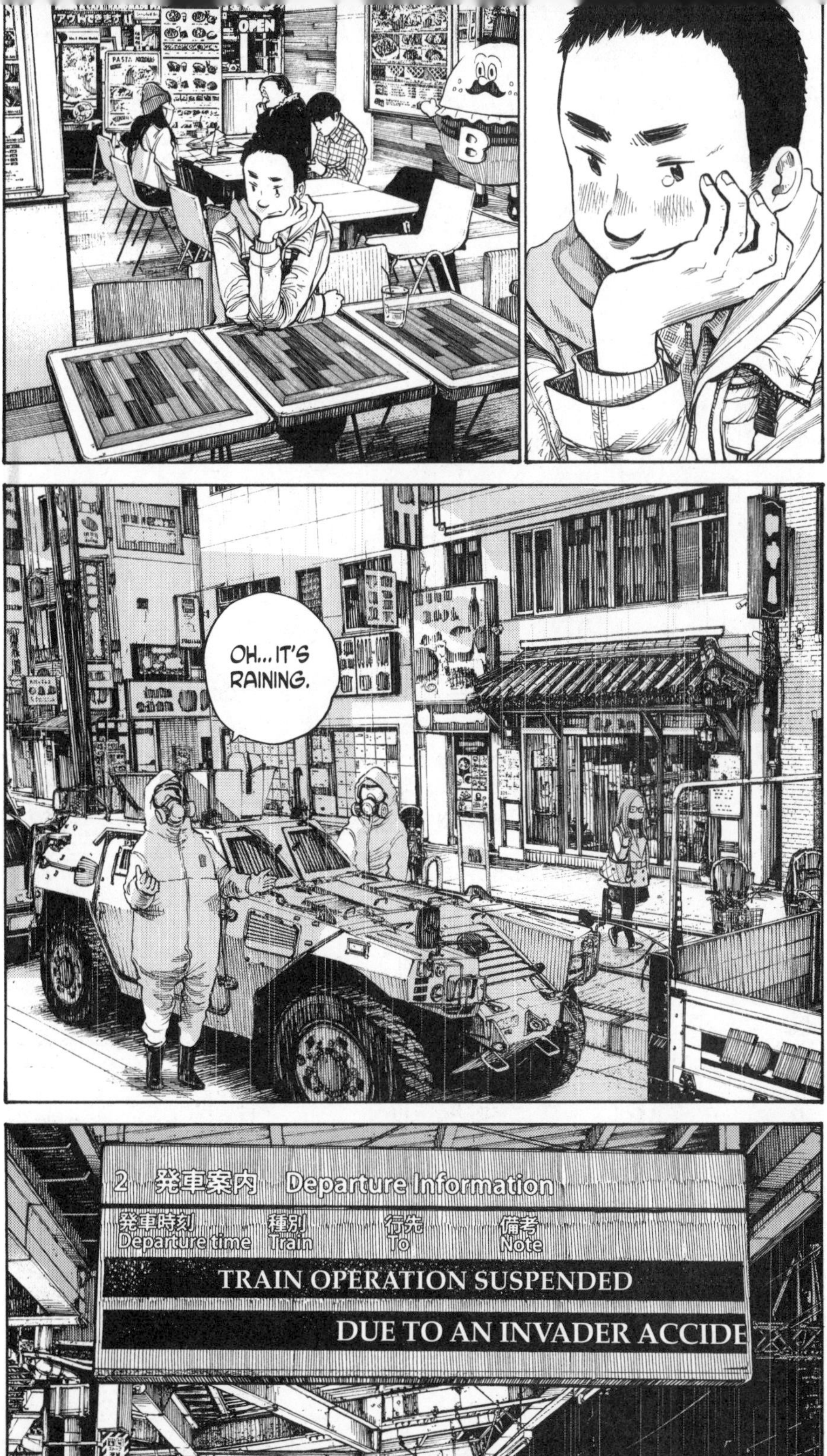
OPEN
PASTA
OH... IT'S RAINING.
2 発車案内 Departure Information
発車時刻 Departure time
種別 Train
行先 To
備考 Note
TRAIN OPERATION SUSPENDED
DUE TO AN INVADER ACCIDE

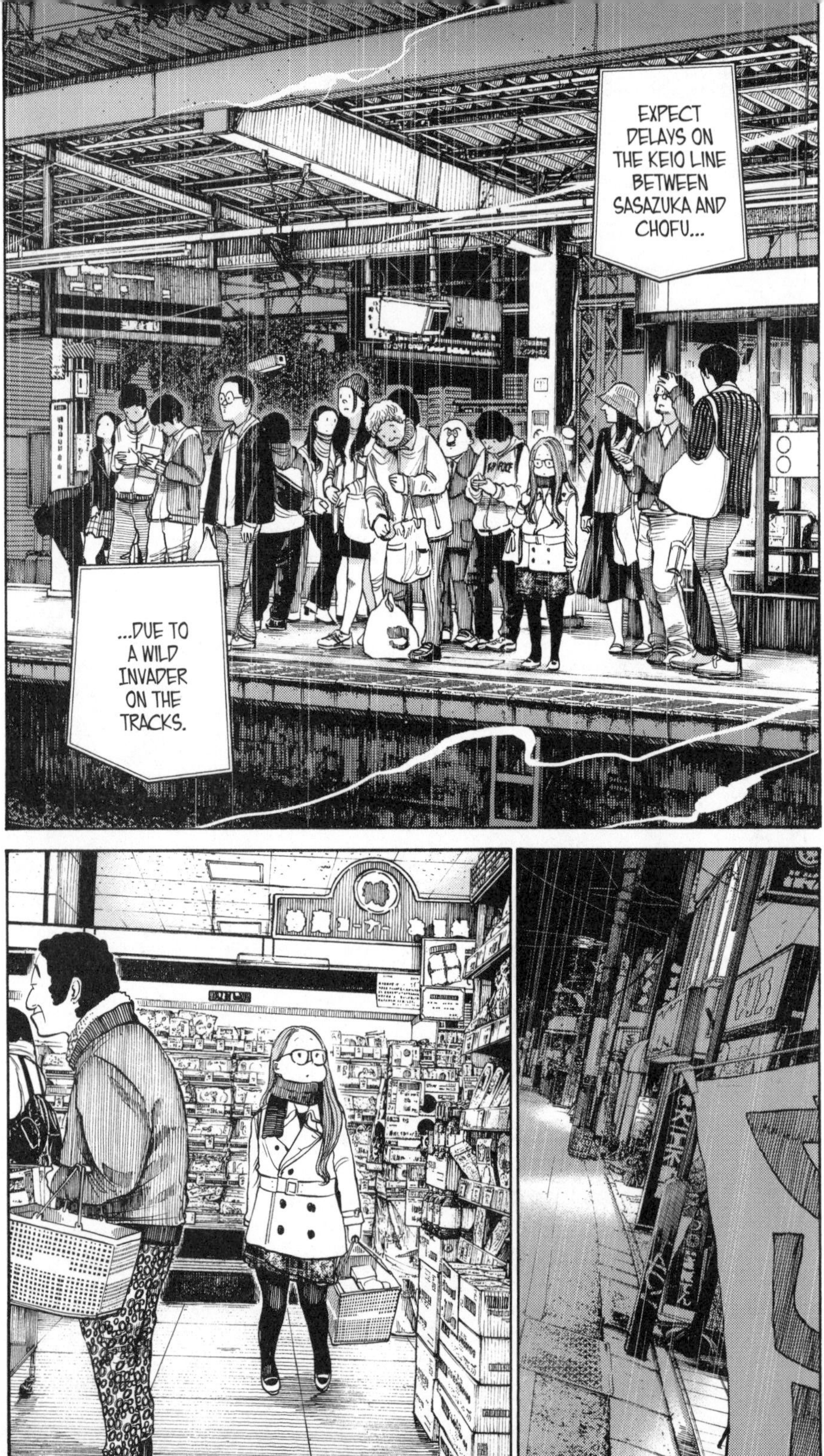
EXPECT DELAYS ON THE KEIO LINE BETWEEN SASAZUKA AND CHOFU...
...DUE TO A WILD INVADER ON THE TRACKS.

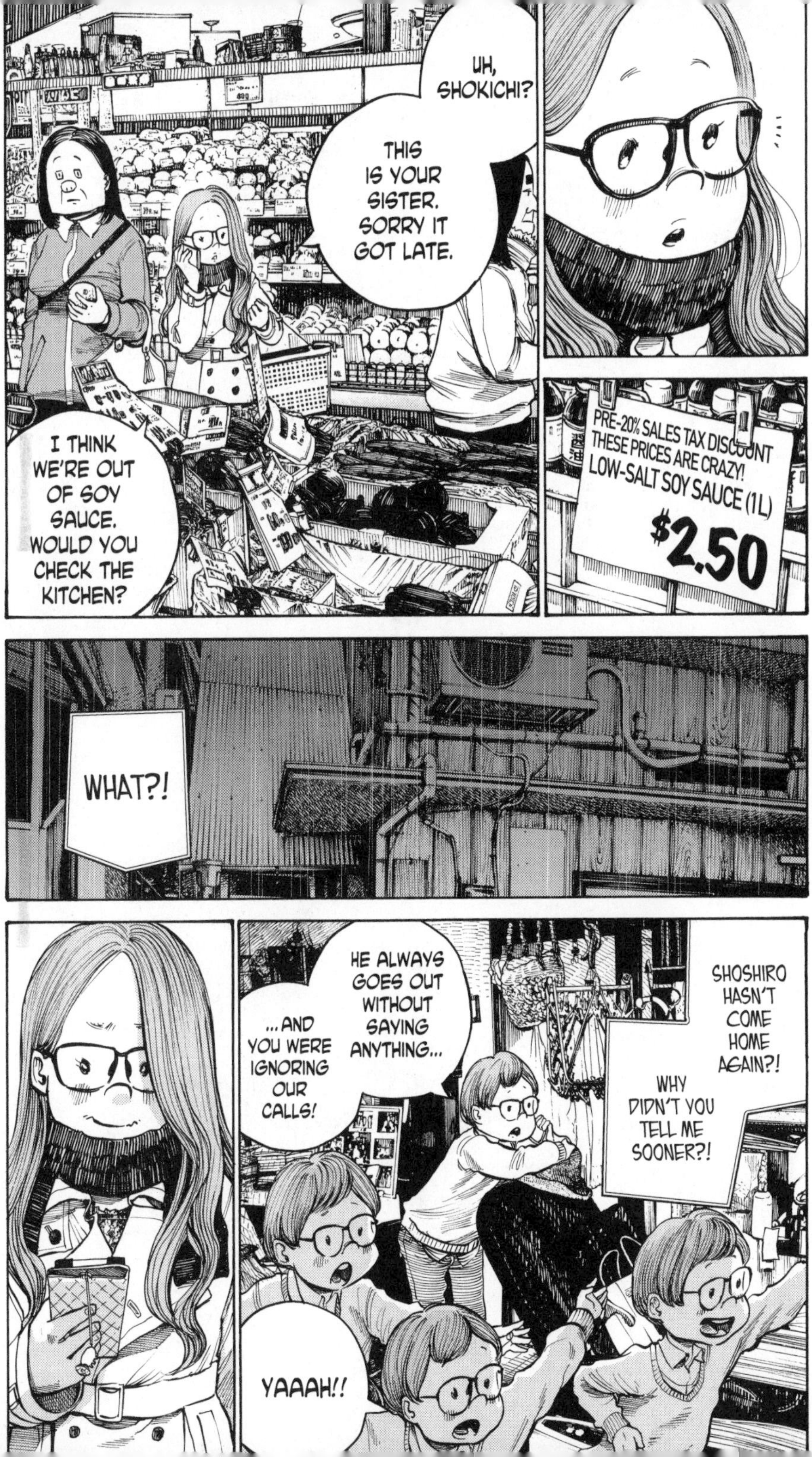

PRE-20% SALES TAX DISCOUNT
THESE PRICES ARE CRAZY!
LOW-SALT SOY SAUCE (1L)
$2.50
UH, SHOKICHI?
THIS IS YOUR SISTER. SORRY IT GOT LATE.
I THINK WE'RE OUT OF SOY SAUCE. WOULD YOU CHECK THE KITCHEN?
WHAT?!
SHOSHIRO HASN'T COME HOME AGAIN?!
WHY DIDN'T YOU TELL ME SOONER?!
HE ALWAYS GOES OUT WITHOUT SAYING ANYTHING...
...AND YOU WERE IGNORING OUR CALLS!
YAAAH!!

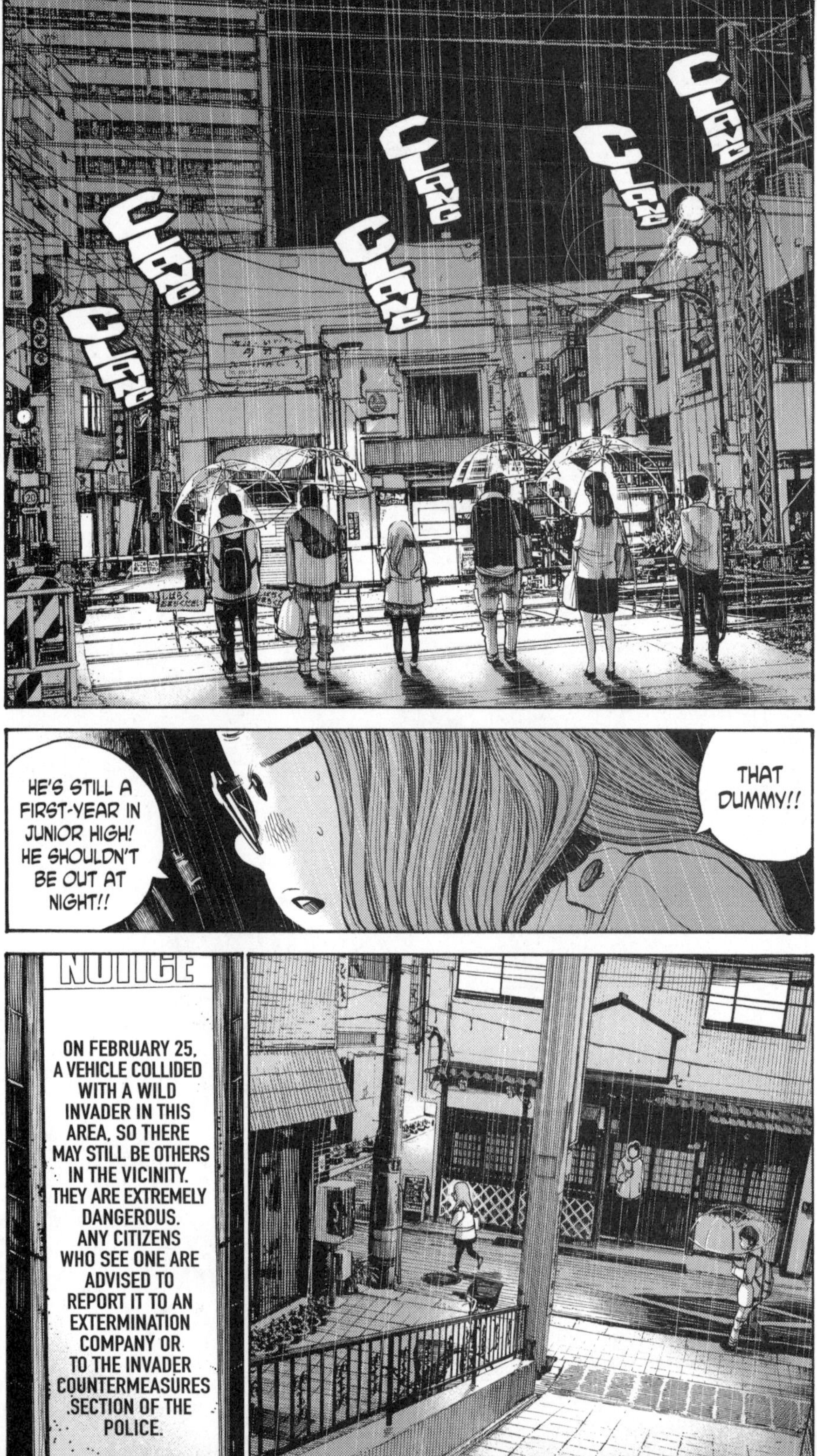
CLANG
CLANG
CLANG
CLANG
CLANG
CLANG
CLANG
CLANG
THAT DUMMY!!
HE'S STILL A FIRST-YEAR IN JUNIOR HIGH! HE SHOULDN'T BE OUT AT NIGHT!!
NOTICE
ON FEBRUARY 25, A VEHICLE COLLIDED WITH A WILD INVADER IN THIS AREA, SO THERE MAY STILL BE OTHERS IN THE VICINITY. THEY ARE EXTREMELY DANGEROUS. ANY CITIZENS WHO SEE ONE ARE ADVISED TO REPORT IT TO AN EXTERMINATION COMPANY OR TO THE INVADER COUNTERMEASURES SECTION OF THE POLICE.

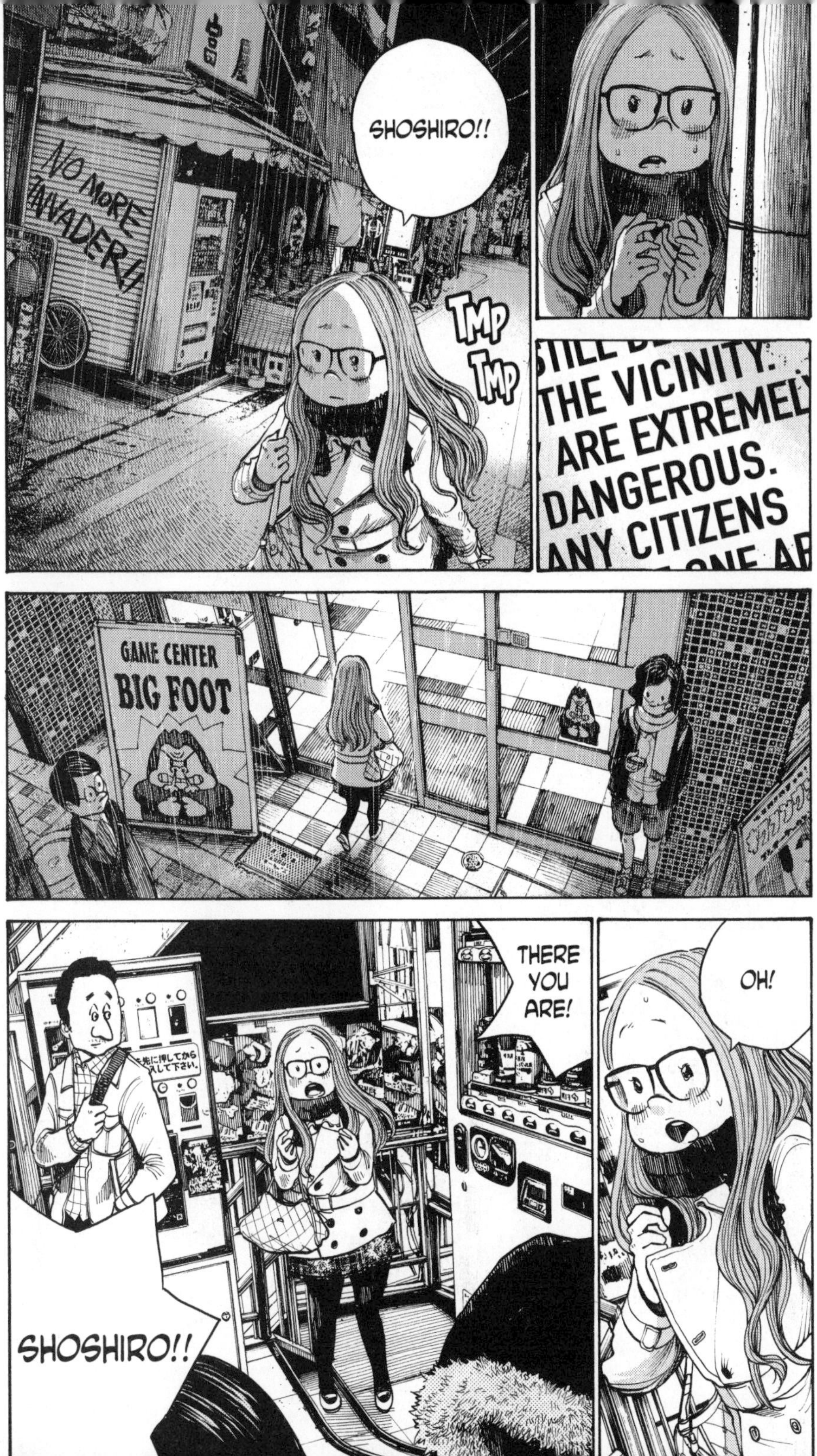
THE VICINITY.
ARE EXTREMEL
DANGEROUS.
ANY CITIZENS
SHOSHIRO!!
NO MORE INVADER!!
TMP TMP
GAME CENTER
BIG FOOT
OH!
THERE YOU ARE!
SHOSHIRO!!

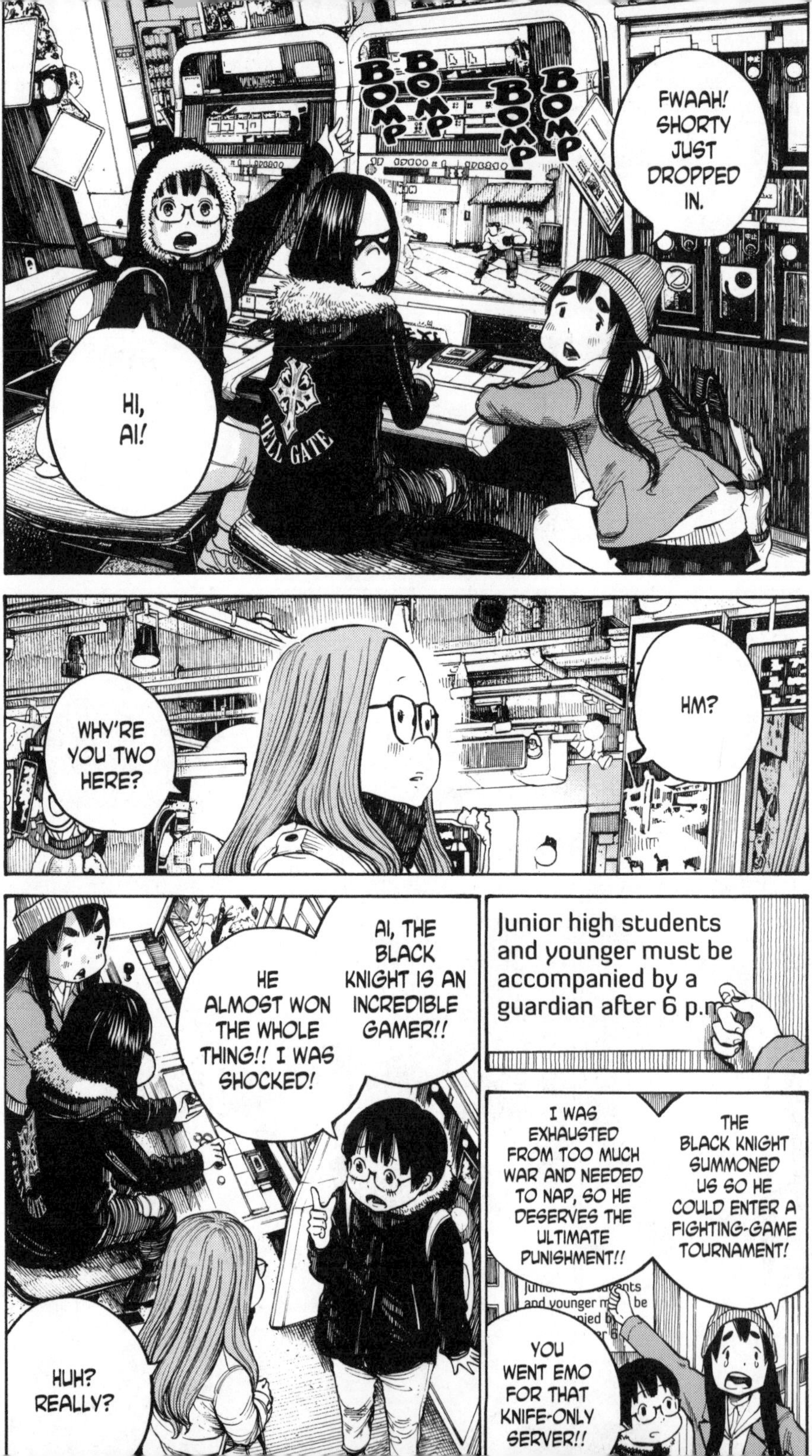
FWAAH! SHORTY JUST DROPPED IN.
BOMP
BOMP
BOMP
BOMP
HI, AI!
HM?
WHY'RE YOU TWO HERE?
Junior high students and younger must be accompanied by a guardian after 6 p.m
THE BLACK KNIGHT SUMMONED US SO HE COULD ENTER A FIGHTING-GAME TOURNAMENT!
I WAS EXHAUSTED FROM TOO MUCH WAR AND NEEDED TO NAP, SO HE DESERVES THE ULTIMATE PUNISHMENT!!
YOU WENT EMO FOR THAT KNIFE-ONLY SERVER!!
AI, THE BLACK KNIGHT IS AN INCREDIBLE GAMER!!
HE ALMOST WON THE WHOLE THING!! I WAS SHOCKED!
HUH? REALLY?

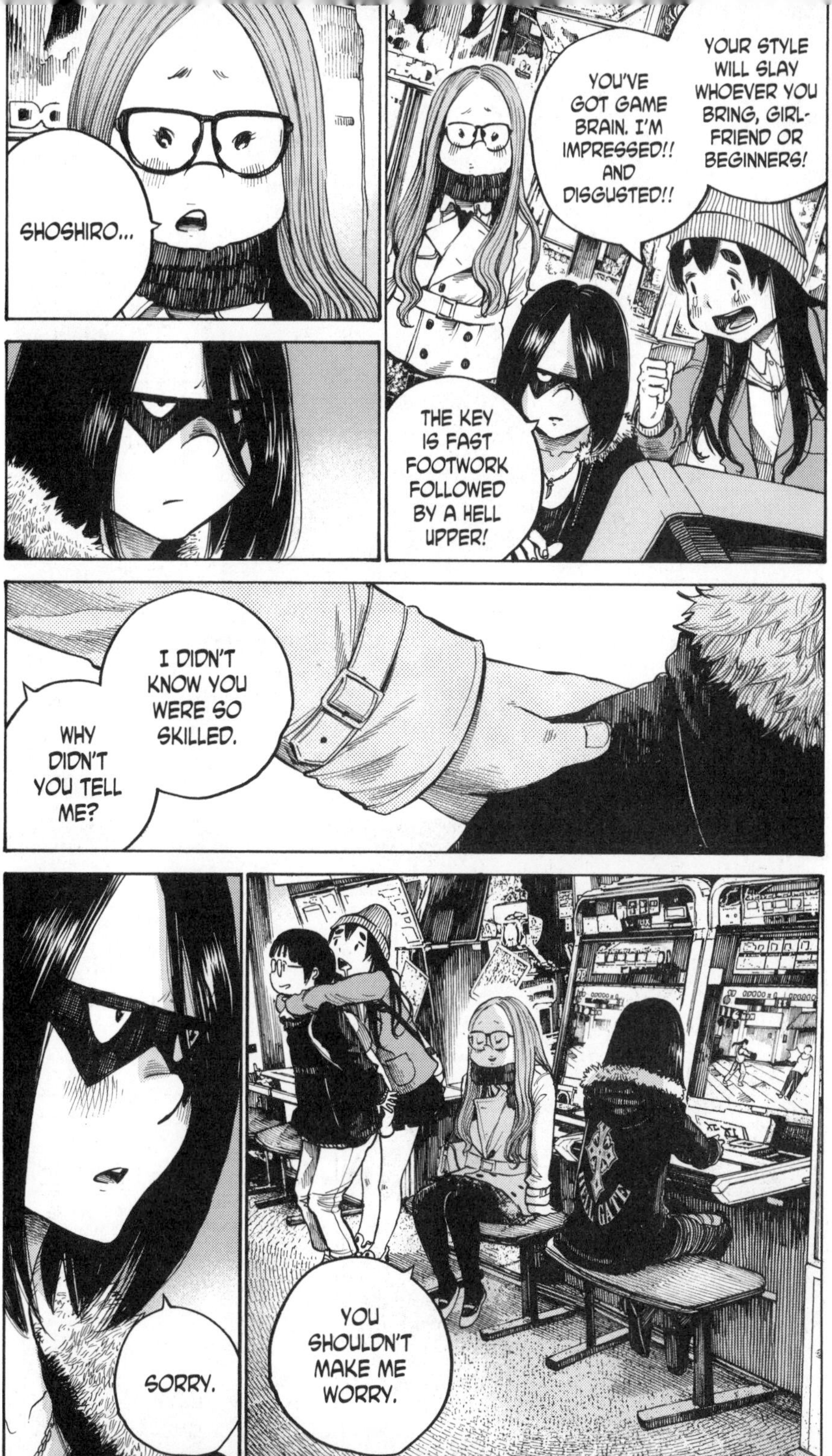
YOUR STYLE WILL SLAY WHOEVER YOU BRING, GIRL-FRIEND OR BEGINNERS!
YOU'VE GOT GAME BRAIN. I'M IMPRESSED!! AND DISGUSTED!!
THE KEY IS FAST FOOTWORK FOLLOWED BY A HELL UPPER!
SHOSHIRO...
I DIDN'T KNOW YOU WERE SO SKILLED.
WHY DIDN'T YOU TELL ME?
YOU SHOULDN'T MAKE ME WORRY.
SORRY.

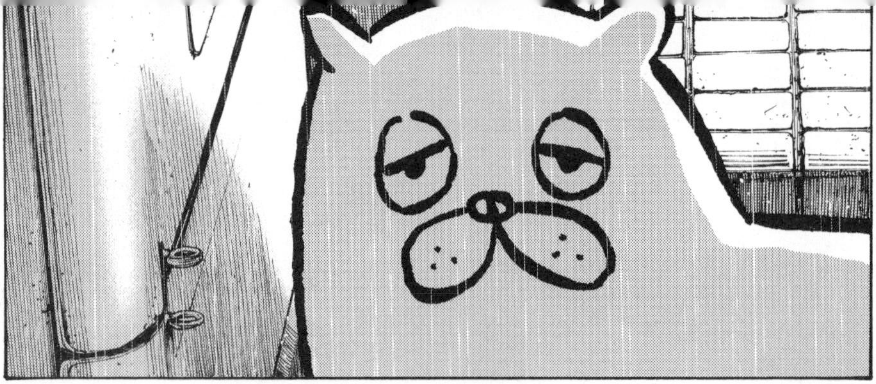

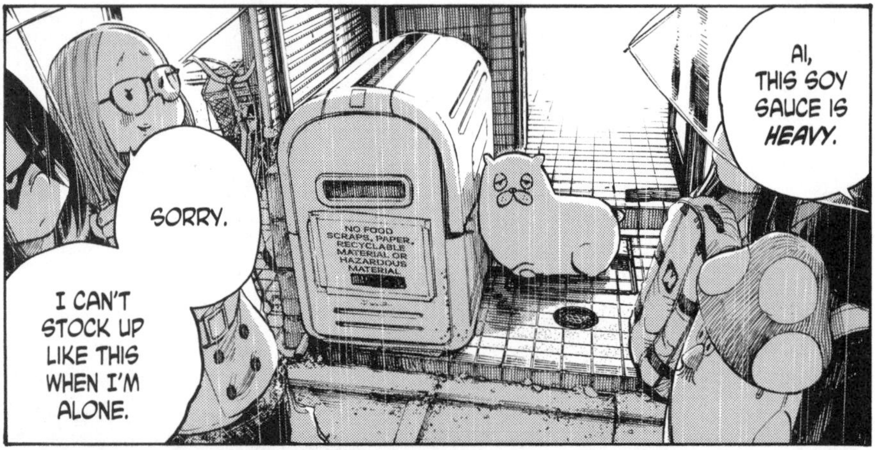
AI, THIS SOY SAUCE IS *HEAVY.*
NO FOOD SCRAPS, PAPER, RECYCLABLE MATERIAL, OR HAZARDOUS MATERIAL
SORRY.
I CAN'T STOCK UP LIKE THIS WHEN I'M ALONE.

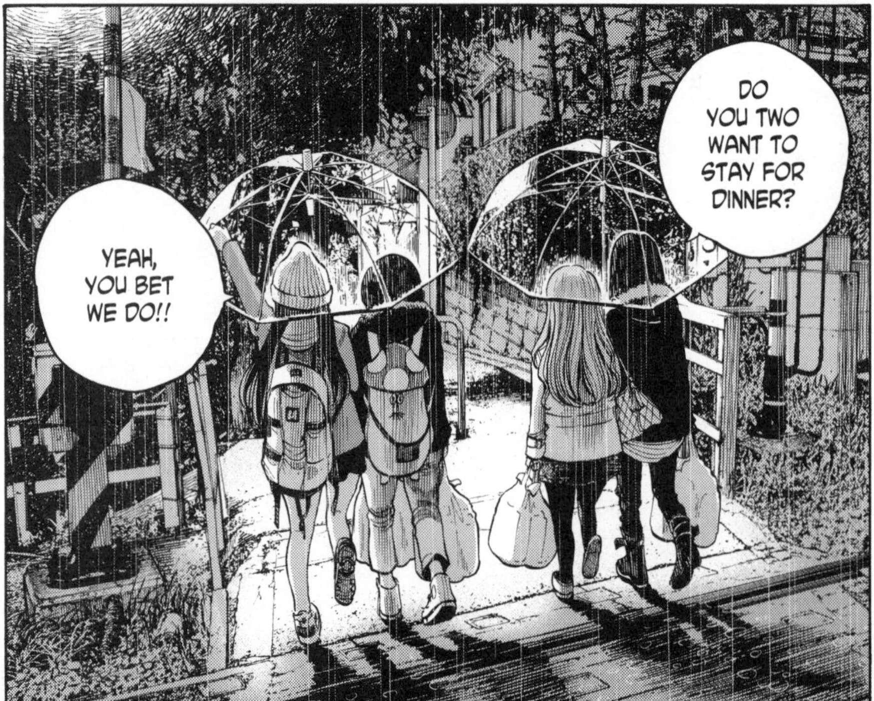
DO YOU TWO WANT TO STAY FOR DINNER?
YEAH, YOU BET WE DO!!

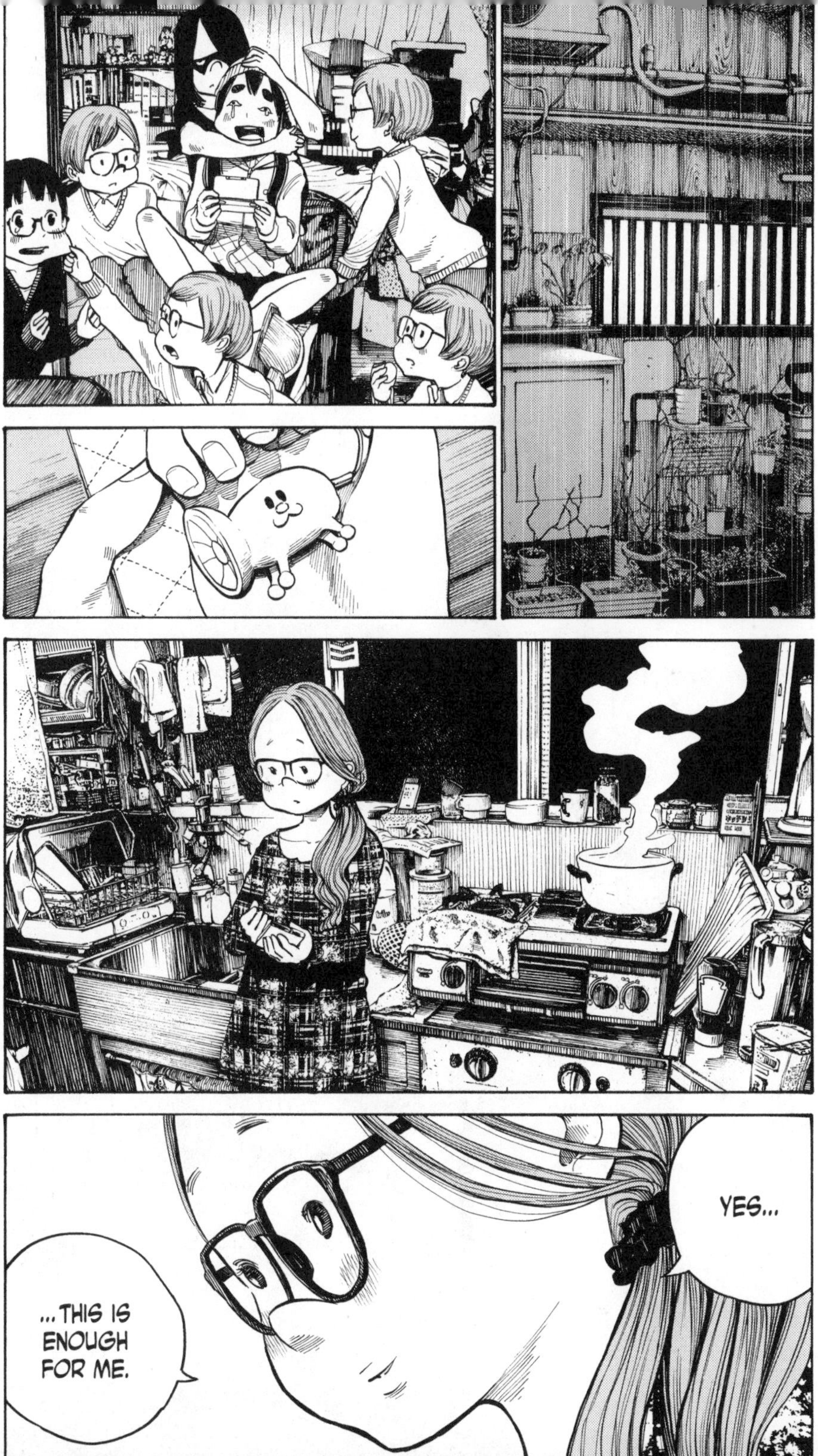
YES...
...THIS IS ENOUGH FOR ME.

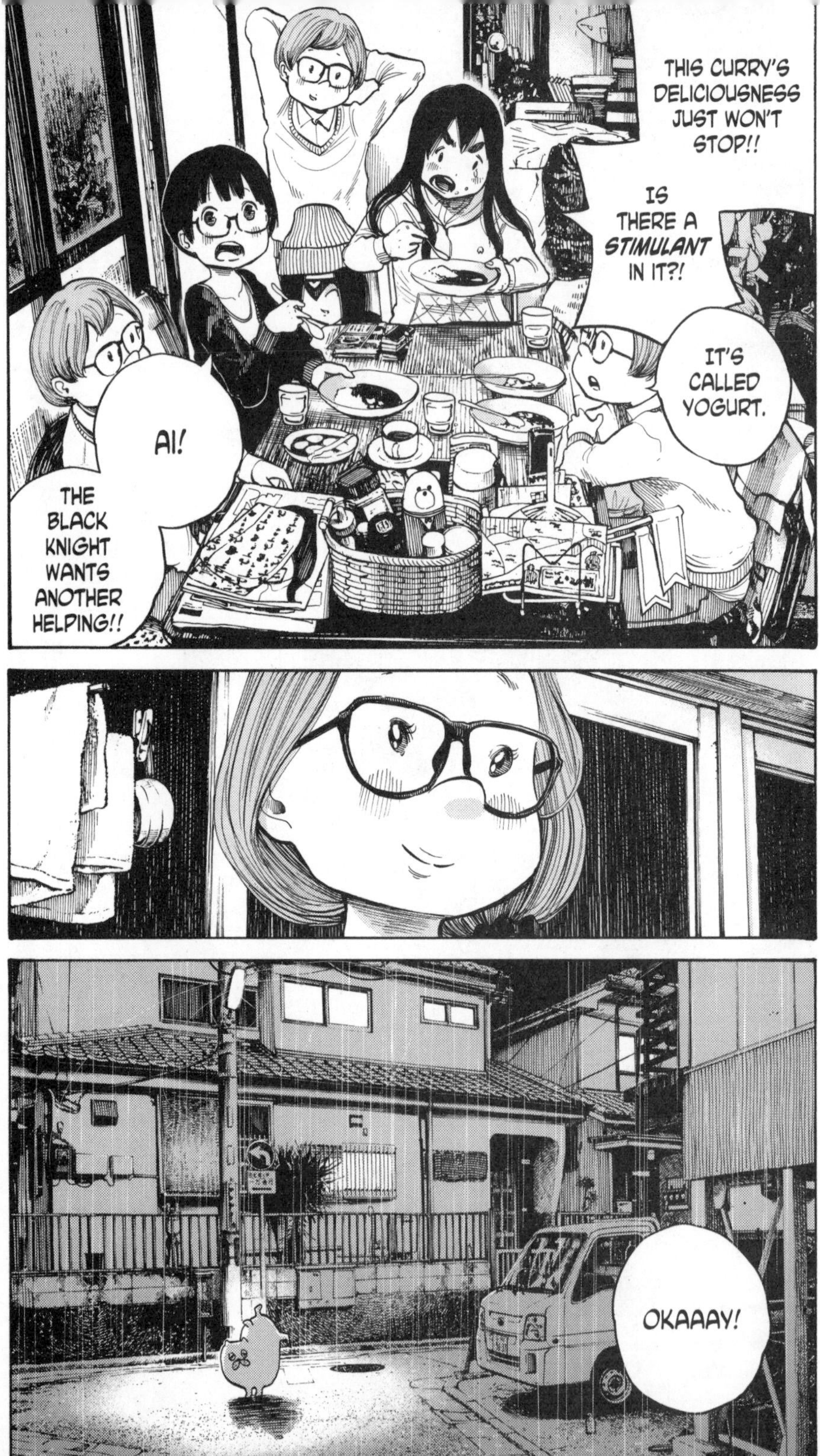
THIS CURRY'S DELICIOUSNESS JUST WON'T STOP!!
IS THERE A *STIMULANT* IN IT?!
IT'S CALLED YOGURT.
AI!
THE BLACK KNIGHT WANTS ANOTHER HELPING!!
OKAAAY!

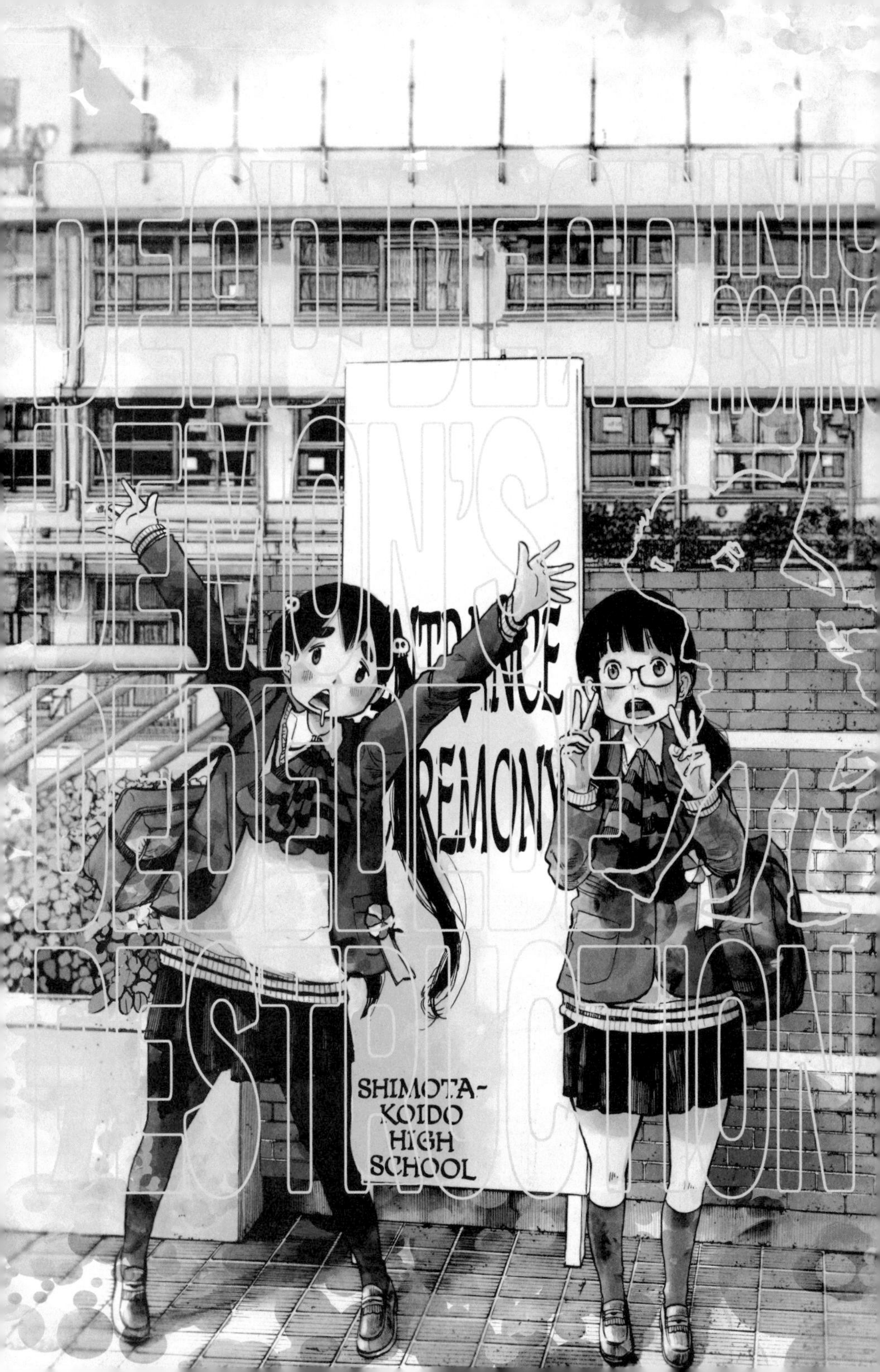
SHIMOTA-
KOIDO
HIGH
SCHOOL

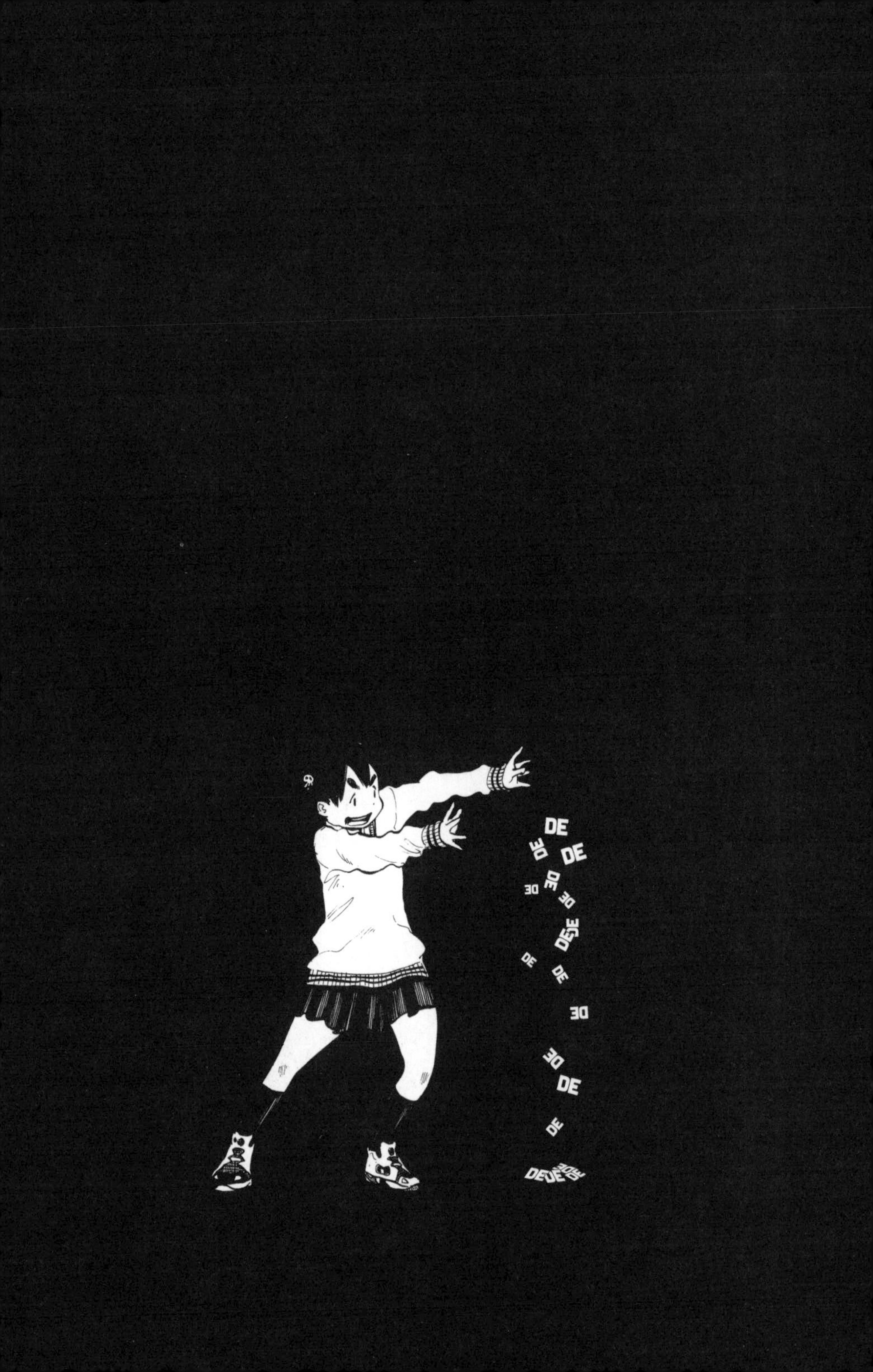
DE DE DE DE DE DE DE DE DE DE DE DE DE DE
DEDEDEDE

CHAPTER 23

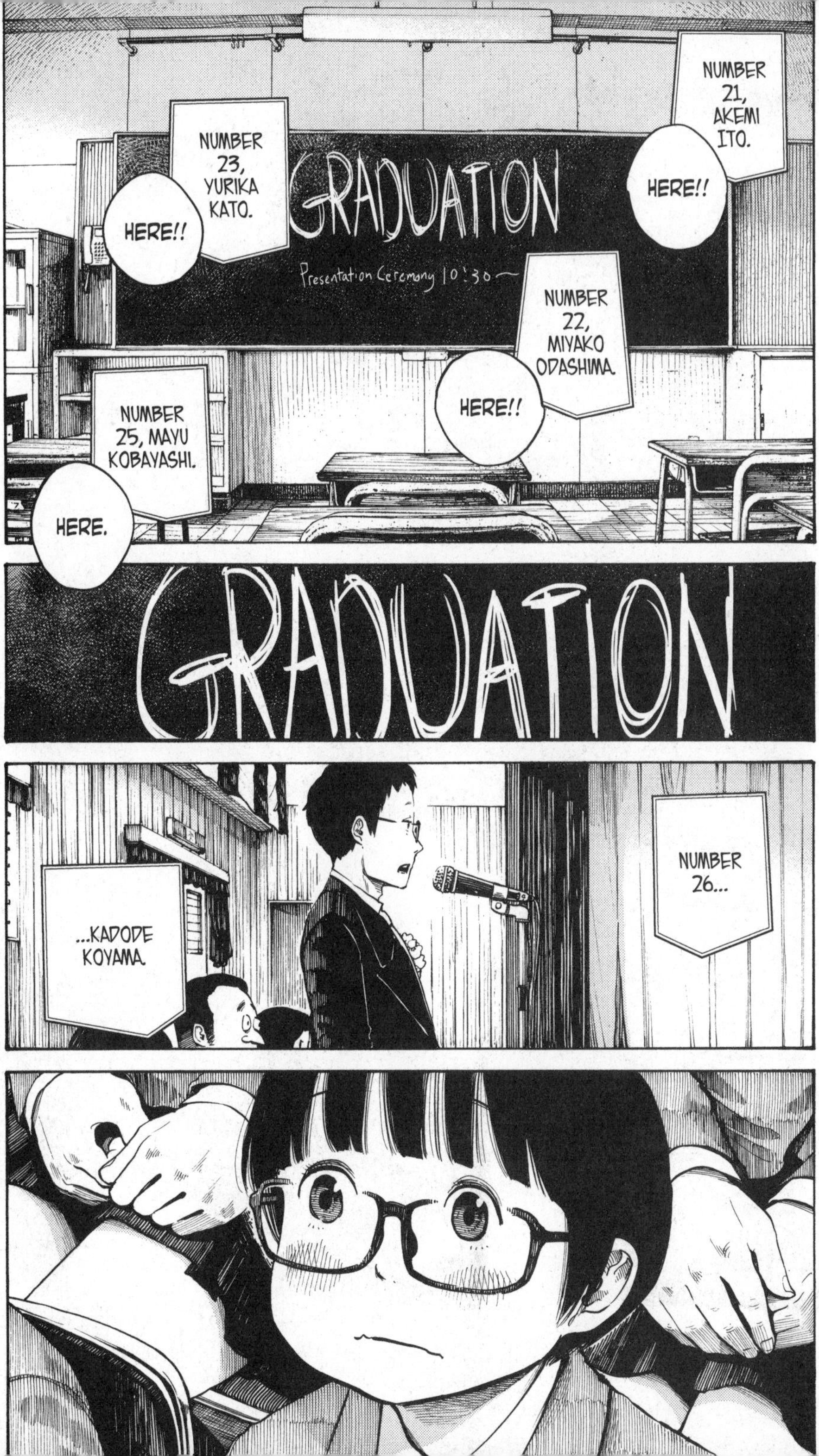
NUMBER 21, AKEMI ITO.
HERE!!
NUMBER 22, MIYAKO ODASHIMA.
HERE!!
NUMBER 23, YURIKA KATO.
HERE!!
GRADUATION
Presentation Ceremony 10:30~
NUMBER 25, MAYU KOBAYASHI.
HERE.
GRADUATION
NUMBER 26...
...KADODE KOYAMA.

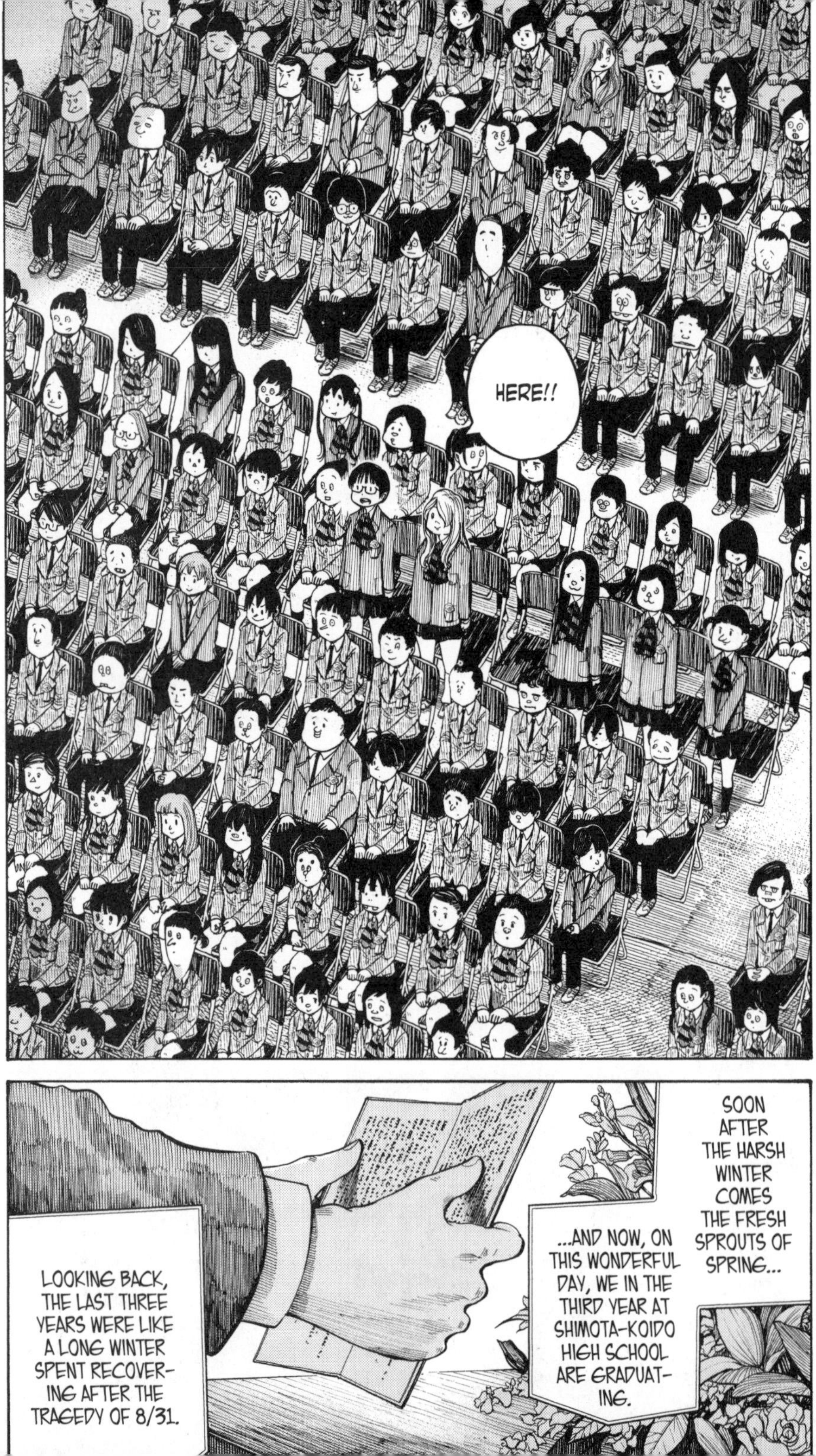
HERE!!
SOON AFTER THE HARSH WINTER COMES THE FRESH SPROUTS OF SPRING...
...AND NOW, ON THIS WONDERFUL DAY, WE IN THE THIRD YEAR AT SHIMOTA-KOIDO HIGH SCHOOL ARE GRADUAT-ING.
LOOKING BACK, THE LAST THREE YEARS WERE LIKE A LONG WINTER SPENT RECOVER-ING AFTER THE TRAGEDY OF 8/31.

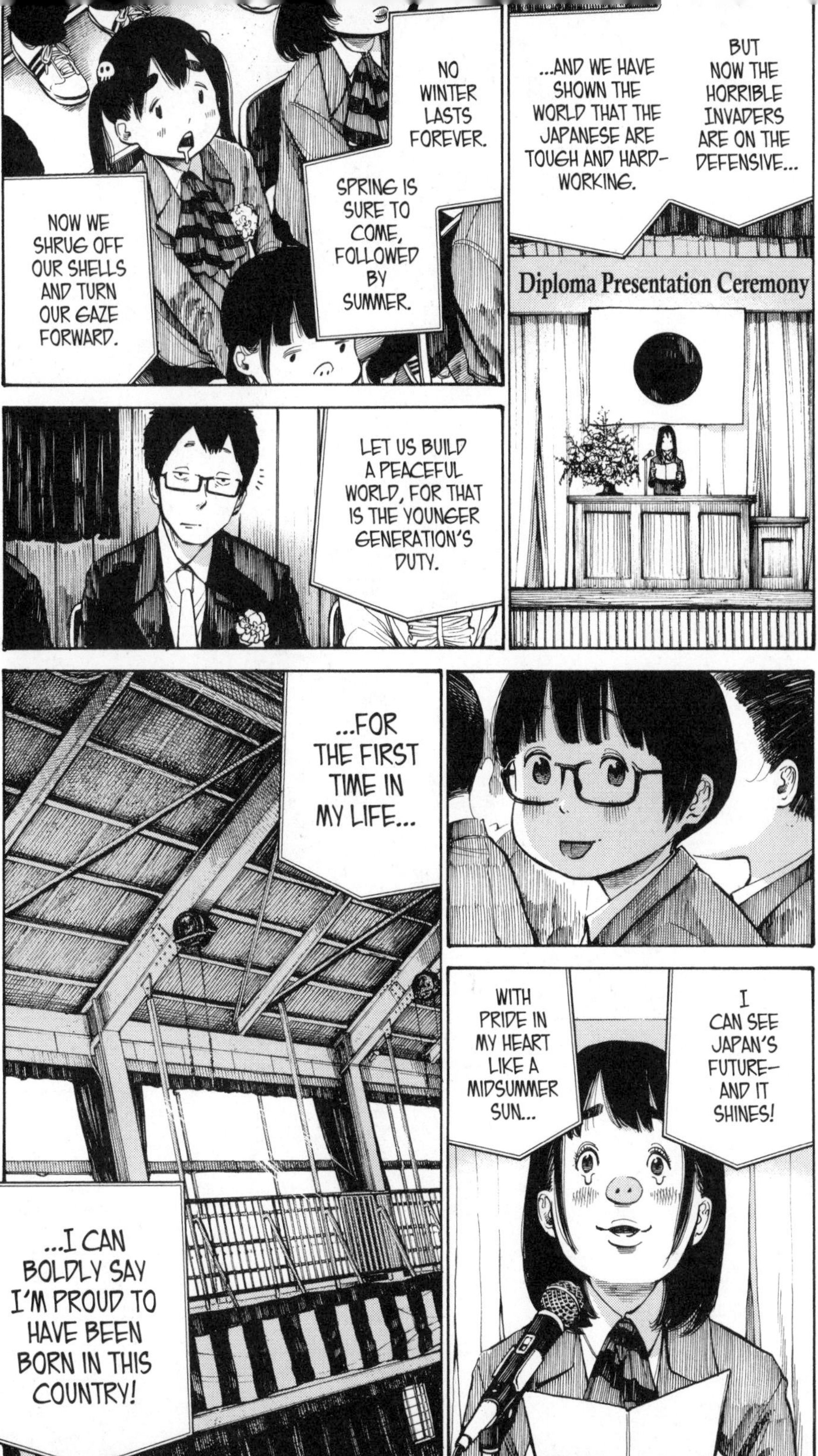
BUT NOW THE HORRIBLE INVADERS ARE ON THE DEFENSIVE...
...AND WE HAVE SHOWN THE WORLD THAT THE JAPANESE ARE TOUGH AND HARD-WORKING.
Diploma Presentation Ceremony
NO WINTER LASTS FOREVER.
SPRING IS SURE TO COME, FOLLOWED BY SUMMER.
NOW WE SHRUG OFF OUR SHELLS AND TURN OUR GAZE FORWARD.
LET US BUILD A PEACEFUL WORLD, FOR THAT IS THE YOUNGER GENERATION'S DUTY.
I CAN SEE JAPAN'S FUTURE— AND IT SHINES!
WITH PRIDE IN MY HEART LIKE A MIDSUMMER SUN...
...FOR THE FIRST TIME IN MY LIFE...
...I CAN BOLDLY SAY I'M PROUD TO HAVE BEEN BORN IN THIS COUNTRY!

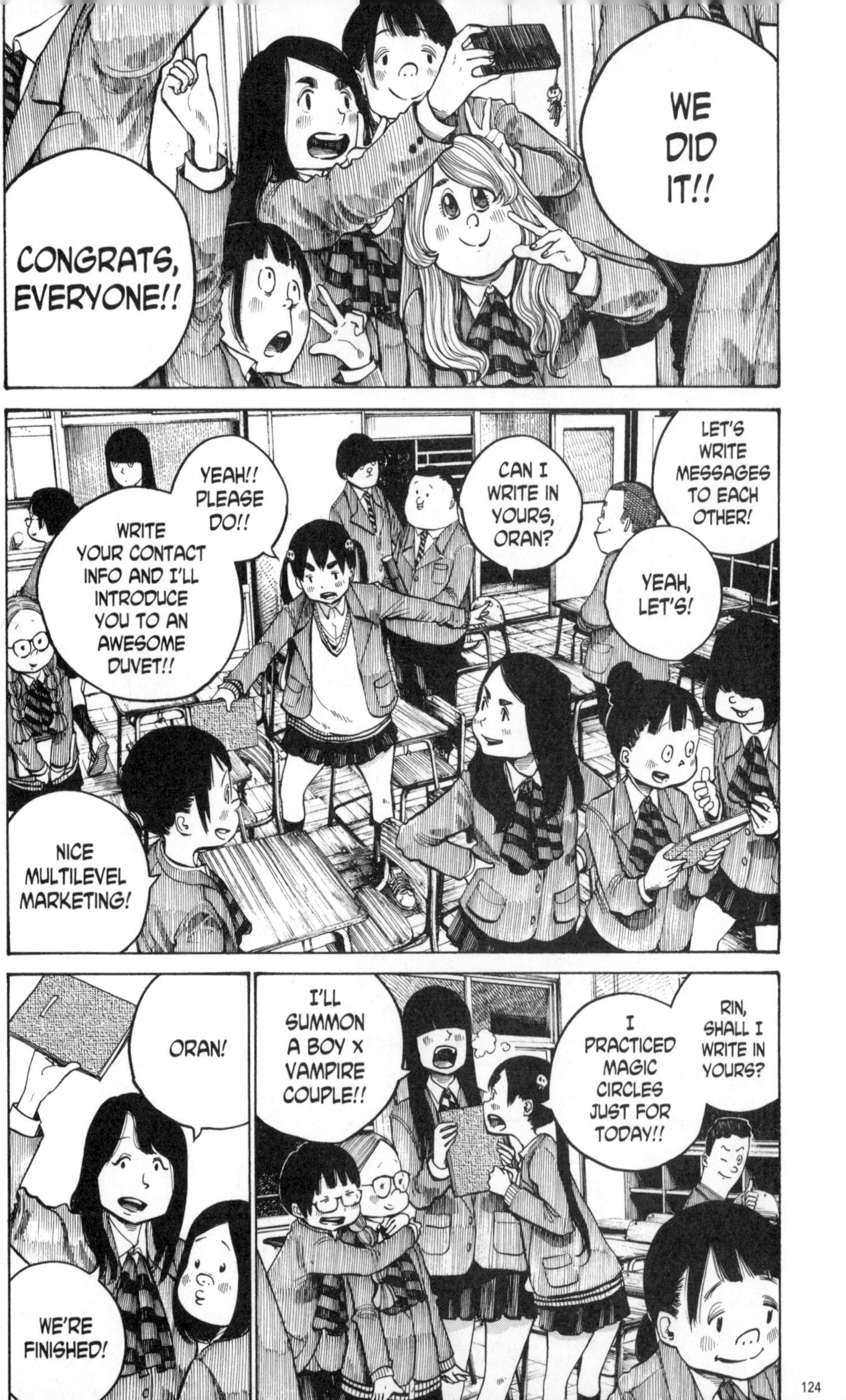
WE DID IT!!
CONGRATS, EVERYONE!!
LET'S WRITE MESSAGES TO EACH OTHER!
YEAH, LET'S!
CAN I WRITE IN YOURS, ORAN?
YEAH!! PLEASE DO!!
WRITE YOUR CONTACT INFO AND I'LL INTRODUCE YOU TO AN AWESOME DUVET!!
NICE MULTILEVEL MARKETING!
RIN, SHALL I WRITE IN YOURS?
I PRACTICED MAGIC CIRCLES JUST FOR TODAY!!
I'LL SUMMON A BOY x VAMPIRE COUPLE!!
ORAN!
WE'RE FINISHED!

3-D
WAKE UP!!
Let's hang out sometime! —Mishima
what the heck is "Hya Hyo foowah!!" Suzumo
I hope I made a friend who becomes famous enough to get in the newspaper. (↑deep thought) -Juinichi
Stay friends with Kadode! —Honda
Hurry up and return to yourself!!
RENA
I SECOND THAT. -SAITO
GAME BRAINZ Koike
Keep up the good work! -Arima
DON'T BECOME A CRIMINAL!! Shimota
I've wanted to ask something ever since we were in the same class in first grade. How long are you going to keep the long pigtails?
Good luck... I guess (lol) -Natsu
I'm worried about your future, Nakagawa. -Kondo
Thank you for everything... -Tsuda
NAKAGAWA, YOU GOING TO BE "FAMOUS" SOME DAY, IN A BAD WAY. —IWAMA
Didn't have much to talk about.
OKAY, HERE GOES!
KOYAMA...

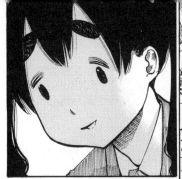

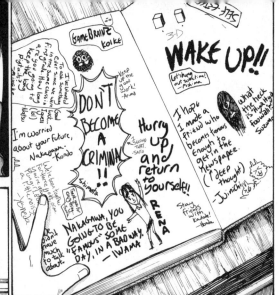

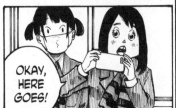

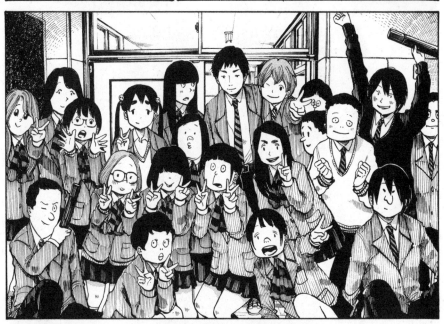

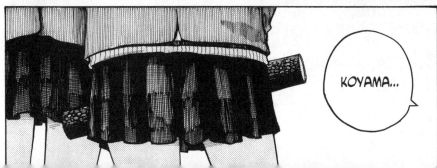

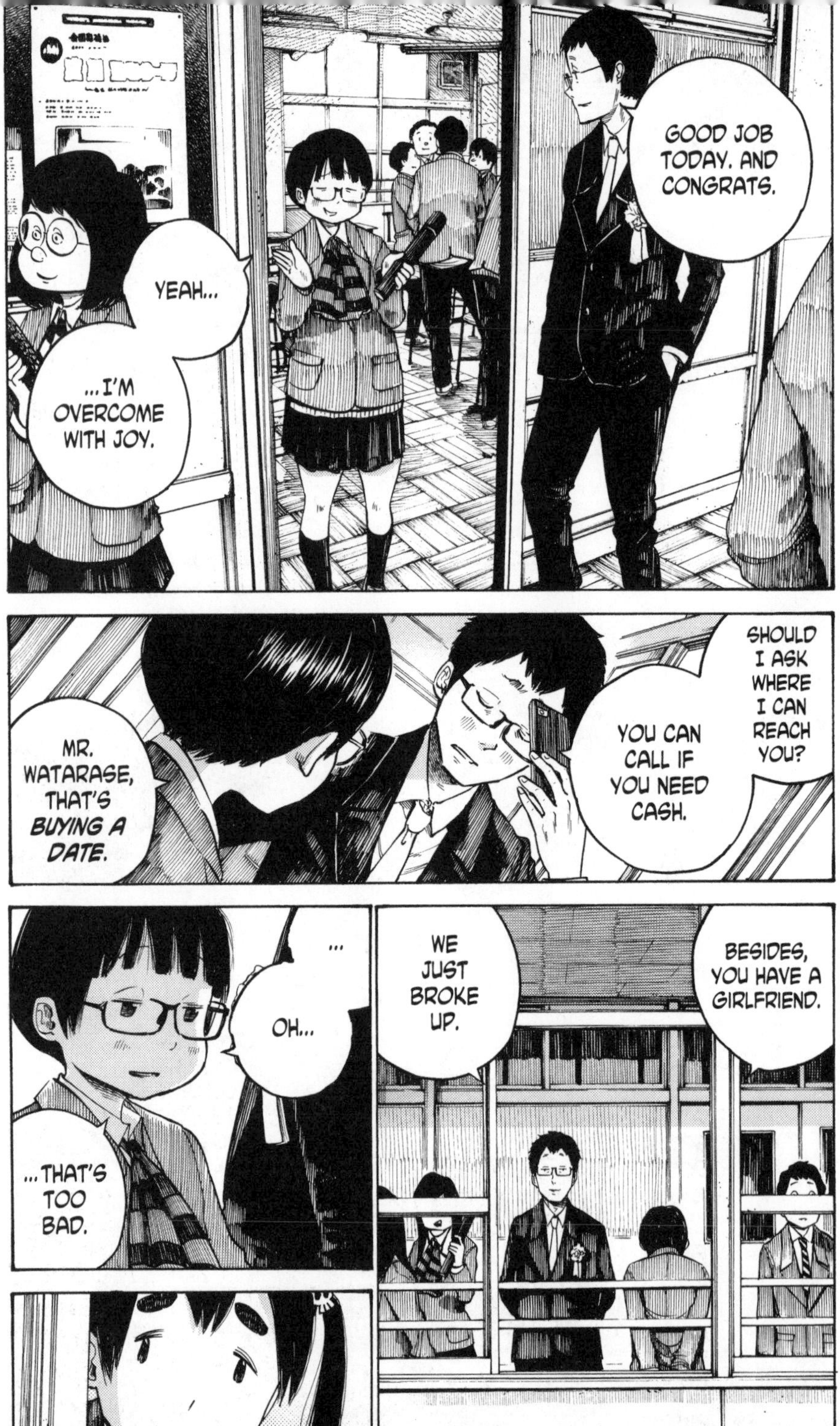
GOOD JOB TODAY. AND CONGRATS.
YEAH...
...I'M OVERCOME WITH JOY.
SHOULD I ASK WHERE I CAN REACH YOU?
YOU CAN CALL IF YOU NEED CASH.
MR. WATARASE, THAT'S *BUYING A DATE*.
BESIDES, YOU HAVE A GIRLFRIEND.
WE JUST BROKE UP.
...
OH...
...THAT'S TOO BAD.

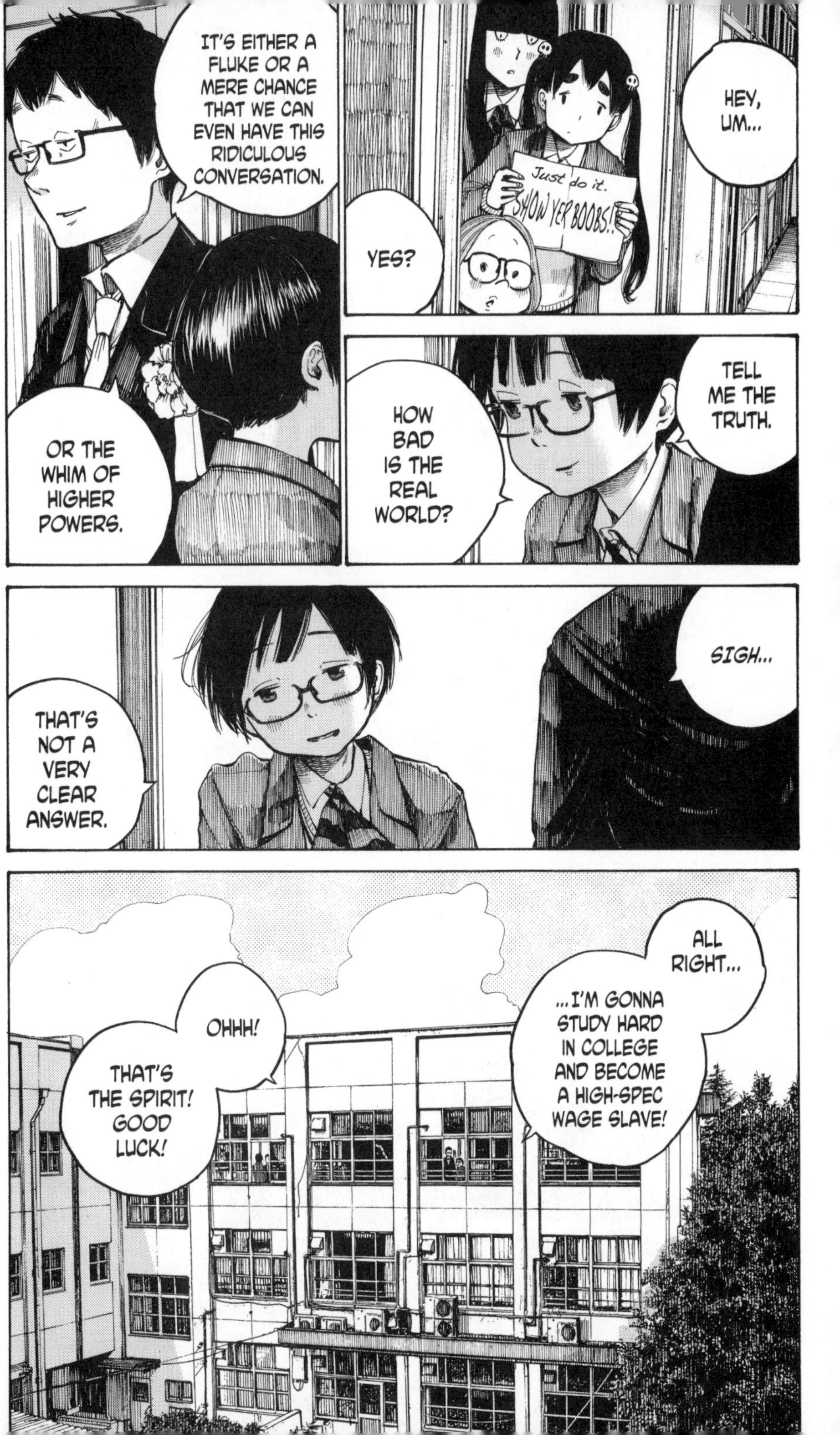
HEY, UM...
YES?
Just do it.
SHOW YER BOOBS!!
TELL ME THE TRUTH.
HOW BAD IS THE REAL WORLD?
IT'S EITHER A FLUKE OR A MERE CHANCE THAT WE CAN EVEN HAVE THIS RIDICULOUS CONVERSATION.
OR THE WHIM OF HIGHER POWERS.
SIGH...
THAT'S NOT A VERY CLEAR ANSWER.
ALL RIGHT...
...I'M GONNA STUDY HARD IN COLLEGE AND BECOME A HIGH-SPEC WAGE SLAVE!
OHHH!
THAT'S THE SPIRIT! GOOD LUCK!

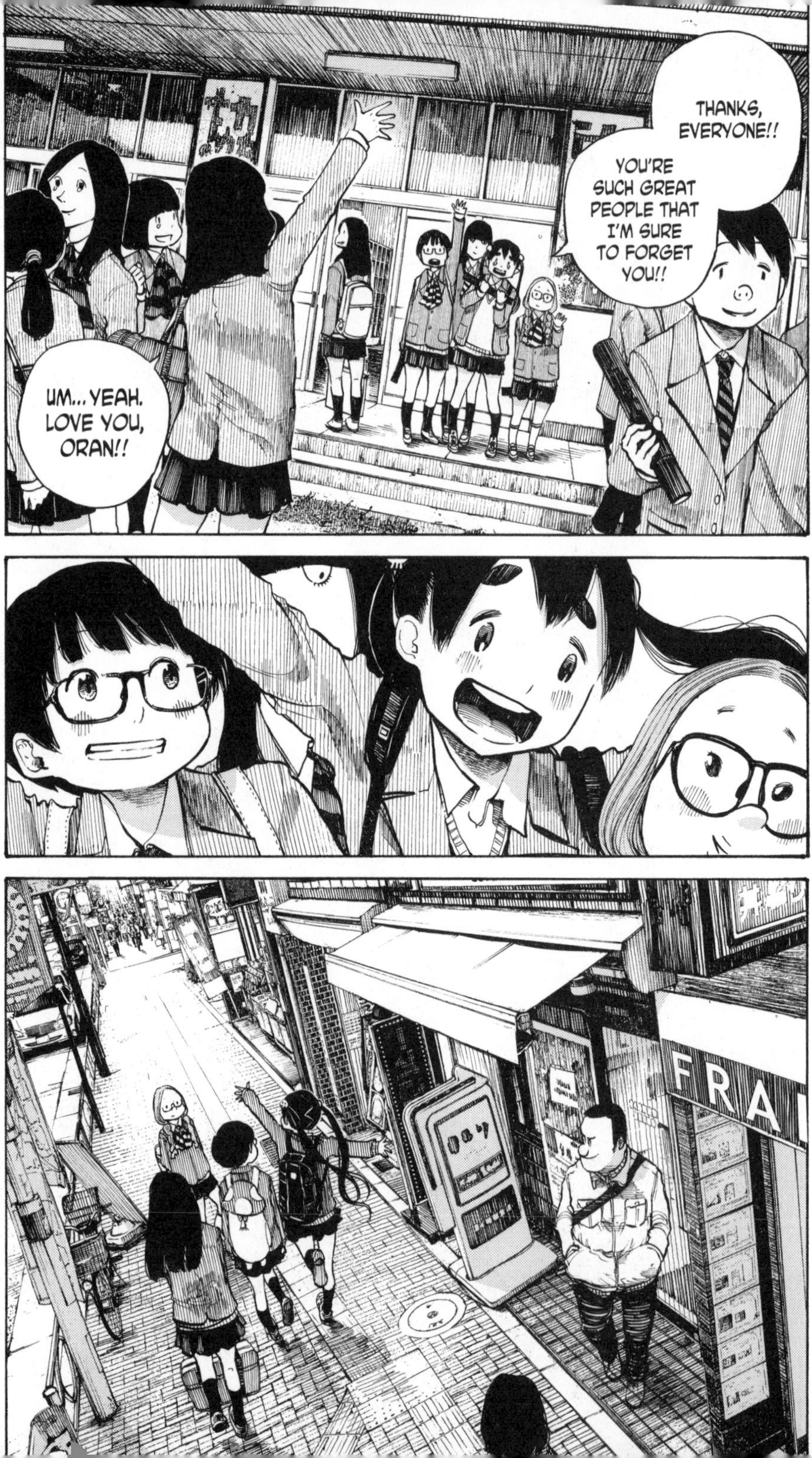
THANKS, EVERYONE!!
YOU'RE SUCH GREAT PEOPLE THAT I'M SURE TO FORGET YOU!!
UM... YEAH. LOVE YOU, ORAN!!

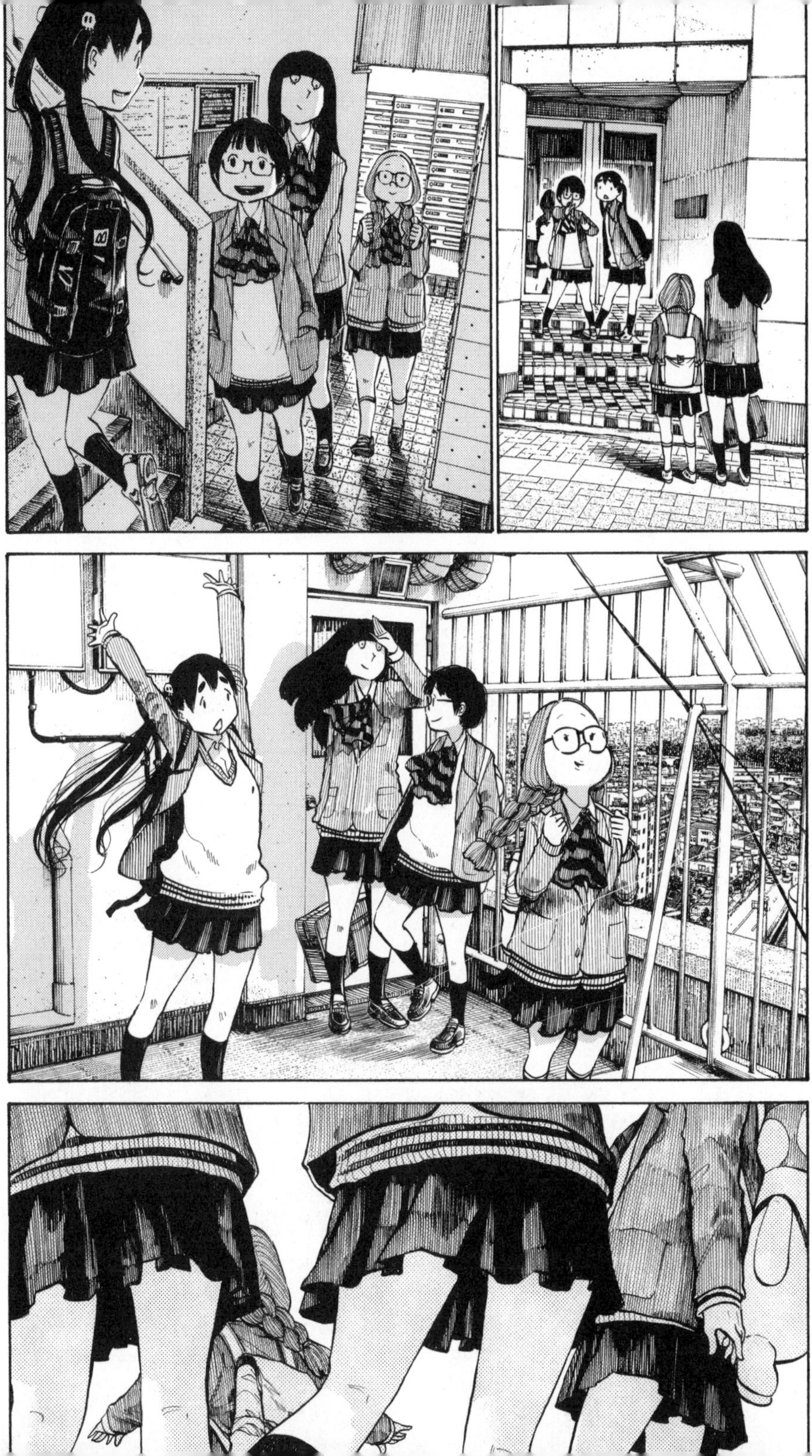

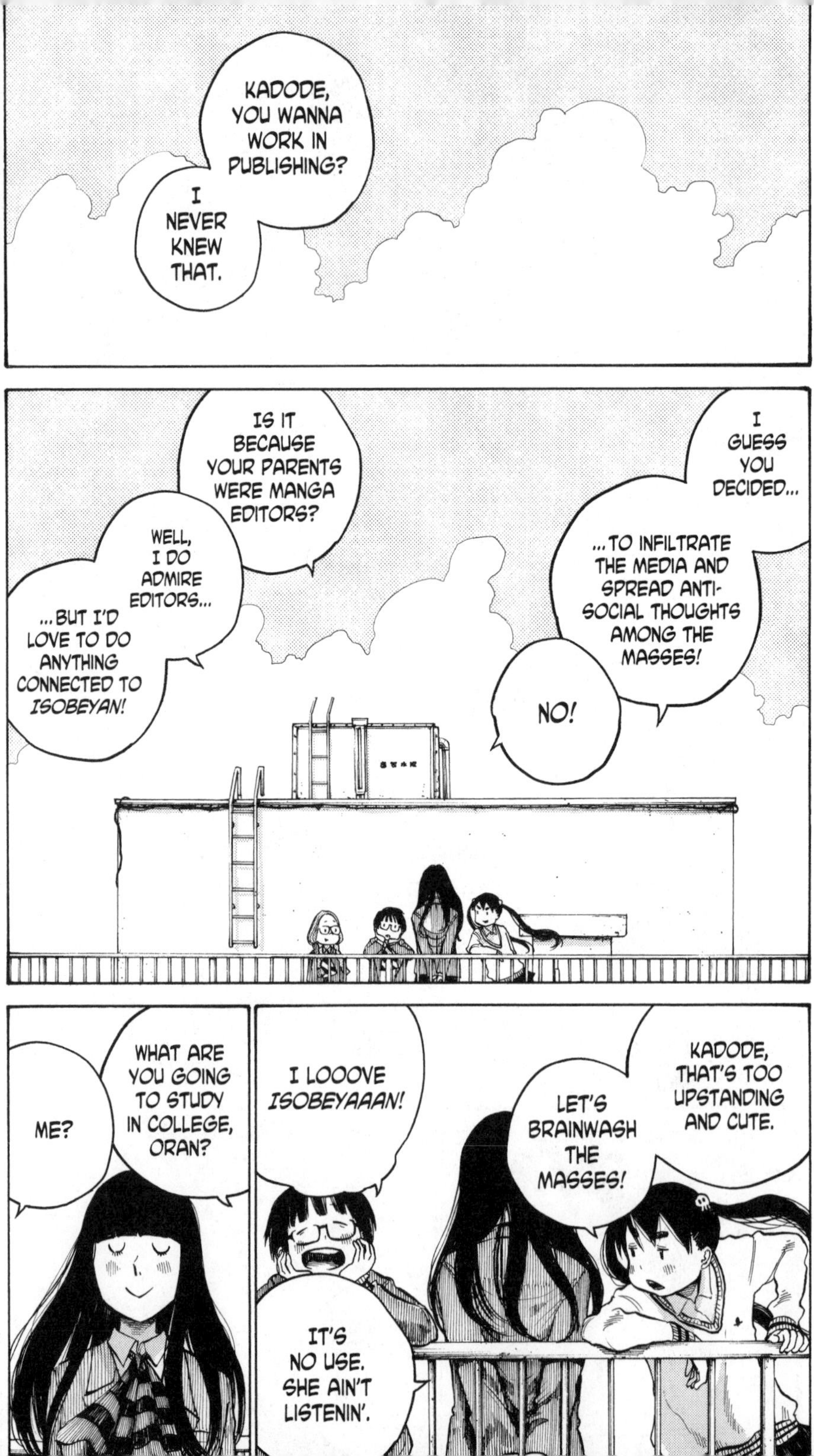
KADODE, YOU WANNA WORK IN PUBLISHING?
I NEVER KNEW THAT.
I GUESS YOU DECIDED...
...TO INFILTRATE THE MEDIA AND SPREAD ANTI-SOCIAL THOUGHTS AMONG THE MASSES!
NO!
IS IT BECAUSE YOUR PARENTS WERE MANGA EDITORS?
WELL, I DO ADMIRE EDITORS...
...BUT I'D LOVE TO DO ANYTHING CONNECTED TO *ISOBEYAN!*
KADODE, THAT'S TOO UPSTANDING AND CUTE.
LET'S BRAINWASH THE MASSES!
I LOOOVE *ISOBEYAAAN!*
IT'S NO USE. SHE AIN'T LISTENIN'.
WHAT ARE YOU GOING TO STUDY IN COLLEGE, ORAN?
ME?

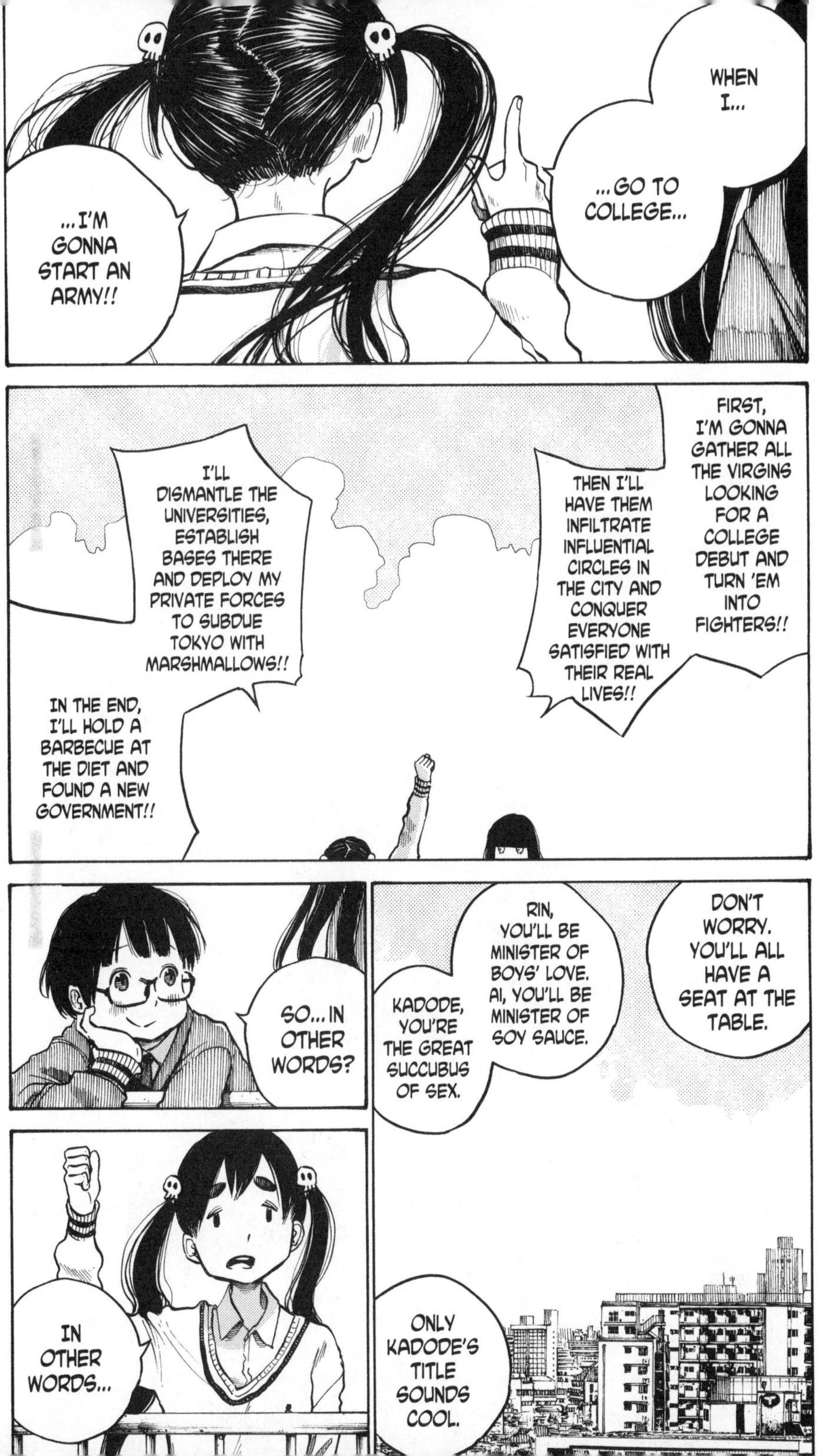
WHEN I...
...GO TO COLLEGE...
...I'M GONNA START AN ARMY!!
FIRST, I'M GONNA GATHER ALL THE VIRGINS LOOKING FOR A COLLEGE DEBUT AND TURN 'EM INTO FIGHTERS!!
THEN I'LL HAVE THEM INFILTRATE INFLUENTIAL CIRCLES IN THE CITY AND CONQUER EVERYONE SATISFIED WITH THEIR REAL LIVES!!
I'LL DISMANTLE THE UNIVERSITIES, ESTABLISH BASES THERE AND DEPLOY MY PRIVATE FORCES TO SUBDUE TOKYO WITH MARSHMALLOWS!!
IN THE END, I'LL HOLD A BARBECUE AT THE DIET AND FOUND A NEW GOVERNMENT!!
DON'T WORRY. YOU'LL ALL HAVE A SEAT AT THE TABLE.
RIN, YOU'LL BE MINISTER OF BOYS' LOVE. AI, YOU'LL BE MINISTER OF SOY SAUCE.
KADODE, YOU'RE THE GREAT SUCCUBUS OF SEX.
ONLY KADODE'S TITLE SOUNDS COOL.
SO...IN OTHER WORDS?
IN OTHER WORDS...

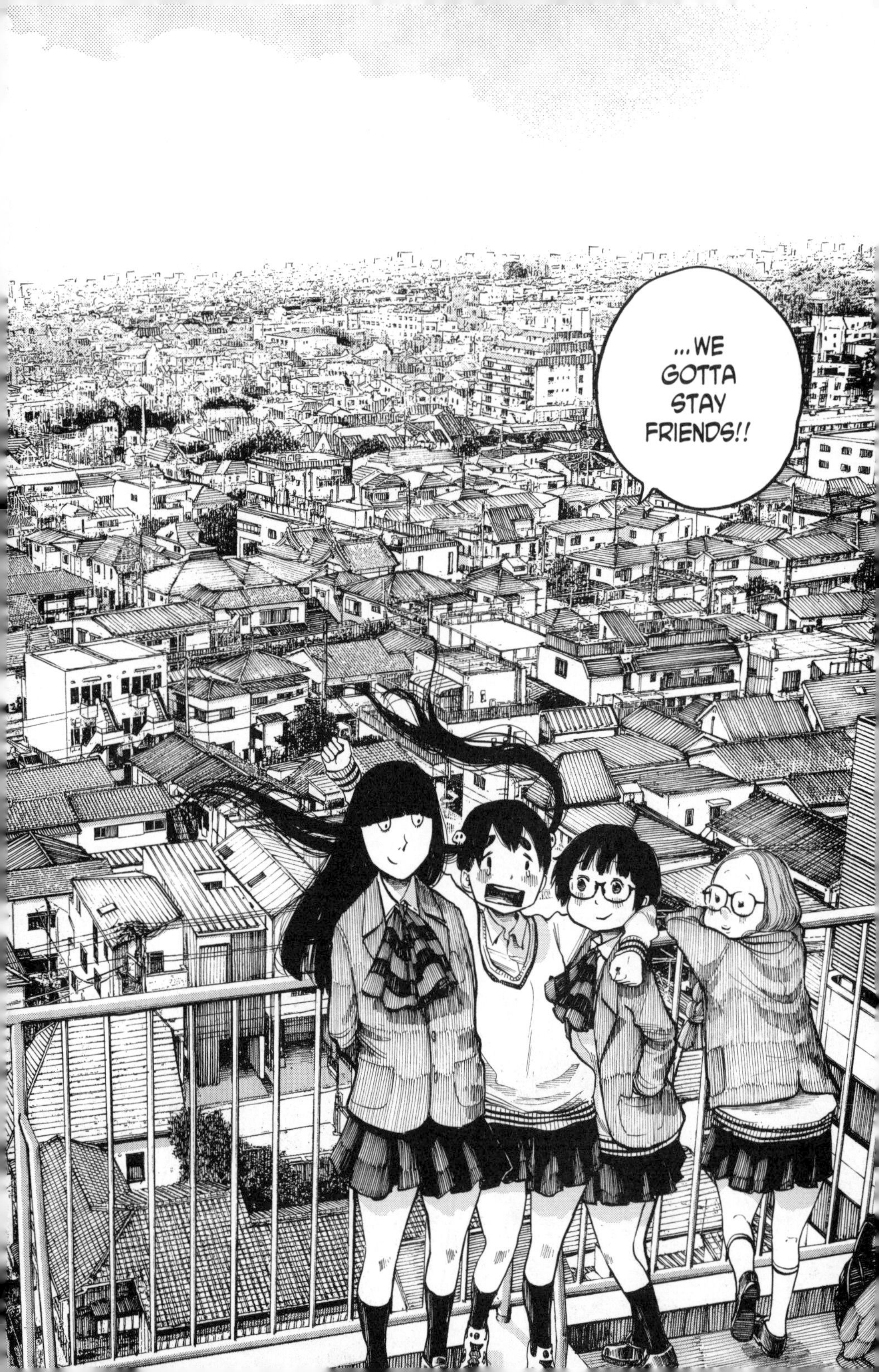
...WE GOTTA STAY FRIENDS!!

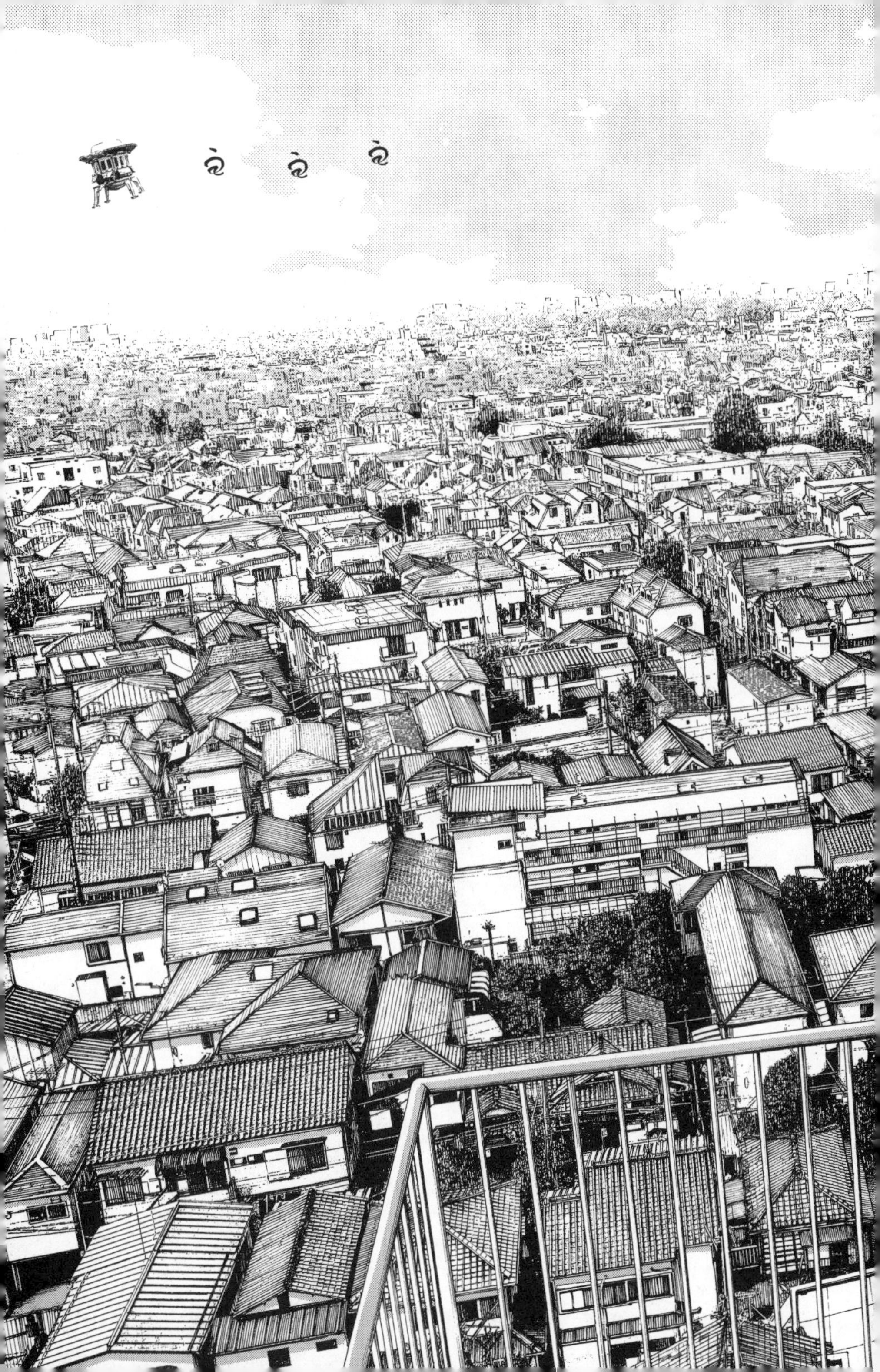

Dead Dead Demon's
Dededede Destruction
Volume 3
Inio Asano

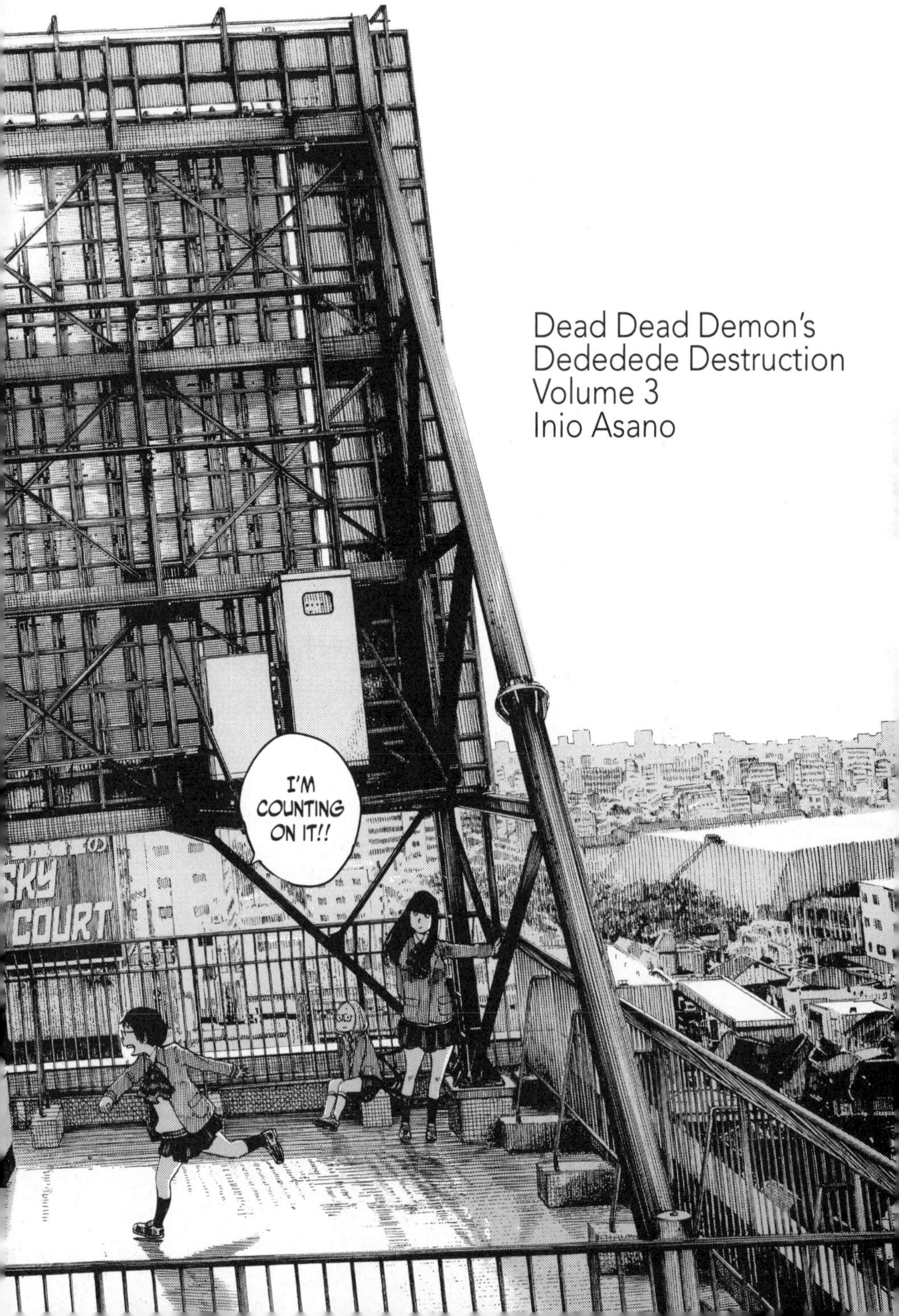
I'M COUNTING ON IT!!
SKY COURT

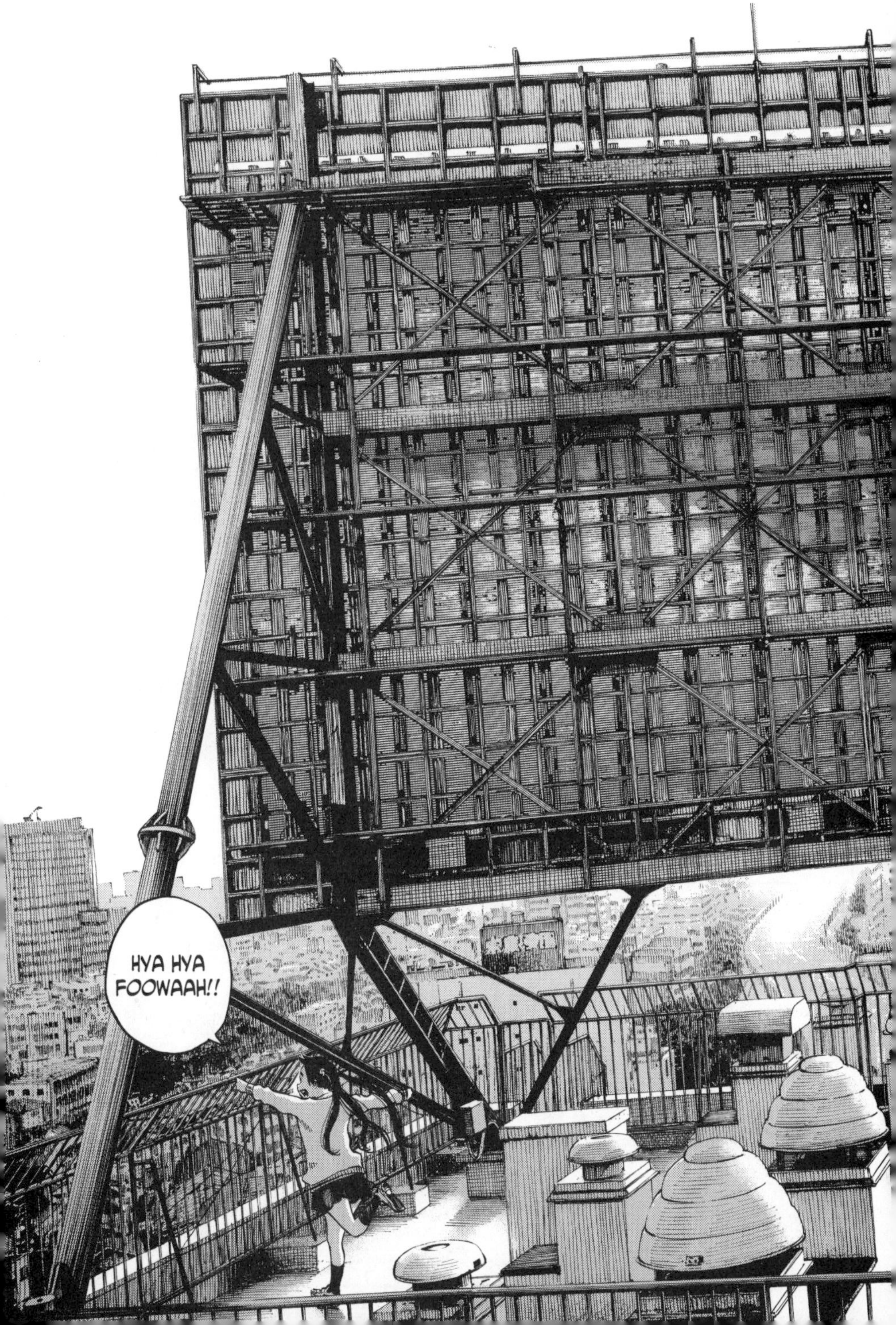
HYA HYA FOOWAAH!!

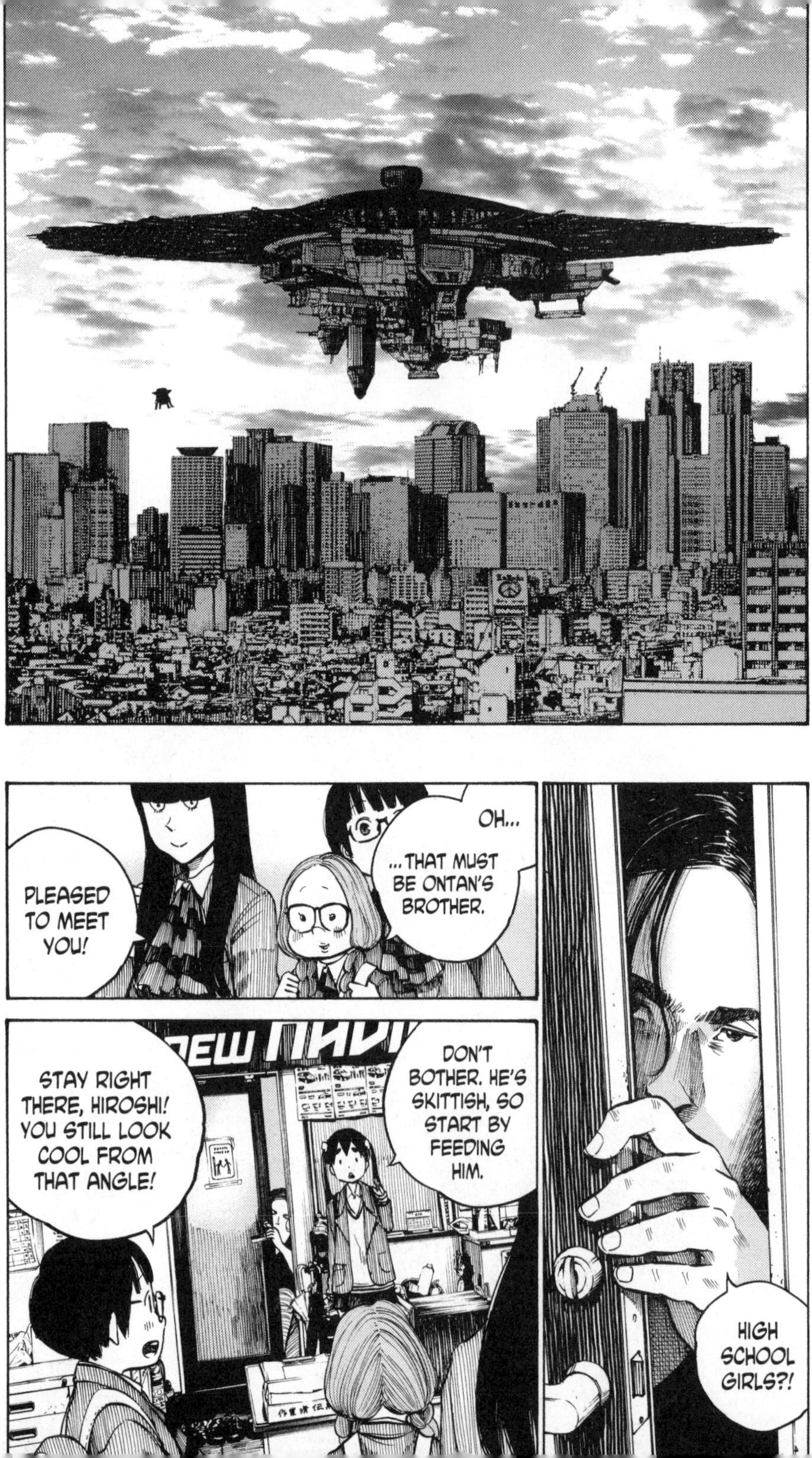
HIGH SCHOOL GIRLS?!
OH...
...THAT MUST BE ONTAN'S BROTHER.
PLEASED TO MEET YOU!
DON'T BOTHER. HE'S SKITTISH, SO START BY FEEDING HIM.
STAY RIGHT THERE, HIROSHI! YOU STILL LOOK COOL FROM THAT ANGLE!

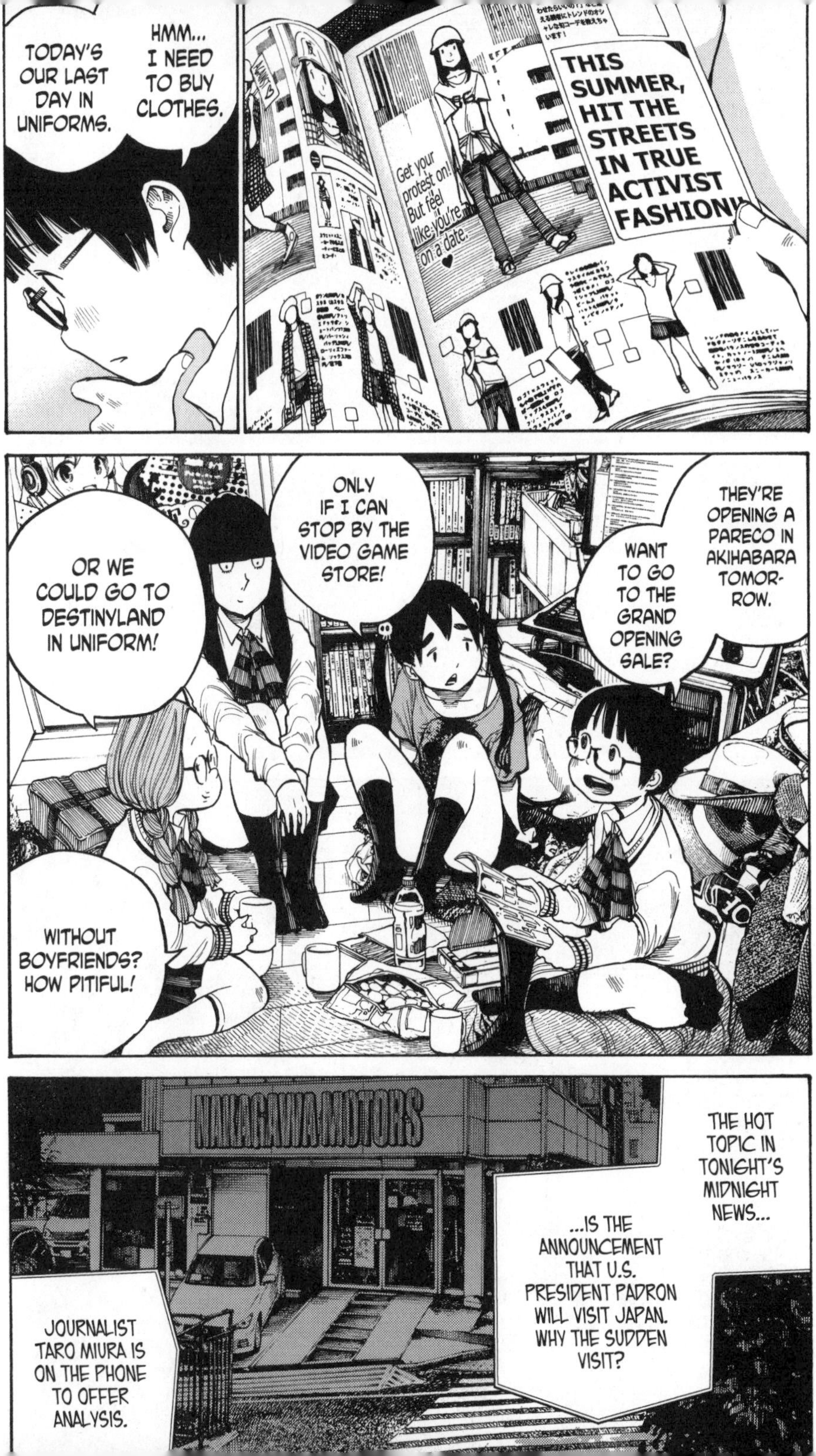
THIS SUMMER, HIT THE STREETS IN TRUE ACTIVIST FASHION!!
Get your protest on! But feel like you're on a date. ♥
HMM... I NEED TO BUY CLOTHES.
TODAY'S OUR LAST DAY IN UNIFORMS.
THEY'RE OPENING A PARECO IN AKIHABARA TOMORROW.
WANT TO GO TO THE GRAND OPENING SALE?
ONLY IF I CAN STOP BY THE VIDEO GAME STORE!
OR WE COULD GO TO DESTINYLAND IN UNIFORM!
WITHOUT BOYFRIENDS? HOW PITIFUL!
NAKAGAWA MOTORS
THE HOT TOPIC IN TONIGHT'S MIDNIGHT NEWS...
...IS THE ANNOUNCEMENT THAT U.S. PRESIDENT PADRON WILL VISIT JAPAN. WHY THE SUDDEN VISIT?
JOURNALIST TARO MIURA IS ON THE PHONE TO OFFER ANALYSIS.

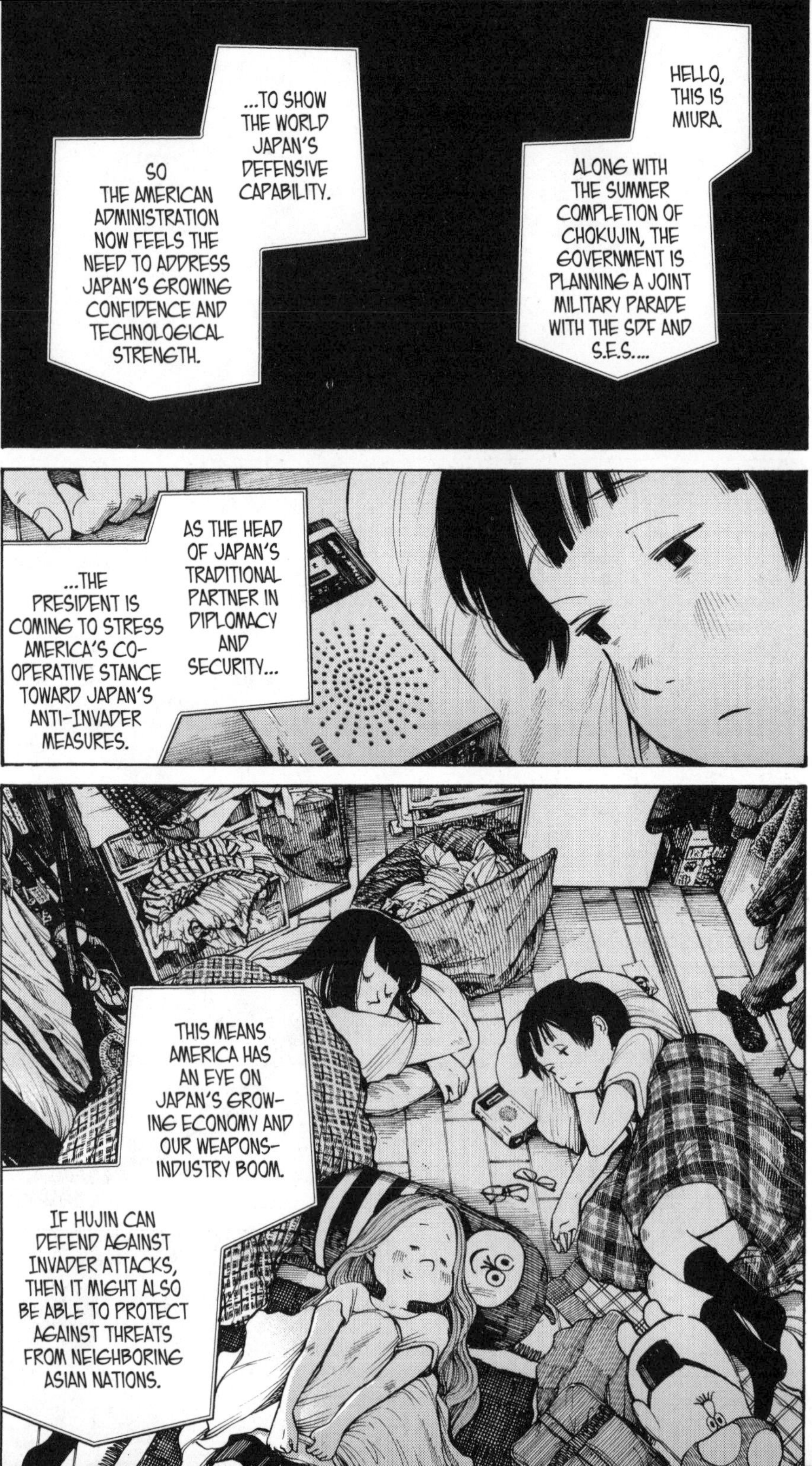
HELLO, THIS IS MIURA.
ALONG WITH THE SUMMER COMPLETION OF CHOKUJIN, THE GOVERNMENT IS PLANNING A JOINT MILITARY PARADE WITH THE SDF AND S.E.S....
...TO SHOW THE WORLD JAPAN'S DEFENSIVE CAPABILITY.
SO THE AMERICAN ADMINISTRATION NOW FEELS THE NEED TO ADDRESS JAPAN'S GROWING CONFIDENCE AND TECHNOLOGICAL STRENGTH.
AS THE HEAD OF JAPAN'S TRADITIONAL PARTNER IN DIPLOMACY AND SECURITY...
...THE PRESIDENT IS COMING TO STRESS AMERICA'S CO-OPERATIVE STANCE TOWARD JAPAN'S ANTI-INVADER MEASURES.
THIS MEANS AMERICA HAS AN EYE ON JAPAN'S GROWING ECONOMY AND OUR WEAPONS-INDUSTRY BOOM.
IF HUJIN CAN DEFEND AGAINST INVADER ATTACKS, THEN IT MIGHT ALSO BE ABLE TO PROTECT AGAINST THREATS FROM NEIGHBORING ASIAN NATIONS.

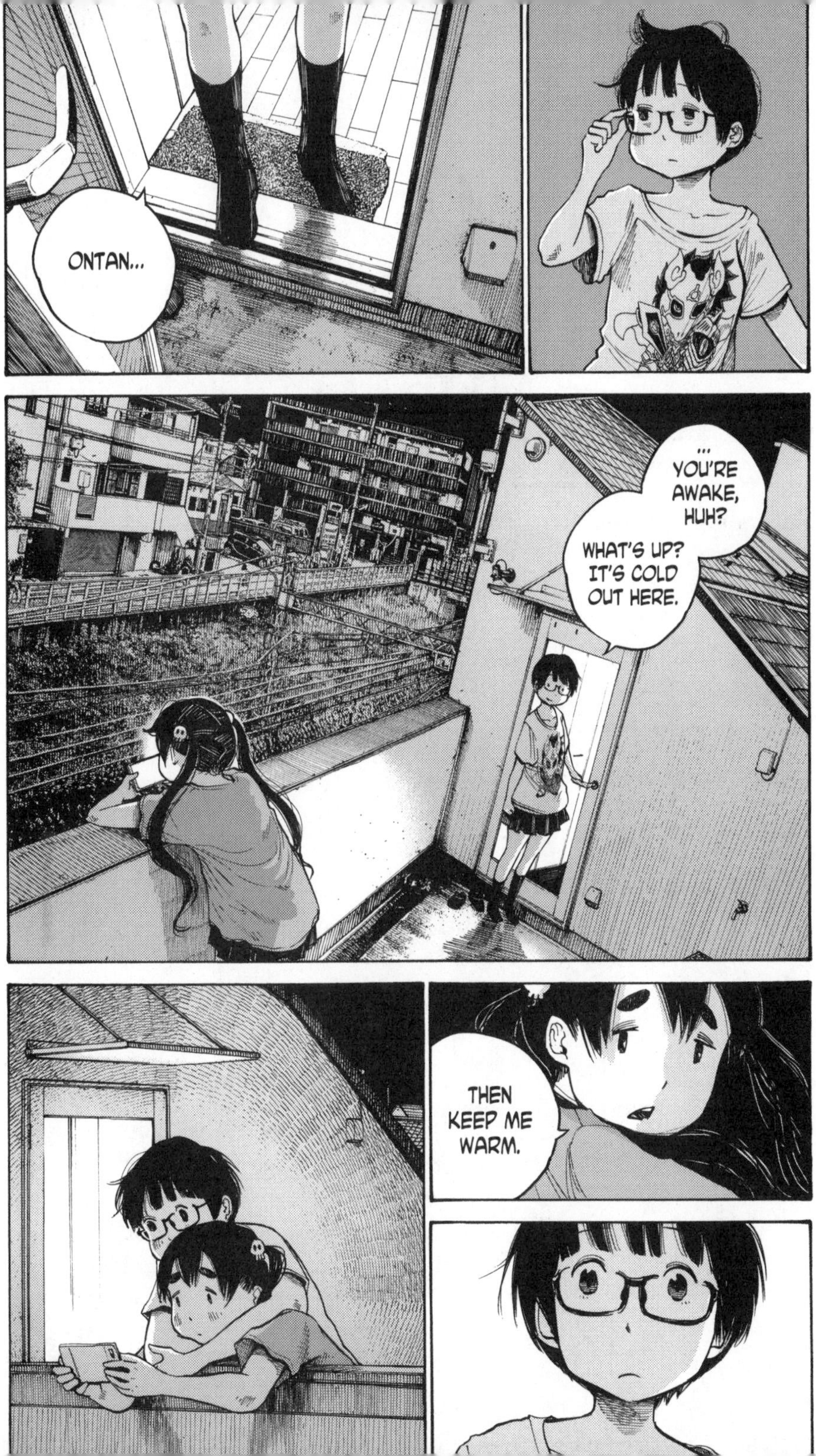
ONTAN...
... YOU'RE AWAKE, HUH?
WHAT'S UP? IT'S COLD OUT HERE.
THEN KEEP ME WARM.

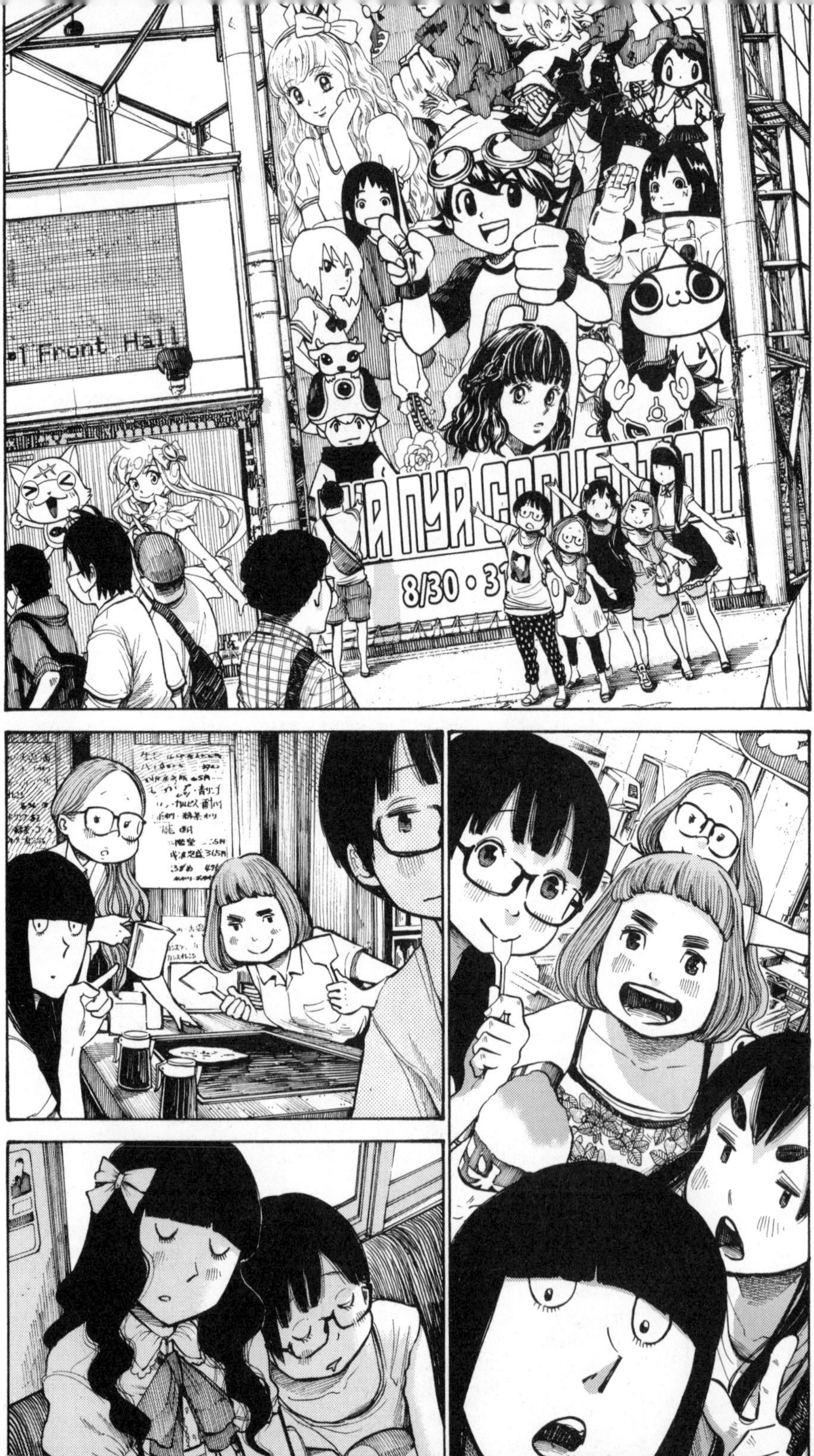
Front Hall
8/30 • 3

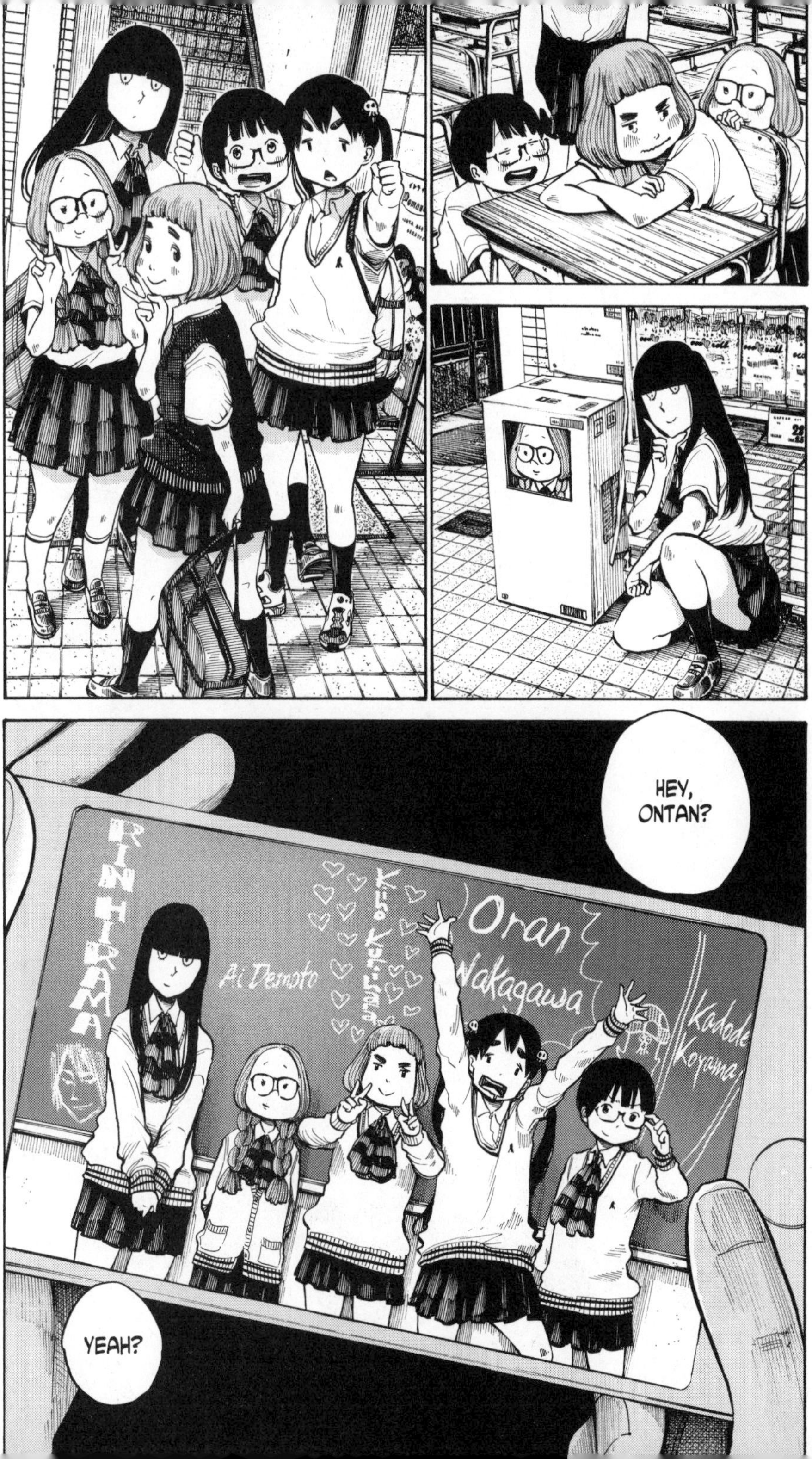
HEY, ONTAN?
Oran Nakagawa
Kadode Koyama
Ai Demoto
RIN HIRAMA
YEAH?

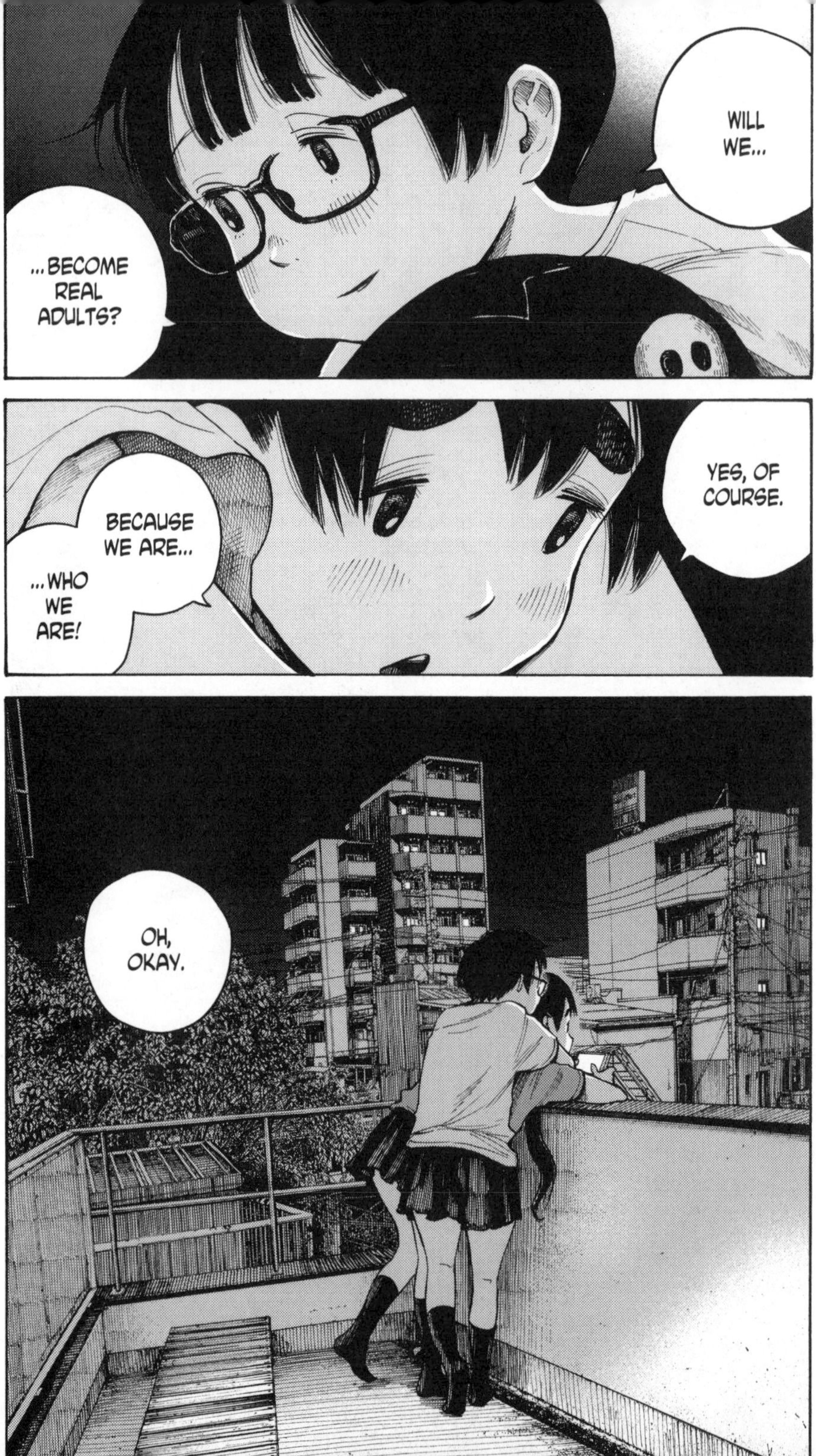
WILL WE...
...BECOME REAL ADULTS?
YES, OF COURSE.
BECAUSE WE ARE...
...WHO WE ARE!
OH, OKAY.

CHAPTER 24

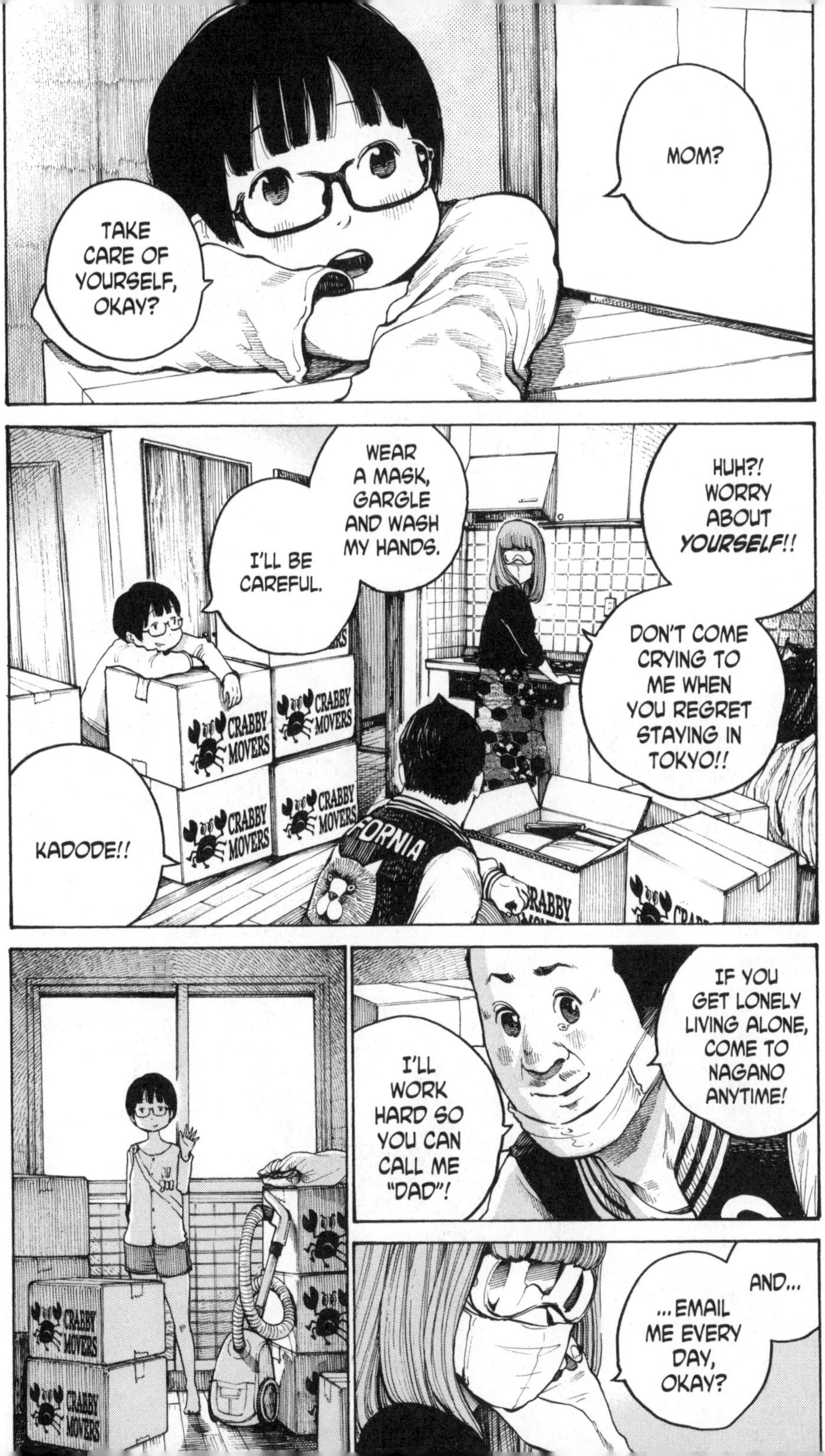
MOM?
TAKE CARE OF YOURSELF, OKAY?
HUH?! WORRY ABOUT *YOURSELF*!!
DON'T COME CRYING TO ME WHEN YOU REGRET STAYING IN TOKYO!!
WEAR A MASK, GARGLE AND WASH MY HANDS.
I'LL BE CAREFUL.
CRABBY MOVERS
KADODE!!
IF YOU GET LONELY LIVING ALONE, COME TO NAGANO ANYTIME!
I'LL WORK HARD SO YOU CAN CALL ME "DAD"!
AND...
...EMAIL ME EVERY DAY, OKAY?

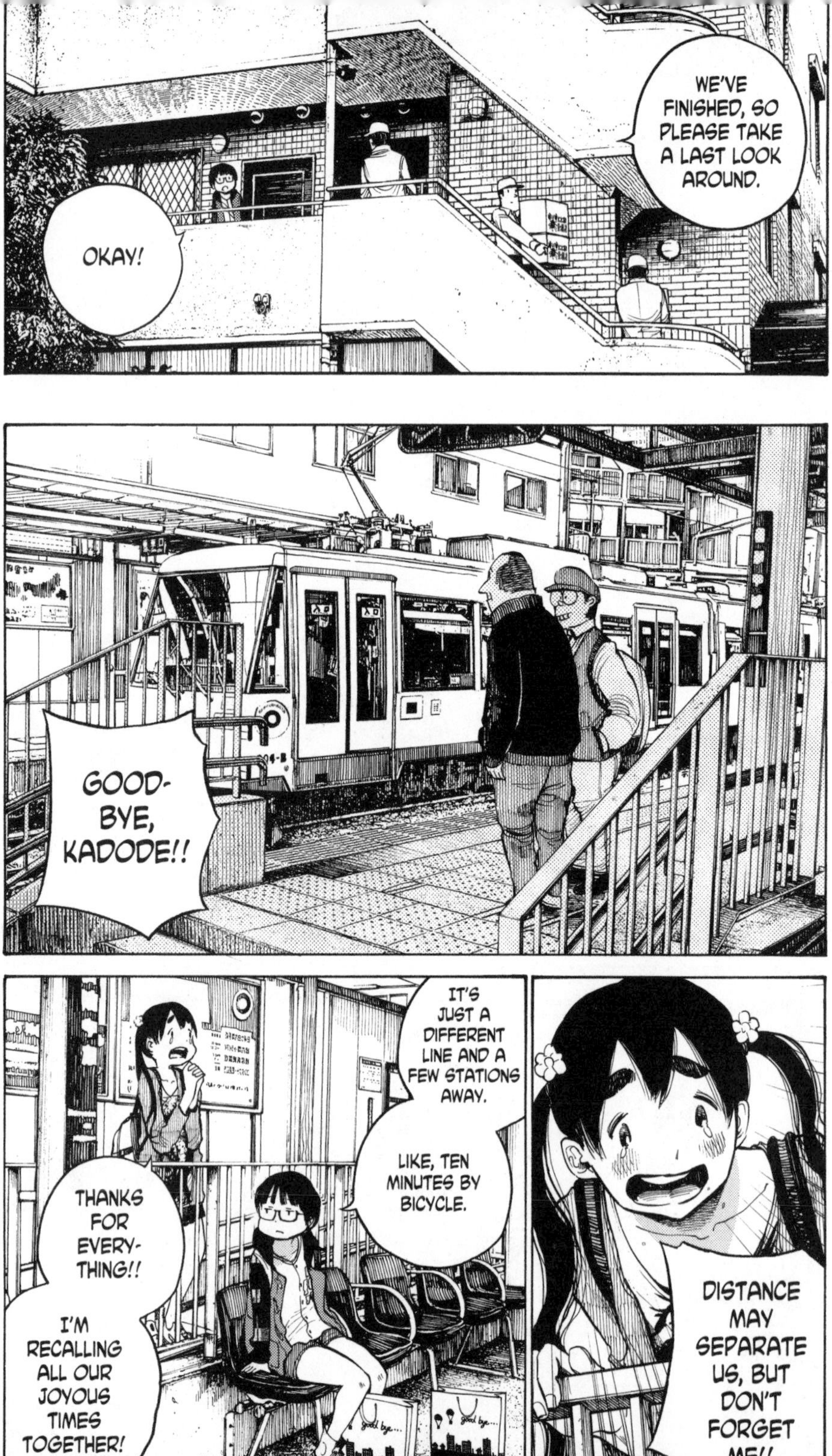
WE'VE FINISHED, SO PLEASE TAKE A LAST LOOK AROUND.
OKAY!
GOOD-BYE, KADODE!!
DISTANCE MAY SEPARATE US, BUT DON'T FORGET ME!!
IT'S JUST A DIFFERENT LINE AND A FEW STATIONS AWAY.
LIKE, TEN MINUTES BY BICYCLE.
THANKS FOR EVERY-THING!!
I'M RECALLING ALL OUR JOYOUS TIMES TOGETHER!
good bye...
good bye...

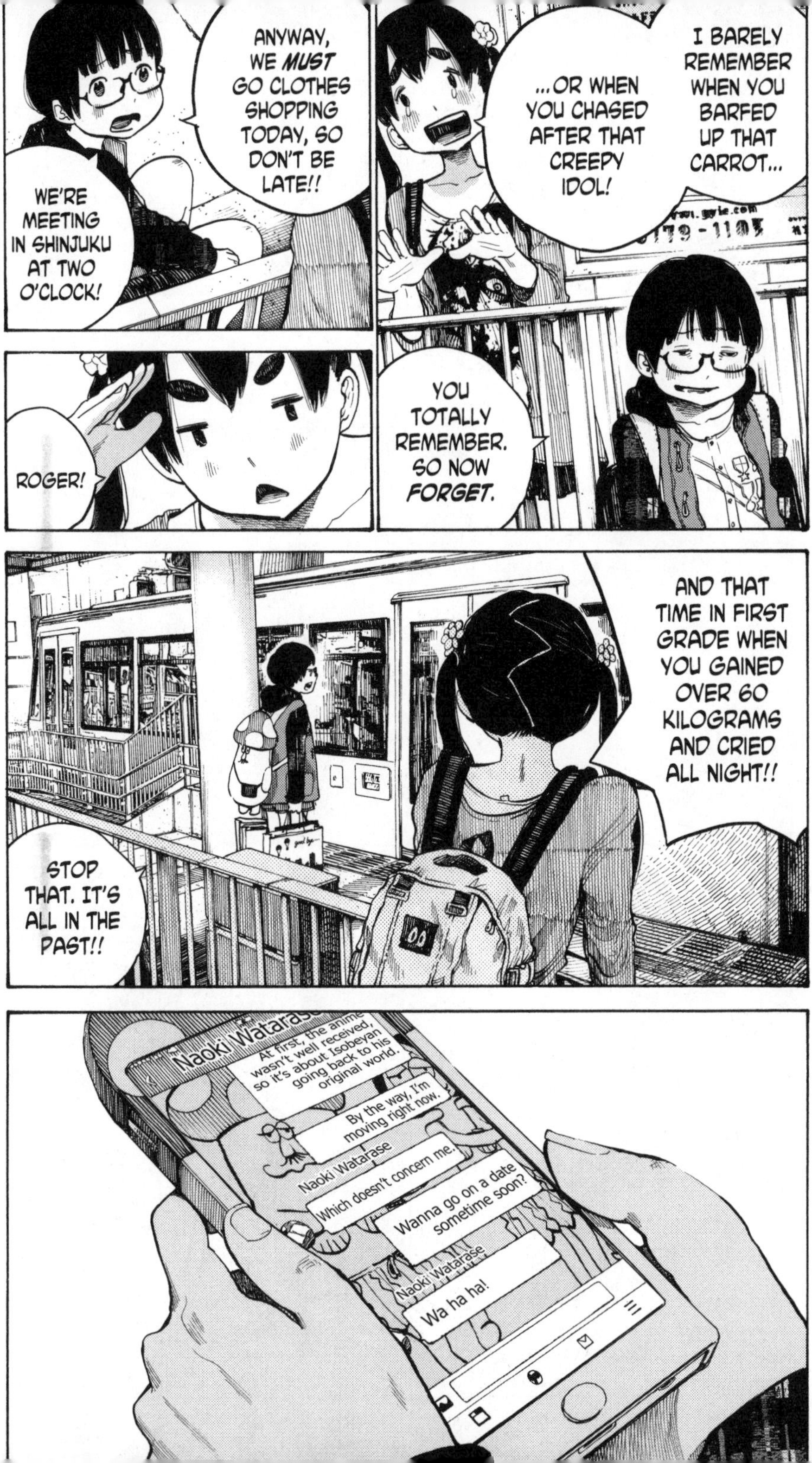
I BARELY REMEMBER WHEN YOU BARFED UP THAT CARROT...
...OR WHEN YOU CHASED AFTER THAT CREEPY IDOL!
ANYWAY, WE *MUST* GO CLOTHES SHOPPING TODAY, SO DON'T BE LATE!!
WE'RE MEETING IN SHINJUKU AT TWO O'CLOCK!
YOU TOTALLY REMEMBER. SO NOW *FORGET*.
ROGER!
AND THAT TIME IN FIRST GRADE WHEN YOU GAINED OVER 60 KILOGRAMS AND CRIED ALL NIGHT!!
STOP THAT. IT'S ALL IN THE PAST!!
Naoki Watarase
At first, the anime wasn't well received, so it's about Isobeyan going back to his original world.
By the way, I'm moving right now.
Naoki Watarase
Which doesn't concern me.
Wanna go on a date sometime soon?
Naoki Watarase
Wa ha ha!

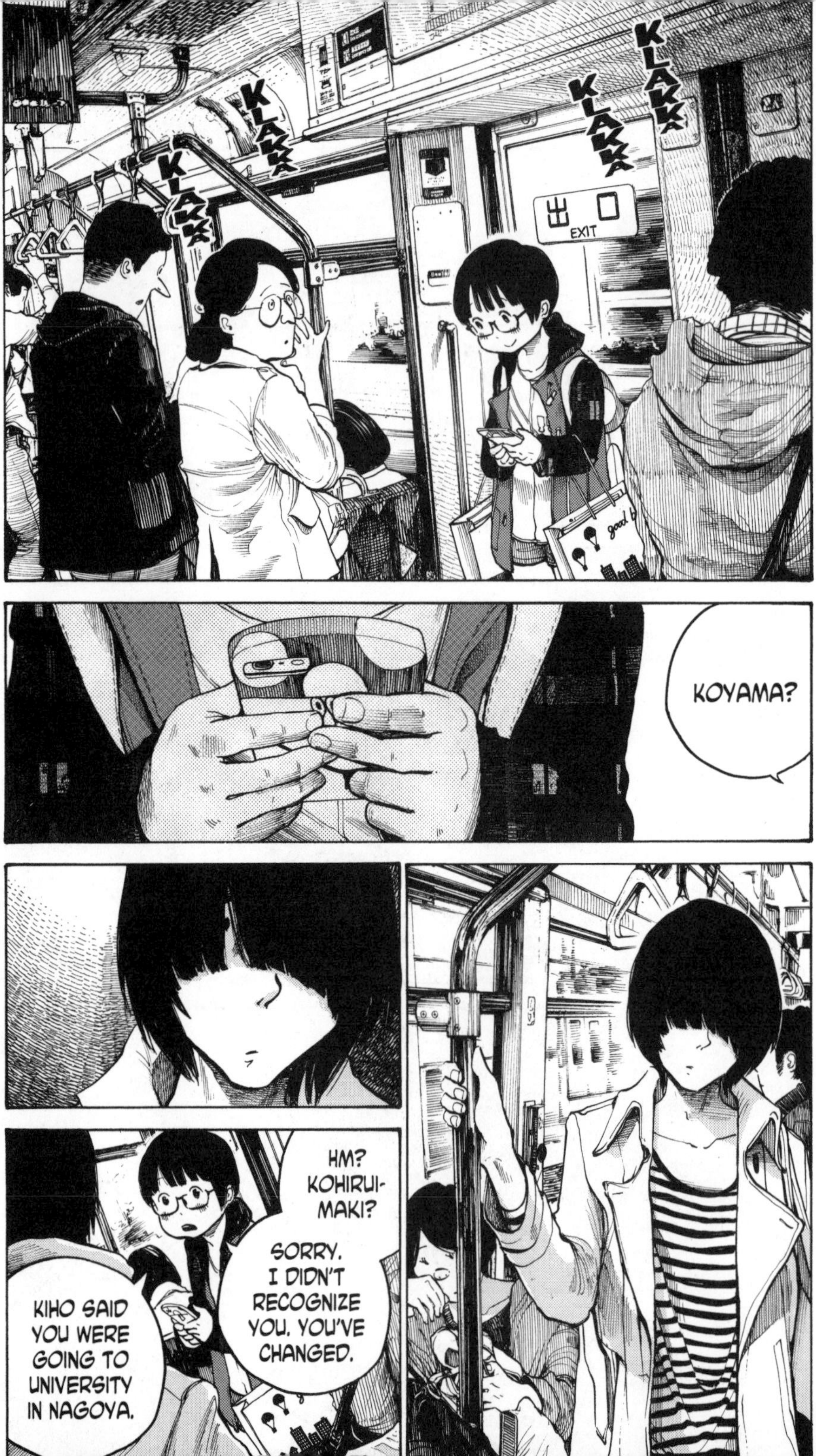
KLAKKA
KLAKKA
KLAKKA
KLAKKA
出口 EXIT
KOYAMA?
HM? KOHIRUI-MAKI?
SORRY. I DIDN'T RECOGNIZE YOU. YOU'VE CHANGED.
KIHO SAID YOU WERE GOING TO UNIVERSITY IN NAGOYA.

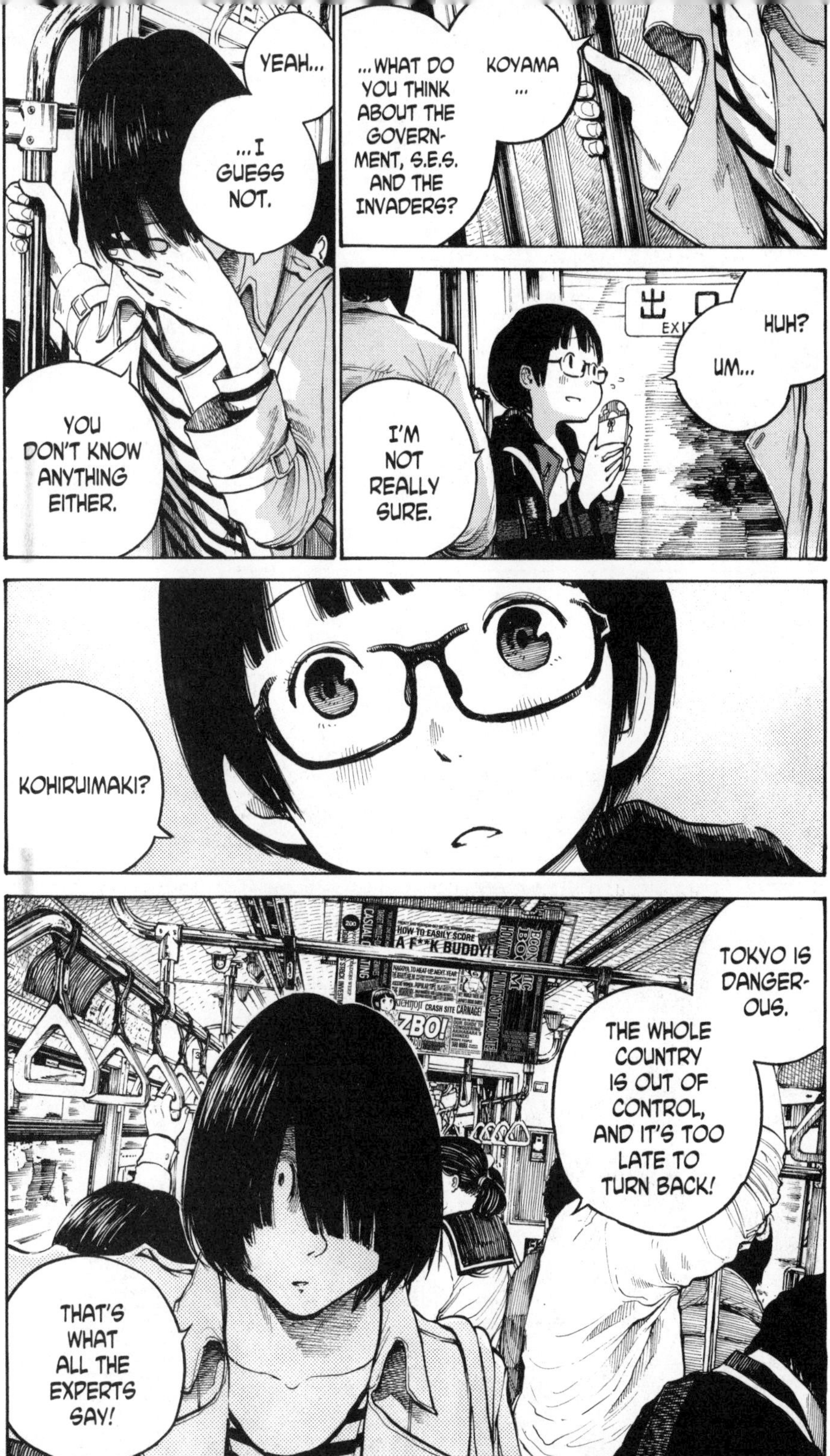
KOYAMA ...
...WHAT DO YOU THINK ABOUT THE GOVERN-MENT, S.E.S. AND THE INVADERS?
出口 EXIT
HUH?
UM...
I'M NOT REALLY SURE.
YEAH...
...I GUESS NOT.
YOU DON'T KNOW ANYTHING EITHER.
KOHIRUIMAKI?
HOW TO EASILY SCORE A F**K BUDDY!
KICHIJOJI CRASH SITE CARNAGE!
ZBO!
TOKYO IS DANGER-OUS.
THE WHOLE COUNTRY IS OUT OF CONTROL, AND IT'S TOO LATE TO TURN BACK!
THAT'S WHAT ALL THE EXPERTS SAY!

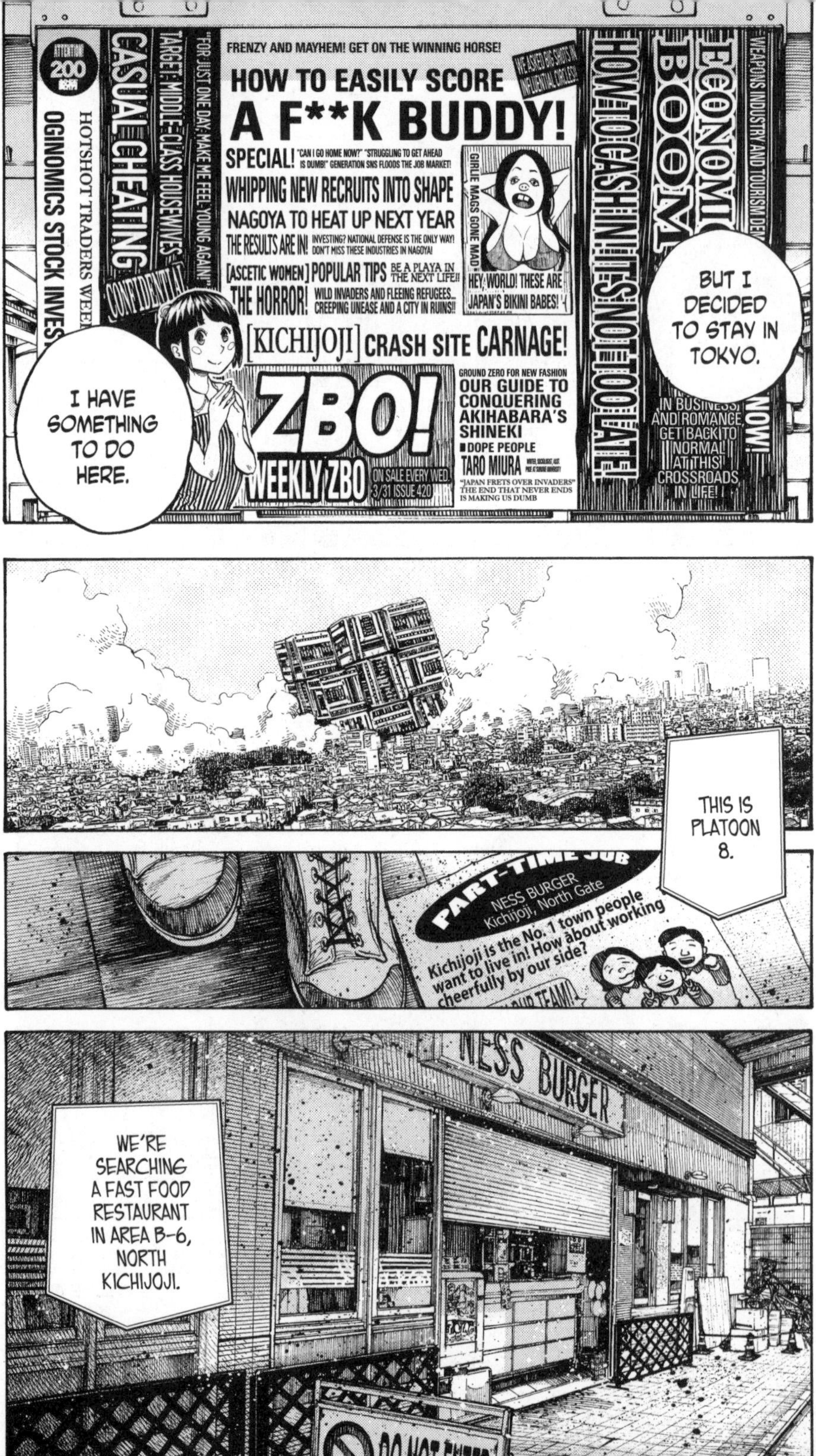

BUT I DECIDED TO STAY IN TOKYO.
ECONOMIC BOOM
WEAPONS INDUSTRY AND TOURISM DE
NOW!
IN BUSINESS AND ROMANCE GET BACK TO NORMAL AT THIS CROSSROADS IN LIFE!
HOW TO CASH IN! IT'S NOT TOO LATE!
FRENZY AND MAYHEM! GET ON THE WINNING HORSE!
WE ASKED BIG SHOTS IN INFLUENTIAL CIRCLES!
HOW TO EASILY SCORE A F**K BUDDY!
SPECIAL! "CAN I GO HOME NOW?" "STRUGGLING TO GET AHEAD IS DUMB!" GENERATION SNS FLOODS THE JOB MARKET!
WHIPPING NEW RECRUITS INTO SHAPE
NAGOYA TO HEAT UP NEXT YEAR
THE RESULTS ARE IN! INVESTING? NATIONAL DEFENSE IS THE ONLY WAY! DON'T MISS THESE INDUSTRIES IN NAGOYA!
[ASCETIC WOMEN] POPULAR TIPS BE A PLAYA IN THE NEXT LIFE!!
THE HORROR! WILD INVADERS AND FLEEING REFUGEES... CREEPING UNEASE AND A CITY IN RUINS!!
GIRLIE MAGS GONE MAD
HEY, WORLD! THESE ARE JAPAN'S BIKINI BABES!
[KICHIJOJI] CRASH SITE CARNAGE!
GROUND ZERO FOR NEW FASHION OUR GUIDE TO CONQUERING AKIHABARA'S SHINEKI
■DOPE PEOPLE TARO MIURA
"JAPAN FRETS OVER INVADERS" THE END THAT NEVER ENDS IS MAKING US DUMB
ZBO!
WEEKLY ZBO ON SALE EVERY WED. 3/31 ISSUE 420
"FOR JUST ONE DAY, MAKE ME FEEL YOUNG AGAIN!"
TARGET: MIDDLE-CLASS HOUSEWIVES
CASUAL CHEATING
CONFIDENTIAL
ATTENTION! 200
HOTSHOT TRADERS WEEK
OGINOMICS STOCK INVES
I HAVE SOMETHING TO DO HERE.
THIS IS PLATOON 8.
PART-TIME JOB
NESS BURGER Kichijoji, North Gate
Kichijoji is the No. 1 town people want to live in! How about working cheerfully by our side?
NESS BURGER
WE'RE SEARCHING A FAST FOOD RESTAURANT IN AREA B-6, NORTH KICHIJOJI.

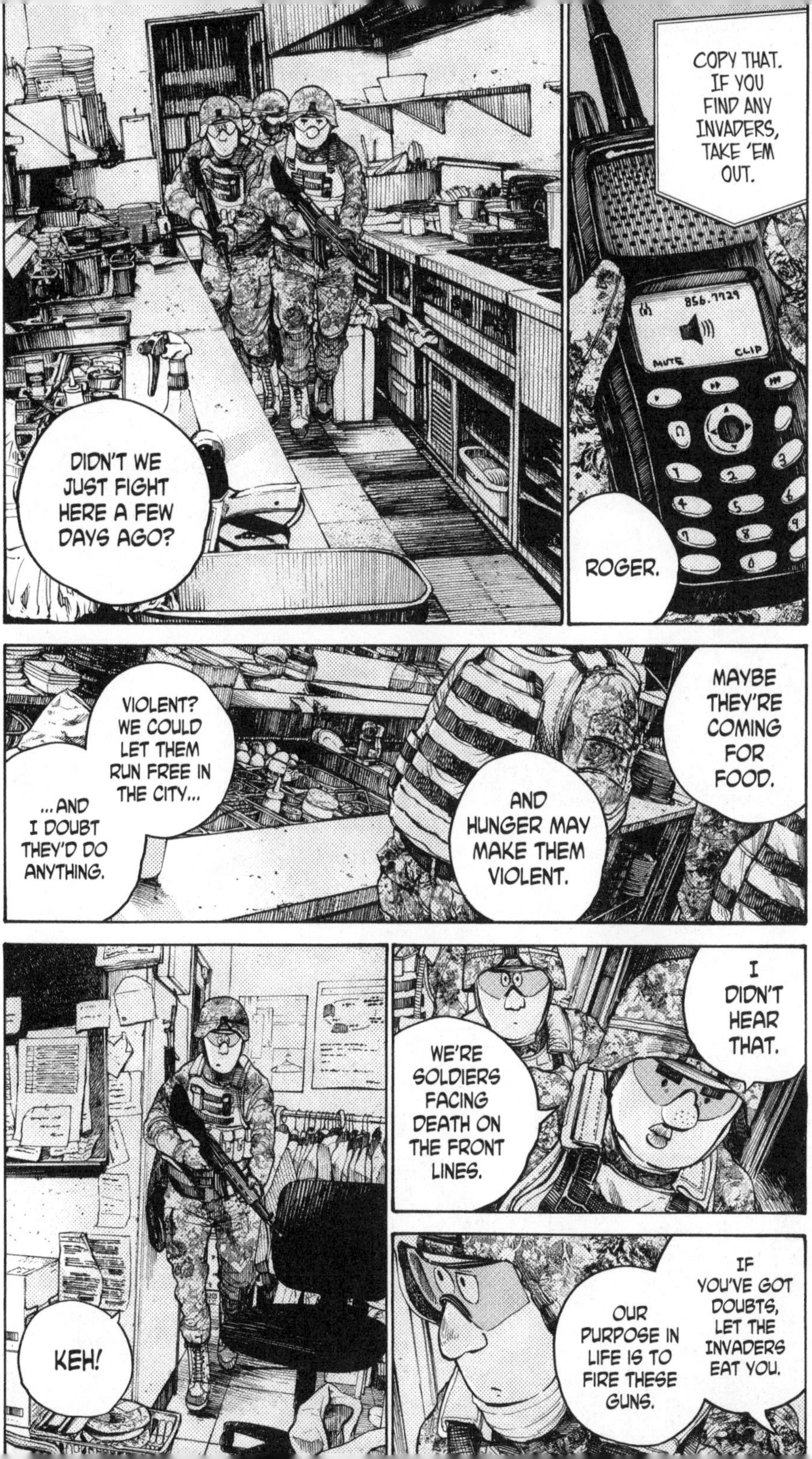
COPY THAT. IF YOU FIND ANY INVADERS, TAKE 'EM OUT.
856.7729
MUTE
CLIP
ROGER.
DIDN'T WE JUST FIGHT HERE A FEW DAYS AGO?
MAYBE THEY'RE COMING FOR FOOD.
AND HUNGER MAY MAKE THEM VIOLENT.
VIOLENT? WE COULD LET THEM RUN FREE IN THE CITY...
...AND I DOUBT THEY'D DO ANYTHING.
I DIDN'T HEAR THAT.
WE'RE SOLDIERS FACING DEATH ON THE FRONT LINES.
IF YOU'VE GOT DOUBTS, LET THE INVADERS EAT YOU.
OUR PURPOSE IN LIFE IS TO FIRE THESE GUNS.
KEH!

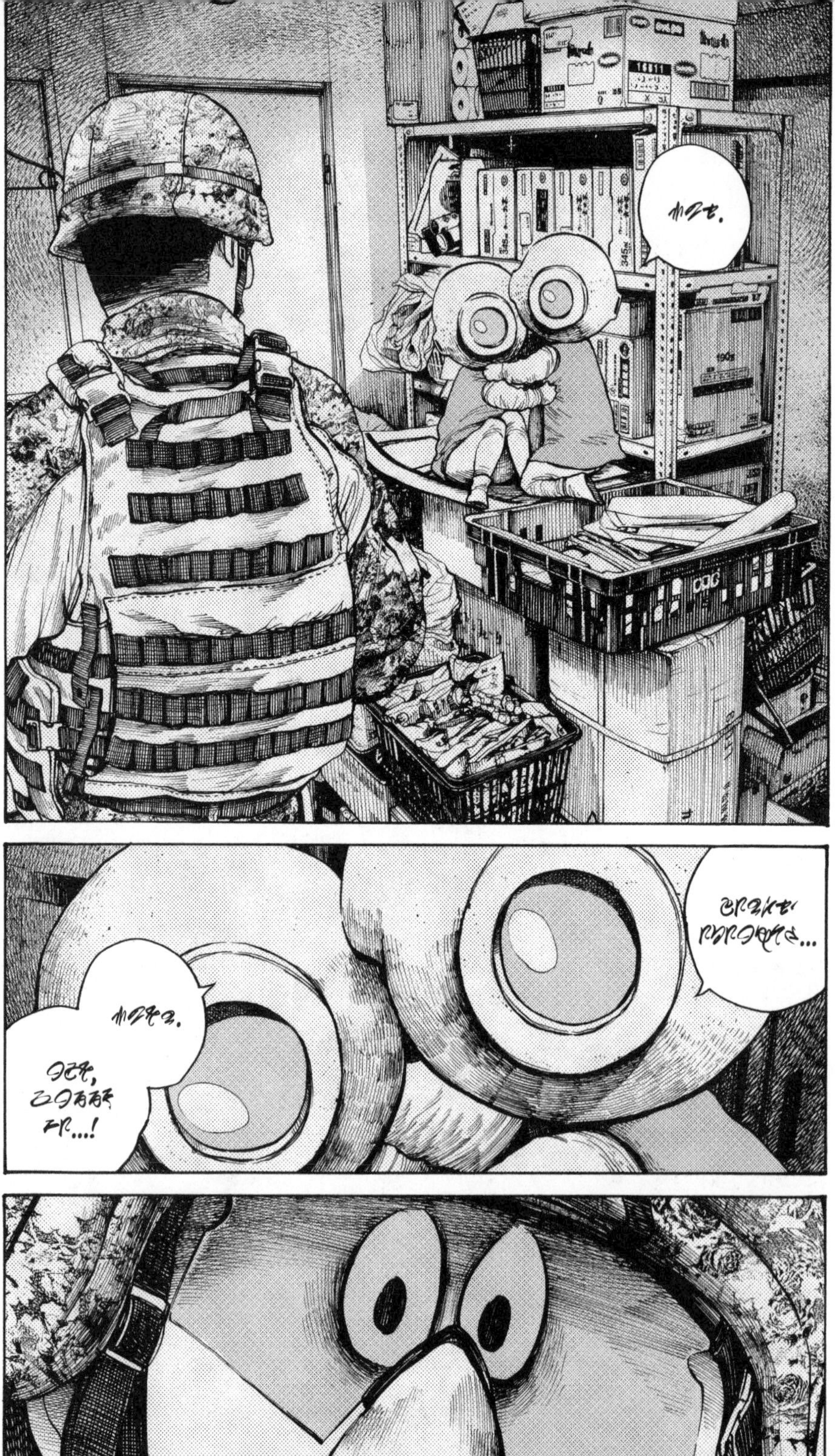

AGH!
WHOA!!
B R AK KA
PT
ONK

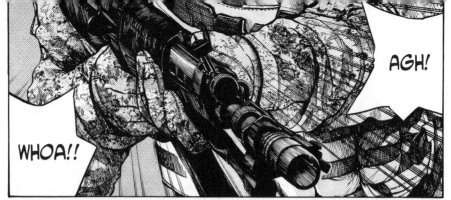

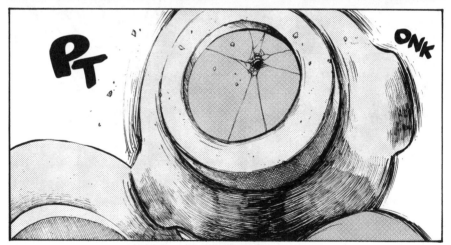

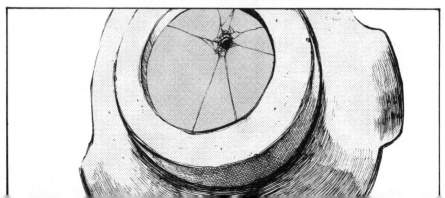

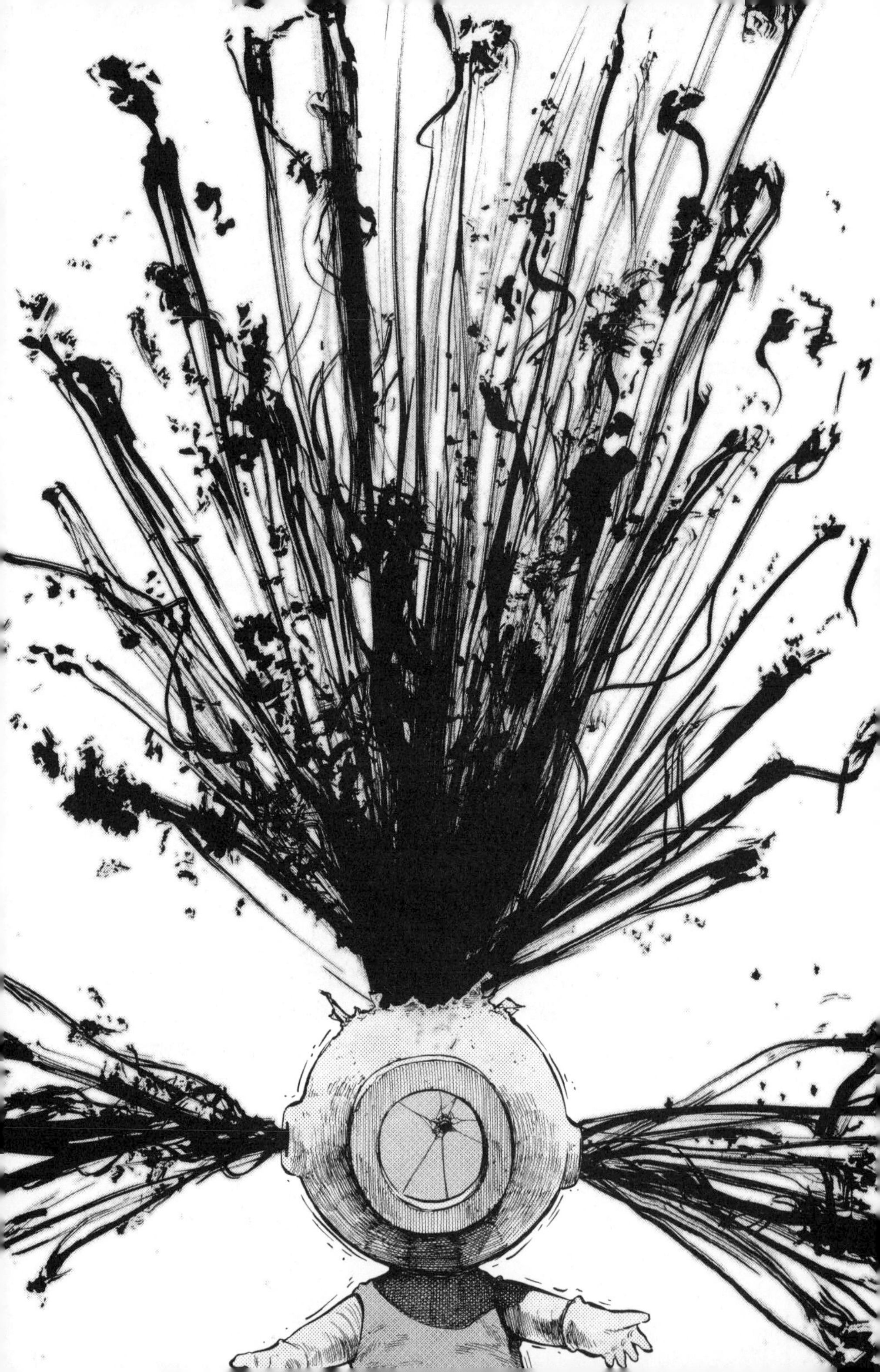

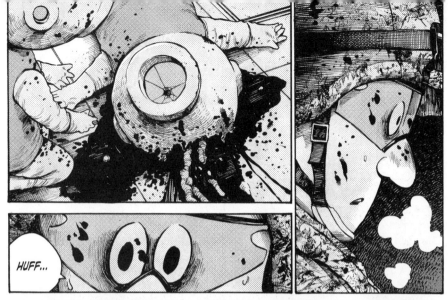

HUFF...

HUFF...

HUFF...

HUFF...

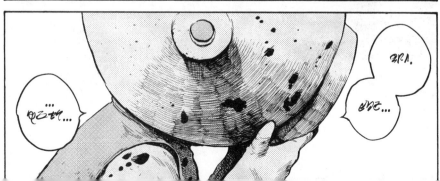

153

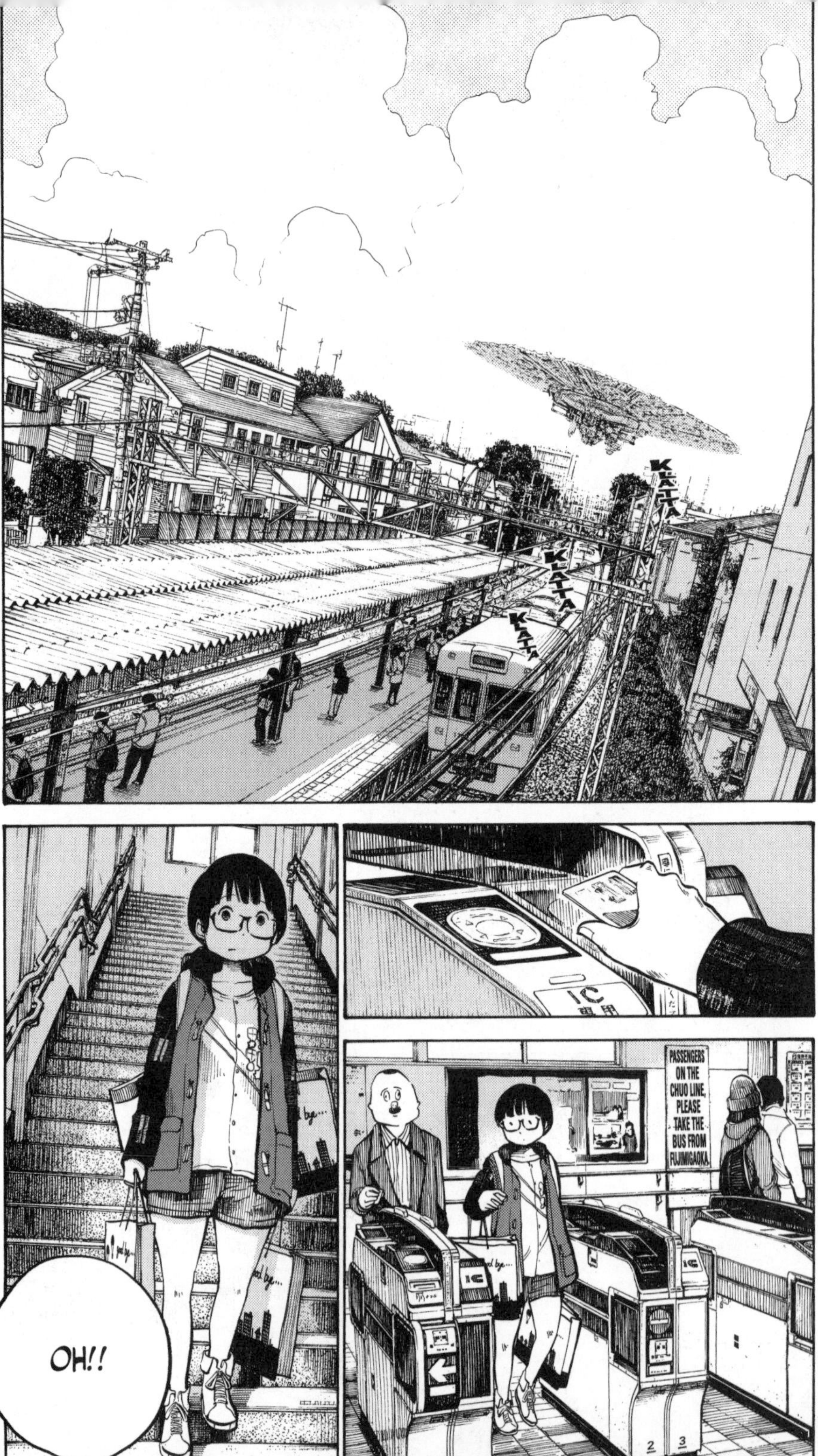
KLATTA
KLATTA
KLATTA
IC
PASSENGERS ON THE CHUO LINE, PLEASE TAKE THE BUS FROM FUJIMIGAOKA
OH!!

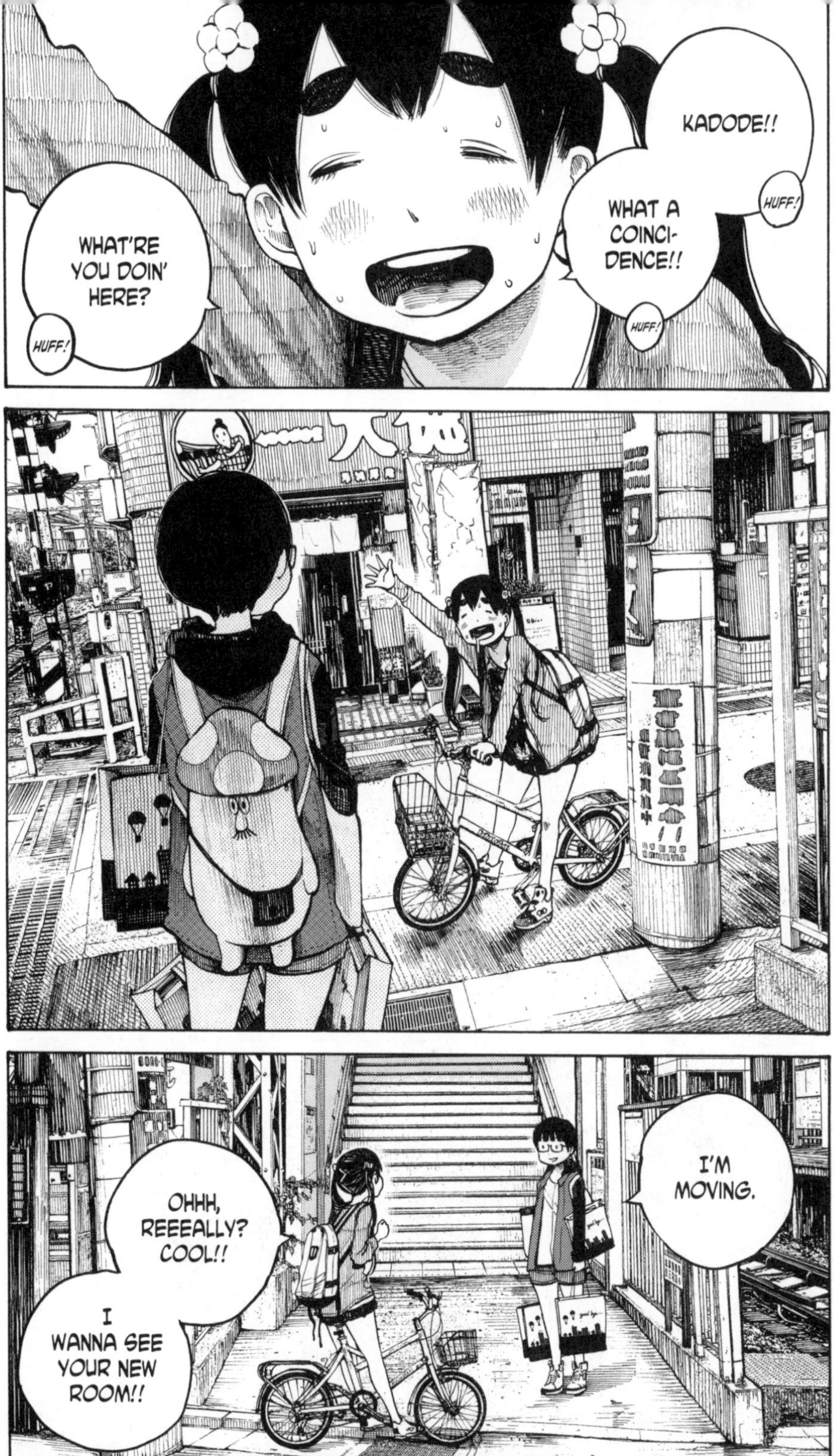
KADODE!!
HUFF!
WHAT A COINCI-DENCE!!
HUFF!
WHAT'RE YOU DOIN' HERE?
HUFF!
I'M MOVING.
OHHH, REEEALLY? COOL!!
I WANNA SEE YOUR NEW ROOM!!

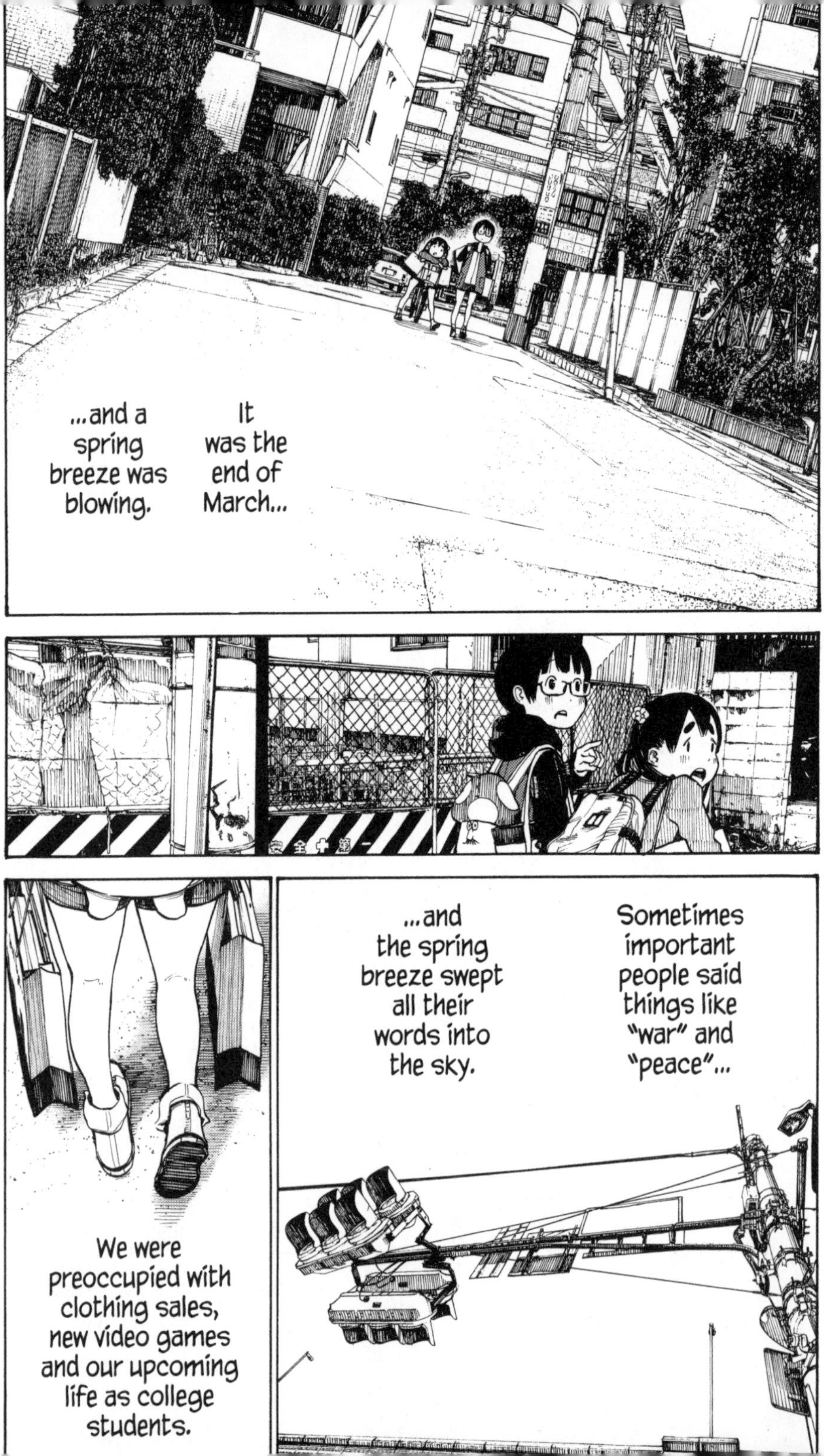

It was the end of March...
...and a spring breeze was blowing.
Sometimes important people said things like "war" and "peace"...
...and the spring breeze swept all their words into the sky.
We were preoccupied with clothing sales, new video games and our upcoming life as college students.

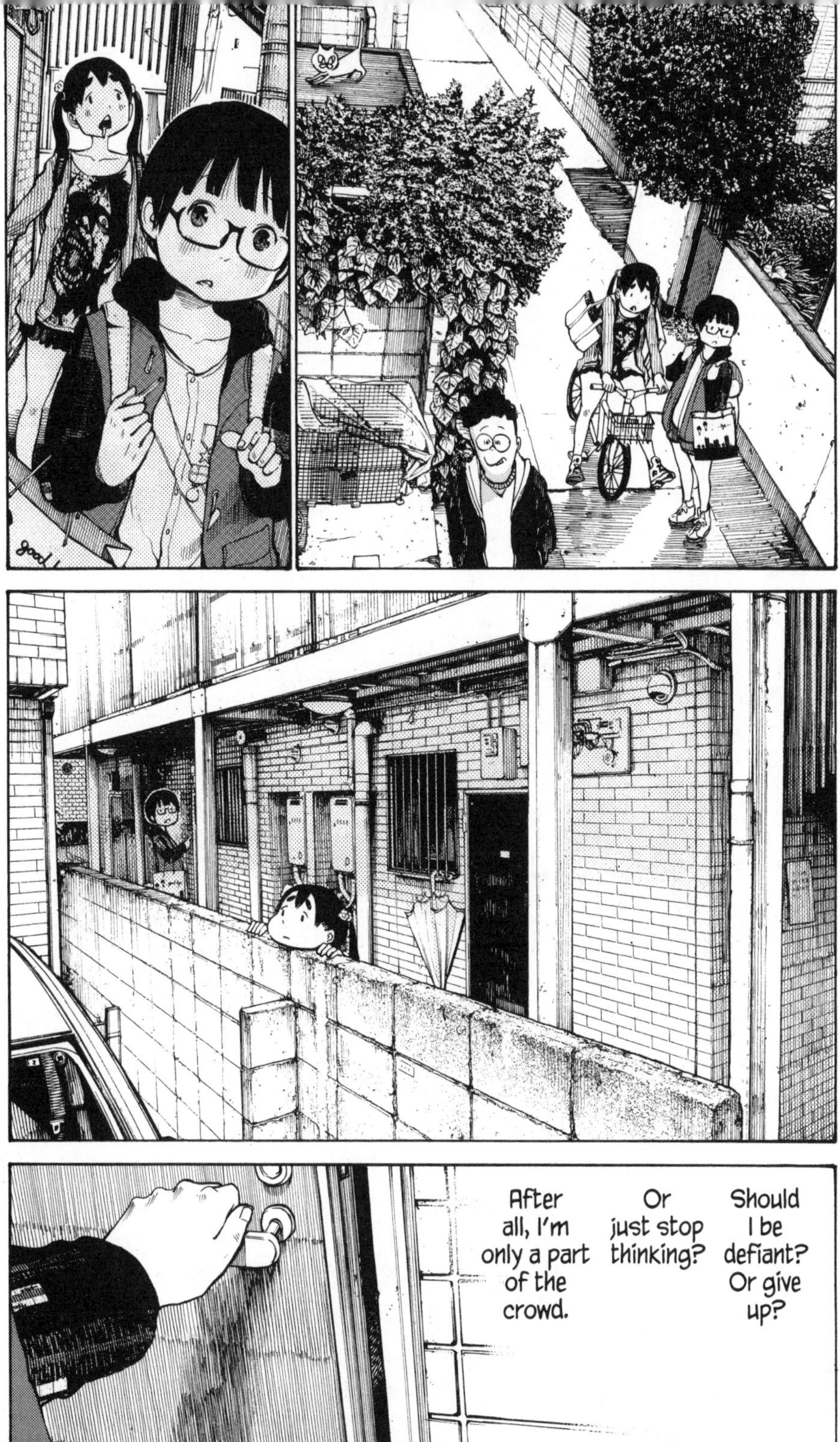
good!
Should I be defiant? Or give up?
Or just stop thinking?
After all, I'm only a part of the crowd.

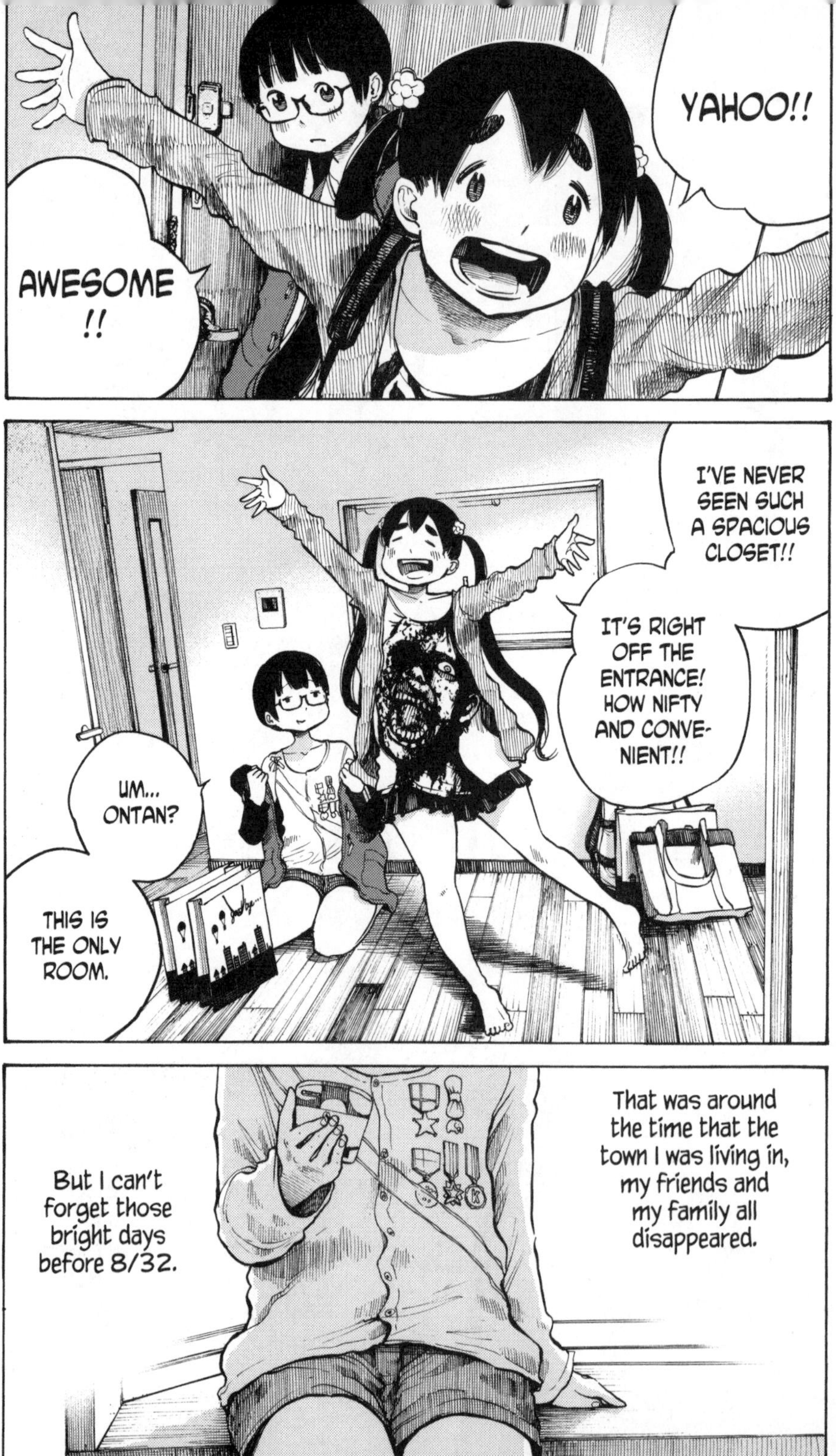
YAHOO!!
AWESOME!!
I'VE NEVER SEEN SUCH A SPACIOUS CLOSET!!
IT'S RIGHT OFF THE ENTRANCE! HOW NIFTY AND CONVENIENT!!
UM... ONTAN?
THIS IS THE ONLY ROOM.
That was around the time that the town I was living in, my friends and my family all disappeared.
But I can't forget those bright days before 8/32.

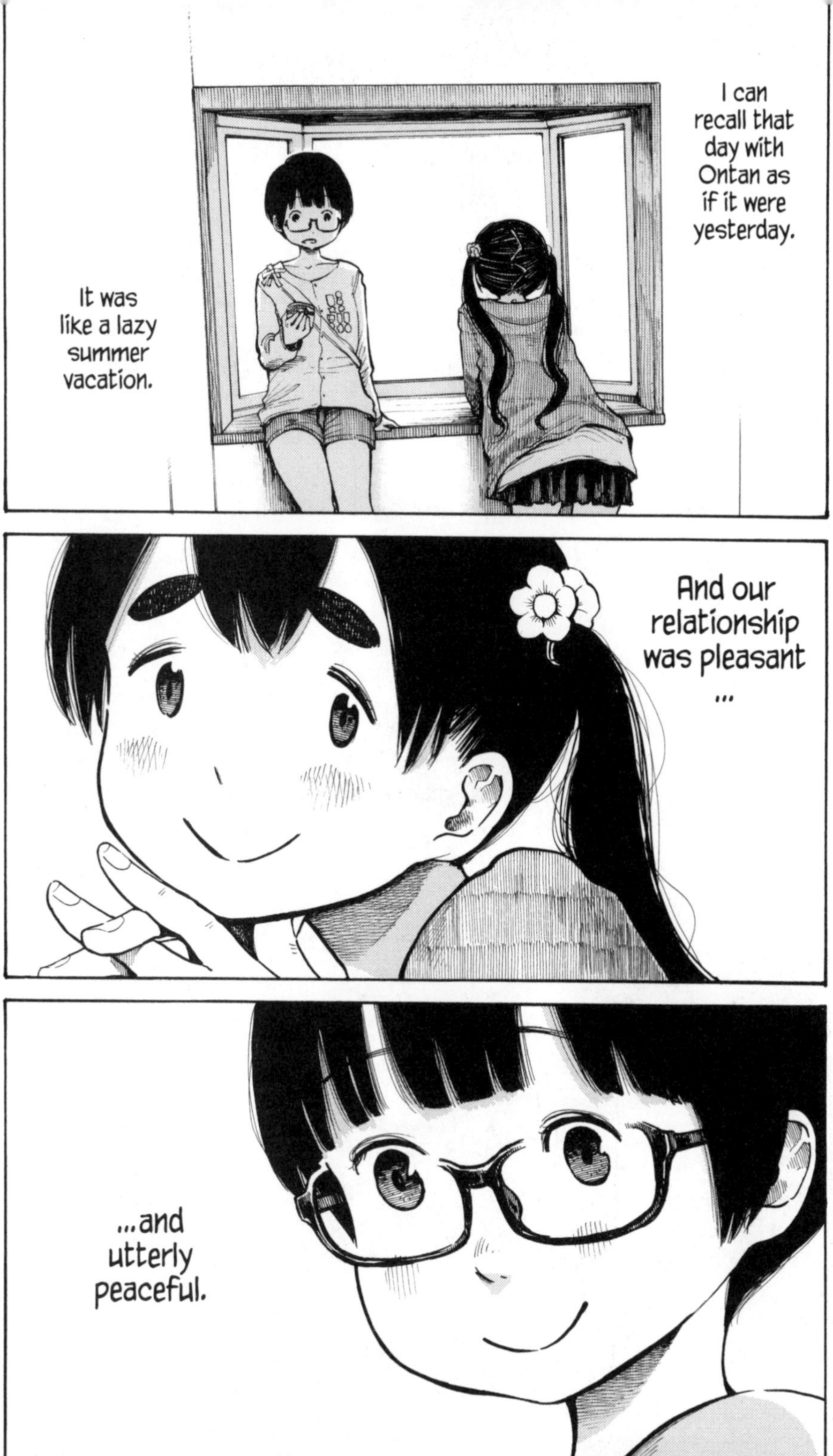
I can recall that day with Ontan as if it were yesterday.
It was like a lazy summer vacation.
And our relationship was pleasant ...
...and utterly peaceful.

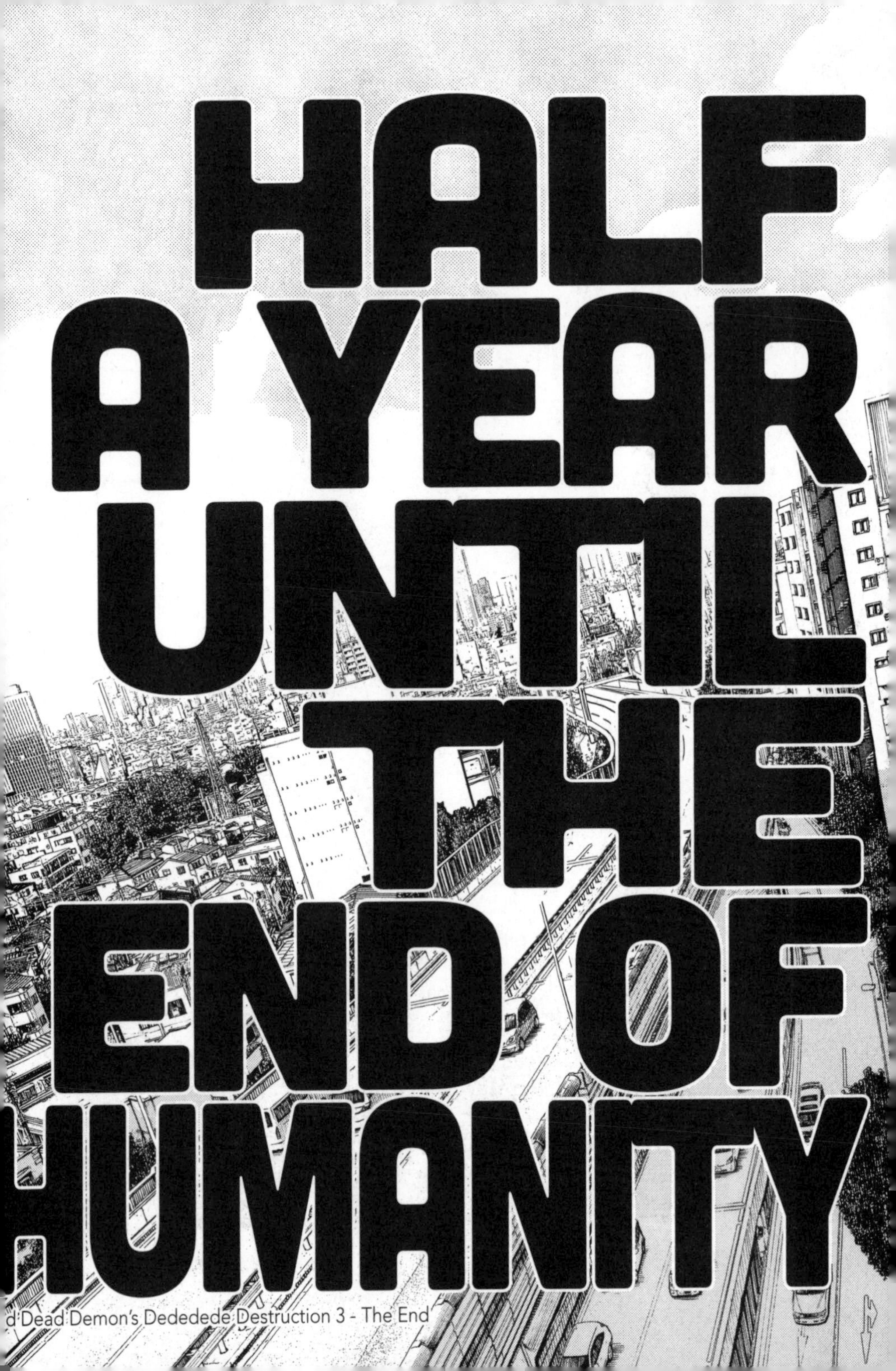
HALF A YEAR UNTIL THE END OF HUMANITY
d Dead Demon's Dededede Destruction 3 - The End

DEDEDEDE

Dead Dead Demon's
Dededede Destruction Volume 3
Inio Asano

Background Assistants: Satsuki Sato
                           Ran Atsumori
                           Buuko

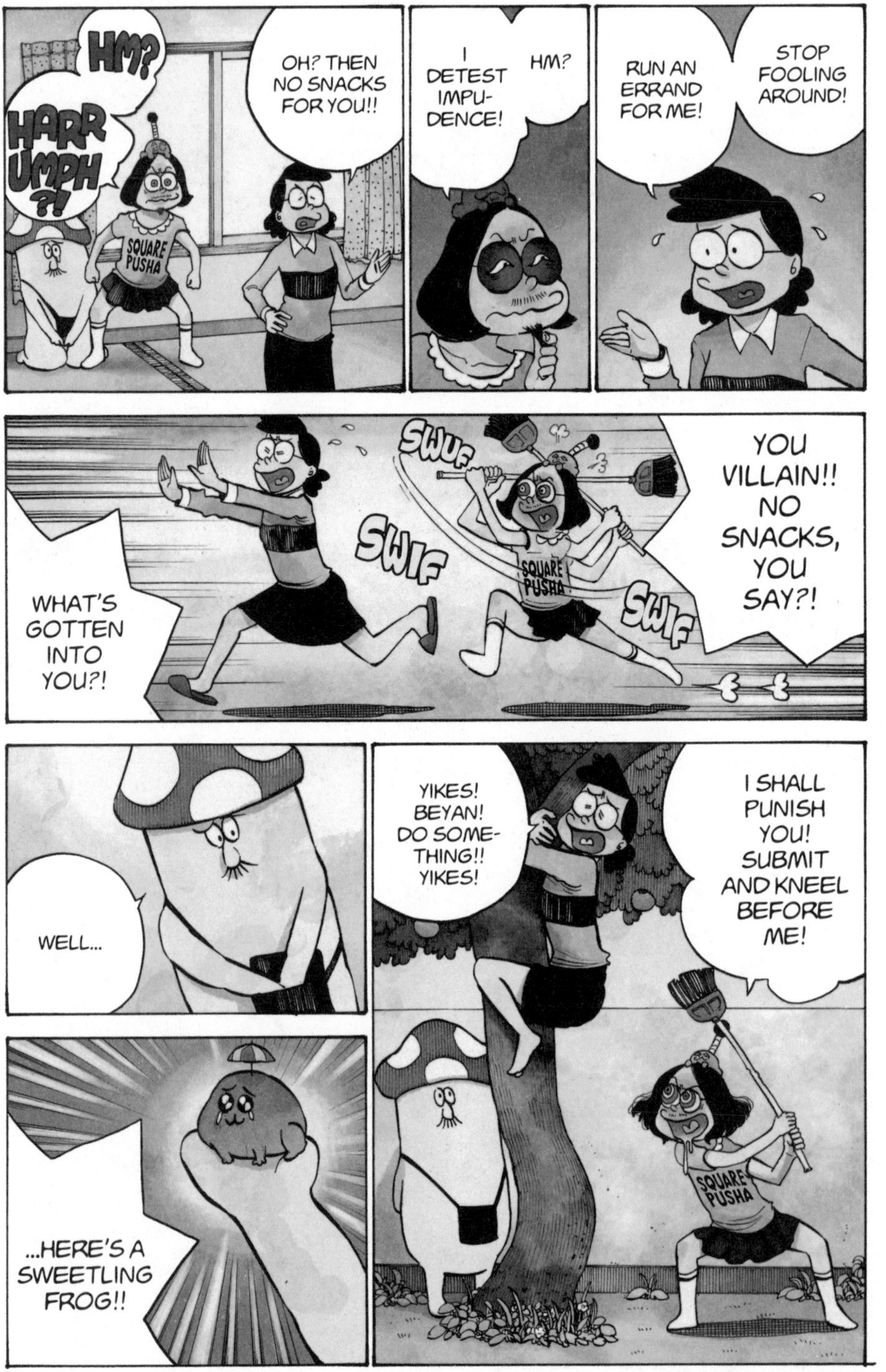
STOP FOOLING AROUND!
RUN AN ERRAND FOR ME!
HM?
I DETEST IMPU-DENCE!
OH? THEN NO SNACKS FOR YOU!!
HM?
HARRUMPH?!
YOU VILLAIN!! NO SNACKS, YOU SAY?!
SWUF
SWIF
SWIF
WHAT'S GOTTEN INTO YOU?!
I SHALL PUNISH YOU! SUBMIT AND KNEEL BEFORE ME!
YIKES! BEYAN! DO SOME-THING!! YIKES!
SQUARE PUSHA
WELL...
...HERE'S A SWEETLING FROG!!

☆Volume 4 goes on sale January 2019! Be on the lookout!

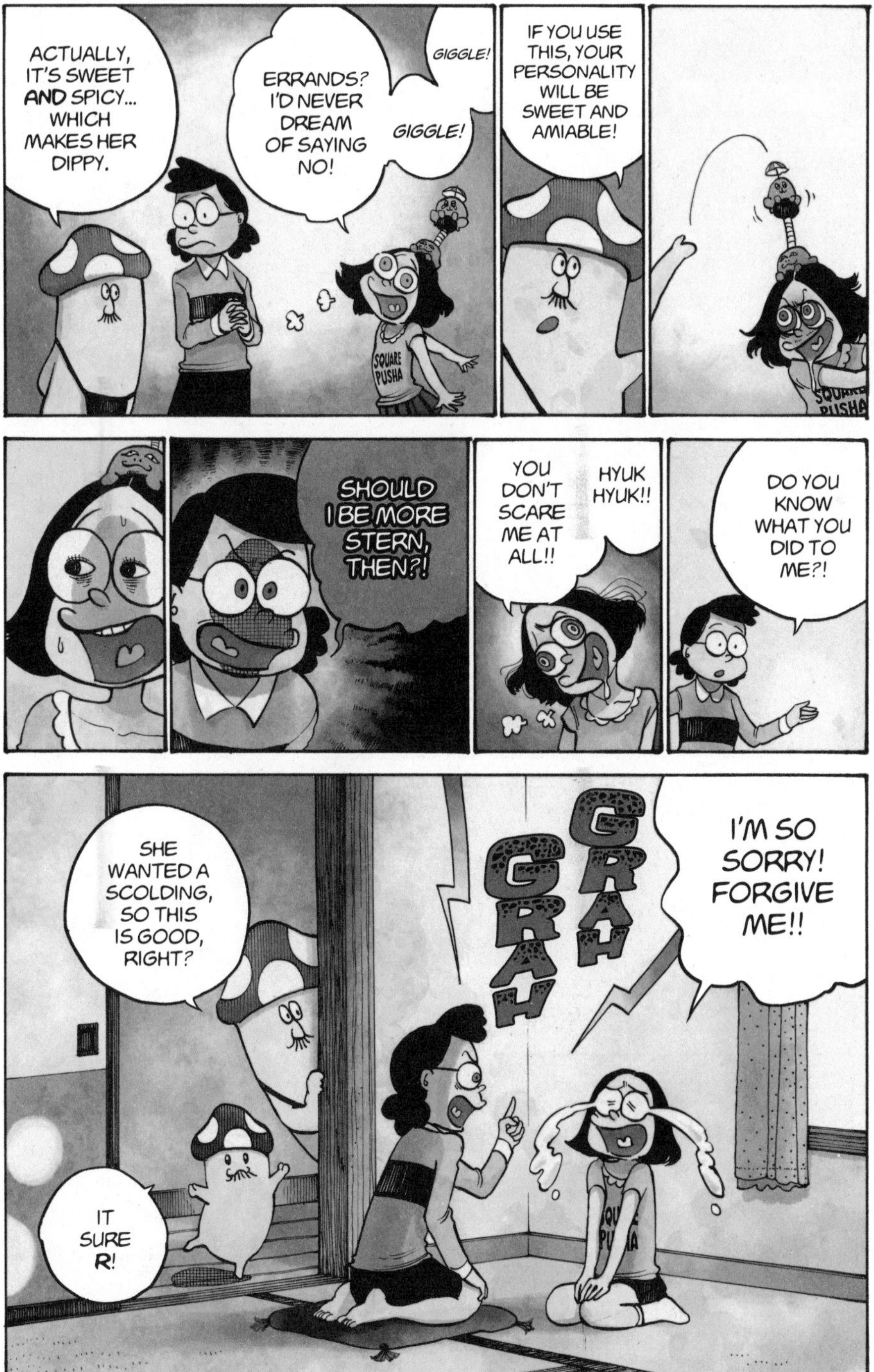
IF YOU USE THIS, YOUR PERSONALITY WILL BE SWEET AND AMIABLE!
GIGGLE!
ERRANDS? I'D NEVER DREAM OF SAYING NO!
GIGGLE!
ACTUALLY, IT'S SWEET **AND** SPICY... WHICH MAKES HER DIPPY.
DO YOU KNOW WHAT YOU DID TO ME?!
HYUK HYUK!!
YOU DON'T SCARE ME AT ALL!!
SHOULD I BE MORE STERN, THEN?!
I'M SO SORRY! FORGIVE ME!!
GRAH
GRAH
SHE WANTED A SCOLDING, SO THIS IS GOOD, RIGHT?
IT SURE **R**!

DEAD DEAD DEMON'S DEDEDEDE DESTRUCTION

Volume 3
VIZ Signature Edition

Story and Art by **Inio Asano**

Translation **John Werry**
Touch-Up Art & Lettering **Annaliese Christman**
Design **Shawn Carrico**
Editor **Pancha Diaz**

DEAD DEAD DEMON'S DEDEDEDE DESTRUCTION Vol. 3
by Inio ASANO
© 2014 Inio ASANO
All rights reserved.
Original Japanese edition published by SHOGAKUKAN.
English translation rights in the United States of America,
Canada, the United Kingdom, Ireland, Australia and
New Zealand arranged with SHOGAKUKAN.

Original Cover Design **Kaoru KUROKI+Bay Bridge Studio**

Printed in Canada

Published by VIZ Media, LLC
P.O. Box 77010
San Francisco, CA 94107

10 9 8 7 6 5 4 3 2 1
First printing, October 2018

VIZ MEDIA
viz.com

VIZ SIGNATURE
vizsignature.com